T0277321

Elephant in the Stadium

Elephant in the Stadium

The Myth and Magic of
India's Epochal Win

Arunabha Sengupta

First published by Pitch Publishing, 2022

Pitch Publishing
9 Donnington Park,
85 Birdham Road,
Chichester,
West Sussex,
PO20 7AJ
www.pitchpublishing.co.uk
info@pitchpublishing.co.uk

A CIP catalogue record is available for this book
from the British Library.

ISBN 978 1 80150 094 4

Typesetting and origination by Pitch Publishing
Printed and bound in Great Britain by TJ Books, Padstow

CONTENTS

TO

The teenaged versions of Anirudha Roy and
Anindya Tarafdar,
with whom I discovered the joys of cricket

ACKNOWLEDGEMENTS

FIRST AND foremost, Abhishek Mukherjee. He has been my collaborator, colleague and friend for more than a decade, and we have even penned a book together. Having decided on a volume of this expanse and ambition, I doubt I could have asked for a better sounding board. The end product would not have been possible without his thorough involvement that encompassed insights, suggestions, fact-checking, an incredible capacity for unleashing trivia linked to events in cricketing history, and enormous help with the appendices. He even compiled the most complex and valuable table in the appendix all by himself.

B. Sreeram is always one of a kind. When every known and unknown source of cricket history fails to cough up what one is looking for, one approaches Sreeram. If Sreeram cannot find it, the chances are a cricketing 99.94 per cent that it did not happen.

Mihir Bose not only did me the immense honour of writing the foreword to the book, he keeps producing splendid volumes covering subject matter closely related to this very work. Looking beyond by standing on the shoulders of giants has never made more sense.

Dilip Vengsarkar, Mike Gatting, Karsan Ghavri, Rahul Mankad, John Jameson and Dennis Amiss were extremely forthcoming in helping me reconstruct the pieces of days long gone by.

Sumit Gangopadhyay is a researcher of rare pedigree and his facility in digging up hitherto unpublished scorebooks from dusty, obscure archives is unmatched. His insights into the socio-political history of India were equally invaluable.

Qamar Ahmed and Vijay Lokapally are two very respected veteran journalists who went out of their way to help with the project.

David Frith, Stephen Chalke and the late Peter Wynne-Thomas were always around for me to dip into their enormous stores of knowledge and also to provide the contemporary accounts of those days.

Mayukh Ghosh and Michael Jones are two others who can be trusted to find missing pieces in a historical jigsaw, which they frequently did.

In the pages that follow we will come across numerous voices, of people who had a ringside view of the world in 1971, some of whom were at The Oval on the final day, and all of whom were touched by the event in one way or the other. I cannot begin to express my gratitude to all those splendid souls.

The Pitch team has always been a pleasure to work with and I am delighted to have been associated with them for this project.

In Richard Whitehead I had an editor who combined scrupulous editing with the most insightful of suggestions and it was a pleasure to work with him.

And finally Coco, a delightful, near-divine companion for nearly 15 years, who provided silent encouragement with a reassuring wag of her luxurious golden tail through the many months that I worked on the book, but was no longer there when it was completed.

FOREWORD

by Mihir Bose

BACK IN 1990 when I published my book *A History of Indian Cricket*, the first narrative history of the Indian game, my main problem was the paucity of material in India to which I could refer. I had to often rely on English sources. Since then, much has changed. A whole new generation of Indian writers has emerged, writing about the game in India. Arunabha Sengupta is one of them. But what sets him apart is that he often takes a very dramatically different approach to the writing of cricket history. His previous two books, *Apartheid: A Point to Cover* and *Sachin and Azhar at Cape Town,* illustrate that beautifully. But even by the standards set by these two books, Arunabha breaks fresh ground with this book. The title itself proclaims that.

Back in 1971 India made history by winning the Oval Test, their first victory over England in England and also their first series win in England, 39 years after making their Test debut. For me it was a very special moment. I was then a chartered accountancy student in London. I had grown up watching and reading about awful Indian defeats both at home and abroad, particularly in England. On that tour I was at Lord's for the first Test where India came close to winning. And while I could not go to Manchester for the second, I kept hoping that rain would continue on the final day as it did to save India. I was at The Oval, which was not far from my bedsit at Clapham Common. The Oval Test saw an elephant paraded round the ground. In *A*

History of Indian Cricket, I started with that victory at the Oval calling my first chapter 'The Day the Elephant Came to the Oval'.

Arunabha has to an extent borrowed that title in calling his book *Elephant in the Stadium*, but in doing so he has cleverly set a new course. He has described the entire epoch-making 1971 tour, starting with the first match against Middlesex at Lord's, but woven into the descriptions of what happened during the tour on the field of play an entire gamut of historical facts that both take the story forward from 1971 and back to the start of Indian cricket.

But what makes this even more special is that during this journey Arunabha, like one of those fabled Indian taxi drivers, take us down many byways which means we read not just about events on the field in 1971, but events going back to the start of Indian cricket and extending far beyond cricket to society, culture, India-British history, activities of far-right groups in Britain, the genocide carried out by the Pakistan army in then east Pakistan in 1971, which led to war between India and Pakistan and the Indian army creating a new country, Bangladesh, and even the prosecution of the D.H. Lawrence novel *Lady Chatterley's Lover*. Churchill and Gandhi also make appearances. And while at first glance all this in a cricket book seems absurd, Arunabha shows how it is relevant to the story of Indian cricket. This makes it a path-breaking book.

The thesis Arunabha presents is that the chronicle of cricket can be skewed due to partial re-telling. One of the best examples he gives is what is known in cricket as Mankading. This refers to what Vinoo Mankad, one of the greatest all-rounders in the game, did during India's first tour to Australia in 1947/48. As he ran in to bowl, seeing the Australian batsman Bill Brown backing up out of his crease, he first warned him and then when he did it again ran him out and under the laws of the game the batsman had to be given out. The Australians dubbed it Mankading, treating it as something that was underhand and not sportsmanlike. Despite Don Bradman finding nothing wrong with what Mankad had done, this still rankles so much in Australia that, less then ten years ago, Vinoo's younger son Rahul Mankad, who was attending a formal luncheon during an Australia-India Test match at Melbourne, was introduced by Paul Sheahan, then president of the Melbourne Cricket Club, as 'son of the notorious Mankad'. Yet, as Arunabha points out, Mankading had been done by many others and went back a long time. It illustrates his thesis about how cricket history is only a partial telling of the story, and who tells the story often dictates what is told, thereby often distorting the picture and creating a false narrative.

In trying to provide a more accurate narrative he has trawled through an enormous amount of material. He has researched many books and sources. Some of the most fascinating bits of information are the many references to contemporary newspapers, and particularly interesting are quotes from the papers of 1971 which reported on that epic tour. It was very interesting for me, having read the papers at the time, to read them again now. It was good to be reminded of how they portrayed Indian cricket then and how Indian cricket was seen as something not deserving top billing, nor any billing at all, and how things have changed since then, reflecting the enormous economic power of Indian cricket. That would have been unimaginable in 1971.

The book also reflects a new generation of Indian writers born long after independence whose attitude to British rule is very different, not only from the generation of my parents but also my own generation, which was born just as India won freedom. Arunabha, like many of his generation, is prepared to raise questions about the past and look at it in a very different way. This shows how the Indian perspective on relations with Britain is changing. This is something that people in this country will have to come to terms with to understand modern India.

1

PROLOGUE: JIGSAW OF ILLUSIONS

IT HAD been an eventful morning for the two-year-old, and she had enjoyed every moment of it. The hour's ride in that cramped vehicle had not been too comfortable, but Bella was used to such excursions. In fact, she was used to much longer journeys. She had already made several trips in her short life. From the port to Birmingham, from Birmingham to Chessington. And before that, the extended voyage across the seas to England. She remembered them all – wasn't remembering supposed to be her forte?

It was unusually loud as she alighted. She had been there the previous afternoon as well, and it had been noisy then. But today she could feel the excitement. The strange headgear seemed a tad uncomfortable at first, but she grew used to it. People were flocking all around as she was led through the crowds, electric excitement buzzed in the air. Soon she found herself in an enormous open space, green expanses stretching in front, with those giant gasometers in the background. And she was set free, allowed to tramp around the perimeter as the huge ground enjoyed the mild sunshine. People fussed around her, and she enjoyed it.

* * *

It is Colonel Hemu Adhikari who spots her first. The manager of the Indian team sits in the dressing-room with the captain, plotting ways to get the 97 runs required to make history. With eight wickets in hand, the task does not look too daunting. But Adhikari knows they have to be cautious. Ray Illingworth's men are sure to make them fight for every single run and a collapse cannot be ruled out. The batting line-up has been brittle throughout the tour.

Captain Ajit Wadekar has scored the bulk of the runs the previous evening. He exudes quiet confidence. Adhikari is glad to see he is not taking victory for granted. Practical, grounded common-sense – the traits that characterise the skipper.

The manager is about to touch upon the plan against Underwood when he sees the young elephant, her forehead decorated with a traditional Indian white caparison, plodding in front of the pavilion.

'Of all things on earth …?' he beckons Wadekar to take a look. 'They've got that elephant here again. It is Ganesh Chaturthi today. Surely this must be a good omen.'

Most of the 7,000-strong crowd are Indians. According to Campbell Page in *The Guardian,* 'Every Indian tourist, businessman, waiter and schoolboy seemed to be at The Oval.' England captain Illingworth will later observe that, in stark contrast to his team, the Indians had the advantage of playing in front of their home crowd.

A few of these Indian supporters have arranged for the trip of two-year-old Bella from Chessington Zoo to The Oval: 24 August 1971 is an auspicious day – the celebration of the festival of Ganesh, the elephant-headed god. Ganesh is worshipped as a remover of obstacles, a source of immense good luck. The deity is also the scribe who wrote down the great epic *Mahabharat,* breaking off one of his tusks to scribble it down as the sage Vyasa dictated the verses.

Today, Bella is there as a symbol of Ganesh, to remove any obstacle that may stand in the way of an Indian victory and to be part of the epic that is being scripted. An epic that will forever rival the *Mahabharat* in re-tellings, in popularity and myth.

Luck has already helped India profusely, without the intervention of either Ganesh or his manifestations – during the Old Trafford Test and also, arguably, at Lord's.

Wadekar will later recall that the sight of Bella sent his hopes surging. 'I went out to bat on my overnight score of 45 with my hopes doubled, and was run out first ball.' (He was actually run out off the first ball of the second over of the day). History is not about to be written without a fair amount of drama.

* * *

The tale of Bella is a fascinating subplot in the saga of the Indian victory. Not often do animals of that size, species and symbolic significance play an important role in a cricket match.

Growing up I had heard the tale some couple of thousand times, along with increasingly mythologised versions of the deeds of the 1971 side. These were men who grew increasingly invincible with each retelling.

It was in the summer of 1986 when cricket for me crossed the fine line between love and obsession. Yes, like every other Indian kid prancing around in his shorts, I had been on the edge of my seat as Kapil Dev's unbelievable catch got rid of Viv Richards at Lord's in the 1983 World Cup final. Like every other 11-year-old's, my spirit too had climbed into the Audi with the earliest versions of the Men in Blue as they had set off on their celebratory drive around the MCG in 1985.

But it was the Test success in England during the summer of 1986 that converted me into an addict. It was then that I started clipping Malcolm Marshall off my toes and watching the ball disappear between the conductor at square leg and the office clerk at midwicket as the bus lurched past nearby playing fields and turned into Cornwallis Street. I played out many an over in my head, perhaps with one or two wristy movements of my hands, as I sat in the classroom or ran on the track during athletics training.

I had already started diving into every cricket book that the school library of Don Bosco Park Circus, and later the British Council, could offer. I had begun borrowing volumes of *Wisden's* compilations of Test cricket scores from the British Council Library. I devoured all the available issues of *The Cricketer*. My early fascination for numbers meant that I began to recreate cricketing action from these current and ancient scorecards. I think I was about 13 when I compiled my first All-Time XI.

During India's 1986 tour of England, on my way home from school and elsewhere, my eyes and ears constantly scanned the crowds to catch the hint of a pocket transistor radio. 'What's the score?' my eternal query. One such query while boarding a bus was rewarded by a transistor-wielding gentleman informing me that Dilip Vengsarkar had followed up his 126 not out at Lord's with an unbeaten 102 on the near-unplayable wicket of Headingley. With that, India were on the verge of taking an unassailable 2-0 lead in the three-Test series.

Memories can be misleading after all these years, but this is what I remember of what took place two days after that Vengsarkar hundred. Three of us, Partha, Anindya and I, all hailing from the rather congested neighbourhoods of north Calcutta, had taken a bus from our school in Park Circus to Sealdah. Waiting for our connection near the noisy flyover, our trained ears kept scanning the nearby street hawkers for the tell-tale crackle of a transistor radio. It did not take long. Sitting in front of his carefully stacked items of clothing, this splendid cricket follower was tuned into the events unfolding at faraway Headingley.

'What's the score?'

We learnt that England were eight down, and they had just about managed to pass a hundred.

'Is Gatting still there?'

The hawker laughed. The target was 408. 'Yes, but will he be able to make all those runs alone?'

Mike Gatting, the new England captain, remained unbeaten on 31 as his men folded for 128. India had clinched the series. Throughout the early 1980s, we had enjoyed our share of limited-over success. But a Test win was rare, especially overseas. An overseas Test series win was almost unheard of. It was the first in my lifetime.

It was time for celebration. It was also time for me to discover the cocoon in which much of Indian cricket nostalgia was stuck; and remains stuck to this day.

I discovered 1971. The first Indian triumph in England.

Not that I had never heard of it. My perusal of cricket literature and scorecards had already told me about the Indian triumph of that year. Especially the scorecards, most of which I knew by heart. Hence, I was rather confused.

'That was *the* great triumph!' I was told. 'This 1986 English side is a poor one. *That* had been a great team. The best in the world at the time.'

I managed to lay my hands on the 1971 Winter Annual of *The Cricketer* in the British Council Library. In it, I read K.N. Prabhu's article on the Indian summer of 1971. '[The English team] was certainly a disappointment to one who had been reared on the legendary feats of the cricketers of the pre-war years, who had seen Compton and Hardstaff, May and Graveney, Dexter and Cowdrey at their best, to notice the decline of standards.'

Of course, with time I have realised that, like many of his fellow cricket chroniclers, the romantically skewed views of Prabhu had a gilt-edged bias for the *glorious* past. However, it was clear that the England team of 1971 had its shortcomings.

Of the top-order batsmen in that Oval Test, only John Edrich and Basil D'Oliveira ended with Test averages of 40-plus. Not the hallmark of the best side of the world.

But that was by no means the only fable that jarred with me about the tour.

'We had Gavaskar and Viswanath.' 'And Sardesai.'

'Bedi, Prasanna, Chandra, Venkat. Spinners who could turn it like a top and win on any surface.' NB. 'They don't make them like that anymore.'

'Our batting overcame the great West Indian pacers in West Indies. Our spinners out-bowled them on wickets tailor-made for fast bowlers. And then we beat the English in their den, on green tops made for their seamers.'

Match scorecards, *Wisden*, Tony Cozier's *History of West Indian Cricket* – all told me that there was no great fast bowler in the West Indies side of 1971. Hall and Griffith had retired; Sobers was 36, had a troublesome shoulder; and he had never really been a great fast bowler. Roberts, Holding and the rest of them would not emerge before the mid-1970s.

I knew the Indians had been caught on a reasonably green top at Old Trafford and only persistent rain on the final day had saved them from certain defeat. Even Sunil Gavaskar's autobiography *Sunny Days* admitted as much.

Yes, England of 1986 was a rudderless and confused side. Yet, I could see that the 1971 side had been no great shakes either. True, they had won the Ashes in Australia, a monumentally long-drawn-out series of six Test matches ending 2-0. However, that Australian side was far from a great one, with a bowling attack in transition.

In the summer of 1971, England had escaped defeat against Pakistan at Edgbaston because of the weather, and had won the series after a very close scuffle at Headingley.

As for the Indian win of 1971, it was nowhere near as comprehensive as the clinical demolition of 1986. The Lord's Test could have gone either way. At Manchester, they had been saved by rain. And the Oval magic had been produced by a freak bowling spell on the fourth morning when England had been right on top.

Besides, the England side had missed the services of Boycott in two of the Tests, Snow in one.

In many ways, it was a triumph that had leaned heavily on chance.

As far as spinning out West Indians on fast wickets and England on green tops, here is Prabhu again in his 1971 article. 'In the West Indies we had expected hard fast wickets. In England we came prepared to battle against pace on green-tops. In both countries our spinners were pleased to find that the pitches suited them better than they did the opposition.'

However, while these insights provided by Prabhu and other journalists had been studiously ignored, some of their other observations, effusively riding on the understandable waves of jubilation, became integral to the Indian cricketing fables. Such as the following Prabhu nugget, 'Throughout the tour we encountered no spinner who could have matched any of the reserves we had left at home.' He was talking about Dilip Doshi, Vithal Joshi, Naushir Mehta and others. Supposedly England had no spinner comparable to these bowlers, let alone the great ones like Bedi and Chandra.

Growing up, we were led to believe that India was the land that produced the best spinners. It was variously attributed, among other things, to the air that we breathed and the warm climate that made our fingers flexible.

Invoking the names of Hedley Verity or Jim Laker is perhaps a journey back in time too arduous for fans. But Underwood ended with a Test record significantly superior to all the members of the celebrated Indian quartet. Illingworth and a clutch of other more or less contemporary English off-spinners enjoyed careers at least comparable to the best of the Indian spinners of that era.

Many of the heroes of 1971 were excellent cricketers, but the near-mythical qualities attributed to them are often far beyond the numbers they left in their wake.

As years went by, I realised that the aura of 1971 was there to stay. Even after all these years, 1986 has never reached the height of nostalgic romanticising that still laces that pioneering triumph. The subsequent series win in 2007 has been all but forgotten. And by the time Covid stopped the 2021 series with India 2-1 up and one Test to play, Virat Kohli's men were expected to win in every corner of the world – overseas wins were getting way too frequent and celebrations becoming too familiar to bother with seasonings of mythologised ingredients.

Also, as years went by, my incurable addiction to scorecards, and later my five years at the Indian Statistical Institute, made me increasingly sceptical about the robustness of visual impression; I-was-there reminiscences and fan memories of the 'glorious past' often do not measure up against solid data.

All these years later, I understand.

I don't believe in the myths that have grown in Indian cricket surrounding 1971, or the rest of the decade that followed. They still jar with one trained in statistical analysis. The favourite cricketing phrase 'it was much more than numbers' does not appeal to me. That, to me, remains a method of believing whatever one wants to.

But now I do understand the 1971 phenomenon.

Distance did help. After several years of working across three continents, wrestling with visas, work permits and residency issues, I finally settled down in Amsterdam and became a Dutch citizen. The perspective lent by time and space helped me make sense of the history that had perhaps been too close for me to look at back in India.

I realised that I had walked countless hours through the serpentine lanes of north Calcutta and under the colonnaded verandas and balconies of the Grand Hotel, taking the contrasts of architectural and urban planning features for granted. Seated in Amsterdam, those everyday images were translated into palpable history. The pillared and porticoed mansions of Dalhousie Square and Chowringhee, originally built for the Europeans, the densely populated sectors towards the north, historically inhabited by Indians, where Partha, Anindya and I grew up among the second generation after independence.

The names of the roads and landmarks became more than mere locations – Cornwallis, Elgin, Lansdowne, Ripon, Dalhousie, Curzon, Outram, Fort William and the Victoria Memorial.

Distance also helped some memories to resurface from long-neglected corners of the mind. The Benson & Hedges World Championship triumph of 1985 for instance, India beating Pakistan in the final at the MCG. I remembered the posters in the stands that day, viewed thousands of miles away on our small television set. One proclaimed 'Down Under, India is Thunder'. Another observed 'Benson 'n Hedges Final. Bus Drivers versus Tram Conductors.'

Seated in a faraway land, I identified with Indians at home and fellow expatriate Indians – also the Indians who came from Guiana, Trinidad, Kenya, South Africa and Uganda to England, and from Suriname to the Netherlands. I also interacted with the Pakistani residents and visitors in England and in the Netherlands.

I sought out others as well, the ones who had come from East Pakistan, and thereafter Bangladesh, with memories of the war of 1971 that cast its looming shadow even as cricketing history was being made under the gasometers at The Oval.

I interacted with several Indians who have been living in England for years, some of whom had seen Bella at The Oval on that day.

I realised that among the schoolboys and waiters and businessmen of Campbell Page, who were rooting for India during that Oval triumph, a significant proportion feared the worst as the Immigration Bill was being discussed in parliament. There were those did not know whether they would be allowed to stay on in Britain, or whether their wives and children would be able to come over and join them. Similarly there were some who had no idea of what would become of their relatives stranded in the genocide-ravaged East Pakistan.

I also spoke to Englishmen who had been there – in whose memory the India-Pakistan War is rather faint, but the trouble in Belfast still reverberates, who remember Prime Minister Edward Heath leading the British team to triumph in the Admiral's Cup and Northern Ireland going up in flames.

Down the years I covered Test tours in England. I wrote innumerable articles and eventually some books on the game. I visited the likes of David Frith, Stephen Chalke, Mihir Bose and others in their homes.

There were reviews of my work, a heady mix of flattering, balanced and critical as can be expected. Alongside, I experienced some baffled and even a few confrontational stares, some face to face, and more from behind firewalls of the two distinct virtual worlds – the worldwide web and time-tinged entitlement. There were more than a few unvoiced, and once in a while voiced, queries: why does an Indian writer write so much about topics such as the Ashes and pre-1970 England-South Africa Test matches?

It did seem quite often that the swim-lanes of cricket history were strictly defined, and other than a privileged few, historians were supposed to go up and down the lanes allotted to them.

This book does not adhere to such conventions.

After the publication of my book *Apartheid: A Point to Cover,* I received an email from a fellow cricket-writer – and an excellent one at that – an Englishman without any prejudice in his makeup. It read, 'I was especially taken by the early chapters in your book about the pre-apartheid history of cricket in South Africa, with the reminder that cricket there was segregated from the beginning, with the collusion of the British.'

This was in 2020. And this realisation is not restricted to just cricket.

Even today the role of the British in the complications of their erstwhile colonies is rather sketchily known by the British themselves – a legacy of a deliberately skewed curriculum that is very recently and reluctantly going through adjustment and correction.

The same unawareness that today manifests itself in a murky trail of social-media footprints, leading to enquiries about and even the axing of some misguided cricketers from the national team. The same unawareness that results in huge controversies in Yorkshire cricket – controversies that are, at least initially, brushed aside as 'mere banter'.

As fellow cricket-writer Michael Jones says, 'The teaching of history in English schools has long been whitewashed, which perpetuates the problem of most of the country being ignorant of the nastier side of its history. I only learnt of some of the worst deeds of the British Empire through subsequent reading and discussions with people from the countries which suffered from them – not from anything I was taught at school.'

Recently more British people seemed to learn of their imperial past from the spate of destruction of statues rather than the academic curriculum.

In the words of Whisky Sisodia in *The Satanic Verses* (stripped of the stammer): 'The trouble with the English is that their history happened overseas, so they don't know what it means.'

The perceptions were way more skewed in 1971.

Even as India played Warwickshire on the tour, British-based Australian journalist John Pilger interviewed the Indian prime minister in Delhi. The resulting article was published in the *Daily Mirror* under the headline 'The Most Powerful Woman in the World'. Pilger's opening question to Mrs Indira Gandhi was, 'The description of India as the world's largest democracy is often used by people in Britain to congratulate themselves on having exported a successful model of Westminster government. Could an Indian, hungry and without hope, really regard himself as a member of a democracy?'

The hunger, squalor, extraordinary economic problems ... all that was beyond question. However, it is fascinating to note that the British still 'congratulated themselves on having exported a successful model of Westminster government' to the Indians.

Perhaps many still do. For me with my Indian background, the patronising tone, along with a palpably fatuous boast, is quite difficult to come to terms with. However, I am sure the question sounds extremely reasonable to some who have grown up during the last days of the Empire, forming long-lasting associations with like-minded contemporaries.

Pilger's query also tells us that such a question, directed at a prime minister from the erstwhile colonies, was normal in those days. Those days ... when India arrived in England with a 0-15 record in the 19 Test matches they had played in the country.

Back home, only six cricketers of the Indian squad had their own cars. The daily allowance on the tour was a *princely* £3.

On the eve of the first Test match, a correspondent of *The Times* was at the Tripura border of East Pakistan. He interviewed a Mukti Bahini general who had been a highly ranked officer in the Pakistan Army and, before that, a grade-two General Staff Officer in the British Indian Army. When informed by this old military man that East Bengal freedom fighters had killed between 15,000 and 20,000 West Pakistan troops, the journalist wrote, 'The figure seemed so high that I would have been altogether sceptical if it had not come from an officer who belongs very much to the old British Army tradition.'

Such perceptions still ruled the world view. The perceptions of superiority and inferiority, of virtues and vices, of truth and lies, that were directly and uninhibitedly linked to racial and national profiling. The decolonisation was all but complete. But the Empire lived on in much of the consciousness.

Material superiority was unquestionable. Through relentless unidirectional syphoning of wealth across several centuries, one nation had got richer, and the other poorer. The game of catch-up started after the 'Transfer of Power', and has since been tracked according to the western definition of 'development'. This game will go on forever. And till then the Pilger-like culture-shock of finding oneself amidst hunger, poverty, heat and dust will continue. A quick restoration of balance is a socio-economic impossibility.

But the illusion of moral superiority demonstrated in the second example is of a strikingly different dimension. It was a remnant of the beliefs that made colonisation such a 'natural and normal' course of history. Beliefs rooted in the archaic concepts of Social Darwinism.

It is quite astounding to reflect that these were very much in vogue just 50 years earlier as I write, even as India toured England in 1971.

While working for Cricketcountry, I wrote mainly about the history of the game. Veteran journalist H. Natarajan (Natty) was my chief editor.

On 24 August, 2013, I wrote an anniversary piece on the triumph at The Oval, 1971. Natty, a stickler for the ideal headline, ran the story as *The Day When India Ended England's Home Rule.*

On that particular day I thought it was over the top, another manifestation of the 1971-fixation. Today, more than eight years down the line, I am not so sure.

It is not that the cricketers were always knowingly taking up cudgels against the prevailing perceptions, the remnants of colonial hangover, eager to strike a blow at the heart of the illusion of superiority. No, as most often happens, they were merely playing cricket.

However, the triumph did merge with the complicated undercurrents of the times to become tinged with a defining hue.

Yes, the resulting fables often distorted facts. But it was also a function of that moment of history and the many years that had led to that point in time.

The myth and magic surrounding the 1971 triumph cannot be understood without taking into account the long and complex interactions between the British and their erstwhile prize colony.

What then about Bella, the elephant in the stadium?

There are many ways in which Bella is an allegory.

In 1885, the Empire was approaching high noon. Imperialist fever was at a high pitch and India was the jewel in the Empire's Crown.

That year, the Indian National Congress (INC) had come into existence – the industry of 70 English-educated Indians who got together in Bombay. These Indian Congressmen tried to change things in the country through the traditional method of submitting petitions. Little came of their efforts. The petitions were seldom read, and scoffed at almost every time they were.

In 1893, tired of the futile efforts of the elite educated Indians of the INC, the fierce nationalist Bal Gangadhar Tilak took the concept of nationalism to the masses. He infused nationalistic ideals into the festival of Ganesh Chaturthi, the festival of the elephant-headed god.

This is not meant to be read as anything more than an icon occurring coincidentally at two different points in history. But the nationalistic Ganesh Chaturthi celebrations of 1893 and the emergence of Bella at The Oval in 1971 do lend scope for historical allegory, and quite a poignant one.

An elephant is symbolic of India – especially the stereotypical image of India.

The English cricketers of yore saw elephants used to roll the pitch at the Maharaja of Patiala's personal cricket ground. Tour after tour saw cricketers riding elephants during their mandatory shooting expeditions.

Almost every western movie made about India featured elephants, be it *Elephant Boy* or *Octopussy*.

In 1997, a shot of an elephant told us that the characters of *Seinfeld* were meant to be visiting the country.

In 2018, *The Big Bang Theory* had Rajesh Koothrapali assuring his American friends, 'Of course there will be elephants' at his wedding.

In 1982, Appu the Elephant became the official mascot of the Asian Games held in Delhi.

In 1992/93, India inflicted the first brownwash on a visiting England side. Battling heat, dust, quixotic selection and a very good Indian side, a miserable Phil Tufnell grumbled, 'I've done the elephants and I've done the poverty. It's time to go home.'

That was 21½ years after the 1971 summer.

The elephant was an apt icon to romp around The Oval that day.

India in England 1971 was a special tour. Pivotal and poignant. And it was a sterling achievement.

Not just because of the result and the cricketing action that led to it, but also because of the way the results combined with the many layers of historical complexity and the kaleidoscopic background to create an indelible impression in popular memory.

This is a story about cricket, but it is also about the reactions, the elation and the reasons for the mythical retellings that followed.

It is not just about 1971. Historical recollection is never just about that tiny window in time.

2

THEY WILL NOT
PUBLISH ANYTHING

'ALL SETTLED WITH THE SIX', blared the front-page
headlines of the *Daily Mirror.*

Only, it had nothing to do with cricket. The six original
Common Market countries had promised Geoffrey Rippon,
Britain's chief negotiator, that they could continue to trade New
Zealand butter and cheese until they had found other markets.
With the livelihoods of Kiwi farmers temporarily taken care of,
the biggest hurdle stopping Britain from joining the European
Economic Community had been removed.

This reads funnily 50 years later, with Britain having
painstakingly jumped back over that and other hurdles. But back
then, just about completing his first year as prime minister, the
Euro-friendly Edward Heath had never wavered from his goal of
finally getting the country across the channel of differences and
false illusions. That was the morning of 23 June, 1971.

The other leading story in the paper was typical *Mirror* – a
41-year-old Roman Catholic priest secretly married a 32-year-old
Roman Catholic nun. Sitting in the lounge of the Bayswater hotel
on that cloudy June morning, Ajit Wadekar could not find any
mention of the match.

Not that the Indian captain expected the tour opener to
make the front page. But as he leafed through the paper, he
could not find anything at all about the game beginning that
day at Lord's.

In the sports pages there was the picture of Margaret Court serving powerfully on the Centre Court at Wimbledon. There was the British hope Virginia Wade taking a tumble on her way to a win against Patti Hogan. The most sensational cricket bulletin was Glamorgan's capitulation for 43 against Leicestershire at Cardiff.

The Test match against Pakistan at Lord's had dwindled to a rain-affected draw, but Peter Laker had written enthusiastically about the name Hutton appearing at the head of England's batting order for the first time in 16 years. Sent in by Ray Illingworth to play out time in the brief second innings, Richard Hutton had enjoyed himself against a posse of Pakistani part-time bowlers, hitting an unbeaten 58. 'Hutton has inherited many of his father's mannerisms. He trots splay-footed up and down the wicket and occasionally tugs absently at the peak of his cap in a way that is startlingly familiar. Even his cover-drive, a free, full-blooded stroke, rolled back the years,' wrote Laker. John Arlott's article in *The Guardian* ran with the headline, 'A Hutton in an Old Mood for England.'

By then Richard Hutton had played more than 200 first-class matches and boasted a batting average in the early 20s. In cricket, as long as we religiously avoid the figures, we are free to see and infer whatever we want to.

It was a while before Wadekar finally noticed it.

In a miniscule square inch or so below the summarised county cricket scores and an advertisement for Wolf electric drills, the cricket in store for the day was announced. Glamorgan played the Pakistanis at Swansea. Following that, there was a one-line notice: *Lord's: Middx v Indians (11:30–6:30).*

That was all. The sports pages were rounded off with a *Mirror Sport Exclusive* explaining why Don Howe would stay on as the assistant manager of Arsenal.

If he had scanned through the entire paper, Wadekar could have concluded that the only article of real cricketing interest was on page 13, where large headlines announced that Nottingham Festival 71 had offered £100 for any witch doctor who could ensure 15 days of dry weather between 10 July and 25 July. The

Indian skipper could do with someone blessed with such powers. Rain had dogged them ever since their arrival five days before. Their only practice had taken place in ex-Surrey bowler Alf Gover's indoor facilities in south London.

Rain was worrying. The Indians had disputed the playing conditions for the series, insisting on covered wickets, but finally they had given in. The vagaries of uncovered wickets in England were well known.

The rain had also been a drag. Other than the previous evening at the Old Taverners', where Jim Laker and Trevor Bailey had kept them entertained and often had them in splits, the players had not been able to go out and enjoy themselves.

The captain, up fresh and early before the rest of his team, now turned towards the dapper 52-year-old man who had come down even earlier.

Some of the senior cricketers resented Colonel Hemu Adhikari. He supposedly got too involved in the cricketing aspects, ceasing to remain just a manager and trying to take on the mantle of a coach. Spartan, regimental, he was perhaps a bit too straightforward for some. Not one to suffer fools gladly.

Wadekar, however, got along with him. The manager's suggestions to him came through as advice, not imposition. Besides, he knew that it had been Adhikari who had presented a solid case when the treasury had been bent on pegging the daily allowance at the ridiculous £1 per day as in 1967. During the last tour, Wadekar's first, many had to seek out cheap restaurants, the vegetarians in the side getting by on nothing but bread and butter. Some saved up enough from even that meagre amount to buy pullovers – the Indian cricket sweaters were not warm enough for the English weather.

One could not take on the English as equals on the field while being miserable and scrounging off it. There was already a huge yoke of the past to deal with without that. The introspective, cerebral Wadekar knew that very well.

This time the players had been allotted £3 per day for lunch, dinner and local transport. They had Adhikari to thank for that.

Now the manager informed the skipper that even *The Times* did not carry anything about the game. Just an announcement about the India-Middlesex match at Lord's. That was all. 'They're too caught up with Wimbledon and the Test match,' the manager said. The underlying message was, 'It's not that they don't take us seriously.'

Adhikari knew that was far from the truth.

Of course, no one expected the type of article that John Woodcock had penned for *The Times* three years before when the Aussies had been about to start their tour. A special interview with Jack Fingleton about why Bill Lawry's men were not to be underrated.

But that had been the Ashes, after all.

Even in 2020, Brad Hogg would claim that the Ashes would ignite public interest far more than any World Test Championship.

However, Adhikari had toured in 1952 as vice-captain of the first cricket team from independent India to visit England. The tour opener, a second-class match against the Indian Gymkhana, had been mentioned in *The Times* along with the names of all the members of the Indian side. On the morning of their first game against a county side, the traditional opening fixture at New Road, Charles Bray had written an eight-paragraph Worcester-centric preview for the *Daily Herald*.

The same journalist had expressed surprise in *The Daily Telegraph* seven years later when Datta Gaekwad's team had turned up late on the eve of the opening tour game, after the nets had been taken down.

Even in 1971, when the Pakistani side had been about to start their tour in Worcester, *The Times* had announced that the groundsman promised a good wicket and new captain Norman Gifford was ready to lead his side, with Basil D'Oliveira and Glenn Turner among his men, against exciting youngsters such as Sadiq Mohammad and Zaheer Abbas.

Of course, Adhikari knew, as did many of the team, that the British media could not entirely be blamed. India had visited England six times, playing 19 Test matches, losing 15 and managing to draw four. Since independence from British rule, they had played 12 Tests in the country, losing 11. The solitary draw had been at The Oval in 1952, when they had conceded a 228-run first innings lead before the skies had opened to swallow the chances of a result.

Could one complain if the newspapers, *Daily Mirror* included, did not print everything?

But Colonel Adhikari, the military man, was probably engrossed in the news from Dacca that was splashed all over the front page of *The Times*. The University halls were being used for guerrilla training. As the story continued on page 6, the correspondent alleged that the army was systematically hunting down the Hindu population. It was curious that India and Pakistan, two countries on the brink of a major conflict, were on tour in England that summer.

The first two England-Pakistan Tests of the series had been drawn. A couple of evenings earlier, the team had been to a nearby Indian restaurant run by Sylheti Bengalis. After all, they were in Bayswater, where West Indians, Indians and Pakistanis seemed to outnumber British people. During dinner, the Indian cricketers had been assured by the proprietor and the waiters, 'We are backing you, not those butchers.'

Dictatorship and war were, understandably, prone to generating such sentiments. Of course, Intikhab Alam's men were not butchers. Adhikari had played against Pakistan in 1952 when the two nations had met for the first time in an emotional encounter. He had scored an unbeaten 81, hauling the score from 263/9 to 372 with No.11 Ghulam Ahmed. And then Vinoo Mankad had wrecked the Pakistan batting with 8-52.

A pity that the teams did not play each other now. The 1965 war had stopped competitive cricket between the countries. Occasionally the players did come across each other. Farokh Engineer had kept to Intikhab in two of the 'Tests' the previous summer, when the Rest of the World had taken on England. But relationships between the two countries were spiralling out of control.

Eight days before, in an interview given to an Italian television team, Mrs Gandhi had said that the tragic events in East Pakistan, and the resulting millions of refugees, had become a colossal problem in India. Two days later, at a meeting with economic editors assembled in New Delhi, she had spoken about the need for immediate action to check any flare-up in the East Pakistan situation.

In fact, just three days previously, Swaran Singh, the Indian foreign minister, had been in London, addressing the heads of Indian missions in Europe. He had vented his frustrations. 'I am fully convinced about the total ineffectiveness of the UNO, whether they are [sic] political, social or human rights. They talk and talk and talk and do nothing.' The response of the United Nations to the developing crisis in East Pakistan had been discouraging, but not really unexpected. They treated it as yet another manifestation of India-Pakistan hostility. India had engaged with United Nations only so that they were not outmanoeuvred by Pakistan on that front. But Swaran Singh knew, as did most of the Cabinet and also quite a few of the citizenry, that this time it was very different.

Many of the cricketers and fans wondered how long it would be before the two countries faced each other again on the cricket pitch.

3

LONGITUDES AND ATTITUDES

THINGS HAD reached breaking point with Operation Searchlight, kicked off by the Pakistani army. On 24 March 1971 the Georgetown Test had ended in a draw, India holding on to their 1-0 lead aided by butterfingered West Indian fieldsmen. In the late hours of 25 March, Pakistani army units had launched their killing spree on Dacca, their American-built M-24 tanks crushing the ramshackle barriers put up by the students.

Asif Siraj, who came to London in 1969 and subsequently worked as a financial analyst, recounts, 'The gravity of the situation was well known. In the beginning of March [1971], Sir Alec Douglas-Home [former prime minister, then Britain's foreign and Commonwealth secretary] had already set up several Pakistan Crisis Units under the South Asia Department. We East Bengalis in Britain did much to create global awareness of the mass murder that was going on in our country.'

British awareness of the crisis was unusually high. It was, however, not merely fuelled by humanitarian concerns awakened by the East Bengalis. A week after Operation Searchlight, Cyril Pickard, the high commissioner in Pakistan, was sending missives to London that the 'eventual end result is likely to be an independent East Pakistan. In terms of investment and raw material sources, our long-term interests may prove to be with a future regime in the East, rather than with the Western rump.'

Chitta Majumdar, who arrived in the 1950s from Sylhet with his parents, has another perspective. 'Many of the British still believed it was a Hindu-Muslim issue. To an extent it was. But the underlying problems were far deeper. It was not really a misreading of the situation on the part of the British, but an easier model for them to understand. The difference in language and culture, the common Bengali heritage, are complex concepts. You see, there were long ongoing riots around the Catholic-Protestant divide in Northern Ireland. Hindu-Muslim divide was a comfortable simplification.'

The British were not alone in this confusion.

In 2014, the Nobel Committee awarded the Peace Prize to 17-year-old Malala Yousafzai and the 60-year-old Kailash Satyarthi. The press release indicated that the committee had chosen the combination of 'a Hindu from India and a Muslim from Pakistan' on purpose, because they 'join in a common struggle for education and against extremism.'

For Satyarthi, the relentless activist against child labour, it must have been quite a shock trying to think of himself as a 'Hindu from India'. As much as it is a shock for me to think of myself as a 'Hindu from India' as I write these lines.

Less than a month before Operation Searchlight kicked off, at the Dacca National Stadium Micky Stewart led an International XI against a BCCP XI. It was the second game of a three-match series. Raqibul Hasan Sr, the East Pakistan batsman, had put a sticker proclaiming *Joy Bangla*' (Viva Bengal) on his standard-issue Gray-Nicholls bat, covering up the mandatory emblem of the Pakistan Peoples' Party. The match was abandoned due to student demonstrations, and the visitors had to be escorted out of the stadium by the army and flown out to Lahore at dead of night. The situation in East Pakistan had been volatile for a long time.

The power vacuum created by the post-war decolonisation had sucked a huge belt of Asian territory into the vortex of Cold War tensions. From the Manchurian Plain in the east, into Indochina's lush rain forests in the south, and across the arid plateaus of Central Asia and the Middle East in the west – according to Professor Paul Chamberlain of Columbia University, 'Seven out of every ten people killed in violent conflicts between 1945 and 1990 died inside this zone.' These were the killing fields in which 14 million people perished as the two superpowers engaged in frigid tests of strength and strategy. The second half of the century has, according to many Eurocentric historical accounts, gone down as a prolonged period of post-war peace. After all, the massacred populations were from the newly coined 'third-world countries'.

In the context of decolonisation and Cold War conflicts, East Pakistan had copped a double whammy.

On one side was the hasty pair of lines scribbled on the map by a British lawyer. That had sectioned off two Muslim majority parts in the east and west of the Indian subcontinent as two halves of Pakistan. It had been a parting present from British rule, with a vicious triple-edged pun on 'parting'. The result had been 14.5 million people uprooted from their homes, massive riots of discontent and retribution, rape, pillage and murder, and eventually a couple of million deaths.

Pakistan was a bifurcated nation at birth. The western half held most of the political power, rested on arid mountains, and was populated by Punjabis, Pashtuns and Sindhis. The more populous eastern half lay in the lush Gangetic plains and comprised the Bengalis. As Salman Rushdie captured it in *Shame*, 'That fantastic bird of a place, two wings without a body, sundered by the land-mass of its greatest foe, joined by nothing but God.'

But was God enough to keep them together? In the intervening years, the folly of creating such a nation linked by religion has been demonstrated several times over.

The two factions had clashed with major consequences when Urdu, preferred by the less populous West Pakistan, had been made the official state language. The language-linked police atrocities that took place in Dacca on 21 February 1952 led UNESCO to declare the date as International Mother Language Day in 1999. The Awami Muslim League, formed to champion the cause of the Bengali language, gained significant power by the end of the 1960s and was getting increasingly vocal about the autonomy of East Pakistan. By 1966, Sheikh Mujibur Rahman had suggested the six-point movement.

And now, on top of the problems of quixotic geography, East Pakistan had to deal with the misfortune of becoming an expendable pawn in the colossal tussle for world supremacy.

The emergence of China as a major power had sparked it off. The 1969 clashes along the Ussuri River had hinted at a Sino-Soviet split contrary to a united communist front. It had suddenly made sense for both Washington and Beijing to consider the prospect of rapprochement after several years of circling each other.

Neither could afford to extend an arm of friendship and thereby risk a rebuff on the world stage. Vietnam was causing enough problems at home for President Nixon, and Chairman Mao was fighting down the ghosts of the Cultural Revolution. An intermediary was required to organise negotiations. Nixon tilted towards Pakistan.

The nation state had always been a US ally during the Cold War. In late 1959, Dwight Eisenhower had even watched a tedious day of Test cricket at the Karachi National Stadium. No other US president has so far emulated him.

Nixon, then vice-president to Eisenhower, had developed close ties with Islamabad. At the same time, he remained suspicious of the Indian prime minister Jawaharlal Nehru, owing to his role in the Bandung Conference, his insistence on championing the No-Aligned Movement and his friendly overtures towards the Soviet Union.

After a significant cooling of US-Pakistan relations during Lyndon Johnson's administration, Nixon was now keen on reviving the alliance. Pakistan and China both looked upon India as a great foe. General Yahya Khan, the Pakistan president, looked to the US for support in its conflicts with India. It made the troubled nation the preferred conduit into China for the US president and his national security advisor Henry Kissinger.

In November 1970, East Pakistan had been devastated by the massive Bhola cyclone. Half a million people were killed. Famine, cholera, typhoid and dysentery loomed menacingly. Relief from Islamabad was scant and indifferent, and, Yahya was inebriated when he visited the area.

When the United States joined a relief effort sending aid, Kissinger deemed it unwise. 'US grants would carry the implication that President Yahya's government in West Pakistan could not ... effectively manage this situation.' Hence, as a diplomatic manoeuvre to ensure the chummy relations with Yahya, lives in East Pakistan were allowed to be lost.

The Blood Telegram

Archer Blood, the American consul general in Dacca, sent regular missives to Washington, alerting them that systematic genocide was in operation. The response was steadfast silent indifference. On 6 April 1971, Blood dispatched his famous telegram, signed by 29 members of the consulate staff. 'Our government has failed to denounce the suppression of democracy ... [and] has evidenced what many will consider moral bankruptcy.'

But the US government answered that the fighting in East Pakistan was 'an internal matter of the Pakistan government.' Kissinger argued that 'the use of power against seeming [numerical] odds paid off'. Nixon agreed, citing the examples of the British in India and Spanish against the Incas. They agreed, 'Yahya must be kept afloat for six more months.' On 2 May, Nixon scribbled a note '*To all hands. Don't squeeze Yahya at this time.*' The word 'Don't' was underlined three times.

This was the first indication of the callousness with which the Nixon and Kissinger duo would handle the East Pakistan situation. However, it was certainly not the first time a major power had stood aside to allow death and devastation. This had been the story in Korea, Vietnam and Indonesia in the Cold War, and would continue to be the story in Cambodia and elsewhere. And, of course, people in the erstwhile undivided Bengal had memories of similar calculated callousness by another major power during the Second World War.

December 1970 had witnessed the first democratic elections in Pakistan. Mujib's Awami League won all but two of the 168 seats. In the west, the Pakistan People's Party, led by Zulfikar Ali Bhutto, grabbed power with 81 seats. With the Awami League pressing for autonomy, West Pakistan military leaders had launched Operation Searchlight, armed with spare military parts and ammunition supplied by the United States.

In the nightmare that followed, Mujib was arrested, and civilians were massacred. The Pakistani army leaders ostensibly tried to round up Hindu men, but the killing was, according to neutral eye-witnesses, without discrimination.

Meanwhile reports of rape, starvation and massacres were splashed across the international press. *Newsweek* had reports of young men being made to lie down on makeshift cots, with needles inserted into veins, and blood drained from their bodies until they died.

Britain's initial stance, even taking into consideration Pickard's cable, had been strict neutrality. Alec Douglas-Home told the House of Commons that the government was 'deeply concerned' about the loss of lives, but they had 'no intention of interfering in Pakistan's internal affairs ... It is the people of Pakistan themselves who must decide their own destinies.' Prime minister Edward Heath was tougher: 'There must be an end to bloodshed and the use of force as soon as possible.'

But the British government suddenly found themselves under unprecedented pressure from public and parliamentary opinion. The East Bengalis, aided by international NGOs [non-governmental organisations], ran most of their campaigns from Britain. One man in particular played a huge role.

Ten days before Wadekar and Adhikari sat in the New Langham Hotel in Bayswater reading their respective papers, Anthony Mascarenhas's report about the East Pakistan situation had been published in London's *Sunday Times*. This Pakistani journalist of Goan Christian descent had been one of the eight newsmen taken on an officially sponsored trip to East Pakistan in the last week of April. The idea was to show 'the patriotic way the army was doing its great job'. Mascarenhas was horrified.

Flying in to meet Harold Evans, the editor of *The Sunday Times*, Mascarenhas explained that the levels of censorship in Pakistan made it impossible for him to report the incident in full. Impressed by Mascarenhas's *'decent Christian passion'*, Evans decided to print the story. Before it was published, the journalist managed to organise the passage of his wife and children to Italy and thereafter into England. He himself took a flight to Peshawar, crossed the Afghanistan border on foot and made his way back to Europe.

'This is genocide conducted with amazing casualness,' announced the article on 13 June. Between March and December 1971, *The Times* ran 29 editorials on the East Pakistan situation, *The Daily Telegraph* published 39, *The Guardian* 37, *The Observer* 15 and *The Financial Times* 15. By early June, Britain, while continuing with the existing programmes, had suspended further economic aid to Pakistan.

With millions of East Bengali refugees making for the Indian border, across which they shared a common language and culture with the Bengalis of West Bengal, the Indian government grew worried. India was a poor nation, not capable of feeding hordes of refugees. Food prices were being driven up, wages pushed down. There could easily be communal tensions. Besides, insurgency was also on the cards because West Bengal had been rife with the Naxalite movement for several years.

The Indian military were already training the guerrillas of Mukti Bahini. On 17 April, at a ceremony carefully orchestrated by the Indian Border Security Force, the government of Bangladesh was formally proclaimed in the presence of Indian and foreign journalists in a mango grove across the Indian border. Syed Nazrul Islam took the guard of honour as acting president. The place, Baidyanath Tala, has now been renamed Mujibnagar.

Recognition of this new government did not come immediately, not even from India. However, at the end of April 1971, in a cabinet meeting, prime minister Indira Gandhi asked General Sam Manekshaw if he was prepared to lead India into war. The military hero replied that he would have to take the monsoons into account. The heavy flooding in the Himalayan passes would be a factor. He had seen the weather as a threat and wanted to set his own date. The prime minister agreed.

Down the years, especially after the passing of Mrs Gandhi, Manekshaw's account of the incident grew more and more imaginative and dramatic with each retelling. Much like the legends associated with the heroes of the 1971 cricket team.

The Witch and the Bastards

The Nixon-Kissinger attitude towards Indians and their leaders would remain constant way after the end of our story. In November 1971, Indira Gandhi visited Washington and met the president in the Oval Office. On the face of it, the conversation was cordial, even banal. However, afterwards Nixon and Kissinger discussed the visit of the lady in no uncertain terms. Both agreed that Mrs Gandhi was 'a bitch'.

'We really slobbered all over the old witch,' said Nixon.

'Indians are bastards anyway,' responded Kissinger, blaming them for starting the war.

From mid-May, New Delhi launched a frenetic diplomatic effort to try and garner international opposition to the Pakistani manoeuvres. Ministers and special emissaries flew to capitals in Europe, North Africa, East and West Asia. Jayaprakash Narayan went around almost like a modern-day John the Baptist. Swaran Singh flew to Moscow, Bonn, Paris, Ottawa, Washington and finally London, expressing his frustrations about the UN at the last stop. All these missions did not really result in much more than sympathetic words and small promises of monetary aid.

On 13 May 1971, Mrs Gandhi sent a message to the White House, explaining the carnage and ethnic cleansing in East Pakistan, and how it had created a massive refugee problem and a major security threat in India. The Nixon administration urged restraint.

In their private talks, Nixon said, 'What the Indians need is a mass famine.' Kissinger agreed, 'They are such bastards, the most aggressive goddamn people around here.' The American administration – even in the Nixon years they were not called the 'Nixon regime' but the 'Nixon administration' – were not the only ones to demonstrate incredible disdain for the Indians.

While India played Essex during the 1971 tour, the British High Commissioner in Delhi sent a missive to the Foreign and Commonwealth Office, calling the Indian government 'a bunch of psychotics'.

The problem was also that not too many Indians thought differently. The nation was still finding its bearings. The optimism of the early post-independence years had given way to struggle against the realities of a huge diverse country. The dreams fuelled by the construction of dams and nationalised heavy industries had now disappeared behind the endless queues for milk and kerosene, decade-long waits for telephone connections, bureaucracy, corruption, increasingly murky politics and an abominable licence raj that made setting up and running businesses an impregnable maze of red tape.

Malnutrition remained a major challenge, and life expectancy hovered around 48.4 (a huge improvement from 32 in 1947). The literacy rate was around 32 per cent. It was a land of contrasts and frustrations, PL480 wheat, bought from the USA, nationalisation of sectors and atrocious import duties.

Wadekar and the rest of the Indian side had grown up watching Peter Sellers and Spike Milligan paint themselves black to play Indians. Indians were not even taken seriously enough to play themselves.

Meeting the English cricketers as equals on the field was not that easy.

4

KICKING OFF WITHOUT THE NOOB

SPORT AND the battlefield were strange bedfellows. Adhikari knew. He had been coaxed out of his military duties at Dharamsala at the age of 39, after a two-and-a-half-year hiatus, to come back into the Indian team and lead them against the West Indies. That had been the winter of four captains in five Tests. Adhikari had scored 63 and 40 and dismissed Hunte, Butcher and Atkinson as India drew the Test. Following that, he had disappeared, never to play again.

Now in 1971, he thought it was curious that the cricket teams of the two countries on the brink of war were sharing the international fixtures of the English summer, as they had done four years earlier.

In 1967, they had both been trounced 3-0 by Brian Close's men. Godfrey Evans had not minced words in *The People* when he had written, 'Cricket fans should not be asked to pay the West Indies-Australian tour minimum price of 7s, 6d. Charge 5s, I say, when the weaker sides are touring. And let one of the big guns share with India or Pakistan in 1971.'

But the same two sides were in England yet again. The only thing that had changed from the Evans narrative was the shillings and pence bit.

On 15 February 1971, the UK had decimalised its currency. Gone were the shillings consisting of 12 old pence. Three new coppers – the new penny (1p), the 2 new pence (2p), and the new halfpenny (½p) were introduced. There were three decimal silver coins – the 50p, 10p and 5p. Not everyone was happy with this. 'How much is that in old money?' asked many.

Harrods, Selfridges and the rest had armies of 'decimal pennies' – girls in 'rakish boaters and blue sashes' or 'in shorts and midi split skirts and other suitably mathematical costumes' – to help confused shoppers. Some made a quick buck selling 'Decimal Adders'. The BBC broadcast five-minute programmes on decimal themes.

Just 46 per cent of the British people were in favour of decimalisation. The most incensed were, of course, the elderly. It was one of the many ways that the country had been going to the dogs since the war. Wherever one looked, one saw long-haired men, bell bottoms, sex, drugs and rock 'n' roll, and excitement about decimal money. And then there was terrorism, the decay of everything British, loud music, and all these 'coloured' people multiplying every day, responsible for inflation, crime, terrorism. Decimal money was the newest vehicle for tradition-bending changes, sure to cripple the economy.

The cricket-minded among the elderly found it symptomatic that in spite of the words of warning of the sideburn-sporting Evans, Pakistan had arrived in late April followed by India one-and-a-half months later.

Wadekar was aware of the terrible record that preceded them. Before the tour there had been a symposium organised by *Sportsweek*, moderated by Khalid Ansari. Not one of the former cricketers had given them much of a chance. Nari Contractor had been the most pessimistic, with an 80-20 prediction against India. Polly Umrigar had been somewhat more charitable with a 60-40 estimate in favour of England. Rusi Modi, suave in his restraint, had declined to forecast. Vijay Manjrekar had not been asked.

And this was after Wadekar's men had made epochal history by defeating the West Indies in the West Indies.

Of course, all this was before the passing of the decades and the gradual juxtaposed mythologising – through which Hall and Griffith of the Sixties and the Roberts, Holding, Garner brigade of the Seventies merged with the faceless Uton Dowes and Grayson Shillingfords to make the 1971 West Indian team, in the collective memory, full of menacing fast bowlers At that point, the cricket world did know that the West Indians were a pale reflection of their great side of the 1960s. The 1971 team possessed one of the weakest bowling attacks in the world and was ploughing halfway through a barren stretch of 31 Tests of which they would win two and lose 10. They did not win a single series after 1966 and before 1973. Recalling the 642 runs he scored in the series, Dilip Sardesai later said, 'I was helped by the fact that they had no pace attack worth the name.'

Yet, toothless bowling and docile wickets notwithstanding, the win was memorable. West Indies, after all, still had the batting big guns in Garry Sobers, Rohan Kanhai and the young Clive Lloyd. It took mountains of runs from the bats of Sardesai and a youthful Sunil Gavaskar to neutralise them. A series win over five Tests could not quite be dismissed as a matter of luck. Wadekar was perhaps justified in feeling a bit let down by the ex-cricketers who refused to go up to an even 50-50.

But he knew their record in England was atrocious. What rankled was perhaps his memory of the previous tour.

Four years before, Wadekar had been on his first tour to England. On the day of the tour opener against Worcestershire, the same *Daily Mirror* that he now held in his hand had splashed a story by Brian Chapman headined, 'India Kick-off without the Noob'.

The Nawab of Pataudi had been afflicted by laryngitis and had stayed back in London while his men had travelled to Worcester. According to Chapman, the Noob's parting order was that his men should put in a full afternoon's stint in the nets, and for three hours they had faithfully followed the behest, disregarding snow flurries that briefly changed bowler Bishan Bedi's turban into a polka-dotted affair of blue and white.

Pataudi's men had arrived with the same dismal Indian record in England behind them and had gone on to add their own sad chapter by losing all three Tests. But a Nawab, even by his absence, had been newsworthy.

That was historical truth, a remnant of the complicated past that was so palpable. Even two decades after the integration of the princely states into India, even after the confiscation of the privileged privy purses.

Wadekar did not quite make it clear whether he was aware of it or not, but he was the first true commoner to take a team to England.

Yes, C.K. Nayudu had led India in their first Test match in 1932. But the tour had been carried out under the leadership of the Maharaja of Porbandar with the Maharaja of Limbdi as the vice-captain. Besides, Nayudu himself had been an officer in the army of the Maharaja of Holkar, employed more because of his cricketing prowess.

Vijay Hazare had led them in 1952, and he had been patronised first by the Maharaja of Dewas and then the Maharaja of Baroda. Hazare's occupations were variously tiger hunter, captain of the Maharaja's army and aide-de-camp. Dewas had even got Clarrie Grimmett to come over and coach Hazare.

The other captains of visiting Indian teams had always been princes with various degrees of proficiency in the game – from the rudimentary cricketing skills in the Billy Bunter form of Vizzy to the accomplished talents of the Pataudis, father and son. And in 1959, there had seen the curious case of Datta Gaekwad conjured out of thin air and pitchforked into the hot seat ahead of Vijay Manjrekar, Polly Umrigar and Pankaj Roy.

In contrast, Wadekar was an out-and-out commoner.

Technically, if Pataudi had made it to the 1971 tour, it would have been as a commoner. He would have registered on the scoreboard as Mansur Ali Khan. That was the ruling of the president of India. Indeed, from the 1972/73 home series, Pataudi played as Mansur Ali Khan.

But even with an 'erstwhile' worn as an invisible regal cloak, the Nawab would probably have held court in the headlines.

Those were not the only items of news that day, though.

Two stories appearing on page 3 provided the defining snapshot of the times.

Mark Bonham Carter, chairman of the Community Relations Commission, expressed disappointment that so few of the amendments he had proposed to the Immigration Bill and the draft rules had been accepted.

The threat of the inflow of 200,000 Kenyan Asians had already resulted in the Commonwealth Immigration Act in 1968. Like the Act of 1962, it had further reduced the rights of citizens of the Commonwealth to migrate to the United Kingdom. The 1971 Bill was about to make immigration even more difficult.

The other story on the third page was about an action taken against Mr and Mrs Patrick Lenehan, proprietors of the Painters Arms, Havelock Road, Luton. In June 1970, five West Indian men had gone to the pub after a game of dominoes and ordered a couple of drinks. Mrs Lenehan had refused to serve them.

There was another pair of supplementary stories.

In Sydney, Springbok rugby legend Danie Craven warned demonstrators against trying the sort of disruptions that had plagued their 1969/70 tour of Britain and ultimately forced the cancellation of the 1970 South African cricket tour. 'If these types come on to the field in Sydney and get mixed up in a loose scrum, God help them,' he said.

In England, the leader of that Stop The Seventy Tour (STST) campaign, 21-year-old Peter Hain, received summonses alleging disruption of four international sporting fixtures. He was handed them at Heathrow, 10 minutes before boarding his flight to Australia. The Australian Anti-Apartheid Movement had sponsored his trip, inviting him to join their campaign against apartheid sport during the Springbok tour of Australia.

Neither Dr Craven's warnings nor the court summons were able to stop him from getting on the plane.

5

HE SHOULD HAVE SAID
THAT TO TENDULKAR

PETER HAIN was 19 when he had led the successful STST movement. The protests had shocked conservatives, and played a leading role in stopping the proposed South African cricket tour of the 1970 summer. Even the MCC, generally as quick off the mark as a slow loris on sedatives, had shown appreciable urgency in replacing the South Africans with a Rest of the World team led by Garry Sobers.

Peter was 70 when I just about managed to pip coronavirus lockdown to meet him at the House of Lords in London. *Apartheid: A Point to Cover* was published in late April 2020, with a crisp foreword by Lord Hain of Neath. Peter's own book on the subject, *Pitch Battles* co-written with Andre Odendaal, was delayed by publishing timelines thrown askew by the pandemic.

Eventually both of us found ourselves in the Chiswick Cricket Calendar's weekly podcast hosted by the two excellent cricket writers, Peter Oborne and Richard Heller. We spoke about cricket, South Africa and the poisoned legacy of apartheid.

A point touched upon during my November 2020 Chiswick Cricket conversation is rather relevant to this book. The question was asked by Richard, just after we had ended the podcast.

South Africa, for complex reasons, had a white monopoly in international cricket. West Indies, yet another land of a long period of white privilege, did not have a white monopoly, but always had a white man at the helm for several decades. It was not so with India, despite it being yet another county with an even longer period of white privilege. Was it simply because of demographics – there not being a big enough white population to sustain first-class cricket in India on its own? Or was it something else?

The answer, I believe, is two-fold.

One of the reasons is pure luck, and I will spend this chapter demonstrating how it was so.

The second reason is more complex and has its root in what David Cannadine termed 'Ornamentalism'. I will cover that in a subsequent chapter.

There are still some who maintain that Lord Harris, the former England captain and governor of Bombay from 1890 to 1895, played a major role in the development of cricket in India. The assertion that Harris is 'the father of Indian cricket' is hotly disputed by several historians. However, it cannot be denied that the British peer was held in a great deal of awe by the pioneers of Indian cricket, the Parsis. M.E. Pavri, the Parsi demon bowler, called Harris the guru of Parsi cricket.

Harris, in his role as a benevolent governor, did do a fair bit for cricket in that community. It was he who persuaded the Gymkhana members to hold the annual Bombay Presidency matches between the Europeans and the Parsis.

With the Hindus joining the fray in 1907/08, the tournament became the Bombay Triangular. With the Muslims coming in from 1912/13, it became the Quadrangular and, in 1937/38, the Bombay Pentangular when the other religions were clubbed into a side called The Rest.

Before all that, from 1892 to 1906, the Parsis and the Europeans faced each other 26 times in bilateral Bombay Presidency matches. The Parsis won 11, the Europeans 10 and there were five draws. The two Parsi tours to England, in 1886 and 1888, had not really seen them set the cricket grounds on fire. But back home, they competed against the Europeans as equals.

Yet, in 1906 Lord Harris, by then back in England for several years, remarked, 'Indians have a good eye and rather long arms, but do not possess the patience and resolution of the Anglo-Saxon.' Therefore, he hinted, they could not become very good cricketers.

When I related this to the Heller-Oborne duo, Richard retorted, 'He should have said that to Tendulkar.'

Curiously, Sachin Tendulkar, perhaps the greatest batsman produced by India, shot to prominence as a 14-year-old schoolboy, hammering a triple hundred and adding 664 with friend Vinod Kambli at the Sassanian ground at Azad Maidan. The two were representing their school, Shardashram Vidyamandir, against St Xavier's High School in the semi-final of the inter-school tournament. The shield they were playing for had a medallion portrait of the erstwhile governor of Bombay in the middle, surrounded by a laurel wreath. It is still called the Harris Shield.

India is full of such contradictions.

The apparent camaraderie with the Parsis was one of the balancing acts that Harris performed to shake off the stigma of insensitivity towards Indians. Harris did not like Indians, especially educated ones. A year into his role as governor, he had written to Viscount Cross in the India Office, 'We can do infinitely more work in their climate than they can ... they get fat and lazy as they rise in rank, whilst our civilians are as active as young men.'

Besides, his attitude towards administration was touched by callousness. There are accounts of his continuing to enjoy cricket at Poona while interracial riots had broken out in Bombay in 1893.

Harris was not alone among his compatriots in his attitude towards Indians – and their cricket. So there was every possibility of Indian cricket following the South African or the West Indian routes, with their entrance into the international scene being usurped or chaperoned by white men.

Of course India was never a White Dominion. Unlike Australia, New Zealand, Canada or South Africa, or even

Kenya, where the attempted White Man's Country experiment went wrong.

The population had nothing to do with it. That had never been a problem. The aboriginals of Australia had been waved aside by the rigorous implementation of *terra nullius*. The native Americans had been variously slaughtered and beaten back. The indigenous African people of South Arica had outnumbered the whites by four to one but had been eventually seconded into seven per cent of the land. The Maori land had been confiscated through Settlement Acts.

However, *terra nullius* and its variants came up with an ineffectual dull thud against a wall of splendour in India when the English sailed right into the Mughal Empire at its full might in the 17th century. When Sir Thomas Roe, an emissary from James I, was presented at the royal court, he was transfixed by the attire of Emperor Jahangir, expending a great number of effusive words on his jewelled belt.

It was not just the emperor's magnificent clothes. The Mughal period saw flourishing cultural life, economic stability and even advances in the field of two different medical systems. Obviously, the *terra nullius* model had hit a stumbling block.

Yet, by the time the Parsis had become the first Indian people to take to cricket, that difficulty had long been overcome. India was way too rich not to be plundered and drained. Inroads had been made through trade, and the gradual takeover of power had followed. Textiles, indigo, salt and other riches were ransacked in exchange for gold bullion from the New World.

At the same time, be it the rule of the East India Company or the subsequent governance of the British Empire, a flaky garb of principle was cobbled together to cover the saga of ruthless money-grabbing. Hence arose the orientalist fables.

The powerful rulers became oriental despots. The farmers who toiled from dawn to dusk under the tyrannical tropical sun became 'the lazy natives'.

Sitting in England, James Mill wrote his *History of British India* in 1818, in which the Indians were referred to as 'the most enslaved portion of the human race'. The conditions existing in India, which he never saw first-hand, reminded Mill of 'rude nations' of the 'Red Indians' or 'primitive Anglo-Saxons'.

The existing riches and administrative order were rationalised by branding India a land in the process of decay after a glorious past. British liberals confidently saw their task as that of stripping off the shackles of 'despotism', 'priestcraft', 'darkness'.

By 1835, Lord Thomas Babington Macaulay was nonchalantly proclaiming, 'A single shelf of a good European library is worth the whole native literature of India and Arabia.' Of course, he did not get around to learning Sanskrit ... or Arabic or Persian or Tamil. However, he had 'spoken to many who knew those languages and none had been able to deny the fact'.

The revolt of 1857 marked a watershed moment, when the jewel from the East made its way from the ledgers of a trading company and found itself ensconced in the glorious crown of the Empire.

The conflict itself was a result of continuous dissent, racial discrimination, blatant annexation tactics such as the doctrine of lapse and pretexts for misgovernance. The revolt, duly suppressed, was paid for by some of the most vengeful atrocities on the rebels ... atrocities buried under the one-sided gamut of interminable fables and myth-laced literature churned out about this 'heroic triumph'. The Mutiny could now be used as an argument in support of virtually any policy. The insecurity of a vastly outnumbered British community as an alien group in a hostile country naturally contributed to the measures thereafter.

By 1858, the Queen had taken over and the British rule was based on a promise of social and economic improvement. This was translated into their annual reports of the Indian government with the obnoxiously arrogant title 'moral and material progress'.

After the revolt, and even before that, black towns emerged in contrast to the British mansions. The social distinction and aloofness of the British as a superior race was marked. Interaction among the races was skewed, limited to the Indian elite and the servant class.

The English in India and Indians abroad

The British rule was marked by a steady diet of devastating famines, terrifying epidemics and contagious diseases. Literacy and social progress remained superfluous luxuries.

However, due focus was provided on the growth of the army – deployed throughout the Empire by the British and paid for by the Indians. That included the cost of the British troops in India, the pensions of the British officials, and the cost of the Indian Office, the Whitehall department from which Indian affairs were supervised.

The troops, amounting to two-thirds of the total standing army of the Empire, had little to do with the defence of India. Before the First World War, they were deployed in China, Ethiopia, Malaya, Malta, Egypt, Sudan, Burma, East Africa, Somaliland and Tibet. They also fought the Boer War in South Africa, but of course only the white troops could participate in that quest.

However, no Indian was permitted to rise above the rank of brigadier.

The Indian Civil Service was formed almost entirely of British officers. On paper an Indian could make the grade. However, the qualifying examination had to be taken in London, which made the proportion of Indians negligible.

The British officers, taken from the hotchpotch curriculum of Haileybury, arrived in India. Confused by a country and culture their courses had hardly prepared them for, they often found solace and nostalgia in the camaraderie of brother officers in their exclusive white clubs and cricket pitches.

Indian villagers, confronted with land fragmentation and agricultural uncertainty, started operating as indentured labourers in Jamaica, Trinidad, British Guiana, Suriname, Mauritius, Fiji, Natal, Malaya, Zanzibar, Uganda and Kenya.

Many of the descendants of these Kenyan Indians were among those rushing to the United Kingdom in the late 1960s, with the Africanisation of the independent government. Soon, in the early 1970s, Idi Amin would drive Indians away from Uganda.

There was segregation at every level of society. Segregating lines drawn in shades of colour. This reflected in the domain of sport as well.

While Indians were more rigidly categorised into castes by the British, even creating criminal castes into which some unfortunates were born, the ruling British became as good as the super-caste of elites. Racial mixing was virtually non-existent and half-castes, the Eurasians born out of mixed parentage, were shunned by society.

The reaction to the introduction of the Ilbert Bill of 1883, and its subsequent compromised implementation, were symptomatic of the racial equation – the very idea of native magistrates and session judges trying charges against European and British subjects was abhorrent.

In late 1889, a band of amateur English cricketers visited India under the captaincy of Middlesex stalwart George Frederick Vernon. This tour has gone down as the first by an English cricket team to India.

They played 13 matches, of which 12 were against sides made of expat Englishmen. None of them have gone down as first-class.

The other match was against the Parsis. In a setting of shamianas, glitterati from the Parsi and the British communities, ceremonially dressed Parsi priests and 20,000 spectators at the Gymkhana Ground, the Parsis triumphed by four wickets, Pavri dismissing seven batsmen.

Three years later, one of the major members of Vernon's side arrived in India with his own team. The Parsis defeated them by 109 runs in the first meeting, Pavri picking up 6-26 in the final innings, and 10 wickets in the match.

This Parsi feat is commendable to say the least. The former member of Vernon's side who led the English team was none other than Lord Hawke, and the team included the immensely gifted future England captain Stanley Jackson. Hawke had been invited to bring a team to India by Harris himself. During the tour, the governor of Bombay entertained Hawke with every bit of lavishness known to the oriental monarchs.

A week after the Parsis had overcome the Englishmen, the two teams met again at the Gymkhana Ground. The visitors rode the brilliance of Middlesex amateur John Hornsby to win a cliffhanger by seven runs. 'The Parsi ladies cried like babies and the crowd did not take the result in good spirit,' wrote Hawke.

Another poignant recollection of these matches dealt with the segregation exercised among the players and spectators. The matches were played in an English ground – it would be 1925 before the English would deign to play on native grounds. The Parsi cricketers and spectators were barred from entering the club on any pretext. The ground was divided into two sections, one for the Europeans and one for the natives, and no native dared to be seen in the European section. While the English team lunched in the clubhouse, the Parsis did so in their own tents.

The rules held even for the Readymoney family, who hosted Hawke and his men in their Malabar Hill mansion.

To come back to the question of luck, and how it played a role in India never consisting of a white team or playing under the captaincy of a white man, let us dwell a while on South Africa.

International cricket arrived at the Cape as an Old Boys' initiative in 1888/89. It was due to the efforts of England rugby international and Western Province Cricket Club supremo William Milton. A team was assembled to visit South Africa – a motley collection of a few average and a few brilliant cricketers. On arrival they were treated to a lavish public dinner attended by a who's who of South African dignitaries – the grandest welcome ever accorded to any visitor to the land.

The tour included the two representative matches that curiously went on to be recognised as Test matches in 1897, a categorisation that decades later had the likes of historian Rowland Bowen frothing at the mouth.

Owen Dunnell, a Port Elizabeth businessman hailing from Eton and Oxford, led South Africa in their first Test match. England were led by Aubrey Smith of Charterhouse and Cambridge. Dunnell's wife embroidered 'SA' on each of the caps of the home cricketers. It could not have smacked of a more domestic, more parochial, and more exclusive Old Boys' club setting. Played at Port Elizabeth, the inaugural Test match not only saw the exclusion of the entire population of non-white cricketers across the land, but Milton also drew flak for ignoring all the deserving white Afrikaner cricketers as well.

As a match it was, as expected, a non-contest, with the skills of George Ulyett and Johnny Briggs proving too much for the home batsmen.

The disdain for the native exclusiveness of the British was as rampant in India. The Old Boys' club connection was no less than in the South African example. Lord Harris, Eton and Oxford, hosted Lord Hawke, Eton and Cambridge, during the 1892/93 tour. The lavishness of hospitality encompassed dinner, entertainment and shooting expeditions.

At the Gymkhana Ground on Boxing Day 1892, the visitors faced off against Bombay. The home team was all-white, with at least one important stalwart in Major Robert Poore. This Hampshire legend later played three Tests against Lord Hawke's Englishmen *for* South Africa in 1895/96. Apart from Poore there was the Gloucestershire cricketer Arthur Newnham, and also a couple of cricketers who had county cricket experience.

If we compare player by player, it was a far better home side that took on the English team than the South African XI had been at Port Elizabeth.

It was plain lucky for Indians that no one was struck with the idea of chalking down this all-white cricket match as the first Test played in India

* * *

A month after their match against Bombay, Lord Hawke's men squared off against a team that was actually called 'India'. It was a side of Europeans alongside a couple of Parsis, led by an Englishman. It included Pavri and also E.H.D. Sewell, the cricketer who gained subsequent fame as a writer. The setting was Allahabad. Once again, one must say that the Indians were distinctly lucky that some old codger fiddling with the scorebooks at the MCC did not have a sudden moment of imperialistic inspiration to brand it a Test match.

Yes, luck did have a role in the first Indian Test team not being a white man's XI. But there was indeed another major reason. A reason strongly linked to the Princes, the Kumars, the Maharajas and the Nawabs.

6

TONGUE-TWISTING NAMES
AND TORMENTING SPIN

AT LORD'S Mike Brearley wins the toss, but very few people seem to care. Only a handful of spectators sit scattered in the stands as Eric Russell and Michael Smith feast on the friendly medium-pace of Abid Ali and Eknath Solkar. The use of Gavaskar as the third seamer, at the insistence of Adhikari, does not quite help the Indian cause.

In the first 45 minutes the experienced opening batsmen raise 53. Russell, who visited India with Ted Dexter's men in 1961/62 and played a Test in Calcutta, looks the more accomplished of the two.

The problems begin when whatever little pace on offer is replaced by revolutions on the ball. On come Bishan Singh Bedi and Bhagwat Chandrasekhar. This is not something the batsmen relish. The pitch, a week old after the just completed Test match against Pakistan, is helping balls tossed up with a rip. Russell, with his penchant for the cover-drive, plays Bedi chest-high to Abid Ali at cover and the catch is floored.

But Bedi has his reward soon enough. The ball, tracing a tantalisingly inviting loop, soon lures Smith into another drive. Abid, now at extra-cover, holds on this time: 89/1 – the first taste of success on the tour.

At lunch it is 92/1 off 36 overs.

At the other end Venkataraghavan, Wadekar's deputy, takes a while to find his length. Twice Russell drives him

57

through the covers. And then the opener is missed twice more, at 38 by Chandrasekhar and at 50 by Sardesai. Wadekar frowns in the slips, Adhikari purses his lips on the dressing-room balcony. This department of the game needs tightening up and fast.

An hour after lunch, the players break for a sip of orange juice. Peter Parfitt and Russell exchange pleasantries with the Indians. They can afford to: 154/1 looks excellent on the scoreboard. The normal Indian tale of struggles on an England tour seems to be happening yet again.

On the resumption, however, wickets fall in a flurry.

Parfitt ventures out to Venkat and is smartly stumped by Krishnamurthy. Ten runs later Russell's luck runs out. He is out in the predictable manner, driving yet another tossed-up Bedi delivery straight to extra cover. Bedi strikes again soon after that, Clive Radley prodding and being neatly held by Solkar at short-leg.

"Bedi is more rounded in shape and craft than when one saw him last," writes John Arlott.

Chandra is coming back after a long lay-off. A scooter accident raised questions about his career. He missed the tour of the West Indies, where, in hindsight, he would have loved to bowl. Until now he has toiled hard without reward with his medium-paced leg-breaks and top-spinners. He now gets one to fizz through and Brearley is caught at the wicket.

It is tea, and suddenly Middlesex have slumped to 205/5.

After the break, the innings lasts just 35 minutes as the last five wickets go down for 28. Chandrasekhar 5-67, Bedi 3-53 from 32 classy overs, Venkat 2-48. Middlesex 233 all out.

Wadekar allows himself a smile. Dr Chandrasekhar Thakore, the Bombay doctor who moonlights as an astrologer, successfully predicted an Indian win in the Caribbean. It could have been the correct alignment of astral bodies, the scientific analysis of the poor run that was dogging West Indies, or simply a lucky wager. But many Indians take him seriously. So seriously, in fact, that when Thakore vouched for the auspiciousness of 17 June, the

Indian cricketing authorities actually pushed the date of departure forward by two days.

The post-tea capitulation of Middlesex is perhaps read as validation of Thakore's astrology skills. But as the Indian team walk smiling back through the Long Room, one of their major stars sit fuming.

E.A.S. Prasanna has misgivings that he is not part of Wadekar's plans. With 124 Test wickets at 27.93, he is the most experienced and the most successful of the spin quartet. Bedi, Chandra and Venkat have not yet hit 100.

But there is a classical left-arm spinner in Bedi, who tosses it up. There are the googlies and top-spinners of Chandra, which have just shown how effective they can be. This leaves room, at least according to the Indian think-tank, for one off-spinner. And in Wadekar's scheme of things, it has to be a stock bowler who chokes things up. Not another man who floats it to buy wickets irrespective of the type of pitches. The elevation of fellow-off-spinner Venkat to the role of vice-captain has been suggestive enough.

Test Status or Social Status?

There is hardly ever any reason that explains categorisation when it comes to cricket and its old scorebooks.

An extraordinary level of cricket was witnessed in the non-white contests between the South Africans and the Kenyan Asians in East Africa in the 1950s. Those were the matches in which a young Basil D'Oliveira led the South African side.

These matches have still not been given even *first-class* status. They remain listed as miscellaneous matches even as every cricketing establishment jumps on the Black Lives Matter bandwagon to provide window dressing for their respective images.

However, the Owen Dunnell/Aubrey Smith farce of 1888/89 enjoys the status of a Test match.

On his return to India, Prasanna will be quick to point out the problems with the 'think-tank'. 'Who chose Venky? Wadekar, Adhikari and Venky himself! They had to include Venky because he was the vice-captain, but haven't two off-spinners played for India before?'

The argument about the inadvisability of four spinners did not cut much ice with Prasanna either. 'Where is the question of my being the fourth spinner? Wasn't I the number one spinner with those 124 Test wickets? Any scheme they drew up should have had me as the number one spinner.'

Later, Dilip Sardesai was scathing in his views of Prasanna's peevishness. 'Pardon my saying so, but Pras's behaviour in England was simply atrocious. It just happened he did not bowl as well as Venky. Venky was bowling like a champion and he bowled like a champion in the West Indies as well. And what a fielder! In the slips, I always asked Ajit to let me stand next to him, for I knew he'd take my catches too.'

Close-in fielding is a vital element in the Indian mix, especially with the team banking on spin.

The 124-wicket argument will also be dismissed by Sardesai.

'Didn't Lance Gibbs have almost twice that number of Test wickets and rate as the best off-spinner when we went to the West Indies? Yet he was dropped because Noreiga was the man in form.' Indeed, when he was dropped against India, Gibbs had 209 Test wickets.

Fitness comes into the picture as well.

Venkat is one of the fittest men in the side and both Wadekar and Adhikari are sticklers on that point. Prasanna just does not believe in that aspect of cricket.

And for all the significance of 124 Test wickets, if we dig deep into the numbers, contemporary or past, the decision will come across as being wise.

In the West Indies, Prasanna was injured during the second Test and came back in the fifth. His 11 wickets were taken at 37.00 apiece. Venkat seized the opportunity to play a more vital role, and picked up 22 at 33.81 in the five Tests.

Wadekar trusts Venkat, especially appreciating his willingness to align his bowling to the captain's game plan.

As for bowling in England, Venkat played one Test in 1967, the only Test in history when all four of India's spin quartet played together. Budhi Kunderan, the reserve wicketkeeper, took the new ball. Venkat sent down 15 overs and took 1/30. Prasanna, the weapon of choice of the Nawab of Pataudi, played all three Tests that series, and his nine wickets came at a high cost of 47.77.

Prasanna is right. The Middlesex match, for all practical purposes, decides the Indian spin attack. In terms of time and space, current form and conditions, Venkat is the better choice.

By the time India start their reply, the light has turned murky. Young Gavaskar walks out with the veteran Abbas Ali Baig.

John Price, with his long, curved run-up is always a handful. At 34 he is not the youthful tearaway of the past, but he is gunning for an England spot.

Gavaskar picks on the less threatening Keith Jones, square driving and hooking him for boundaries. '... a hint of how he came to be so prolific last winter,' is the retro-fitted speculation of Woodcock.

Amritt Harrichand Latchman

Of Indian roots and born in Kingston, Latchman belonged to the Windrush generation. Coming to London in the 1950s, he went to school in Shepherd's Bush. He played for Middlesex for nine seasons, capturing exactly 400 wickets. In 2015 he became the president of the club.

On 22 June 2020, Windrush Day, Middlesex CCC listed the Caribbean-born cricketers who had represented them on their website. The group contributed to almost 55,000 runs and accounted for 2,600 wickets. Latchman stood shining alongside Wayne Daniel, Wilf Slack, Roland Butcher, Norman Cowans and others. He remains the only West Indian of Indian origin to have played for the club.

But at 22, Price strikes. Baig snicks to slip. The captain walks in and is greeted by a bouncer. Wadekar hooks impulsively. The ball does not come as quickly as he expects on the sluggish pitch. The resulting skyer comes down safely into the hands of short leg. Sardesai, Mr Dependable after his Caribbean heroics, comes out to thwart the hat-trick.

In the dying moments of the day Gavaskar, stroking the ball excellently, falls unexpectedly. It is a loose ball from leg-spinner Harry Latchman that he can put anywhere and ends up hitting straight back to the bowler.

India end the day at 41/3, the loss of quick wickets dimming the brightness of the deeds on the field.

* * *

The Indian showing at Lord's was, however, not the biggest cricket news of the following morning. The headlines screamed that John Snow was 'too busy' to turn out against the Indians in their tour match against Derrick Robins's side. Struggling with fitness issues since his triumphant Australian tour, and dropped by Sussex for 'lack of effort', Snow cited having 'personal things to attend to'. The fast bowler seemed to be giving up a grand opportunity of getting back into the Test side.

In *The Guardian,* Arlott curiously began his piece, 'Bedi, Gaveshkar [sic], Chandrasekhar and Venkataraghavan, the spin bowlers who are the most effective arm of the Indian team, showed their strength when they took the last nine Middlesex wickets for 79 runs at Lord's.' Among Gavaskar's considerable list of achievements in a long career, this perhaps remains the only instance of his being listed as a stalwart among the Indian tweakers of that era.

Wadekar did find mention of India's match in that morning's *Daily Mirror.* Under the Snow article and elbowed to a corner by the news of Geoffrey Boycott's double hundred against Essex, there was the headline 'Chandra, Bedi put Middlesex in spin.'

Peter Laker started his report, 'The Indians opened their tour at Lord's yesterday in a welter of tongue-twisting names and tormenting words that threatens to ruffle English feathers this summer.'

Venkataraghavan was perhaps the greatest of the tongue-twisters. When he joined Derbyshire in 1973, Rent-a-wagon was preferred as a phonetic substitute.

Middlesex v Indians, Lord's – 23, 24, 25 June
Middlesex 233 (Russell 84, Smith 54; Chandra 5-67, Bedi 3-53)
Indians 41/3.

7

KINGS, PRINCES AND BRUTES

THE FIRST major tongue-twisting Indian name English cricket encountered was, of course, Kumar Shri Ranjitsinhji. Even 'Ranji' did not quite help. The nickname derived by consensus was the plebeian 'Smith'.

Ranji delighted the English with lightning flashes of his oriental blade. The wristy magic that can perhaps be approximated from the batsmanship of latter day artists like Viswanath, Azharuddin and Laxman.

It was our old friend Lord Harris who blocked Ranji's proposed Test debut at Lord's in 1896. On his return from his post as governor of Bombay, Harris became president of the MCC in 1895. After that he virtually ruled English cricket through his position as the Kent cricketing supremo and various offices held in the MCC.

In those days the club hosting the Test match selected the England side for that particular game. When Ranji was discussed for the Lord's Test against Harry Trott's Australians, Harris objected. He said that he did not like migratory birds.

The following Test was held at Manchester. At Old Trafford, the Lancashire Cricket Club, headed by A.N. 'Monkey' Hornby, had no such featherweight reservations. Ranji, however, insisted they ask the Australians. Trott simply responded that it would be a pleasure. Was Trott influenced by his own heritage? He was the grandson of a manumitted slave hailing from Trinidad. But that is mere speculation.

Thus Ranji made his Test debut at Old Trafford and scored 62 and 154 not out. Within another decade, the cricketing world did not struggle to pronounce his name. In fact, while Ranji had been shackled with the mundane English nickname of Smith, 'Ranji' itself became a common nickname in the cricketing world and beyond.

The Australian googly bowler H.V. Hordern was called Ranji because of his swarthy complexion. Another man to boast the nickname 'Ranji' was Nathaniel Arthur Wilson, an All Black rugby star of English and West Indian parentage.

Labuschagne, Steve and Kevin

The malaise of tongue-twisters continues to this day.

John Glennie Greig, the legendary English cricketer who was born and played in India, was indeed nicknamed 'Junglee' Greig. But that was before the internationalisation of the game.

Today commentators from the subcontinent have little difficulty – and persevere even if they do – in pronouncing names as exotic as Marnus Labuschagne and Jason Krejza without seeking a shortcut. However, many of their occidental counterparts still hesitate to go beyond Murali to refer to the man with 800 Test wickets.

There have even been suggestions to simplify the three-syllable Pujara to Steve. Even Che-tesh-war comprises of three syllables, with only one of them unfamiliar to the occidental tongue.

And of course the supposed Yorkshire use of Kevin for all cricketers of Asian origin, by some accounts a dogged preference for the name, has taken the issue to another dimension.

Unlike Wilson, who in spite of his Caribbean roots was born in Christchurch, Harris himself was, rather surprisingly, born in Trinidad. His father, the third Baron Harris, was then the governor of the island. With a convert's zeal, our man developed a fanatical fetish for forced adherence to birthplaces within county boundaries to qualify for county sides. This policy delayed the first-class career of Wally Hammond by two years.

But migratory birds were not the only sentient beings to which Harris took a dislike. Lionel Lord Tennyson, writing in 1933 in his exquisitely named *From Verse to Worse*, was quite scathing in his analysis of the man, 'The late Lord Harris was never exactly what one might call a friend of mine. For nearly half a century he had occupied every position of importance in the council of the MCC, and consequently what he said there was absolute law ... I believe, had I been more friendly with him, and had he liked me more, I might have captained both a side to Australia and to South Africa.'

We must say Harris was rather colour blind when it came to whimsies of likes and dislikes, and it is therefore difficult to attribute his blocking of Ranji as racist. However, colour blind or not, he was not blind, and with time he had to become aware of Ranji's brilliance. By 1906, when Harris dismissed native Indian cricketers as feeble aspirants to a great game due to their lack of Anglo-Saxon qualities, Ranji had completed his Test career with a batting average of almost 45, incredible for those days of non-standardised wickets. By then he had also hit 62 first-class centuries in England, and three more in Australia.

Why, then, did Harris continue to look upon the Indian cricketers with such disdain? The answer lies in the concept of Ornamentalism.

A look at the scorebooks available in the Sussex Museum from Ranji's first season throws light on the issue. In his first few appearances, he is jotted down like any other gentleman cricketer: Mr K.S. Ranjitsinhji. After a few matches, this changes, and for the rest of his career he becomes Kumar Shri Ranjitsinhji.

'Kumar' denotes 'Prince'. It pitchforked the Indian darkie into the ranks of the English gentleman. A leading Mr was rendered superfluous.

The British had never ruled the whole of India. About one-third of the people were, right until the end of the Raj, under 'indirect rule' of the British, administered by hundreds of independent princes. These were personal fiefdoms ruled by Rajas and Maharajas, Nawabs and Nizams. Queen Victoria's dictum had been 'respect the rights, dignity and honour of native princes as our own'. They were supposed to be the natural leaders of South Asian society.

The British thus ruled a third of India by princely proxy. These 'native states' administered themselves under British paramountcy, with residents from the Indian Political Service assigned to them as advisers. They were outside the government of India's tax base. They were insulated by their own autocracy from nationalistic agitation. And most importantly they contributed substantially to the Indian army.

And they were given the status of English gentlemen.

In 1887, when Queen Victoria celebrated her Royal Jubilee, she held court at Windsor Castle for the reception of the Indian chiefs visiting England to tender their personal congratulations. Alongside dignitaries, such as the Duke and Duchess of Connaught, Prince and Princess Christian and Prince Henry of Battenberg, there were Maharajas and Nawabs galore.

This was during the same period when the sahib in India was disciplining his *punkha coolie* with kicks and blows, or bagging a native 'by mistake' while out on shikar. No fewer than 81 such 'shooting accidents' were reported between 1880 and 1890, the killings punished with ridiculously light sentences.

There were less brutal but equally explicit examples of discrimination in more or less every walk of life.

However, yet again when the Queen celebrated her Diamond Jubilee Day on 22 June 1897, Rajput princes stood next to Australian troopers as London witnessed a parade of the spectacles of the Empire.

This dichotomy between race and class was, thus, a feature of India. Race did play a big role in the plight of the common Indian man. However, when it came to the princes, class trumped race.

Hence Lord Harris, his distaste for migratory birds aside, could at once appreciate the beauty and substance of Ranji's batting while dismissing the native Indians as less than cricketing material. To an imperialist, himself steeped in feudal hierarchy, it was not irrational.

Two-way Cricket

The extension of privilege and respect was two-way. In late 1896, while recovering from a congestion of the lungs, Ranji sent for a shorthand writer and dictated his thoughts about the game. He was helped by some of his friends, including his great mate C.B. Fry. And thus was born his magisterial book on the game.

Due to the year of publication, Ranji decided to call it *The Jubilee Book of Cricket*.

The phenomenon is encapsulated by this comment made in 1881 by the German crown prince, the future Kaiser, to his brother-in-law, the Prince of Wales, the future Edward VII. Referring to King Kalakua of Hawaii at a party given by Lady Spencer, Friedrich Wilhelm Viktor Albert said, 'Either the brute is a king or he's a common garden n*****.'

The archetypal Indian prince lived a luxurious life with a large harem, dazzling parties, frequent trips to Europe. And he indulged in sports, some of which were borrowed from the British. Hunting, riding, polo, pig sticking … and cricket.

Ranji was an exception. Prince or otherwise, very few men have batted like him. Down the years a few Indian princes did dazzle on the cricket field, Ranji's nephew Duleep proving to be as brilliant as his uncle. However, many others ended up looking ordinary, even pathetic. But they played a very, very important role as patrons.

Nripendra Narayan, the Maharaja of Cooch Behar, was a cricket fanatic who ran three teams, two in Calcutta and one in the Himalayas. He maintained an excellent ground at his palace in Cooch Behar and sponsored another at Alipore in Kolkata. He recruited two Sussex professionals, George Cox and Joe Vine, to coach his cricketers and play for his side. Later, during the Great War, he recruited Harry Lee.

The foremost patron of the game in India, however, was the House of Patiala. In 1895, having built a formidable polo team and an excellent stable of race horses, the Maharaja Rajendra Singh turned his attention to cricket. He recruited the stalwart Middlesex and England bowler J.T. Hearne and the Surrey professional William Brockwell. An English amateur batsman, Arthur Priestly, also played for his side. On the home front, he employed Parsi stars Colonel K.M. 'Clem Hill' Mistry, champion bowler Captain A.H. Mehta and 'Schoolboy Scorcher' B. Billimoria.

In the 1898/99 season, the Maharaja even engaged Ranji when the maestro wintered in India. The side fielded by Patiala against Calcutta Rangers in December 1898 has to be one of the strongest of the time, including all the cricketers mentioned. The all-European Rangers team, incidentally, included the grandfather of Colin Cowdrey.

The match ended in a tense draw, with Calcutta Rangers managing to bat out time with one wicket remaining.

Patiala vs Rangers, Dec 27 and 28, 1898
Match Drawn

Patiala First Innings

W Brockwell	c Forbes	b Preston	23
KM Mistri		b Preston	12
Prince Ranjitsinhji	c Strong	b Forbes	16
HH the Maharaja		lbw Forbes	15
B Billimoria		not out	34
Badesi Ram	c Strong	b Preston	4
Priestley		retd hurt	5
JT Hearne	c Warden	b Preston	0
Mehta		lbw Forbes	0
Mansoor	c Mahomed	b Preston	5
Williams		b Forbes	8
Extras			20
Total			142

Calcutta Rangers Club First Innings

G Cook	c Hearne	b Mehta	9
J Forbes		c&b Mehta	36
G Reakes		b Hearne	0
SN Powell		c&b Brockwell	23
E Stewart	c Sub	b Hearne	8
CV Warden		not out	35
H Strong		b Hearne	1
JB Clarke	c Sub	b Hearne	0
E Cowdrey		b Hearne	17
W Hill		not out	11
E Preston		b Brockwell	11
Extras			**20**
Total			**157**

Patiala Second Innings

W Brockwell		c&b Preston	22
H Mistri		b Preston	11
Prince Ranjitsinhji		b Hill	56
Badesi Ram		b Stewart	31
B Bilimoria		b Hill	38
F Priestly	c Reakes	b Hill	5
JT Hearne		b Preston	15
HH Maharaja		b Hill	2
J Williams		b Hill	0
J Mehta		b Hill	6
Mansoor Mahomed		not out	0
Extras			**8**
Total			**196**

Calcutta Rangers Club Second Innings

G Cook		b Mehta	6
J Forbes	c Maharaja	b Mehta	5
G Reakes		b Brockwell	2
SN Powell	c Hearne	b Brockwell	6
E Stewart		b Brockwell	9
CV Warden		b Hearne	13
H Strong	c Mistri	b Hearne	7
E Cowdrey	c Maharaja	b Brockwell	0
W Hill	c Billimoria	b Brockwell	18
JB Clarke		not out	11
E Preston		not out	1
Extras			**8**
Total		(for 9 wkts)	**86**

By the 1910/11 season, Ranji had ascended the throne and become the Maharaja of Nawanagar. That winter he took a combined Jodhpur-Jamnagar side to Calcutta to engage in a 12-a-side match against Nattore. The Maharaja of Nattore was yet another major promoter of the game, and a cricketing rival of Cooch Behar.

Nattore's team included fantastic Indian talent. The 'untouchable' left-arm spinner Palwankar Baloo, his brother, the batting mainstay Palwankar Vithal, the brilliant wicketkeeper Kilvidi Seshachari, the Parsi left-arm spinning all-rounder Jehangir Warden. All these men toured England with the Maharaja of Patiala's side in 1911.

But it is Ranji's side that makes one sit up and take notice. There were the Relf brothers Albert and Bob, the former a Test cricketer. There was Tom Killick, another formidable Sussex professional. And there was Archie MacLaren, the very embodiment of the heroic amateur of the Golden Age.

At that time, the former England captain had for a few years held the post of personal assistant to Ranji. The portfolio was vague, often including duties such as riding elephants and hunting tigers. Ranji was funding the hard-up MacLaren and paying for the education of his two sons at Elstree and Harrow. The Indian prince was the godfather of MacLaren's elder son.

Also in the Jodhpur-Jamnagar side was Harry Simms, the Australia-born Sussex all-rounder. This again was to be expected, since Simms took over the duties of Ranji's secretary, whatever such duties entailed, from MacLaren.

Of course, Ranji later employed yet another English captain as his private secretary – his inseparable friend C.B. Fry.

Back in Britain, it was a morose period for the aristocracy. Lloyd George's People's Budget had been passed after the House of Lords had stalled it for over a year. Death duties raise to unprecedented levels, a new series of exactions on land, and rapid clipping of the wings of power wielded by the landed gentry – all this had hit the upper class hard. The Parliament Bill would be introduced in February 1911, removing the right of the House of Lords to veto money bills.

Nattore XII vs Jamnagar-Jodhpur Combined XII

Natore Park, Calcutta
22, 23 December 1910

Match Drawn

Nattore XII First Innings

MD Umriga	c AE Relf	b Simms	5
Prince Hittie	c MacLaren	b AE Relf	14
KA Date		b AE Relf	1
JS Warden		b AE Relf	2
P Vithal		b Simms	0
A Massie		b Simms	19
CV Mehta	not out		14
Prince Victor	c Pyara Khan	b Simms	9
P Baloo		b Simms	19
K Seshachari		b Simms	1
Maharaja of Natore		b Simms	0
KB Mistri		lbw Simms	4
Extras	(4 b, 10 lb)		10
Total			98

AE Relf 13-2-32-3, Simms 12.3-3-33-8 (incomplete)

Jamnagar-Jodhpur Combined XII First Innings

RR Relf		lbw Baloo	5
Oghad Shankar	c Prince Victor	b Vithal	24
EH Killick		b Baloo	9
AE Relf		b Warden	30
HL Simms		b Warden	7
AC MacLaren	lbw Baloo	1	
Maharaja of Nawanagar (Ranji)		not out	24
Ijazuddin	c Prince Victor	b Baloo	1
Maganlal Vyas	lbw Baloo	9	
Hanumant Singh		b Warden	1
Pyara Khan	c Umrigar	b Baloo	1
P James		lbw Warden	1
Extras	(4 b, 7 lb)		11
Total			124

Baloo 22-5-68-6, Warden 19.5-5-34-4, Vithal 4-1-16-1 (there is a slight discrepancy between the bowling figures and the runs scored by batsmen)

Nattore XII Second Innings

CV Mehta	lbw	15
MD Umrigar	b	6
KA Date	b	4
P Vithal	b	0
P Baloo		13
Prince Victor		26
A Massie	b	45
JS Warden	b	40
K Sesachari	b	5
KB Mistry	b	5
Maharaja of Natore	not out	0
Extras		25
Total		184

Jamnagar-Jodhpur Combined XII second innings

RR Relf	st	12
Oghad Shankar	not out	15
EH Killick	b	7
Extras		0
Total	(for 2 wickets)	34

It must have been eerie for the English cricketers to witness that at exactly the same moment, in a far-off corner of the Empire, titled aristocrats such as Ranji and Nattore were exuding the most regal pomp and splendour as they faced each other on the cricket field.

It was curious for another reason. The proposed partition of Bengal had been announced in 1905 by the then viceroy Lord Curzon. The ostensible reason was ease of administration of a large and complex state, but in reality there had been plenty of acts of nationalism in the state and the partition was an effort to divide Bengal along communal lines. This proposal had sparked further nationalist protests not only in Bengal but across the country. Fanned further by the Japanese victory over Russia, the first time an Asian nation had overcome a white power, the uprising became volatile and spread into the *Swadeshi* movement ... every British-manufactured product was boycotted.

The situation remained tense until partition was overturned in 1911. And all this while, with the simmering volatility around them, Nattore and Ranji engaged in cricketing contests, the latter with a veritable army of English cricketers.

The greatest name among the princely patrons of Indian cricket was Bhupinder Singh, the man who became Maharaja of Patiala in 1900 when Rajinder Singh died after falling off his horse during a polo game.

The new Maharaja of Patiala was a towering figure in the early history of Indian cricket. He was also a sexual predator, who reputedly started his day with a virgin. He married often and slept with numerous women who were not his wife. Many of these women were the wives of other men. According to a 1929 indictment, not all of them went to bed with the Maharaja willingly. Some perturbed husbands developed the curious habits of disappearing, dying or ending up in prison. The charges against his treatment of some unwilling women read as rather horrendous.

However, Bhupinder Singh was too important a prince for such reports to lead to significant action. His enthusiasm in raising men, money and material for the Great War was invaluable. He was a representative at important war councils, including the Indian War Conference at Delhi, the Imperial War Conference and War Cabinet. He was the leader of the Indian States' Delegation at the Round Table Conference of 1930 and was Chairman and Chancellor of the Chamber of Princes from 1926 to 1931 (Ranji took over from 1931 until his death in 1933, underlining the potency of cricketing diplomacy).

Hence, when a 200-page charge sheet – consisting of several counts of murder, rape, assault, cruelty and misuse of power – was brought up against him with the full force of witnesses, it seriously alarmed Viceroy Lord Irwin. In the end J. Fitzpatrick, agent of the governor general, held the inquiry and explained, 'His Highness does not deny youthful indiscretions and is willing to make monetary amends.' The same lax measures that allowed white officers to get away with the murders of natives were extended to the Maharaja. It was one of the most definitive illustrations that the Indian princes had been accepted as equals of the white gentlemen.

All-India in England, 1911

Viewed purely from a cricketing point of view, the tour was disastrous. The Indians lost 10 of their 14 matches, winning against Leicestershire and Somerset, and drawing the remaining two. Even the university sides trounced them. However, in the 14 first-class matches, Palwankar Baloo captured 75 wickets at 20.12. His brother Shivram was one of the centurions of the tour. H.D. Kanga captained the side most often, scoring 163 in the win against Leicestershire.

Patiala himself played only in three of the first-class matches. He was too busy, attending garden parties hosted by the likes of the Countess of Jersey, the Sheriff of Middlesex and Lady Crump, the Duchess of Northumberland. He went to polo matches, attended the Trooping of the Colour and even had a private audience with the King. During the match against the MCC, he was summoned from the ground by the Secretary of State, and the tea break was extended by half an hour with All-India nine wickets down in the second innings so that the Maharaja could have a bat.

The excessive indulgence involved in such lavish parties took its toll. Patiala fell ill and withdrew from the tour. As a result, his private secretary, the excellent all-rounder Colonel Mistry, had to withdraw as well.

But Patiala had understood that cricket, a sport for which he anyway had truckloads of passion, could be used diplomatically for power and privilege during the Raj.

In cricketing terms, the Indian princes were at par with the amateur cricketers of England. Hence, it was the same Maharaja of Patiala who led the first All-India team to England in 1911. In a microcosmic reflection of British rule in India, the team was selected by two Hindus, two Muslims, two Parsis and the selection committee was chaired by John Glennie Greig.

The arrival of the side and their accommodation at the Imperial Hotel, Russell Square, were reported in the papers. On the day the team was scheduled to start their first match against Oxford University, *The Times* did mention the event with names of the cricketers of the two sides – in stark contrast to the cold shoulder accorded to Wadekar and his men 60 years down the line.

On 22 June, Bhupinder Singh was among the glittering group of Indian chiefs and notables to attend the coronation of George V. The list of dignitaries published in the papers ate up column inches by the yard just to include the full names and titles, and necessary details such as 'The Gwalior Imperial Service Troops now consist of 1,897 cavalry and 1,794 infantry, including a transport corps of 446 men'.

This was important. The Princes would be vital in the Great War, with the Indian troops playing a pivotal part in the outcome.

As the years rolled on, Patiala recruited major stars. Wilfred Rhodes spent as many as six winters in India, George Hirst was there in 1921/22, Roy Kilner in 1922/23, Maurice Leyland in 1926/27, even Harold Larwood in 1936/37. Frank Tarrant, the Australian, was another major import, a stalwart figure in the history of inter-war Indian cricket. Apart from playing and organising, he was also entrusted with coaching Patiala and his son Yadavinder. It stretches the truth somewhat to categorise Bhupinder Singh as a decent cricketer. The young Yuvraj, however, benefited from the coaching and became a good batsman.

Patiala also bankrolled tours. The first representative MCC side to tour India in 1926/27 had an enormous role to play in the country achieving Test status. Arthur Gilligan's men were sponsored by his Highness.

Players who avoided that tour included the celebrated duo of Jack Hobbs and Herbert Sutcliffe. Four years down the line both were playing for another princely side, turning out for the Maharajkumar of Vizianagaram's team in India and touring with the team in Ceylon. The Kumar, who has gone down in notoriety for his antics in the 1936 tour of England, personally visited Hobbs's sports shop in London to persuade the Master and his celebrated accomplice to make the trip. Vizzy also tried to poach Bradman, but the attempt was unsuccessful.

Hobbs did have problems with playing on Sundays; Vizzy was most accommodating, allowing him to be off the field and absent while batting. Neither Hobbs nor Sutcliffe, professional cricketers both, could hope to be treated as regally in England as they were during the trip.

Another magnificent cricketer, Learie Constantine, was employed as a coach in Hyderabad by Nizam Moin-ud-Dowlah and also played for Vizzy's side.

The 1932 tour of England, where India played their first Test match, was paid for by Vizzy. Patiala, by then 41, had sponsored the training and selection and had been named captain before dropping out at the last moment. The official captain on the tour was the Maharaja of Porbandar, who managed scores of 0, 2, 0, 2, 2. But a royal touch was required for captaincy, much as some ordinary amateur hand was needed to lead the Hobbses, Sutcliffes, Hammonds, Huttons and Comptons of the England side.

In 1935/36 Patiala bankrolled yet another tour, this time the unofficial 'Test' side of the Australians, led by Jack Ryder, including ageing stalwarts such as Charlie Macartney, Bert Ironmonger, Ron Oxenham, Stork Hendry, Hammy Love and others.

Thus foreign cricketers and teams being sponsored and lured to India with money did not start with either the BCCI or IPL.

And as long as men like Patiala, Vizzy, the Maharaja of Cooch Behar and others were recruiting international talent and sponsoring tours, it created a hurdle to prevent cricket from being projected as a purely English game and to made into the monopoly of the white ruling class.

Ornamentalism did tilt the balance in favour of Indian representation.

However, the role of the princes did not begin and end with recruitment of foreign cricketers and sponsoring tours. They played their part in developing local talent as well.

The Maharaja of Nattore maintained his ranks of homegrown stars. Patiala's father recruited Mistry as a colonel. The son continued as his patron, making Mistry his private secretary.

Bhupinder Singh also acted as a patron of future Test cricketers Nazir and Wazir Ali, Lall Singh and Mohammad Nissar. Lala Amarnath, Indian cricket's first centurion, initially received patronage from the powerful Rana family of Lahore before being absorbed by the Patiala house.

The Nawanagar state, the seat of Ranji, supported the likes of the superb Lala Amar Singh, Ladha Ramji, K.S. Meherhomji and Sorabji Colah. Patronage continued after Ranji's death in 1933 through his heir Digvijaysinhji. Ranji's nephew, the great Duleepsinhji, spotted the talent of Amar Singh, and later Vinoo Mankad.

Vijay Hazare, as mentioned earlier, was supported by the Maharaja of Dewas. Hazare later received support and employment from the Maharaja of Baroda.

Even in the 1950s, Salim Durani was employed by the house of Mewar (cricketers were employed like racehorses, he supposedly confided to Richard Cashman).

And in the 1960s, Digvijaysinhji's heir, Satrusalyasinhji, not only turned out for Saurashtra, but also funded men such as Uday Joshi and Dhiraj Parsana to play in England. One of the other cricketers whom he sponsored for his travel to Sussex for county experience was Eknath Solkar, a vital cog of the 1971 side.

Some of the Princes did end up with rather decent deeds in the international arenas. Ranji and Duleep were exceptions, whose feats could be matched by few, but plenty of princes kept playing the game, and also continued getting into the Indian team, many of them on merit. No princely family kindled the Indian imagination as much as the Pataudis.

Cricket and Print Capitalism

While luck and Ornamentalism are two major reasons for the Indians emerging unchaperoned into the international fold, historian Sumit Gangopadhyay does put forward a third angle.

He attributes it to the rise of the Indian middle class in the late 19th century as a result of a form of capitalism from Britain, termed 'print capitalism' by Benedict Anderson in *Imagined Communities*. The clubs, schools and colleges of this community were developed on the basis of Western structure and rules, but independent of direct British influence. A lot of the middle-class sports organisations were formed in this way.

This community went through a significant modernisation of outlook in the aftermath of the First World War. This led to the formation of independent sports associations in Bengal and Bombay, with the support of, but not directly controlled by, the British.

8

TIGER IN A TUNNEL

THE NAWAB of Pataudi had been a Wisden Cricketer of the Year in 1968. His performances during the 1967 tour had been steady, the 64 and 148 at Leeds particularly splendid. The tour itself had been disastrous and apart from Pataudi, the only other Indian batsman to manage a semblance of consistency had been Wadekar.

* * *

Now Wadekar sits tense in the Lord's dressing room as the Indians struggle. Sardesai, after a prolonged period of strokelessness, hits a Latchman long hop to midwicket. Nightwatchman Venkat snicks one from the leggie and is brilliantly caught by Parfitt at slip. Solkar does not last long, hitting a ball from Jones straight back.

The Indians are 94/6. Titmus has been laid low by his leg injury, otherwise Middlesex could have considered themselves on top. But even as the lack of form of the Indian batsmen makes itself apparent, the dapper, neat, wristy form of Viswanath starts to set the ground alight. Heartened by the ease of his young partner's cuts and drives, Abid grows in confidence. Latchman is played off the back foot, in contrasting styles, mostly through the covers. Runs flow after lunch, 50 coming at a run a ball.

After a 66-run partnership, Abid tries something too fancy to a ball on the off stump and is bowled by Parfitt. Viswanath, having hit an excellent 60, tries a single to short third man, not really knowing whether his partner has responded or not. Price comes back to knock over the final two wickets and India, for all the good work of the first day, trail by 65.

With Russell nursing a torn fingernail, Smith is accompanied by Radley. The openers extend the lead by 24 before tea. However, as the sun beats down after the break, welcome warmth spurs the Indian spinners to success. Radley pushes at Bedi to be well-caught by Gavaskar low down at midwicket. Smith is bowled by Venkat, who goes on to dismiss Featherstone and Brearley off successive balls. It is Bedi attacking from one end, Venkat playing the role of the stock bowler, but somehow the latter is picking up the wickets.

Wicketkeeper J.T. Murray counterattacks for a brief while, but a smart stumping does for him. Venkat, taking a break from picking up wickets, catches Parfitt's attempted sweep off Bedi at backward short leg. It is left to the injured Russell to come out and brave the last few minutes. The day ends with Middlesex on 99/7, 164 ahead with three wickets in hand.

Middlesex v Indians, Lord's – 23, 24, 25 June
Middlesex 233 (Russell 84, Smith 54; Chandra 5-67, Bedi 3-53) and 99/7 (Chandra 4-27, Bedi 3-24); **India** 168 (Viswanath 60; Price 4-31, Latchman 3-53).

* * *

The Indian High Commissioner, Appa Sahib Pant, was known to be a philosopher by nature and a mystic at heart. Moreover, he was a confirmed Gandhian. One of the first recipients of the Padma Shree Award, he had held diplomatic posts in multiple countries. But for all his accomplishments, no one expected him to predict cricketing results à la Dr Thakore.

However, that evening, at a party given by the MCC, Appa Pant said that he hoped one of the Tests would be drawn, the other washed out by rain, and the third won by India. In retrospect, no prediction could have been more accurate.

The high commissioner had been born to a princely family in Aundh in 1912. He did his MA at Oxford and passed the bar exams at Lincoln's Inn Fields. He had one of those princely lineages so abundantly common in the Indian diplomatic ranks of those days.

At the party, Wadekar exuded sophistication, charm and played the role of an Indian captain to the hilt. However, these were the settings Pataudi would have fitted into with effortless élan. He had relished such evenings in 1967. If manager Keki Tarapore was to be believed, he relished them somewhat more than the other responsibilities of captaincy.

By 1967, Pataudi had been leading India for five years. Not many believed there was an alternative when it came to leadership. To have a prince such as him at the helm seemed the natural order of things.

However, batting success in England notwithstanding, as the time approached for the announcement of the team for the Australia and New Zealand twin tour of 1967/68, a strong rumour surfaced that Tiger had fallen out of favour. Tarapore had supposedly filed a negative report about his captaincy and player management. The attitude 'The Test cricketers should be able to look after himself' was perhaps not the best model to follow when leading in foreign lands, especially where inexperienced men were looking up to the captain because of his long familiarity with the country.

However, according to Budhi Kunderan, Tarapore himself was part of the problem. 'He did not organise any training. He went around telling the English: we have come to learn, we have come to learn. He was always crawling to the English.'

Kunderan's description of Tarapore may or may not have been accurate. One of the few Parsis to have played Test cricket for India, Tarapore had been the manager of the Indian tour of the West Indies earlier in 1971. In his account, Wadekar calls him 'a man of the world with a taste for the good things of life'. But Kunderan's description does match many Indians of that, previous and subsequent generations.

And the attitude did not stop with the Indians. During official dinners in England, the 1971 Pakistanis heard their manager

Masood Salahuddin thank their English hosts for civilising them, teaching them to play cricket and to eat with knives and forks.

In his autobiography, Pataudi writes, 'On my return from East Africa in 1967, I became engrossed in the development of real estate and farming in Pataudi, a project important to the community in which I live, as well as to myself.' He hints that was the reason why he surprised everyone by suddenly declaring that he wanted to retire from Test cricket.

However, some argue that the announcement shrewdly pre-empted what promised to be a heated discussion about his captaincy, and the counter-claims of Chandu Borde.

On the eve of selection, Pataudi was back, playing for South Zone against West Zone in the Duleep Trophy final at the Brabourne Stadium. Walking in at 20/2, he put his head down and batted 10½ hours to get 200. South Zone secured a first innings lead and thus the trophy. It was held aloft by M.L. Jaisimha. Of course, Pataudi did not lead Hyderabad or South Zone. He just led India, and the Rest of India in the Irani Trophy. And of course Sussex, the county that had become a haunt of the eastern princes.

So it was Pataudi who led India to Australia. They lost all four Tests, making it 17 losses in a row away from home, 11 of them under Pataudi. And the captain once again enjoyed one solitary heroic Test, scoring 75 and 85 at the MCG. The first innings was played with a pulled leg muscle after coming in at 25/5, a knock people have not stopped talking about.

India did win 3-1 in the New Zealand leg of the tour, but then the Kiwis were rather easy meat in those days. It was India's first ever overseas success, but primarily because it was their first ever tour of the beautiful island country. Had Lala Amarnath's side visited in 1947/48 the first victory could perhaps have come much earlier.

For the time being, however, the Pataudi legend was revived. After all, the Indian team had had some success during his stint. The impulsive decision to insert England in the final Test of 1963/64, which he justified as his desire to 'do something different after four drawn Tests', could have led to another man being crucified. Not Pataudi. A nawab, hailing from a famous sporting family, was born to lead. In Pataudi there was an unpredictability. There were no fixed batting position of his batsmen. In Tests under him Surti had batted in nine different positions in 40 innings; Nadkarni seven in 34; Durani eight in 27; and Budhi Kunderan has either opened or batted at No.8 or below. The explanation was regal capriciousness.

People respected that he was one of the best outfielders of the world. There was the enigma of what might have been if he had not damaged one eye in that accident. There was the nickname Tiger which laced his persona with majesty and esoteric powers. There was national euphoria over his wedding to Sharmila Tagore, which interlinked the glamorous worlds of cricket and Bollywood, with the inter-religion alliance adding to the mystique.

Most believed he was a great captain. The belief continues to this day, his rather ordinary win-loss record notwithstanding. That wins under his captaincy remained rather rare was neither here nor there. Many players who rubbed shoulders with him still vouch for the genius of his leadership.

As one Hyderabad player told me in an interview: 'And then Tiger [Pataudi] would phone Bhopal and ask them to prepare jeeps for *shikar*. Jai, Mumtaz Hussain, Abbas … we all would go with Tiger for hunting immediately after the match. Tiger would drink a bottle of gin every day. Some of us would join him. Once Pataudi was arrested while shooting deer in Warangal and was taken to the house of the Collector, who happened to be my uncle. He wanted to know from Tiger how I was doing in cricket. Everything was settled amicably. Those were wonderful days.' The player in question never played a single game under Pataudi's captaincy. In domestic cricket he had always been led by Jaisimha. The memories are of the regal display which left him bedazzled. The regalia remained hallowed, above the law, quite like it had been before in the old days.

Unlike his fans, Pataudi himself had no illusions about his captaincy. 'India has never had a great captain. In the land of the blind, the one-eyed man is the king,' was his standard self-effacing rejoinder.

By 1969/70 things heated up once again. The failure to win the series when New Zealand visited was magnified even further because of the enormous conspiracy of weather, groundsmen and umpires required to rob the Kiwis of a deserved win at Hyderabad, Pataudi's home ground. Pataudi nevertheless went on to lead in all five Tests against Bill Lawry's Australia. But India lost the series, and Pataudi's bat was far from commanding or consistent.

The signals were strong. By 1970, Wadekar had been appointed captain of Bombay. For the Irani Trophy showdown at Eden Gardens, the only fixture apart from Test matches in which Pataudi captained in India, the selectors had named Borde as captain.

Pataudi skipped that crucial encounter. The reason given was influenza. Not many believed it. Wadekar batted for six hours to get 164.

Ten days after the match, Pataudi was back at the venue that had seen him rescue his position in 1967/68. At the Brabourne Stadium, West Zone met South Zone in the Duleep Trophy semi-final. With Wadekar not playing, Borde led West. The selectors, in another tell-tale move, had appointed Venkat as South Zone captain ahead of Jaisimha.

It was a comfortable 188/3 when Pataudi walked in to bat and started stroking the ball about with aplomb. Borde beckoned forward young fast-medium bowler Syed Ahmed Hattea. An aspirant for a place in the team bound for the West Indies, the strapping youngster ran in and bounced. Pataudi hooked him for six. He pointed at the spot where the ball had pitched, almost asking the youngster to bowl him another.

Hattea charged in again. Pataudi was dropped at gully off the next ball. The delivery that followed cut away from leg to middle and struck him in front. Hattea screamed his appeal and umpire Sunil Banerjee was convinced. Pataudi was out for 14: no double hundred for him this time.

Six days after the dismissal, the selectors met to decide on the captain for the tour to the West Indies. Vijay Merchant and Bal Dani wanted Wadekar; C.D. Gopinath and Madhavsinh Jagdale wanted Pataudi. Hence, it was up to Merchant and his casting vote as chairman. He nodded towards Wadekar. The Bombay man became the skipper.

On the following day, 9 Jan 1971, the Duleep Trophy final kicked off between East Zone and South Zone at the Brabourne Stadium. Pataudi had made himself unavailable. Three days later, a telegram reached the selection committee. Pataudi was not available for the West Indies tour. He had lost his captaincy … and he had lost his title and privy purse.

It is rumoured that on losing his privy purse, Pataudi complained that apart from being a nawab, he was not really trained to do much else.

Unusually for a nawab, he decided to take on the problem in a thoroughly democratic manner. While the Indians played in the West Indies, Pataudi stood for the Lok Sabha elections from the Gurgaon constituency against the Congress Party candidate Bansi Lal.

'You want to vote for Pataudi?' his opponent taunted during the campaign. 'What good will it do to you if he wins? To meet him you'll have to get into the stadium first. And you know how difficult it is to get into a cricket stadium in this country. Granted you get in, what will he give you? At most a bat and a ball.'

One has to hear or imagine the speech in rustic Hindi to get the full force of rib-tickling appeal. Pataudi was duly trounced. It had been a bad couple of years for him.

Princely titles and privy purses

The 565 princely states of India had to be dealt with after independence in 1947. The bigger ones had even retained their armed forces. Many of the departing British were convinced that India would soon crack into several nations. In *Nineteenth Century and After,* a magazine that no longer exists, Sir Percival John Griffiths, Indian Civil Service and later adviser to British business in India, confidently wrote of three or four countries in place of British India and a federation of South Indian states.

However, the minister of home affairs, Vallabhbhai Patel, and his aide V.P. Menon, ensured a smooth transition. Simple accession preceding complete administrative merger, plush privy purses to the princes themselves.

Mergers and acquisitions followed, and force was used only in the odd case, like the powerful Hyderabad state with the obstinate Nizam.

The privy purses were paid until 1970. Six states received more than 1,000,000 rupees (£10,000 according to 1970 exchange rates). These were Hyderabad, Mysore, Travancore, Jaipur, Baroda and Patiala. Most states, however, received a maximum of Rs 100,000 (£1,000).

A motion to dismiss the privy purse was brought before the Parliament and failed to clear the Upper House by one vote. The President of India, V.V. Giri, passed an order for the immediate stoppage of the rights, privileges and the privy purses of rulers. The Supreme Court ruled that this was unconstitutional.

However, a relief was shortlived, and following the Lok Sabha elections in early 1971, Indira Gandhi brought in a series of changes that included abolition of the privy purses.

9

ABSENTEE PRINCES

THE NAWAB of Pataudi Senior, Iftikhar Ali Khan, had been a Wisden Cricketer of the Year 36 years before his son, in 1932. In the 1931 season, he had amassed 1,454 runs at the average of 69.23 with six hundreds.

In the same summer, another Indian Prince was setting English grounds alight fire. K.S. Duleepsinhji hit 2,684 runs at 54.77 with 12 hundreds, including 109 at The Oval in a Test against New Zealand. He had already played 12 Tests for England, scoring 995 runs at an incredible 58.52.

In the summer of 1932, I.A.K. Pataudi and Duleepsinhji were among the best batsmen in England.

As far back as in the 1928/29 season, Duleep, fresh from his six hundreds for Sussex in 1928, had been approached by the newly formed Indian Cricket Board with the request to play a greater role in the development of Indian cricket. This had included an offer to captain the 1932 side to England. Following his uncle Ranji's advice, however, Duleep declined. Playing for England would allow him much better cricketing opportunities. Duleep made his debut for England in 1929 , and hit that magical 173 at Lord's against Bill Woodfull's side in 1930.

In the 1931/32 winter, Duleep travelled to India again, this time to spend time with an ailing Ranji. Co-opted to the Indian selection committee that season, it was Duleep who can be credited with the discovery of the exceptional fast-bowling all-rounder Amar Singh.

That winter he also played for the Viceroy's XII against the Roshanara Club XII, hitting 173 in the second innings. In the same innings, Pataudi scored 91 and the two shared a 189-run stand.

The 1932 Indians were known as All-India – because the cricket team represented British India as well as the princely states. The concept of India as a country was alien to the British. In a speech to the Constitutional Club in March 1931, Winston Churchill had remarked, 'India is a geographical term. It is no more a united nation than the Equator.'

The opening first-class encounter for the visiting side was against Sussex. It was Duleep who led the county against his countrymen. The match immediately before the Test match at Lord's was against Worcestershire. It ended in a close three-wicket win for India with Amar Singh taking 11 wickets. For the county, Pataudi batted at No.3 and scored 83 in the first innings.

Halfway through the following month, the major fixture of the season was contested at Lord's – Gentlemen v Players. For the Gentlemen, Duleep hit 132 and Pataudi 165; the pair added 161.

The visiting Indians must have wondered what might have been if their batting had been bolstered by these two impeccable batsmen. And those two were not the only batsmen they missed.

Back home, following the Civil Disobedience Movement, Mahatma Gandhi had been arrested in early January 1932. The Viceroy, Lord Willingdon, had outlawed the Congress Party.

In protest at Gandhi's arrest, the Hindu Gymkhana had boycotted the 1932 tour. That meant Vijay Merchant had not been available for selection. It also meant that the other major batting stalwart, L.P. Jai, could not travel.

The tale of India's inaugural Test is well known – at least the tale of the first 20 minutes. Spearheaded by the excellent new-ball duo of Nissar and Amar Singh, and some electrifying fielding by the Malay-born Lall Singh, England were reduced to 19/3. Fighting knocks by Douglas Jardine and Les Ames ensured that they recovered to 259. But when India ended the day on 30 without loss, they were off to a rather good start in Test cricket.

However, the following day, from an excellent position of 110/2, they collapsed to 189 all out and the rest of the Test was a saga of surrender. Only Amar Singh's half-century from No.9 in the second innings provided a bright spot. The bowlers had done a wonderful job, matching their experienced English counterparts in potency and effectiveness. But with Nayudu nursing an injured hand, the batting lacked depth and class.

Quickest duck

Not all the fomenting protests were non-violent.

In Bengal, former England captain Sir Francis Stanley Jackson, was presiding as the governor. On 6 February 1932, while addressing a convocation at the Senate Hall in Calcutta University, he had been shot at by a 20-year-old female graduate student, Bina Das, with a revolver hidden in her convocation gown. The shot fired from almost point-blank range was off-target and Das was sentenced to nine years of imprisonment.

Later on, when nerves had been restored, Jackson joked that it had been the 'quickest duck he had ever made'.

So what if the two absentee princes had decided to play for India? If they and Merchant had been around, things could have been very, very different.

They had not known it then, but illness and a frail constitution meant that Duleep's career was on the verge of ending. His was one of the first names on the team list for the tour of Australia, but he could not go. Neither did he play first-class cricket again after that 1932 season.

Pataudi eventually did make his debut in Australia, scoring a sluggish hundred in the Test. Famously he refused to stand in the leg-trap, prompting Jardine to say, 'I see His Highness is a conscientious objector.' As David Frith pointed out, subsequently Pataudi did field close in on the leg side. He was dropped after the second Test, but it remains a mystery whether that was due to his confrontation with Jardine or because of his inability to force the pace. The strike rate for his 122 runs in that series was, after all, 24.

That was not the end of Jardine's interactions with the princes of Indian cricket. The rest of it was more characteristic of the chaos, luxury and indiscretions associated with Indian regalia and the controversy associated with the England captain.

By the time he took the MCC on their first official Test tour of India, Jardine knew his cricketing days were numbered. Dominion diplomacy and the duplicity of men such as Plum Warner had already ended the career of his Bodyline henchman Harold Larwood. Jardine knew, even as MCC President Lord Hailsham and Treasurer Lord Hawke informed him of his Indian assignment, that the Australians would not be keen to play against him in 1934 and the MCC would toe the duplicitous diplomacy line.

The Indian tour almost resulted in another diplomatic disaster, but due to events quite different from Bodyline.

The lavishness of the Maharaja of Patiala's hospitality had managed to squeeze the milk of human kindness even out of Jardine's spartan spirit. Patiala was now 42 and had already donated the national trophy for Indian cricket named after Ranji. And even middle age, which hurtled towards him in a mad rush due to his intemperate lifestyle, had done little to temper his womanising.

In a grand ball at Simla, he had made an inebriated pass at the unmarried daughter of the Earl of Willingdon, then Viceroy of India. Willingdon had been furious. At the annual Delhi cricket festival that followed, the cricket-mad Patiala did not turn up … the princely pair of Vizzy and Porbandar took his place. The reasons were not disclosed, but were plain enough.

When Jardine's men reached Patiala for their encounter with the local side, the Maharaja entertained the team with extraordinary relish. The enormous collection of jewellery, often exhibited by Cartier, was displayed to the cricketers. Shikar was arranged, and Nobby Clark bagged a cheetah. Several other

Englishmen shot deer and partridge. There was abundant flow of the famous Patiala pegs of whisky.

The match itself was well-contested. The Patiala side, reinforced by a number of Test cricketers, had the better of the draw. Much of it had to do with the relaxed structure of the game. The time of the scheduled start was adjusted. On one day play ended at lunch, so that the players could get away to the Simla Hills for shooting. On another, a banquet lasted till 4am; the Englishmen were then aroused at seven for a deer hunt. Only after their return did the cricket continue.

The hospitality also rippled into on-field reciprocation. During his innings of 37, the Yuvraj was clearly caught by Fred Bakewell at short leg. The batsman indicated to the umpire that the catch had not been clean and the prince was allowed to continue.

However, the Maharaja's great victory came off the field. Charmed by his hospitality, Jardine offered Patiala a place in the team to play the Viceroy's XI. Given Willingdon's relations with the Maharaja, this was tantamount to diplomatic dynamite. Technically, Patiala was a member of the MCC, and hence eligible to play. However, news of this invitation had Willingdon frothing at the mouth.

When he tried to use his viceregal prerogative to persuade Jardine not to include Patiala in his team, the England captain just kept fiddling with his pipe. As a last-ditch effort, Lady Willingdon was set on him. She took Jardine for a walk in the Mughal Gardens and tried to talk him out of it. But the skipper was adamant.

In spite of his obstinacy, Jardine was perhaps aware of the diplomatic implications of playing the Maharaja. He included Patiala in the MCC side against Delhi and Districts. While he batted, play was held up for several minutes as groundstaff and cricketers searched for one of his missing ear-rings. But when Jardine's men took the field against the Viceroy's-XI, there was a huge sigh of relief on finding that Patiala was not among them.

The government shut down the Secretariat and Legislative Assembly for the game played at Feroz Shah Kotla. Huge crowds gathered, and Lord and Lady Willingdon graced the occasion with their presence.

But Willingdon had rubbed Jardine up the wrong way. No one could tell him what to do with his team. Besides, on the morning of the match Jardine also found that the pitch had been rolled for 20 minutes instead of the allotted 10, so that the Viceroy's team would have it easy when they set off. He was livid. In fact, Christie, the groundsman, was persuaded to apologise to the captain by the viceroy himself. 'My dear fellow, you are dealing with a tough proposition, the toughest that even the Australians had come up against ...'

Back at his most ruthless, Jardine set Verity and Nichols on the home batsmen. The team included some stellar names, with Wazir Ali, C.K. Nayudu, A.L. Hosie and Mushtaq Ali in their midst. Amar Singh and Nissar were there as the opening bowlers. However, they managed just 160 and 63 while the MCC amassed 431.

When the MCC men left Delhi, Willingdon wrote to his sister. 'The cricketers have left us for elsewhere thank goodness ... I don't like Jardine and don't wonder at the Australians hating him. He is a fine cricketer and very good captain, but he is the most self-opinionated man I've ever met, full of wind in his head, talks to all of us as if he and not we know much about India.'

Jardine probably did know somewhat more about India. He had been born there, and during the tour he accompanied the former butler of the Jardine family to the old cemetery. He was also attracted to Hinduism during his last days. His experiences were not limited to the Lutyens-designed viceregal mansions and official functions with dignitaries. Willingdon, as the viceroy in India, generally did little of importance other than inciting people through some of his acts, and was, by all accounts, a thoroughly disagreeable person.

However, Jardine did have an incredible aptitude for ruffling important diplomatic feathers.

The Indian cricket team played their first home Test match at the Bombay Gymkhana ground. It was there that Lala Amarnath hit the first Test century by an Indian, prompting Maharajas to make gifts of money, and ladies to tear off and throw their jewellery at him. The club still has frames displaying giant blown-up photographs of captains Jardine and Nayudu smiling at the camera for the occasion.

An exception was made for the Test and the Indian cricketers were allowed to use the clubhouse. However, for all intents and purposes it was a European club where natives were still not allowed. Seating arrangements for the Europeans and the Indians remained separate.

The umpires engaged for the match were Bill Hitch and Frank Tarrant. For all his chumminess with Patiala and cordiality with his family butler, Jardine drew the line when it came to Indian umpires.

As Vinay Lal, professor of history at the University of California, Los Angeles, says, 'It is striking that during the course of their presence in India, most particularly after around the late-1700s, the English had very little contact with Indians in the ordinary course of life. They associated throughout only with the princes or with those whom they could command with impunity, that is the "servant class"'.

Recall Jardine's associations with Patiala and his old family butler. This was 50 years after the Ilbert Bill, and just 38 before the 1971 tour.

Complex Equations

To be fair Jardine also found problems with lbw decisions given by Tarrant as well as the Australian's audacity in suggesting that bouncers at Yuvraj constituted unfair tactics. The Australian professional had to be replaced by the Worcestershire amateur John Higgins for the third Test of the tour.

Jardine's equation with Australia was perhaps complex enough to override all other parameters.

10

TURNING DEFEAT INTO VICTORY

AT LORD'S, Middlesex are 131 all out. Bedi 6-29 from 25.2 overs, Venkat 4-41 off 17. John Woodcock wonders if they could have done it faster had Abid Ali and Solkar not been allowed to bowl 12 overs with the new ball.

'Conclusively their spinners – even without the mastermind Prasanna – were the major power of the match,' writes Arlott.

'Their game was clear from the first match of the tour against Middlesex,' Prasanna will fume later. 'It was played on a spinner's track. Surely, as our number-one spinner, I should have been the first choice.'

He is not the first choice, at least as far as captain Wadekar is concerned. Set 197 to win, India make colossal heavy weather of it. Baig falls to Black early, making his Test spot more uncertain. Ostensibly selected because of his experience in England, he last played here in 1962. At the other end Gavaskar is amazed that someone who played Trueman in his pomp can look so helpless against quick bowling.

He himself starts promisingly once again, and Wadekar looks solid at the other end. However, at 34, Price picks up two wickets in two balls – the fourth consecutive day he has done so. Gavaskar hits him to wide mid-on and Sardesai snicks to the wicketkeeper.

Five runs later Viswanath, the hero of the first innings, turns one from Jones and the catch is held fast and low at backward short leg.

At 39/4, the left-handed pair of Solkar and Wadekar steady the ship. The captain wisely avoids anything outside off stump and grows in confidence as the innings progresses. The score reads 79 when Solkar dabs to short third man and sprints down the wicket. Wadekar can hardly react and is stranded. The skipper walks back with plenty of runs still to get. A precursor of the dramatic finale.

Abid Ali is a handy man to have in such situations, a scrapper to the core. The pitch, which seemed spiteful when the Indian spinners bowled, suddenly turns rather tame with Latchman and Parfitt in operation. The Indian all-rounders bat with pluck and street-smarts, presenting the full face of the bat and striking the fuller deliveries with carefully directed strokes. Seam has to be reintroduced in order to get the next wicket. Solkar is caught at midwicket, driving Jones a bit too early, but his 41 has been invaluable.

There are still 62 runs to get with the vice-captain at the crease. There are occasions when Venkat gives the impression of being a rank tailender. And there are occasions when one wonders whether he can be thought of as an all-rounder. In 1971, he is in the middle of a purple patch of sorts with the bat.

At Port-of-Spain, he struck his first Test half-century. Four months before that he had used his captain's prerogative to bat at No.6 for Tamil Nadu and hit 137 against Kerala. Of course, the Kerala bowling was club-class, but it was a first-class century.

Venkat has come out thinking like a batsman. The phase of play that sees him and Abid get India closer and closer with quiet confidence is vital, not only for the match but beyond that, for the entire tour. They are just five runs away when Brearley turns to the occasional off-spin of Featherstone. Abid hits a full toss straight to the Middlesex captain at silly mid-off. He walks back for 61.

A run later, Venkat heaves at a straighter one from Parfitt and is bowled – 194/8. This means Krishnamurthy and Bedi are at the wicket, with only the notorious batting skills of Chandrasekhar left in the bank.

Bedi clinches the issue in his straightforward manner. The ball from Parfitt is short and a beefy pull finds the midwicket fence.

The Indians have won, the first time they have done so in the opening match of a tour of England

Middlesex v Indians, Lord's – 23, 24, 25 June
Middlesex 233 (Russell 84, Smith 54; Chandra 5-67, Bedi 3-53) and 131 (Chandra 4-41, Bedi 6-29) lost to **India** 168 (Viswanath 60; Price 4-31, Latchman 3-53) and 198/8 (Solkar 41, Abid 61) by 2 wickets.

Brown bar

Ashok's brother Rahul arrived in Essex four years later, in 1975. He was in England to play for Cleckheaton in the Bradford League on Saturdays. On Sundays, he turned out for Woodford Wells in the Essex League.

'I had heard a lot about playing and learning in England from my father and brother as they had spent numerous summers there. Needless to say, I was very much looking forward to my stint in England,' he recalled.

That was the time when there was a huge influx of immigrants from East Africa, mainly Uganda. There were incidents of racial tension in the country with riots in Brixton, Southall and Notting Hill in London and in several cities around Britain.

'The economic situation was getting worse, Right-wing parties were adding to the tension by blaming migration. There was the coal miners' strike too. Migrants became soft targets,' says Rahul.

Based on his performances in the Essex League, Rahul made it to the Essex Second XI the following year.

'Our home ground was at Chelmsford. After a game I went to the bar as I wanted to buy an orange juice. I was ignored at first and then refused to be served at my own club! Thankfully, one of team-mates saw this and ensured that I was served and treated better.'

There was not much time to engage in celebrations. The team started off on the coach towards Colchester where they were playing Essex the following day. For the newcomers, it was their first good look at the English countryside, and it could not have been a more scenic route. Much of the drive was through Epping Forest.

The two entertainers of the team, Ashok Mankad and Syed Kirmani, put on a nice little musical performance to liven things up. However, by the time they reached the Dickensian-looking inn, the cricketers were dead tired and the weather had become worse.

Opening *The Times* the following morning, Adhikari saw Woodcock's report headed 'Indians turn defeat into victory'.

In the inside pages there were the ominous words of the Indian foreign minister Swaran Singh. 'India might go into war if the crisis in East Pakistan and the refugee problem were not resolved by a satisfactory political solution in the near future.' The article was accompanied by a disturbing picture of families of East Bengal refugees at a Calcutta camp, extending their arms to grab a piece of bread.

Another piece of news must have caught the military man's eye.

At St Paul's Cathedral, the Queen had unveiled a memorial to the Indian Army – the tablet recording the deeds of the army that began with Clive and ended with two million volunteer soldiers in the Second World War.

The memorial stood beside the colossal monument of the Duke of Wellington, who began his army service in India with the 73rd Regiment, and opposite the plaque of Lord Roberts of Kandahar, who was born at Cawnpore and won the VC during the Indian Mutiny.

The article mentioned the short history of the Indian army penned by Colonel F.L. Roberts of the Punjab Frontier Force, now chairman of the Association of British Officers of the Indian Army. 'In its relationship between British officer and native soldier it was one of the happiest armies of all time.'

It ended with the words 'the soldiers and officers turned out in force yesterday to support the claim.'

No one really asked why there was no scope for a corresponding cordial relation between the native officer and the British soldier or the native officer and the native soldier or the native offices and the British officer in what was essentially an Indian army. It did not ask whether the deeds of the army under Clive should be glorified even as decolonisation was virtually complete and past events could be perhaps viewed without pink Imperial tints.

Too many concepts taken for granted for years were yet to be questioned.

11

A TALE OF THREE BOOKS

AS FAR as imperialist concepts are concerned, the Patiala-Jardine-Willingdon incidents were not really exceptions. The records left by the English tours over the years make for most intriguing reading.

On the declaration of Queen Victoria as the Empress of India, the first great Durbar was held in 1877. Lord Lytton, the viceroy, selected a historic site outside Delhi to build a temporary city, acting out a Disraelian extravaganza. Maharajas, nawabs, elites thronged there to take part in a spectacular display of pageantry, rulership and homage. This magnificent show of wealth and expense took place during the great famine of 1876 to 78.

The Durbar was repeated in 1903, for Edward VII. The viceroy, Lord Curzon, provided the princes with a much more active role. In the amphitheatre specially designed in Indo-Saracenic style by Swinton Jacob, they paid homage to the King-Emperor. The viceroy declared that the princes were 'pillars that help to sustain the main roof'.

In 1900, as the Indian army was being deployed in China to crush the Boxer Rebellion, the fractious and lengthy Boer War raised questions about the invulnerability of the British Empire. And Curzon said, 'We could lose all our [white settlement] dominions and still survive, but if we lost India, our sun would sink to its setting.'

While Curzon was raising the contribution of the princes to the roof, there arrived in India the third English cricket team after

Vernon's and Hawke's. It comprised the members of a private club at Oxford University called the Authentics. Led by the Surrey cricketer K.J. Key, the Authentics had in their midst the great lob bowler George Simpson-Hayward. Cecil Headlam, the wicketkeeper of the side, produced the tour book, *Ten Thousand Miles Through India and Burma*.

The book contains the now oft-repeated quote, 'First the hunter, the missionary, and the merchant, next the soldier and the politician, and then the cricketer – that is the history of British colonisation.' After the quote, Headlam continues, 'And of these civilising influences the last [cricket] may, perhaps, be said to do least harm. The hunter may exterminate deserving species, the missionary may cause quarrels, the soldier may hector, the politician blunder – but cricket unites, as in India, the rulers and the ruled. It also provides a moral training, an education in pluck, nerve and self-restraint valuable to the character of the ordinary native.'

The Authentics were trounced by the native community of the Parsis by eight wickets. They went on to play European sides, mixed sides and Indian sides. They encountered the cricketer-turned-missionary C.T. Studd, then a pastor at the Union Church in Ootacamund, and persuaded him to turn out against them for the Gentlemen of India. And they attended the Durbar.

There are several pages on the Durbar in Headlam's book, including a detailed description of the ceremony, the viceroy and his entourage, the wondrous series of great and little chiefs arrayed in every sort and kind of dress and magnificently profuse in their display of jewels.

At the same time the book included several sections discussing ordinary Indians and what Headlam and his mates thought of them.

'On landing we were met by our hosts and by a crowd of rascally-looking natives who, on consideration of an exorbitant fee, were willing to give us their services.' These were people, Headlam explains, who act as *khitmagar,* bearer and courier, valet and butler in one. He continues, 'If he is comparatively honest, you are lucky … for all servants in India are thieves.'

The tone metamorphoses to near-obsequious when he describes the Indian commander-in-chief of the forces of his highness, the Nizam of Hyderabad, who arranges elephants for them to go around the city. And then suddenly social dissection starts with passages such as: 'Thieves in India form separate castes. There are definite brotherhoods and tribes and robbers, and every member of them is born a thief. They glory in their calling and can follow no other ... For a member of these tribes, to be honest would be wrong, impious even.'

Much of this fanciful concoction seems to be influenced by British literature set in India – *Thugee* and its poor imitations – rather than actual experience. Unfortunately, the fables promoted by such reports are read so often that they are hard to shake off from reality.

As the tour reaches Madras, Headlam writes, 'The country is redolent with great names ...' and the very first example of such great names he provides is Clive. 'It teems with small posts ... from which a few hundred brave Frenchmen and Englishmen, using petty, discordant rajahs as their tools, fought for the supremacy of their indifferent countrymen in India.' As we have seen in the previous chapter, Clive remained a great name even in 1971.

Then comes the infamous chapter 'Indian rails and the Babu'. We soon read of 'the aimless babble that every low-caste native must raise on every occasion'. There follows a detailed description of how to hit a native when the occasion demands, for example if he lurches along in front of your tum-tum, refusing to get out of the way of the sahib. 'You learn that you must be very careful how you hit a man in India. Nearly every native suffers from an enlarged spleen, and any blow on the body is very likely to prove fatal. ... It is best to carry a cane and administer rebuke therewith upon the calves and shins, which are tender and not usually mortal.'

After such practical advice, there is the description of the way he himself dealt with a clerk, an English-educated babu, at the railway ticket counter, when a ticket-buying operation, which would have taken a minute and a half at Euston, went on for over an hour.

Big Game

Before leaving for Burma, several of the Authentics went for their usual shooting expedition in Kashmir. Shooting and hunting reverberate through cricketing accounts down the years. The cricketers under Hawke went on shooting expeditions arranged by Harris. The Authentics had their European friends who made the *bandobust*. Down the years men like Patiala and Vizzy arranged hunting expeditions for their cricketing guests. Jardine even stayed back in India after the tour for some extended shooting. The Sussex County Cricket Club Museum has an excellent collection of photographs of Ranji's life, and a significant percentage are quite gruesome images of the animals bagged during the hunts with Ranji and his European friends gallantly posing with their kills. During the Great War, Ranji lost an eye to a gun wound. It was while shooting grouse.

Lionel Tennyson, who took an unofficial England side to India for a series of high-quality cricket in 1937/38, was the last visiting captain to be entertained by Bhupinder Singh, the Maharaja of Patiala. Two months before his death in 1938, Patiala arranged a shoot for Tennyson and his men, all mounted on elephants, as his army beat for them. Tennyson also visited Jamnagar and was entertained by Digvijaysinhji, the heir of Ranji, and there too was treated to big-game hunting and black-buck shooting. However, once Tennyson supposedly shot a goat instead of the targeted tiger.

And then we have the Nawab of Pataudi Junior calling up his palace at the end of a match, ordering the jeeps to be readied because men would go hunting.

Hunting formed an indispensable part of the Indian experience. In 1906, the Prince of Wales and the future King George V visited India. Around 14,000 people with 600 elephants escorted him on shikar, and a road 50 miles long was built to connect his two hunting camps. It was a grand success, with his party shooting, according to official statistics, 39 tigers, 18 lions and four Himalayan bears in a single day. (It was still possible to get tigers and lions in the same region in Indian forests. Sustained hunting ultimately stopped this majestic confluence.)

'This was too much. I put the toe of my riding boot round the rear leg of his three-legged stool and gave it a sharp jerk. In a second it capsized, and my Aryan brother capsized with it. Never shall I forget the look of mingled astonishment and awe upon the faces of his gaping underlings, never the look of fear and injured pride upon the countenance of that sprawling and obese black gentleman. Without saying a word, he got up, bowed, and deferentially led the way to the ticket office. In two minutes I had my tickets and paid for them.'

There was no cricket book award in 1903. But I do have a sneaking suspicion that, with such tales of English gallantry and the re-manufacture of old myths, this book would have been a prime candidate.

Things perhaps never quite reached the extent of arrogance as in Headlam's book, but visits to India remained steeped in both race-class dichotomy and protracted grumblings about people and facilities.

In 1948/49 the West Indians under John Goddard toured the country. Alongside the black stars, Everton Weekes, Clyde Walcott and an over-the-hill George Headley, there were stalwart white cricketers such as Goddard, Gerry Gomez, Jeff Stollmeyer and Denis Atkinson. That was the series when Weekes took his number of consecutive hundreds to five. The 1971 Indian manager Hemu Adhikari saved India from defeat in the first Test with determined unbeaten knocks of 114 and 29.

It was Stollmeyer who documented the tour in his book *Everything Under the Sun*. Bhupinder Singh had passed away after bequeathing the Brabourne Stadium to Indian cricket. The erstwhile Yuvraj, Yadavinder Singh, was the new Maharaja. Even after independence – and by now Patiala had acceded to the Indian government and the Maharaja was actually the Rajpramukh – he hosted and entertained the visiting team.

He led North Zone against the tourists at the Bardari Ground in his estate. His turban changed frequently (azure, cream, fuchsia, as Stollmeyer recounts) and he batted well enough to score 22. Patiala's private regiment, colourfully dressed, marched across the field playing their bagpipes at close of play. The players were guests in the Maharaja's palace, with a 37-room kitchen catering for them. Stollmeyer assures us that they were wonderfully looked after.

However, outside the Maharaja's palace things are not so luxurious. Stollmeyer complains about long journeys (the complaints read a bit strangely given that the West Indians travelled first-class and the Indian cricketers had to make do in general compartments; Stollmeyer was also one of the six lucky West Indians who were given air tickets). He goes on to grumble about cold, dark, damp rooms in hotels.

There are elaborate descriptions of stolen clothes and money, too many people and the disparity between the rich and the poor. It is, however, the post office that stands out in his litany of grievances.

'A visit to the Post Office was interesting from the point of view that to get there one wandered through a back street tripping over the odd goat, curry fire, and prostrate form, then up a dingy and absolutely pitch black staircase which opened up into a small room, covered inches in dust inhabited by two dirty men who had obviously never heard of the West Indies.'

Stollmeyer did not kick the stools from under them as Headlam had done, but his account of the Indians – both the regalia who were reduced shadows of themselves, and the masses – smacks of Imperialist hangover. The only thing missing was perhaps the customary hunting trip.

There is another rather striking example of the difference of world views in Tennyson's second autobiography *Sticky Wickets*. Published in 1950, it tells of the cricket and travels of the England captain. What makes it remarkable is that this is one of the rare cricket books to contain photographs of topless women.

While sauntering through Bali, Tennyson uses his camera with relish to capture the images of several Balinese women clad only from the waist down. He provides some tongue-in-cheek captions as well. A group photo of three beauties with naked breasts is called *A Balinese Study*. A topless Balinese damsel is captured on frame next to an artwork in a temple, and Tennyson cannot resist quipping, 'We were lucky to be in Bali.'

While the photographs of similarly dressed (or undressed) European women would relegate the book to levels of pornography or, at the very least, erotica, the Tennyson book is just another cricketing memoir, with pictures of the Balinese dames ending up as studies of a strange world, perhaps akin to exotic fauna.

12

A LEAGUE OF
EXCEPTIONAL PLAYERS

COLCHESTER IS cold. The wind is blustery, almost a gale. Ted Dexter's article in *Sunday Mirror* reads, 'The Indian cricketers are midgets in size, but don't under-rate them.' He explains, 'Among its many virtues, cricket is as kind to those who lack poundage and inches as rowing and Rugby are cruel.' Whether the assessment will still be valid in the era of T20 is a different question, but as they reach the ground to take the field against Essex, the Gavaskars and Viswanaths seem in danger of being blown away by the wind.

In cricketing terms, they almost are. The wicket is a typical English green top. Prasanna, playing in place of Bedi, cannot have been enthralled at the prospect of having his first bowl of the tour in this setting.

The Essex attack, on the other hand, is in the able hands of West Indian Keith Boyce and an expert of these conditions, John Lever. Most of the Indian batsmen have never seen a wicket like this one.

With the last ball of his first over, Boyce gets Gavaskar with an excellent outswinger. Jayantilal plays down the wrong line to Lever and is lbw – 0/2. A single later, in the same over, the captain tries to cut too close to his body. With the second ball of his second over, the left-handed Lever sends down a yorker and Viswanath cannot get his bat down in time.

After 20 balls, it is 3/4. Four ducks. As Michael Melford writes in *The Sunday Telegraph*, 'It would take a genius to find any resemblance between a windy East Anglian hilltop and the sultriness of the Brabourne Stadium in Bombay and the new ball swung and bounced just enough to upset batsmen still groping to find their way.'

India do fight back. Sardesai, back to his old dependable self, plays late and deals with the moving ball. Mankad is determined, if painstaking, until he gets a questionable lbw decision. Indians believe he has got a touch while trying the attempted sweep. But he has done enough to stake his claims as Gavaskar's partner ahead of Baig and Jayantilal.

Sardesai and Solkar, perform another of their rescue acts. They have done it three times in the West Indies.

Sardesai-Solkar partnerships in the West Indies, 1971

Wicket	Runs	Start	End	Venue
6	137	75/5	212/6	Kingston
5	114	186/4	300/5	Port-of-Spain
6	32	246/5	276/6	Georgetown
7	186	70/6	256/7	Bridgetown

The latter is rather aggressive, enjoying himself against the faster men. The hundred is raised with five men down, quite a feat from 3/4.

But Sardesai gets a bit too adventurous against left-armer Ray East. Stepping forward, he hits the ball back for the bowler to hold a superb return catch. Venkat tries to play another good hand, but Boyce comes back to wipe the tail, 164 all out.

A seam attack of Solkar and Gavaskar is just not good enough in response. Essex end the day at 50/1.

The second day starts with sunshine, and the Indian spinners look a bit happier. However, a cloudburst added to the freezing wind that sees the Indians pile on four sweaters means a wet ball and numb fingers for the tweakers. They keep at it, but the conditions are loaded against them. While Chandrasekhar bowls exceptionally well, catches go down and lofted strokes fall in no man's land. By the time Keith Fletcher comes in it is 95/2. He proceeds to bat with clinical professionalism, shaping well for his cuts and drives, using the sweep to good effect. His third century of the season underlines claims for a Test spot.

Later in the day Lever goes berserk, slamming three sixes and a couple of fours in an innings of 37, adding 51 unbeaten runs with Fletcher in just 24 minutes. Essex declare, having exactly doubled India's score; Venkat 3-100, Chandra 3-115, Prasanna 2-85.

In the limited time left in the day, Boyce sends back Jayantilal. and Gavaskar bats out time with nightwatchman Kirmani.

Poor Kirmani. There is always an understudy for the regular wicketkeeper on an important foreign tour. But on this tour his role is even less significant. He knows that he does not stand a chance of playing a Test, even if Krishnamurthy gets injured or fails miserably.

In fact, even Krishnamurthy does not have much chance of playing a Test. He kept in all five Tests in the West Indies, and Rusi Jeejeebhoy had been sent as his understudy. Farokh Engineer had not been selected for the tour because of 'policy'. He had not played in the 1970/71 domestic season, because he was busy turning out for the Rest of the World in Pakistan. The selectors had followed 'policy' and handed Krishnamurthy the big gloves.

However, the 'policy' has been revised. Engineer is there in England. He is playing for Lancashire. He knows the conditions better than anyone else. Due to his contract with Lancashire, Engineer can play only in the Test matches. That means poor Mohinder Amarnath has had to make way for a reserve wicketkeeper, and two stumpers have been sent. A real pity, because at this stage of his career, Amarnath is being seen as a promising seam bowler who could be useful on English tracks.

So, for all intents and purposes, Kirmani is the third wicketkeeper for India on the tour. Only the extreme joviality of his character allows him to take it with a smile.

He does not last too long on the following morning. Trying to force leg-spinner Robin Hobbs, he treads on his wicket. But the pitch is a lot easier by now, the sun is out and Boyce and Lever are hardly the menace they were on the first morning. Batting through the day is not really a tough ask, especially with Gavaskar looking in good touch and Wadekar showing signs of settling down.

However, the young opener starts taking too many risks in his duel with Hobbs. Luck sides with him for a while; he is dropped twice and India progress to 112/2. But then he steps out once too often and wicketkeeper captain Brian Taylor whips off the bails.

Taylor is in action again when Wadekar tries to sweep Acfield. Down on his knees, the Indian skipper misses the ball and the bails are taken off. Umpire David Constant adjudges that his toes are in the air.

Mankad grafts cautiously yet again, but Acfield is now getting some help from the wicket, and more from the batsmen. Viswanath is out to a bad shot. Sardesai is the victim of a tough decision. After all his resolve, Mankad gifts his wicket to East.

With the end in sight, Taylor beckons to Boyce and Lever.

* * *

Two years earlier, in the summer of 1969, a 19-year-old Peter Hain and his fellow protestors had entered the Carreras Ground, Basildon, in order to interrupt the match between Essex and Wilf Isaac's XI. It was a sort of warm-up for the South African rugby and cricket tours due in the next few months.

Wilf Isaac, the South African entrepreneur, had brought over a side led by former South African wicketkeeper-batsman John Waite. It included some raw talent, such as the towering young swing bowler Vintcent van der Bijl. The star appeal was provided in the form of Graeme Pollock.

Running into the ground, Hain had been intercepted by a policeman on duty. However, the other demonstrators had made it to the pitch and stood there holding up the game. Taylor had beckoned Boyce over and asked him to bowl at the protestors. An embarrassed Boyce had refused.

Taylor lived for the game, had been at it for more than two decades, and also enjoyed his football. He might just have been annoyed at the demonstrators. However, asking a black man to bowl at anti-apartheid demonstrators was more than a bit naïve.

* * *

However, today there is no awkward request. Boyce obliges by dismissing Prasanna; Lever uproots the stumps of Chandra.

Essex need 68 to win in 18 overs. Should he go on the defensive, Wadekar asks Adhikari. The military man shakes his head. 'Make a match of it. Start with Prasanna and Chandra.'

Wadekar has seen Prasanna and Chandra toil without success on the wicket. He decides that Venkat's flatter, faster deliveries will be more useful. He hands the new ball to Solkar and asks Venkat to bowl from the other end.

It pays off. Taylor has promoted himself to push for the runs. He is bowled by Venkat for a duck. Bruce Francis is run out in the heat of the chase.

At 6/2, Fletcher, in at No.3, plays another vital hand. Boyce, promoted to use the long handle, keeps the scoreboard moving. The fielding does not help. Kirmani fumbles a few. Prasanna drops a catch. In the penultimate over, Viswanath drops a skier.

Venkat bowls magnificently, 3-36 from nine overs. Solkar keeps runs in check. However, an over each from Chandra and Prasanna prove expensive. Fletcher, with an unbeaten 38, takes Essex home with five balls to spare.

Essex are a leading team in the Sunday League. They know how to chase.

The familiar tale of struggle on seaming wickets in chilly weather seems to have returned. Has the Lord's win been a false sign?

Essex v Indians, Colchester – 26, 28, 29 June
India 164 (Sardesai 53, Solkar 53; Boyce 4-33, Lever 3-13) and 231 (Gavaskar 55; Acfield 3-30) lost to **Essex** 328 (Ward 55, Fletcher 106*; Venkat 3-100, Chandra 3-115) and 68/4 (Venkat 3-36) by 6 wickets.

Cigarette Cards

The Sunday League, or the John Player League. So named after the sponsors – the tobacco and cigarette manufacturers inseparably linked to cricket long before the Sunday League, through their collectible cigarette cards featuring famous cricketers of the day.

In 1904, John Player produced a 'British Empire' series of cards. In 1938, alongside Bradman, Hammond and other cricketers, they produced a set of cigarette cards on 'Military Uniforms of the British Empire Overseas'.

They were not the only ones, though. W.D. and H.O. Wills had 'Builders of the British Empire' in 1898, 'Indian Regiments' in 1907, 'Arms of the British Empire' in 1910, 'Governor Generals of India' in 1911, several 'Overseas Dominions' in 1915, 'Picturesque People of the Empire' in 1926, 'Flags of the Empire' in 1926 and again in 1929. Gallagher's had 'Scenes from the Empire' in 1939.

The subjects of cigarette cards revolved around sport, music-hall performers (later film stars), transport, armed forces and the Empire.

Film critic Philip French asserted that in the 1930s he learned as much about the world from cigarette cards as he did from the cinema. John Julius Cooper, Second Viscount Norwich, wrote that while he was growing up, the Empire 'was all around us, celebrated on our biscuit tins, chronicled on our cigarette cards, part of the fabric of our lives. We were all imperialists then.'

Cooper was born in 1929. He was 41 when the Indians toured in 1971. French was born in 1933, he would turn 38 four days after the conclusion of the Oval Test.

There were many active men and women in the prime of their lives who had grown up playing with Empire toys. They had grown up with pictures of exotic Indian subjects of the Empire as curiosities – Indian maharajas, Indian armies, Indian people. And, of course, elephants.

13

SPLENDID CAPTAIN AND HALF-NAKED FAKIR

IN 1936, All-India (still known by that name) had also lost to Essex, by a hefty margin of seven wickets. But Lala Amarnath had come in at No.3 and hit 130 out of 184, scoring at a run a minute. When Essex had batted he had captured 4-54. In the second innings, Amarnath made 107. When Essex chased down the paltry 61-run target, he picked up two of the three wickets to fall.

It was a tremendous feat of all-round brilliance by one of the most talented Indian cricketers on tour.

What took place after that has been repeated often enough. Within a few days, against Nottinghamshire, Amarnath found himself batting at No.5. Against Minor Counties, he had been relegated to No.7, after the likes of Amar Singh and C.S. Nayudu, with C.K. Nayudu batting at No.10. The batting orders set by the Maharajakumar of Vizianagaram were difficult to explain. It has been argued that some of this was a deliberate ploy by the prince to prevent Nayudu and Amarnath from getting runs. Vizzy also supposedly tried to deny Amarnath the double.

Besides, there were occasions when the little rotund man in glasses refused Amarnath the field he wanted. It led to the choicest Punjabi epithets from the young all-rounder, Vizzy's subsequent complaint to the manager Major Brittain-Jones, and soon, even before the first Test, Amarnath was sent home on disciplinary grounds. (His replacement C.S. Nayudu became the first cricketer to arrive by trans-continental flight.)

That was not Vizzy's only controversy on the tour. It was rumoured that insecurity about his own sporting prowess made him goad Baqa Jilani into insulting C.K. Nayudu at the breakfast table. The promise made to Jilani, duly kept, was a Test cap.

There was also the occasion when he asked Mushtaq Ali to run Vijay Merchant out. Merchant had openly proposed C.K. Nayudu as captain in the Tests, and Vizzy had not been amused. As they walked out to bat, Mushtaq spilled the beans. 'Try it if you can,' Merchant laughed. They ended up adding 203, Mushtaq bringing up the first overseas Test hundred for India and Merchant soon following him to the three-figure mark.

During the tour, Vizzy gifted a gold watch to the opposition skipper during a tour match. The unnamed recipient is supposed to have recalled, 'I gave him a full toss and a couple of long hops, but you can't go on bowling like that all day, not in England.' In today's terminology, this would have gone down as spot-fixing.

However, at the same time, early in the tour at a dinner given to the All-India team at Lord's, Vizzy was elected a member of the MCC.

Just after the match against Essex, it was Vizzy who opened a new playground at the Hornsey YMCA Boys' Club at Tottenham Lane, Crouch End. He was welcomed by Lord Rochdale, Lord Lieutenant of Middlesex. After the inauguration he, along with Nissar and Jahangir Khan, bowled to the boys.

On 24 June, a couple of days after Amarnath had been sent home, the members of the two Houses of Parliament who made up the Parliamentary cricket team entertained the Indian cricketers to lunch at the House of Commons. Presided over by Lord Ebbisham, the company included the prime minister. Stanley Baldwin, R.A. Butler, our old friend Lord Willingdon, and former England captains Stanley Jackson and H.D.G. Leveson Gower. The prime minister was invited by Lord Ebbisham to propose the health of the popular Indian team and toast the name of 'their splendid captain Maharajkumar of Vizianagaram'.

On 15 July, at Buckingham Palace, King Edward VIII conferred a knighthood on Rajkumar Vijaya of Vizianagaram.

He remains the only Indian cricketer to have been knighted. In the three Tests of the tour, the only ones of his career, he managed 33 runs at 8.25 with a highest score of 19 not out.

Vizzy was not the ruler of a major state like Patiala. He was not even a ruler. Many western – and even Indian – writers make the mistake of referring to him as the Maharaja of Vizianagaram. He was not the Maharaja, but Maharajkumar – a relation to a princely family who lived apart on his estate near Benares. As Mihir Bose explains, he was like just another duke.

Yet the effect of Ornamentalism was in full force here. Poor performances and misdemeanours notwithstanding, he was toasted by the British prime minister as the 'splendid Indian captain', inaugurated sports venues and was knighted by the King. Amarnath, the sparkling talent, was sent back because of problems with him.

But, Vizzy's story also tells us something else.

After India's independence in 1947, Vizzy gave up his knighthood. He continued to play a major role in Indian cricket, acted as president of the BCCI, and, curiously, even appointed Amarnath captain. In 1958, he was awarded the Padma Bhushan for sports, one of the highest civilian awards of India. To date, apart from Vizzy, the Padma Bhushan has been awarded to C.K. Nayudu, Vinoo Mankad, Sunil Gavaskar, Lala Amarnath, pre-Test era cricketer D.B. Deodhar, Kapil Dev, Chandu Borde, Rahul Dravid and M.S. Dhoni (only Sachin Tendulkar has received the higher award, the Padma Vibhushan. After retirement, Tendulkar has also received the Bharat Ratna, the highest civilian award of India).

While the list reflects the arbitrariness of the bestowal of the award and a blatant discrimination against bowlers, it also tells us that Vizzy continued to be treated with immense respect in cricketing and other circles even a decade after independence. He remained a rather tiresome voice on All India Radio during cricket matches. And, of course, he continued to hunt. It led to the famous Rohan Kanhai quip – when Vizzy was in the process of an elaborate story of how he shot a tiger, Kanhai supposedly said, 'Oh, I thought you just left a radio on and bored him to death.'

Ted Dexter says in his latest autobiography that he had seen Vizzy a year before his death and he looked shorn of the life force that one associated with him. When asked, Vizzy explained that he had fallen from an elephant during one of his hunts.

Vizzy passed away in December 1965, just five and a half years before the tour of 1971. Hunting on elephants, controlling cricket and getting awarded for being one of the privileged princes associated with the game – all these were still very much a part of the Indian cricketing scene even as the Empire was tottering on the brink of its final demise.

The princes did not quite disappear from Indian cricket after independence. Apart from the flamboyant example of Pataudi, there were others. Some were talented enough to make their marks on merit. Jayasinghrao Ghorpade, one of the finest fielders of the era, played in the 1950s. Datta Gaekwad was the captain during the 1959 tour to England. K.S. Indrajitsinhji, a scion of the Ranji family, kept wicket for India in a handful of Tests and did not do too badly. Hanumant Singh, a centurion on debut, played 14 Tests and perhaps did not do justice to his immense talent. Anshuman Gaekwad emerged as a gutsy opening partner of Gavaskar. Yajurvindra Singh Bilkha was another excellent batsman who played four times for India, and created history by holding seven catches in a Test match, a record for a non-wicketkeeper.

And then there were the ones who did not quite make a great mark as cricketers, but were powerhouses of cricket administration. The same election in 1971 that saw the defeat of Pataudi also saw the triumph of Madhavrao Scindia, who made his native Gwalior a major cricketing centre and became the president of the BCCI. Jackie Baroda – or, to use his full name, the Lieutenant-Colonel Farzand-i-Khas-i-Daulat-i-Inglishia, Shrimant Maharaja Fatehsinghrao Prataprao Gaekwad, Sena Khas Khel Shamsher Bahadur, Maharaja of Baroda – the last titular ruler of Baroda, became a powerful president of the BCCI.

Raj Singh Dungarpur was, surprisingly for a prince, an opening bowler for Rajasthan and also led the state team. He was not quite good enough to make it to the Test level, but for all intents and purposes ruled Indian cricket for almost a quarter of a century from the mid-1980s till his death in 2009. His question to Mohammad Azharuddin, *"Mian, Captain banoge?"* (*Monsieur, do you feel like becoming the captain?*) is part of the country's cricketing folklore. Raj Singh was perhaps the one who came closest in India to what Lord Harris was to English cricket. Of course, the comparison has its limitations.

While Vizzy was being feted for being the 'splendid' prince-captain of the All-India team, the British understanding of the Indian people and their own privileged place in the world did not go through too many changes.

In 1933, the British Empire reached its pinnacle in terms of the area occupied under the Union Jack. Following his appointment as Professor of Greek at the University of Sydney in 1938, a 26-year-old Enoch Powell travelled from England to Australia making about 20 halts on the way.

He later exclaimed that only one of those stops was not under the British flag. 'Alexandria, the Lake of Galilee, Habbaniya, Basra, Abu Dhabi, Mekran, Karachi, Jaipur, Allahabad, Calcutta, Akyab, Rangoon, Penang, Singapore – one was witnessing the ubiquity of a power on which the sun had not yet set. I saw, and I marvelled.'

The year of the Indian tour saw Malcolm Balcon produce *Rhodes of Africa*. The previous year had seen *Clive of India*. The Anglophilic Hungarian director Zoltan Korda would direct *The Four Feathers* in 1939 with a fascinatingly imperialist theme. Sussex bowler and England-captain-turned-Hollywood-actor Charles Aubrey Smith played one of the major roles in the movie. Aubrey Smith also managed to get a walk-in role in this movie for Archie MacLaren, who, 30 years after Ranji had employed him as secretary, had drifted virtually penniless to the New World.

A 1935 advertisement of Gossages' Magical Soap, with the tagline 'Makes Black White', featured a smiling African, half of his face washed fair.

As Bryan Magee remembers in *Clouds of Glory: A Hoxton Childhood*, 'It was taken for granted that England was the leading force for good in the world because it provided decent government to people who were not yet developed enough to govern themselves, training them for eventual self-government when they would become democracies like us.'

In India, self-government was being stalled. The Government of India Act had been implemented with grudging dissent from the British, and the Congress Party had swept the polls. The same Congress Party Curzon had once declared 'an unclean thing.'

They had passed a motion weeks after the accession of King George VI to boycott any plans for another Royal Indian Durbar. However, in the King's speech of October 1937 the monarch proclaimed, 'I am looking forward with interest and pleasure to the time when it will be possible for me to visit My Indian Empire.'

Five years before Vizzy's tour, another Indian man was in the news in Britain. On 17 February 1931, Mahatma Gandhi, huddled in a shawl in the cold Delhi winter, walked up the palatial steps of the viceregal palace to meet Lord Irwin who was waiting 'not as a viceroy but as a man'.

The old imperialists back home were horrified at this example of 'taking tea with treason'. In Parliament, Winston Churchill declared, 'The nauseating and humiliating spectacle of this one-time Inner Temple lawyer, now turned seditious fakir, striding half-naked up the steps of the Viceroy's palace ... to negotiate and parley on equal terms with the representative of the King-Emperor.'

Gandhi could have been the Great Soul or Mahatma. But he was no relative of royalty like the Maharajkumar of Vizianagaram.

14

CONSTANTINE AND ROBINS

DERRICK ROBINS has hired a side stronger than most counties. Hylton Ackerman, the South African, Kerry O'Keeffe the Australian, Mushtaq Mohammad the Pakistani, Tony Greig the South African recruit for England; alongside a host of local talent. There is Parfitt, Russell and Smith, whom India have already played against. There is Richard Hutton. There is another Yorkshireman, a young fast-medium bowler who will break into the England side within another year and half and end with 143 Test wickets – Chris Old.

Captaining the side is the 57-year-old Robins himself. He played twice for Warwickshire in 1947, as a wicketkeeper and without distinction. In the decades that followed he became an entrepreneur-par-excellence, turning Banbury Buildings into a major public company. In 1960, he became chairman of Coventry City FC, hiring Jimmy Hill as manager and transforming the side into a First Division team.

In the late-Sixties, he took over the organisation of Captain L.C. Stevens's XI in the Eastbourne Festival, before performing some sort of an acquisition act in this domain as well. In 1969, he suddenly appeared in first-class cricket once again, at the age of 54. Against Garry Sobers and his West Indians, he captained the D.H. Robins' XI. In 1971 he is paying his players £30 per game plus expenses.

The Indians reached Eastbourne late at night and drove around the sea front trying to find their hotel. They managed to locate it at 1am. Now they are rather miffed when Wadekar loses the toss.

The captain makes up for his wrong call with a superb sprawling left-handed catch to dismiss Russell. It is off the young Hyderabad fast-medium bowler Govindraj. The pace bowler, finally given a game, gets Smith to edge to Krishnamurthy and ends his first spell with 2/20 off 12 overs.

Not that Govindraj expects to get into the side, even in English conditions. 'It was an era when the new ball was rubbed on the ground to take the shine off so that the spinners could come on to bowl quickly!' Govindraj told me three decades later. 'In the tour matches I bowled well. I had a very good outswinger. But because of our poor slip fielding, edges would go for boundaries. Two or three catches would go down in the first two overs, and then I would be taken off and the spinners would come on.'

But weren't there great close-in fielders in the side?

'We hear a lot about the quality of close-in fielding in that era, but actually it is a lot better now. It was horrible then.'

Perhaps Govindraj is bitter even after all these years. However, it does question one of the myths about the 1970s. Of course, we cannot deny the greatness of Solkar, with photographs of the full-length dives to show for his brilliance. It was probably the case that close catchers excelled to the bowling of the spinners but seldom got any opportunity to hone their catching skills to pace bowlers.

Indeed, even in this game, despite Govindraj and his early success, Bedi and Prasanna are soon bowling in tandem. They are the only two spinners playing. Prasanna castles Parfitt and gets left-handed Ackerman to edge to Wadekar, who holds another fine catch at slip. Mushtaq skips down the track to lift Bedi over long-on for six. The canny Sikh changes his length and the Pakistani maestro snicks his attempted cut to the keeper.

There is a 34-run association during which the 6ft 5in Hutton and the 6ft 7in Greig tower over the Indians. But Bedi and Prasanna fox them before tea, and soon after the break the hosts are eight down for 157.

But O'Keeffe and Old produce some entertaining batting. The former a genuine all-rounder, the latter always a handy lower-order batsman; theirs is the highest and most exciting stand of the innings. The spinners are swept, and Govindraj, brought back to knock them over, is driven with contempt. They both are unbeaten on 35 when the innings is closed at 228/8, leaving the Indians to bat out half an hour. Prasanna 4-61, Bedi 2-64.

Gavaskar and Baig open, with Jayantilal and Mankad slotted to come in down the order. All four openers are in the game, three of them fighting to be Gavaskar's partner in the Tests.

Perhaps the desperate competition prompts Baig to hook Hutton for six and then force him for four. By the end of the day, India are 28 without loss.

Baig's is a curious career. Brimming with talent, he was a star Oxford cricketer in 1959 when asked to do national duty at Manchester by stepping into the large – in the Indian context – shoes of Vijay Manjrekar. He responded with 112 in the second innings. In his fifth Test he hit a couple of fifties against Australia. During the course of the second fifty, a young woman ran out on to the ground and planted a kiss on his cheek. On All India Radio, a bemused Vijay Merchant lamented, 'I wonder where all these enterprising young ladies were when I was scoring my hundreds.'

All that took place during the first five months of his Test career.

He went on to play Tests off and on for another six years, and remained hovering around the doors of the side for several more. As we can see he went on the 1971 tour to England. But he never got another half-century.

Lala Amarnath, Deepak Shodhan, Kripal Singh, Abbas Ali Baig and Hanumant Singh. This had been the sequence of five Indian centurions on debut. None of them scored a second Test hundred. It made people uneasy about the great talent that was Viswanath.

Viswanath will eventually overcome the bogey, but not until 1973. But on the second day of the game against D.H. Robins' XI, he becomes the first Indian batsman to get a century on the tour.

The bowling unit is a strong one, with Old, Hutton and Greig providing the pace and O'Keeffe and Mushtaq two varieties of leg-spin. Baig and Jayantilal do nothing for their chances of a Test slot, one losing his stump to Greig, the other to Old. But Wadekar bats beautifully. Starting with a hook and a drive off Greig, he enjoys himself against O'Keeffe, looks solid against Old and soon overtakes Gavaskar. However, having hit Greig for four fours in an over, he falls leg-before to Hutton. It was disappointing to be dismissed when timing the ball so well, but he does not mind going into the pavilion and watching Evonne Goolagong play extraordinary tennis to overcome Billie Jean King in the Wimbledon semi-final.

After seeing off the threatening bowlers, Gavaskar falls, snicking Mushtaq to the wicketkeeper. With Mankad not lasting long, it is 144/5. But Viswanath finds an able partner in the feisty Abid. While there is assurance with wristy cuts and shots at one end, Abid drives the faster men with plenty of flamboyance and pulls O'Keeffe for six. They add 84 and the scores are level when Abid falls, chancing his arm once too often against the Australian leggie.

Govindraj now comes out to put the long handle to good use. With Viswanath picking up silken boundaries, the paceman finds a few with slashes. They add 62 before Govindraj departs, with Viswanath now in the 80s.

That Wadekar allows the innings to continue does not go down well with Robins and his men. It is Eastbourne, and the focus is on exciting cricket. But Wadekar has to think of his side. Some of the members can do with a break. Besides, the wicket does not look like producing a result anyway.

He eventually declares as soon as Viswanath reaches his hundred. India lead by 77. By the end of the day Smith and Russell clip the lead by 12.

This is the day when Baron Learie Constantine passes away in Hampstead, London.

* * *

Constantine and Constants

Learie Constantine was a man whose cricket seemed to sparkle with the combination of sun, surf and the music of his homeland, under whose bubbling and ecstatic spirit simmered the hunger for freedom of his people.

'He revolted against the contrast between his first-class status as a cricketer and his third-class status as a man.'

Constantine had broken the colour barrier through his cricket, delighting the crowds at Nelson with his uninhibited strokeplay, his exciting fast bowling and his electric fielding. He gained acceptance in the Lancashire town well before the days heralding pretence of racial equality. He was a welfare officer of the Ministry of Labour and National Service in 1943 when he arrived in London with wife and daughter to take part in a few war-time cricket matches at Lord's and Guildford.

At the Imperial Hotel, where he had been assured he would be treated with the utmost respect, he was informed that he and his family could stay only one night. The American servicemen staying at the hotel had complained about their presence. Arnold Watson, a colleague of Constantine at the Ministry of Labour, attempted to intervene. The manager of the establishment, a lady named Margaret O'Sullivan, exclaimed, 'We are not going to have these n•••••s in our hotel.'

When Watson pointed out that Constantine was a British subject and government employee, O'Sullivan responded, 'He's a n•••••'

Constantine stayed the night in another hotel. The following day he captured 7-37 for the British Empire XI at Guildford. A couple of days later he sued the Imperial Hotel.

Justice William Norman Birkett, who later served as the alternative British judge during the Nuremberg trials, ruled in his favour. The penalty levied on the hotel was just five guineas, but it did mark a landmark in the race relations in Britain.

Or did it? Thirty-seven years after the incident, well beyond the timeline of our story, two international cricketers were playing as professionals in the Lancashire League, just like Constantine had done.

It was 1980, and the Indian all-rounders Karsan Ghavri and Madan Lal were in England. Ghavri was turning out for Ramsbottom, Madan for Enfield.

'Whenever you went to restaurants in a group, the smiles of the waiters vanished,' Ghavri recalls. 'The faces became long. It was as if they were being forced to serve us.'

Ghavri was once refused a second pint of beer in a pub next to his house in Ramsbottom. 'I just wanted a second pint of lager. The man behind the counter looked at me and told me to try any other pub. I asked why and he simply said, "You'll not be served".'

The Lancashire League matches were held at the weekend. Their club mates worked on weekdays. The two Indian cricketers found time lying heavy on their hands. Especially Ghavri. Madan was at least newly married and had his wife Anju living with him.

'It was just a short drive to Madan's place. I went down, and we decided to have some beer. Since his wife was in the house, we decided to go to a nearby pub. In his hurry to leave, Madan came out fully dressed but wearing his bedroom slippers.'

They went to the pub and had a drink.

'Behind the counter was a typical old English guy wearing a tie. He came out from behind the bar and started inspecting our attire before going back in. After a while we asked for another pint. He refused. We asked why we were being refused. He said, "You're not properly dressed. No one comes here to look at your feet." Madan got angry. He said, "When your people visit our country they walk around in shorts and go to the beaches and swimming pools in trunks and bikinis." The guy said, "That's not my problem. You can tell your authorities."'

This was 1980; those were different times.

Or were they?

The following day, addressing the Parliamentary Committee on Communalism, Indira Gandhi stressed that the stories of Hindus being forced out of East Pakistan gave the situation a communal hue. 'If the correct perspective is put across, it has nothing to do with communal problem, but it is a national problem for Bangladesh.'

* * *

At Eastbourne, Govindraj and Abid strike once each in the first hour, removing the openers, but Robins has instructed his batsmen to go for quick runs. On a wicket that has become easier, the Indian spinners get some punishment. Bedi has 0-58 in 15 overs, Prasanna 0-56 in 12. With the batsmen throwing their bat at everything, Mankad and Gavaskar pick up a wicket each. Ackerman and Parfitt are particularly severe in their rollicking 139-run partnership in 135 minutes.

Robins sets the Indians a target of 182 in 130 minutes. They do make an attempt to go for the runs. Baig strikes six fours in a quick 38 before responding late to the call for a single. Wadekar also sends in Govindraj at No.3 to speed things up. But, Robins keeps his fast men on with the field set defensively.

With 17 overs left, India are 82/2, 100 more required, Gavaskar and Mankad at the wicket. But, the next three overs see them scratching around for seven runs. With that, the chase practically ends. Wadekar decides to call it a day with 50 required off four overs, Hutton and Greig bowling down the leg side. Gavaskar remains unbeaten on 55, his second half-century in as many matches.

On the last day, the cricketers are met by Mrs Tara Cherian, wife of the late Dr P.V. Cherian, who had been the Governor of Bombay some seven and a half decades after Lord Harris. The Indian Tea Board have sponsored some awards and Mrs Cherian presents them to Viswanath and O'Keeffe for performances in the match, and to Robins for promoting cricket.

It is late in the evening when the Indians leave Eastbourne. By then Evonne Goolagong has become the first indigenous Australian to win the Wimbledon.

D.H. Robins' XI v Indians, Eastbourne – 30 June, 1, 2 July
D.H. Robins' XI 228/8 dec (Prasanna 4-61) and 258/5 dec (Ackerman 80, Parfitt 76) drew with **Indians** 305/8 dec (Viswanath 100*, Gavaskar 46, Wadekar 45, Abid 40; O'Keefe 3-71) and 132/4 (Gavaslar 55*).

15

ILLUSION OF PERMANENCE

EASTBOURNE WAS a favourite holiday destination for royalty. One of the rare 1935 film clips preserved by Reuters shows King George V and Queen Mary returning from their holiday in Eastbourne to Buckingham Palace. The voiceover narrates, 'The weather has been exceptionally lovely since their majesties went away, and it is hoped that the change will give them the strength and energy for the arduous days of the Jubilee Celebrations to come.'

A regular guest of honour on the occasion for both the monarch's coronation in 1911 and the Jubilee in 1935 was none other than Bhupinder Singh, the Maharaja of Patiala. Of course the maharaja was leading – in a relaxed sense of the word – the All-India cricket team in England during the Coronation of 1911. In 1935, as the royal couple travelled in an open carriage to a service at St Paul's cathedral, the Maharaja of Patiala sat next to them, resplendent in his medallion-covered formal attire and the decorated turban.

Bhupinder Singh was also with the King during the Imperial Durbar of 1911. The winter following the coronation, Lord Hardinge, the new viceroy of India, orchestrated the great event in Delhi. Held in December 1911, this Durbar marked the only visit of the ruling British monarch to India during the Raj. The King, with his fond memories of the bag of tigers, lions and Himalayan bears of 1906, presented himself and his queen to their Indian subjects. Bhupinder Singh's wife – one of them anyway –

presented Queen Mary with a magnificent necklace on behalf of the ladies of India. The act encapsulated Ornamentalism, cricket and the Raj in one gesture.

The pageantry, camps and amphitheatre created for the 1911 Durbar were once again incredibly exorbitant. The viceroy stepped into the shoes of the Mughal Emperors and the King and Queen appeared in the Mughal Red Fort. The British conception of the appropriate style of governing India was being played out with full regalia even as Indians cried for increased self-rule. It perhaps outdid the 1903 Durbar on which subject Cecil Headlam had filled so many pages.

The Durbar was also the chosen event to announce that the decision to partition Bengal, which had led to so much heartache and fomenting of nationalism, was being reversed. At the same time, a subsidiary announcement followed that Delhi was going to be made the seat of governance, changing the British base from Calcutta.

The new capital, to be known as New Delhi, was to be located to the south of the old Mughal city. The planning was entrusted to architects Sir Edwin Lutyens and Sir Herbert Baker.

The virtual cloak of Mughal glory was an important element in how the British saw themselves as rulers of India. Also, the nationalistic hotbed of Bengal had left Calcutta simmering with freedom fighters, a city prone to conspiracy, sabotage and terrorism.

The shifting of the capital in 1911, the elaborate shenanigans and the immense expense associated with the same, underline the illusion of permanence the British entertained about their Indian future. It took more than 15 years for the magnificent viceregal palace to be completed.

Two years before the 1911 Durbar, the Morley-Minto Reforms in India had established the electoral principle to membership of the imperial and local legislative councils in India. In spite of his liberal outlook, John Morley, secretary of state for India, said, 'If I were attempting to set up a parliamentary system in India, or if it could be said that this chapter of reforms led directly or

Mohun Bagan, Yorkshire and the sense of History

Calcutta, 1911. The hotbed of nationalism.

While cricket did play a role in the nationalist movement in a subtle manner, it was football, the sport of choice of the Bengalis of that period, that really kindled the sentiments that same year.

The Indian Football Association (IFA) Shield had been played since 1893, and had till then been dominated by British army teams. In 1911, the local Mohun Bagan Athletic Club, a team of barefooted Bengalis, overcame the Ghaziabad-based East Yorkshire Regiment 2-1 to become the first Indian side to triumph in the tournament. Mohun Bagan, one of the oldest clubs of India and based out of Calcutta, added more than their share of fuel to the fire of the nationalistic fervour of the time.

However, some of the effect of the victory has, like the 1971 triumph at The Oval, been over-mythologised. Not everyone in Bengal or Calcutta was a patriot; nor were all the footballers who played for Mohun Bagan that day. For example, Sailendra Nath Basu, the general secretary from 1906 to1914, was a Subedar-major in the British army, and gave up his role in the club once the Great War broke out.

Mohun Bagan remained extraordinarily traditional, in a manner quite similar to Yorkshire. While their arch rivals East Bengal recruited foreign players as early as 1942, and continued to field footballers from Pakistan, Sri Lanka, Burma, Nigeria, Iran and even Ireland and Brazil, Mohun Bagan remained staunchly Indian. They broke out of this mould only in 1991 when the Nigerian star Chima Okorie donned the green-and-maroon jersey for the first time.

Or so it was believed.

In 1921, a team of Natal-Indians from South Africa visited India to play a series of football and cricket matches.

The visitors did not quite represent the cream of South African Indian cricket, partly because the focus was on football and partly because several of the best cricketers could not get four months leave from their jobs.

In the cricket matches, they drew against Presidency College on 14 January 1922. The following Sunday, 21 January, they lost to Mohun Bagan's cricket side by eight wickets.

After the second match, Billy Subban, the captain of the Natal side, and Baboolal Maharaj, the vice-captain, were requested to turn out for Mohun Bagan in a club game against Ballygunge.

This was 69 years before Chima played for the club in 1991.

I mentioned this in *Apartheid: A Point to Cover*. While digging into the South African past, the diligent Kolkata-based researcher Sumit Gangopadhyay and I stumbled across this factoid in one of the ancient newspaper clippings that have almost fallen off the pages of time.

Not only is Mohun Bagan one of the oldest and most successful football clubs in India, but its cricket team has also been represented by several Indian stalwarts. Virat Kohli, Javagal Srinath, Sourav Ganguly, Vinoo Mankad, Lala Amarnath, Dattu Phadkar, Mushtaq Ali, Vijay Hazare, Subhash Gupte, Madhav Apte, Vijay Manjrekar ... all these men have played for the club. To put it in a nutshell – it is kind of a big deal.

However, the importance of this and quite a few other such facts mentioned in that book escaped most readers and reviewers. Non-Anglo-Australian cricketing facts often fail to register in the domain of cricket history.

Imagine the reactions in cricketing societies and associations if someone discovered that Yorkshire had recruited a foreigner in the 1920s.

necessarily up to the establishment of a parliamentary system in India, I, for one, would have nothing to do with it.'

Lord Minto, the viceroy, concurred that India must depend on 'the supremacy of British administration, and that supremacy can in no sense be delegated to any representative assembly'.

The British, however, were depending upon the sheer numbers of the Indian army forces in the Great War. A million or so Indians served in the conflict, playing a major role on the Western Front. In exchange the moderates wanted a status on a par with the white Dominions of Australia, Canada and New Zealand. The radicals wanted complete independence from the shackles of the Empire.

In August 1917, Edwin Montagu, the Secretary of State in India, did announce that the objective of British rule in India would be the 'gradual development of self-governing institutions with a view to the progressive realisation of responsible government in India as an integral part of the British Empire.' After all, Montagu argued, the people of India are 'intellectually our children'.

Exactly how 'gradual' was this 'gradual development'?

The Montagu proclamation developed as 'India Reform: Formula of the New Policy', discussed at a British war cabinet meeting. Before the meeting, foreign secretary Arthur Balfour warned in his memo that the racial equality that the governments of Canada, Australia and the Cape worked under was unfortunately too much of a stretch in India. In India, there was far too great a difference between the various races. 'Nor will education provide a sufficient remedy, for education cannot fundamentally alter the material on which it works, and it is the essential character and variety of that material which is the bar to political advance along the rather narrow and specialized lines which have been found to yield good results in Europe and America.'

Note the use of the word 'material'.

Lord Curzon, the former viceroy, also made it clear that India was very different from the white dominions. 'Of one thing we may be sure, [the political unity of India] would disappear altogether if the protecting power were withdrawn; and no language should be used that might, even inferentially, encourage such a belief.'

In the actual war cabinet meetings, it was stated, 'the expression "ultimate self-government"... probably contemplated an intervening period that might extend to 500 years ... Everybody who had experience of India, knowledge of the people, and sympathy with their aspirations, knew that, for the good of the country, England must continue to rule unless India were to relapse into chaos or be dominated by some other nation less qualified to guide its destinies.'

The estimate of 500 years was wrong by some 460. However, it was not only the war cabinet members, riding high on the euphoria of imperialist success, who subscribed to such views.

In 1946, with India in the grip of religious riots, the cricket team led by I.A.K. Pataudi was in England. After a speech on relations between Britain and India delivered by Vijay Merchant, a young John Arlott asked the Indian master whether India really deserved independence in view of the on-going religious riots. 'Shouldn't the white man stay on to secure the peace?' Merchant reminded his friend that the British had to undergo a civil war to obtain their own political liberties.

Arlott was as far as possible from being a racist, as can be very well understood from the relations he developed with the Indian cricketers, the way he stood up to the South African immigration officers, the way he lambasted apartheid on the BBC and later the help he extended to Basil D'Oliveira. In 1970, he was one of the first to announce that he would not be interested in broadcasting the cricket if South Africa were invited. However, before his human qualities made him question the system, the world-view constructed during his formative years in the epicentre of imperialist supremacy had led him to subscribe to the general thought-process.

That was true with many. Not all had Arlott's inherent qualities to come out of the cocoon and question the system. Many who followed in Arlott's cricketing footsteps have still not done so.

The Montague-Curzon-Balfour comments were from 1917. That was 54 years before 1971. As I wrote, we are already 51 years on the other side.

16

BALANCING THE MAGNANIMITY

KENT ARE the county champions. For Colin Cowdrey, the previous summer was a dream. Sadly, he has now been laid low by pneumonia.

Mike Denness leads the side. India, too, has a change at the helm as Wadekar rests and Venkat takes over. Once again Prasanna is left out and it is back to Bedi, Chandra and Venkat.

It could have been an early showdown between these Indian spinners and Derek Underwood. However, the left-armer is rested.

Cowdrey and Underwood aside, Asif Iqbal is missing from the side. He is with the Pakistan team, taking the field against Derbyshire. But in spite of the absences, Kent remain a formidable team.

Venkat starts his first game as captain by dropping Luckhurst at slip. Denness takes a heavy toll of the Indian attack. Govindraj has strained his side, so India are back to a new-ball attack of all-rounders who can send down a few overs of medium-pace. Abid and Solkar both look ordinary, and when Venkat comes on he is tonked over midwicket for six by Luckhurst.

Kent put on 125 for the first wicket, with only Chandra looking likely to make an impression. Luckhurst presses on to 118. At Lord's, Boycott hits 182 against Middlesex; and at Taunton, the Somerset bowling is flayed for an unbeaten 195 by John Edrich. The three English top-order men seem to be in fine fettle.

When Chandra and Venkat somehow reduce Kent to 209/4, Knott and the Barbadian all-rounder John Shepherd add 96 in quick time. As the lower middle-order go hammer and tongs, Bedi cashes in, capturing three late wickets. Denness calls his men in at 394/8: Venkat 3-93, Bedi 3-101, Chandra 2-93.

Gavaskar is sitting out the match and Baig opens with Jayantilal. The Kent pace attack is strong, and soon Jayantilal is gone for a duck. Mankad, batting at No.3, leaves for 6. Helped by the resilience of Kirmani in his perennial nightwatchman role, Baig manages to see through to the end of the day at 32/2.

It has not been a happy day on the field for India, but elsewhere sub-plots of their epic tale are being scripted. At Sandown Park, three-year-old Mill Reef gallops ahead of Caro and Welsh Pageant to win the Eclipse Stakes in record time. Before the end of the summer, he will become the most famous horse known to the Indians since Rana Pratap rode Chetak into battle.

On the Sunday, the Indians rest while Underwood captures 2/21 in seven overs against Yorkshire at Maidstone as Kent win the John Player League encounter by 83 runs.

* * *

But the biggest cricket news of the day harked back to the days when the likes of Vizzy and Patiala had dominated the sports pages. At RAF Cranwell in Lincolnshire, Prince Charles trotted in to bat at No.6 for the RAF against the Lord's Taverners. He literally trotted in, seated on a chestnut pony, waving a polo stick, as 10,000 spectators laughed at royalty. He scored 10 before trying to force Ken Barrington through the off side and lost his off stump. The prince, however, had his revenge when he got Barrington out with his underarm offerings. The Taverners won the match by taking eight runs off the prince's final over.

* * *

On Monday, the woes of the Indian side continue at the beautiful Canterbury ground. Norman Graham, who has taken both wickets to fall, now bowls Kirmani. His new-ball partner, the left-armer John Dye, castles Sardesai. Off the following ball, Viswanath offers his pads and the ball trickles on to his stumps.

At 52/5, the Indian batting looks brittle. Baig and Solkar avert further disaster, but more by chance than composure. They slash and the ball frequently travels through the slips. Shepherd gets Baig caught after a 60-run partnership, and then proceeds to run through the tail. Solkar's cavalier unbeaten 50 takes the score along to 163. Denness does not make India follow on. If he did, saving the match would have been more than a tough ask. As it is, even with this lavish dose of generosity, they only manage to escape by a whisker.

Kent do score quickly, Alan Ealham leading the way with 87. Bernard Julien, their new recruit from the Caribbean, is promoted to No.4, a manoeuvre of speed that hits a bump. A total of 176 in 49 overs is brisk; it would have been brisker, but Bedi is incredibly difficult to hit. Perhaps Denness does not think the Indians, without Gavaskar and Wadekar, are capable of batting through the last day.

But they do. Jayantilal is pushed down the order as Wadekar wants to try out Mankad as an opener. Baig and Mankad add a sedate 53. Viswanath at No.3 relishes the challenge. Mankad digs in at the other end, and soon Viswanath is stroking away freely. When they go in to lunch on the final day, he is 52 to Mankad's 47.

There are flutters after the break. At 146, Shepherd has both Mankad and Sardesai caught in the slips. Solkar plays his strokes and hits a brisk 32 before running out of luck. Along the way, Abid falls, Jayantilal at No.7 fails again, and Venkat is castled for a duck. But Viswanath carries on and plays out time with Kirmani, in the process reaching his second successive hundred. An innings of the highest class, full of wristy on-side strokes and deflections.

A draw. But would it have been possible without the misguided magnanimity of Denness?

Balancing Act

Perhaps Denness balanced his act 31 years down the line.

That was at Port Elizabeth 2002 when he was the match referee. Virender Sehwag was banned for a Test match for using the f-word (crude and offensive language, according to the official version). Deep Dasgupta, Shiv Sunder Das and Harbhajan Singh were served with suspended one-Test bans and docked 75 per cent of their match fee for excessive appealing. Captain Sourav Ganguly was fined 75 per cent of his match fee due to his inability to control his players. And, to top it all, Sachin Tendulkar was docked 75 per cent of his match fee and served with a suspended one-Test ban for ball-tampering.

The reaction was one of outrage. The cricket world was practically divided once again, as they had been on the South African issue in the 1960s. Along colour lines.

Malcolm Speed, the ICC president, was rather standoffish while rebuffing the Indian journalists. He faced them when changing planes in Mumbai. 'Rules are there for a reason,' he said, with a shrug of sorts. This Headlam-like attitude did not endear him to the Indian cricket fraternity, many of whom saw discrimination writ large on the incident.

All these years later, when I evaluate Speed's statement rationally, I find it full of holes when applied to cricket. There have been too many rules, under the garb of laws, littered through the history of the game without any semblance of a reason.

Ehsan Mani, the Pakistan-born ICC president-elect, commented that while there was no racism involved, 'What we have is an enormous communication problem. There is also a big cultural gap between Asian culture and white culture.'

An editorial in the generally balanced *Hindu* thundered, 'Denness's sense of fairness dates back to the Victorian era when Britannia ruled the waves. In the event, Denness truly believes – in the manner of his forefathers who ruled this land with such cunning for so long – that there are always two sets of rules. Nothing has changed since the days when the sun never set on the British Empire.'

The Indian politicians got a whiff of a juicy bit of news and everyone was soon snapping for a bite.

Scyld Berry described BCCI President Jagmohan Dalmiya as 'the control freak, the player of political games, the man who destabilises, then poses as the saviour of the Indian tour by telling his players to play on'. On the other hand, Harsha Bhogle, who admiited he had been rather emotional while on air the morning of the verdict, said that Dalmiya was 'a reflection of the Indian mood'.

The impasse was temporarily solved by the agreement of the Indian and South African boards to sack Denness, and play an unofficial Test match with Denis Lindsay officiating as match-referee.

An all-South African team playing a touring team in an unofficial 'Test'. Not the sort of déjà vu anyone would have wanted.

Nineteen years later, Abhishek Mukherjee and I discussed the incident in our book *Sachin and Azhar at Cape Town*. We pondered whether there was a racial bias involved in the Denness decisions. We concluded, in agreement to Ehsan Mani, that it was more of a case of unfamiliarity.

For Denness, and the umpires Russell Tiffin and Ian Howell, a young, warm-blooded white athlete like, say Shaun Pollock, appealing in that manner was perhaps completely normal. That is how boys will be and that sort of thing. But the facial expressions of Sehwag and the other Indians, as they appealed, could have seemed unfamiliar, oddly threatening or lewd in a subliminal way.

This is a major cause of cultural misunderstanding and often the stepping stone to most racial problems.

Cultural differences, inter-cultural unfamiliarity. By 2002, the world was already being talked of in terms of a global village, but such issues were still predominant. Thirty-one years before that, the skew was far more pronounced.

Kent v Indians, Canterbury – 3, 5, 6 July

Kent 394/8 dec (Luckhurst 118, Shepherd 76, Denness 59, Knott 49; Venkat 3-93, Bedi 3-101) and 176-4 dec (Ealham 87, Nicholls 57) drew with **Indians** 163 (Baig 58, Solkar 50*; Graham 3-60, Shepherd 4-33) and 264/7 (Viswanath 115, Mankad 53).

17

INDIA, PAKISTAN AND
THE WEST INDIES

IT WAS still more different around the turn of the century, when immigrants were starting to flock into England from Russian Poland. Successive governments pondered a good deal about it. Anti-immigrant pressure groups such as the British Brothers League were set up, which were to a great extent instrumental in formulating the Aliens Act of 1905. Supporters included the writers G.K. Chesterton and Sir Arthur Conan Doyle. The problem then was not really colour-linked, but had to do with Jewish migration and German phobia. Britain had historically been more of an emigrant nation than immigrant. It is difficult to realise that as we walk the streets of London or Birmingham today.

Yes, there were immigrants, a mixture of Caribbean and Indian sailors, Indian students, Germans, Poles, Russians, Arabs and Jews. There were the lascars. G.W. Steevens, star reporter of the *Daily Mail,* described the lascar seamen, 'They are a specimen of the raw material. Their very ugliness and stupidity furnish just the point. It is because there are people like this in the world that there is an Imperial Britain. This sort of creature has to be ruled, so we rule him, for his good and our own.'

It was not unusual to spot an Indian student in London or Cambridge. Gandhi, Nehru and Jinnah were all there, as was Vinayak Damodar Savarkar. In other domains there were mathematicians such as Ramanujan and Mahalanobis, cricketers such as Bangalore Jaya Ram and M.E. Pavri.

Stepney, Canning Town and Spitalfields were among the poorer areas housing immigrant groups. Salut e Hind, the first recorded Indian restaurant in 20th-century London, was already established in Holborn in 1911. The Veeraswamy Indian Restaurant, the first South-Asian eaterie aimed at British diners, opened in 1918 with great success.

There were Indian politicians, too. Dadabhai Naoroji became the Liberal MP for Central Finsbury. S. Krishnavarma, the Irish-influenced Indian nationalist, launched the Home Rule Society in 1905 aiming for absolute freedom from British control.

The Great War meddled with the immigration equation. Wounded Indian soldiers were a common sight in Brighton, and many were cremated on the funeral pyres of the Sussex Downs. While demobilised West Indian servicemen settled down in Britain way before the *Windrush*, there were a number of Indian servicemen doing the same at the end of the First World War. Sikh pedlars and door-to-door salesmen were quite common sights in the late-1910s and the early-1920s.

By the mid-1930s, there were Indian import-export businesses, based mainly in Manchester and London. According to *Indians Abroad*, a 1934 survey by S.A. Waiz, as many as 48 business organisations could be designated as Indian. There was also a continuation of political representatives. Shapurji 'Sak' Saklatvala came to Britain in 1905 for medical treatment. Joining the Independent Labour party and subsequently the Communist Party of Great Britain, he sat in the Commons for Battersea until 1929. Krishna Menon arrived in 1924, a student at the London School of Economics, and subsequently became an anti-Imperial activist in the Indian League.

From 1935, Amar Singh, that fantastic Indian fast-bowling all-rounder, forged a successful career in the Lancashire League. Right up to the last season before the Second World War, he played as the professional for Colne, and one season for Burnley, scoring more than 3,500 runs and picking up 437 wickets. There were memorable occasions when he squared off against other famed professionals in the League, such as Learie Constantine and Manny Martindale. Once in a while he was pulled in by English sides for a first-class match or two. He turned out under Arthur Carr for Sir L. Parkinson's XI against Leicestershire, batting alongside George Headley and bowling in tandem with Ted MacDonald. In a landmark performance, he bowled for an England XI against the 1938 Australians at Blackpool, capturing 6-84, restricting the visitors to 174.

However, neither the Indian politicians nor the Indian businessmen or the occasional Indian sportsmen were really representative of the general Indian population of Britain between the wars, just like Learie Constantine and Paul Robeson were not typical representative of blacks.

The general subcontinental immigrant continued to be working class, mainly employed by the shipping industry, often unemployed because of race-linked discrimination. Perceived racial distinctions were rampant – from creating problems in obtaining accommodation to the manifestation of socio-sexual fears and persecution of the half-caste populations.

During the Second World War, both the Caribbean and Indian population witnessed marginal increases. Manpower shortages led to a few hundred West Indians being brought into England to boost the economy's workforce. It was also a method of projecting the best face of the Colonial Office to the world. People from India were recruited into the merchant marine – seamen came ashore looking for factory work. In 1939, Birmingham housed approximately 100 Indians, including 20 doctors and students. By 1945, this figure had grown to 1,050. Under a scheme started by Ernest Bevin, the minister of labour, a number of Indian trainee munitions workers arrived to undergo instruction at government training centres in Letchworth and Manchester.

It all changed after the Second World War.

Westminster and Whitehall recognised the full brunt of Attlee's statement, 'We are a poor nation.' The reconstruction of the British economy required an injection of additional labour, as cheap as possible. The answer lay in the British West Indies. On 8 June 1948, the SS *Empire Windrush* left Kingston with

492 passengers. They were the pioneers. Other ships *Orbita* and *Georgic* soon followed. The 1948 British Nationality Act helped their cause. The flow was accelerated when the 1952 McCarran-Walter Act limited the number of British West Indian Immigrants to the United States to a maximum of 800 per year.

In 1956, the London Transport Executive liaised with the Barbadian Immigrant's Liaison Service. In 1966, London Transport began to recruit workers from Trinidad and Jamaica. There were other companies, too.

The West Indian immigrants sang calypsos as Ramadhin and Valentine destroyed England in 1950; quite a few turned up at The Oval in 1971 to witness the Indian win. By the time Clive Lloyd lifted the first World Cup in men's cricket at Lord's, 1975, Arlott would describe the ground as 'seething West Indian delight'.

However, life was by no means all calypsos and delight for them. Alongside them, there were the people from the Indian subcontinent. At the end of the Second World War, a number of former prisoners of war from the Japanese-occupied territories arrived in Britain, some of whom decided to stay. This was just a minor addition. But then they came in waves throughout the 1950s and 1960s.

There were the East Pakistanis from Mirpur and Sylhet, driven away by poverty and the volatile situation. Mirpuris were known for service in the British army as well as on British vessels at sea. Sylhetis were well known on British merchant ships. There were the Campbellporis, the West Pakistanis who had been recruited by the British army as bearers, cooks, batmen and caterers on the North-West Frontier.

The developing pressure on land resources following the partition of Punjab led to a steady inflow of Sikhs. The Gujaratis travelled due to the economic pressure in new India. And then there were the refugees who lost everything during the Partition of India and Pakistan.

The East Pakistan government's decision to build a dam at Mangla led to 250 villages being submerged in the Mirpur district. Homeless families made a beeline for Britain to join relatives who had already settled. A community of Sylhettis in Spitalfields, for example, with shops and institutions of their own, would have migrants sent to them in exchange for cash oayments back home. These were from a network of East Pakistani villages called *Londoni*.

Until the Second World War, the black and South Asian populations had been concentrated in specific areas of London, the seaports and near universities. During the following decades they shifted to the West Midlands, Lancashire and West Yorkshire. The Indian and Pakistani immigrants worked unpopular night shifts in textile mills, as labourers, in the furnaces and foundries.

They preferred living in close-knit communities, and were often forced to do so because of housing discrimination and, frequently, the antagonism of local people. The Moss Side area of Manchester, formerly a middle-class Victorian suburb, had by the Sixties acquired the nickname 'Black Belt'. Nicholson Street in the Gorbals, Glasgow, was now dubbed 'Burma Road'.

Most immigrants had never been compelled to think of their colour as a badge of identity. But now, they were physically identifiable as strangers in a country where black and brown people were generally regarded as inherently inferior.

Veteran Pakistani cricket writer Qamar Ahmed says, 'I arrived in England in January 1964. There were not many non-Europeans in London at the time. There were mostly West Indians working in London Transport as indentured migrants. Most of the Indians and Pakistanis were in the Midlands factories and also transport workers. It was tough for the Asians and West Indians to get accommodation with white landlords and landladies in London or elsewhere. When I tried my luck in the Birmingham League, I had to stay with a Gujarati family in Walsall and later with a Sikh family in Smethwick.'

Of course, Britain was not South Africa. In many respects conditions were far better for the coloured people than in the United States. In 1949, when Eben Dönges, one of the architects of apartheid, introduced the Prohibition of Mixed Marriages

Bill in South Africa, 30 states in the United States had similar legislation. In 1961, when Ann Durham of Wichita Kansas married the Luo Kenyan economist Barack Obama Sr, a couple of dozen US states prohibited such marriages. President Dwight Eisenhower spoke with considerable sympathy about the fears of the Southern whites with respect to mongrelisation of the race. As late as 1970, the state of Louisiana passed a law that made 1/32 fraction of 'Negro blood' the dividing line between white and black. The law was repealed only in 1983.

In contrast, there was friendliness and tolerance for the immigrants from many British quarters through much of the 1950s. Discrimination did take place and immigrants were officially advised to expect the same. But it was never backed by legislation and very seldom by politics. The National Council for Civil Liberties, the Institute for Race Relations and other bodies strived to make their lives better. Liberal politicians were welcoming, liberal publications supporting.

Some clubs and restaurants did impose the colour bar. The Indian student V.K. Das Gupta, for example, was refused admission to the Scala Ballroom in Wolverhampton. But this was never done with official sanction.

There were a few politicians who raised their concerns. Such as Conservative backbencher Sir Cyril Osborne, MP for Louth, who cried himself hoarse, and once literally cried, that disease, prostitution and crime were rampant and if something was not done 'Britain will soon cease to be a European nation and become a mixed Afro-Asian society.' But he and his ilk were not taken seriously for most of the 1950s.

Basil D'Oliveira made England his home. He arrived from the Cape barely a week after the Sharpeville massacre. He looked for the compartment of 'his people' after boarding a train. John Kay, the *Manchester Evening News* cricket correspondent, explained, 'Things are not done that way here.' For D'Oliveira and his wife Naomi, being treated as equals took a lot of getting used to.

Racism, however, was abundantly, and rather crudely, mixed in the curious mishmash of cultural confusion. A Liverpool taxi driver commented, 'I can take them or leave them, the same as anybody else. I don't mind having a drink with a coloured chap. I've met some very nice coloured people. But with regard to intermarriage, I think I'd draw the line there.' On 18 July 1956, the *Daily Express* asked, 'Would you let your daughter marry a black man?'

The 1962 Commonwealth Immigration Act stemmed the flow of people into Britain. The West Indian, and to a lesser extent subcontinental, migrants rushed to beat the embargo and this resulted in a cruel game of moving people. In 1961, 66,000 people arrived from the Caribbean, a further 49,000 from India and Pakistan.

The threat of immigration controls in the mid- to late-1960s led to the arrival of women and children from India and Pakistan, resulting in family reunions and re-creations of cultures from the subcontinent. And there were the Kenyan Asians who flocked to Britain from 1967.

British life ceased to be what it was. Multi-racial society had been thrust on the population before they knew it.

By 1971, there were 264,905 people in Britain who had been born in the Caribbean, 240,630 who had been born in India, and 127,565 born in Pakistan. Besides, there were tens of thousands of others who were second-generation British from these communities. In all, more than 650,000 inhabitants of Britain traced their roots to the West Indies, India or Pakistan.

Before *Windrush*, there had been just about 75,000 black and Asian citizens living in Britain.

This sudden scaling up in the immigrant population gave rise to insecurities, fear, racial stereotyping, xenophobia, politicisation, discrimination ... even riots and violence. It did. Britain from the late-1950s had taken a pretty depressing turn for the immigrant Asians and West Indians.

These were the immigrants who came to the cricket as India toured in 1971, and along with them came Bella the elephant to The Oval.

18

SUNNY DAYS AT LEICESTER

TOWARDS THE end of the first day at Grace Road, Ajit Wadekar goes back to Jack Birkenshaw and essays a fierce pull. The ball sails over fine leg, over the picket fences, and crashes through the window of the members' lounge. The sound of splintered glass echoes the click of everything falling into place for the tourists.

The atmosphere helps. The sun is back and so is warmth, weather-wise and otherwise. A large number of migrant Gujaratis in the crowd cheer the Indians along. There is the initial toothless bit with the new ball, during which Krishnamurthy spills a catch, and the less-than-formidable duo of Barry Dudleston and John Steele add a quick 60. But after that the match proceeds like a dream.

Prasanna, Venkat and Chandra are selected for this match, and all three soon get into their grooves. Prasanna is finally back near his best. Venkat is steady, as he has been all through the tour. And Chandra finds the Grace Road surface particularly to his liking.

The fielding remains keen. Even as Krishnamurthy continues to have an off day, missing a stumping off Prasanna and a catch off Chandra, the men close-in are sharp and the outfielders are quick. Baig runs Dudleston out from cover, Wadekar catches a well-struck pull at silly mid-on, and the Rhodesian Davison is snapped up by an acrobatic Solkar.

Apart from Dudleston's 51, only Clive Inman, the Ceylonese left-hander with a stance that reminds the Indians of Bapu Nadkarni, figures substantially on the scorecard with 49. Leicestershire 198, Prasanna 2-42, Chandra 5-63, Venkat 2-39.

In reply, by the end of the first day, India are 120/1. Gavaskar starts off by driving the Australian paceman Garth McKenzie and his partner Robin Matthews, and reaches 54 by stumps. Baig throws it away once again, this time frustrated by the shackles imposed on him by Birkenshaw. However, Wadekar comes in and quickly progresses to 36.

* * *

That same day, in Huddersfield, West Yorkshire, Enoch Powell voiced his reservations on the question of Commonwealth immigrants. With his famed use of rhetoric, he argued, 'As the voice at the end of *The Republic* says: "The blame is the chooser's; destiny is blameless."'

Immigration was not diminishing, he claimed. 'The Government, the Home Office, the race relations propagandist all want that to be believed, but it is not so. Net immigration from the New Commonwealth in the last 12 months was over 40,000, more than 10 per cent higher than in the corresponding previous 12 months.'

He estimated an increase in the 'coloured' population in 1970 of at least 91,000, a total of natural increase plus net immigration.

Before the mid-1960s Powell hardly ever spoke on immigration. By 1968, however, he had made his infamous 'Rivers of Blood' speech in Birmingham, and, as a result, had been sacked from the shadow cabinet by Edward Heath.

In the spring of 1969, a Gallup poll had found that Powell was the single, most-admired man in the country. At the turn of the century, a BBC poll to find the greatest Britons of all time saw him miss the top 50 by a whisker.

* * *

The following morning dawns bright and sunny, and the two Bombay batsmen send the hosts on a leather-hunt. The Gujaratis are back in the crowd, and Gavaskar harks back to the habit of mammoth knocks he cultivated in the West Indies. Wadekar thoroughly enjoys himself on the docile surface.

For the general English cricket fan, however, the focus shifts to Headingley for the third and final Test against the Pakistanis. John Woodcock warns that the groundsmen have prepared a brown and cracked surface that reacts like plasticine to the bounce of the ball – something similar to the pitches in Dacca, Kingston and elsewhere, but never seen in England. Illingworth goes in with three spinners, himself, Gifford and Hobbs.

As Boycott sets himself up for a century at Leeds, at Grace Road Gavaskar and Wadekar get theirs in the first session. Wadekar, in particular, is severe on anything loose and by lunch the Indians are 245/1.

It takes a stunning catch by Birkenshaw to get rid of the Indian captain for 126, a knock studded with 18 fours and a six. As so often happens with batsmen who wait for hours with their pads on, Sardesai is quickly in and out. But with Gavaskar now scoring at will, Mankad becomes limpet-like at No.5. The second new ball is taken with the score on 320/3.

Gavaskar finally falls to Matthews, tickling him too fine down the leg side, where Tolchard dives to hold the catch. The opener walks back for 165, to a raucous ovation from the Indians in the crowd. Wadekar declares at 416/7, after Venkat has essayed a cameo of 38. Mankad remains unbeaten on 43. Importantly, he has impressed the team management with his handling of the second new ball.

Before the end of the day, Chandra strikes again, hitting Dudleston's stumps.

Sadly, not much of the batting of the Bombay duo gets a mention in the papers. Britain is too caught up with the Queen visiting Princess Anne as the latter gets an ovarian cyst removed at a hospital named after her great-great grandfather. At the same time, speaking at the jubilee dinner of the Institute of

Marketing at London, Prince Philip warns that as a nation they are getting poorer.

For cricket-lovers, Boycott has hit 112 on his home turf and England have finished the first day at 309/9.

The third morning dawns misty. And in spite of conditions almost ideal for Govindraj, Wadekar tosses the ball to Chandra.

It pays off, like most of what Wadekar does that day. Chandra strikes at 54 and then twice at 66. There ensues stubborn resistance by Balderstone and Tolchard. The wicket is as flat as ever and the sun is now beating down. The score progresses past 100 and when Chandra returns in an effort to dislodge the partnership Solkar drops Tolchard at short square leg.

Wadekar now turns to Gavaskar, a surprise present on the eve of the young man's birthday. 'You've been bragging about your leg-breaks all through the tour. Here, have a go. But it'll be just one over.'

Gavaskar, thus far used as a medium-pacer, now comes off three steps. A half-tracker cries out to be dispatched to the pickets on the off side. Tolchard unleashes a cut and somehow manages an edge. It ricochets off Krishnamurthy's gloves to Wadekar at slip. The captain is happy enough to give his newly discovered leggie an extra over.

The rest of the Leicestershire batsmen fold to Chandra and Venkat. The Indians complete a victory by an innings and 50 runs: Chandra 6/64, eleven for the match, Venkat 3/31, Gavaskar 1/7. Prasanna 16 overs for 21 and unlucky not to get a wicket.

Brian Chapman in *The Guardian* describes Chandra aptly. 'His main weapon is the googly, which the Leicester batsmen could not sort out from the top-spinner. He bowls both at quite remarkable speed, sometimes as fast as Underwood bowls his cutters. To add spice, he has the knack of skidding the occasional ball through very low.'

Wadekar is suffering from an embarrassment of riches, even discounting the sudden two overs of Gavaskar's leg-spin.

Bedi and Prasanna have played three matches each, Chandra and Venkat four apiece. At this stage of the tour:

- Bedi has 15 wickets at 22.07
- Chandra 21 at 21.09
- Venkat 22 at 19.77
- Prasanna 8 at 33.88

He will keep switching and changing, trying to see which combination is optimal. But his mind is pretty much made up and the figures are eloquent in support.

His bigger problem is Gavaskar's partner for the Tests.

- Baig has 184 runs at 26.29
- Mankad 201 at 33.50
- Jayantilal has managed just 10 at 2.50

The 18 innings played by the three have resulted in two half-centuries, and seven single-digit scores.

The 'opener' question weighs far more heavily in Wadekar's mind as they proceed to Birmingham.

Leicestershire v Indians, Grace Road – 7, 8, 9 July
Leicestershire 198 (Dudleston 51, Inman 49; Chandra 5-63) and 168 (Balderstone 63; Chandra 6-64, Venkat 3-31) lost to **Indians** 416/7 dec (Gavaskar 165, Wadekar 126, Mankad 43*) by an innings and 50 runs.

19

RIVERS OF BLOOD

IT WAS in Birmingham, at lunchtime on 20 April 1968, that Enoch Powell walked into the Midland Hotel to address the West Midlands Conservative Political Centre. He had prepared the speech with characteristic diligence and his wife Pam had typed it up. 'Just a good speech, a forceful speech,' she had said.

It was indeed forceful. Laced with rhetoric like any Powell speech, it was scintillating and impressive. The impact was, however, more than that of a merely good speech.

It was a decade earlier, in 1958, that the sparks of anti-immigrant feelings were witnessed during the Notting Hill riots. 'N***** hunting' and 'n***** baiting' came to the fore. The press slammed the occurrences as a Hooligan Age, with the 'teddy boys' branded as villains. However, that was not the last of it.

Immigration was not a major issue in the 1959 elections, and Cyril Osborne's bill to control 'coloured immigration' was laughed away by most. But unsavoury incidents continued to occur, such as white mobs going around in Middlesbrough in August 1961 chanting, 'Let's get a wog,' smashing the windows of houses of immigrants, and setting a café owned by a Pakistani family on fire even as the owners hid in cupboards. An outbreak of small-pox in Bradford in early 1962, with the source traced to the Pakistani community, did not help matters. A Gallup Poll in May 1961 revealed that 73 per cent were in favour of immigration control.

The 'never had it so good' phase of the 1950s was over and crisis packages were being introduced. Economic, social and political influences played their distinct roles in the 1962 Immigration Control Act. The 1948 British Nationality Act, catering to the British Commonwealth citizens, was now being waylaid for Britain's proposed entry into Europe as part of the European Economic Community. The Commonwealth citizens who were not white were caught in the crossfire.

According to Zygmunt Layton-Henry of the University of Warwick, this was on top of a pre-existing history of hostility towards the West Indians and the people from the Indian subcontinent, rooted in the sense of white supremacy nourished over many years of a complex Imperial tradition.

In 1963, the West Indian cricket team under Frank Worrell delighted spectators in one of the most thrilling Test series ever. At Lord's, one of the greatest Test matches of all time was played to a draw amidst nailbiting tension. David Allen played out the final two express deliveries from Wes Hall as Colin Cowdrey, arm in plaster-cast, stood at the non-striker's end with nine wickets down and five runs to win. Ten miles away from Lord's at Southall, where thousands of Punjabis had settled in the Fifties, a local residents' association was formed to campaign against the immigrants. Demands were made for segregated schools, and estate agents were encouraged to sell to 'whites only'.

In the 1964 General Election, the politicisation of immigration was taken to a new level by the Conservative candidate for Smethwick in the West Midlands, Peter Griffiths. His opponent, Peter Walker, had been a Labour spokesman against the 1962 Act. Griffith's eventual win rode on the slogan 'If you want a n***** neighbour, vote Labour.' Conservative canvassers even spread rumours that Walker's daughters had married black men, and that since black people were prone to leprosy there were two secret leper hospitals in town.

Harold Wilson, leader of the Labour Party, dismissed Griffiths as a 'parliamentary leper' and called the Smethwick result 'a disgrace to British democracy'. However, there were letters to the editor of Wolverhampton's *Express and Star* newspaper that described Griffiths as an ideal MP because 'he was not afraid to speak his mind on coloured immigration.'

In 1964 and 65, a British version of the Ku Klux Klan made a brief reappearance. The Racial Preservation Society was established for the purpose of maintaining racial purity. In 1967, an attempt was made to weave together various strands of racial nationalism into the National Front. Clause 8 of their programme emphasised the need to preserve 'our British native stock' by 'terminating non-white immigration'.

It was during the 1964 election that Enoch Powell, the Wolverhampton Tory, began to change tack on the subject. The industrial town of Wolverhampton had thrived on an inflow of immigrants and had a higher concentration of recent immigrants than anywhere outside London. Powell, sophisticated and brilliant, had always been silent on the immigration issue, and implicitly supportive. He now claimed that he was not suffering from any colour prejudice or racial intolerance, but the fact remained that only if substantial further addition to immigrant population was prevented would it be possible to properly assimilate the immigrants who were already here.

By 1965, he was advocating opening the doors for a reverse flow for immigrants who suggested life in Britain was a misery. Powell suggested that Commonwealth immigrants and their families should be treated as 'aliens'.

In 1967, with the prospect of a serious inflow of Kenyan Asians into the country, Powell took his agitation to the next level. His campaign was to 'turn off the tap'.

Former Tory minister Duncan Sandys said that 'the breeding of millions of half-caste children would merely produce a generation of misfits and create increased tension.' Powell could never be as crude as that. He was subtle, but the content of his rhetoric suggested that racial difference was an undeniable truth and immigrants who were not fitting in should return to the country where they belonged. 'No amount of misrepresentation, abuse or unpopularity is going to prevent the Tory party, my colleagues and myself from voicing the dictates of common sense.'

In March 1968 the Commonwealth Immigration Bill was passed, further restricting the rights of people from the Commonwealth countries to migrate to Britain.

In the meantime, the proposed Race Relations Bill had come into focus. This was to prohibit discrimination in housing, employment and commercial services. According to two major studies in 1966 and 67, the Indian, Pakistani and West Indian populations were suffering mainly due to the discrimination in British society that restricted employment, housing and services. There had been evidences of colour bar among workers, such as at Paddington and St Pancras stations. There were also increasing incidents of physical violence directed towards Indians and Pakistanis.

It was in these circumstances that Powell walked into the Midland Hotel to deliver his speech.

'Those whom the gods wish to destroy, they first make mad. We must be mad, literally mad, as a nation to be permitting the annual flow of some 50,000 dependants, who are for the most part the material of the future growth of the immigrant-descended population. It is like watching a nation busily engaged in heaping up its own funeral pyre,' he fumed. '... Like the Roman, I seem to see "the River Tiber foaming with much blood". That tragic and intractable phenomenon which we watch with horror on the other side of the Atlantic but which there is interwoven with the history and existence of the States itself, is coming upon us here by our own volition and our own neglect ... Only resolute and urgent action will avert it even now. Whether there will be the public will to demand and obtain that action, I do not know. All I know is that to see, and not to speak, would be the great betrayal.'

This has gone down in history as 'the rivers of blood' speech, although Powell himself never used that phrase. The following night Heath called Powell to inform him that he had been sacked from the Shadow Cabinet.

However, that was hardly how the country reacted. The *News of the World* predicted that most British people would agree with

Powell. 'We can take no more Coloured people. To do so, as Mr Powell says, is madness', the paper declared in block letters.

The Wolverhampton offices of the *Express* and *Star* received thousands of letters in support of Powell. According to a Gallup poll conducted at the end of the month, 74 per cent agreed with what he had said; a mere 15 per cent disagreeing. Eighty per cent wanted stricter immigration controls. In the 1970 elections, the Conservative win had a lot to do with Powellism.

On the one hand, Britain was playing to the Common Market galleries by proposing to end immigration restrictions for all EEC citizens once they themselves were in that club. At the same time, the next Immigration Act was already being thrashed out. This landmark Act, passed in October 1971, was the pulling up of the drawbridge. It allowed Commonwealth citizens with patrial status unrestricted entry into the United Kingdom, while the entry for citizens from the Commonwealth who did not have patrial connection was dependent on the issue of a work permit.

'Patrial' essentially meant a native of any country who, by virtue of the birth of a parent or grandparent in Great Britain, had citizenship and residency rights. As A. Sivanandan points out in *A Different Hunger*, 'patrial' was for all intents and purposes a euphemism for white Commonwealth citizens.

Indeed, Home Secretary Reginald Maudling told his colleagues that since assimilation was 'all but impossible' for Asians, immigration ought to be limited to people from a 'cultural background fairly akin to our own.'

20

TWIST IN THE TAIL

STRANGELY AT Birmingham, a city where the Indian population throbs with numbers and life, very few people come to watch the game. The wicket, on which Indians play three seamers along with Bedi and Prasanna, is a perfect one.

The previous year John Jameson heard those incredible whispers. Having been with Warwickshire for more than a decade, the opening batsman suddenly got to know from an England selector that he was being thought of as a contender for the Indian Test team. The reasons were India's continuing search for an opening batsman and, more importantly, Jameson's Indian birth.

However, now he walks out to bat against the Indians on a belter of a wicket and produces a blistering double-hundred. Early on, he survives a confident shout for leg-before by Govindraj. And for some reason, while he flogs Abid Ali at the other end, Wadekar removes the faster man from the attack.

Of course, Abid fits into Wadekar's plans for the Test side. One has to play seamers in England, and it will be the best of a bad bargain to play a couple who can contribute significantly with the bat and in the field. Abid and Solkar thus form a limited seam attack with considerable utility value. This morning, however, Wadekar is not really elated to see Abid thrown off his length because of experiments with his action. Following the advice of Alf Gover, he has switched from his usual round-arm to an overhead action. As a result he is neither on length nor is he swinging the ball. On this slow track, he is hammered by Jameson and Whitehouse.

The Sporty Jamesons

Jameson was not simply born in Bombay. He belonged to one of those British-Indian families who had lived and worked there for generations. His father Jimmy was born in Belgaum, Karnataka. Mother Sylvia was born in Deolali, Maharashtra.

Both were excellent sportspeople. Jimmy was a regular feature in the Aga Khan hockey tournament and played for 25 consecutive years. He later umpired in the Tokyo and Mexico City Olympics. In Parel, Bombay, teams played for the Jimmy Jameson Trophy until the early years of this century. Sylvia was a tennis star and a swimmer.

John Jameson himself lived in India till 1955 before moving to Taunton. 'Playing for India after years of growing up in England would be unfair,' he said many years later.

When the spinners come on, Jameson hits them with the spin over the in-field. He does not really time all his strokes, but even the ones he mistimes fall in vacant spaces. Once he is all but stranded mid-pitch and Sardesai throws to the wrong end. By lunch he is 72, and Warwickshire 130/0. It is not reassuring for the Indians that the next man in is Rohan Kanhai.

After the break, Bedi strikes by removing Whitehouse, and Kanhai lasts just three balls. But Jameson is now joined by former England captain M.J.K. Smith and the run feast continues. In a little less than two and a half hours, the two add 241. Jameson hits Bedi, Prasanna, Abid and Govindraj for a six apiece, the last one into the hands of Prasanna at long leg, who then steps over the ropes. Smith's strokeplay is graceful, cultured, a far cry from his two visits to India. In 1961/62, Gupte tormented him, and two years later, as captain, he drove everyone to despair by thrusting his pads forward.

Jameson finally falls leg-before to Bedi for 231 in less than four and a half hours. Captain Alan Smith closes the innings immediately, with the score on 377/3; Bedi 3-106, Prasanna 0-96.

Against a benign attack on a flat wicket, India reply with plenty of spirit. Gavaskar and Baig are both gone by the end of the day, but the score rises to a healthy 94/2.

* * *

That same day, England and Pakistan were locked in a tense tussle at Headingley. And the 400m world-record holder Marylyn Neufville disclosed that she was flying back to Jamaica, leaving Britain forever.

'I have been called a black bastard and a n*****. White people here have actually asked me whether I live in trees and exist on bananas and nuts. Say what you like, there is still a lot of hypocrisy in England when it comes to accepting people of a different colour. Stay here a lifetime and you still would not be accepted.'

* * *

The following morning Wadekar and Sardesai do to Warwickshire what Jameson and Smith have done to the Indians. They add 214 for the third wicket, Wadekar enjoying himself with 77. But more pleasing for the team is the return to form of Sardesai. The home bowlers help matters along by bowling short, and Sardesai cuts and pulls with a touch of mastery. The Bombay batsman duly completes his hundred, compiling a neat 120 in four hours, adding 118 more with Viswanath. When Smith takes the second new ball, the pair hammer 50 off the first 10 overs.

The little man from Karnataka is on his way to his third successive hundred on tour. When he is missed at 57, it seems he is riding on the wings of fortune. But at 90 he hits one back to, of all people, Jameson.

At 421, Solkar skies Jameson and is caught by Hemmings. The opener has batted through the Warwickshire innings, caught Gavaskar, Baig and Wadekar, and dismissed two Indian batsmen.

India end the day on a mammoth 510/6.

The front pages were splashed with the shock of a British soldier killed by a terrorist sniper in Belfast. The sports pages were lamenting the omission of Underwood. Pakistan, needing 231 to win at Leeds, had ended the fourth day at 25 without loss. But reports did speak about how the Indians had hammered the Warwickshire bowling and sounded a warning ahead of the Tests.

* * *

There was other Indian news as well. This was the day when *Daily Mirror* carried the interview of Mrs Gandhi by John Pilger.

On entering the red stone Parliament House built by the British, Pilger had seen a man in the doorway that led to the prime minister's office trying in vain to listen to the cricket score from England. Having entered the office and met up with the lady he called the 'most powerful woman in the world', he had asked the question already mentioned in the first chapter: 'The description of India as the world's largest democracy is often used by people in Britain to congratulate themselves on having exported a successful model of Westminster government. Could an Indian, hungry and without hope, really regard himself as a member of a democracy?'

Vinay Lal, Professor of History at UCLA, agrees with Pilger's comment about the self-congratulatory British. 'He was entirely right in saying that Britain congratulated itself for having exported the Westminster model to the benighted Indians.' It was widely believed that this export had allowed India to survive so long. 'How often have I myself not heard, going back to the early 1970s, that India was not likely to survive?'

And it was not only the British who seemed to have such thoughts. Lal continues, 'I also recall reading, every now and then, some Indians of the middle-class suggesting that India had been governed better under colonial rule. This was not, it must be underscored, the view of the overwhelming majority.'

Bullion, cotton, democracy … the British and their exports to India. And their perceptions of the world. What they had failed to export, and which the Indians of 1971 needed in large quantities, perhaps was the uniquely British arrogance.

Lal, however, is prepared to take a lenient view of Pilger: 'We should also perhaps recall Swami Vivekananda's remark that one cannot preach to hungry souls. Some people will take Pilger's remark in this spirit and therefore reach a conclusion that he is being less condescending than what one might think.'

* * *

To the chagrin of many, Wadekar allows the innings to run its course. With hindsight, the captain will claim that he had this surprise up his sleeve. The real reason is perhaps to allow Abid, 74 not out overnight, to complete his century. But Krishnamurthy departs early, and Abid's race for a century against the incompetence of the Indian tail ends when he is last out for 93.

India 562: a lead of 185. The cavalier manner of the match continues with Whitehouse taking two boundaries off the first Govindraj over. Jameson is batting with the momentum of his mammoth first innings pulsating through his veins. Abid's long hop is too inviting. A swivel, a hook, and Bedi at long leg latches on to it.

It seems to be a minor hiccup. Kanhai looks good, his initial hesitation against Bedi overcome with two fine sweeps. The few who have made it to the ground look set for some entertainment from the ageing star. Bedi's guile gets Whitehouse at 64, but Kanhai is joined by Smith, intent on carrying on from his unbeaten innings in the first essay. There is a moment of concern. Kanhai, in his eagerness to dominate Bedi, swings him to leg, Solkar runs round the fence at long leg and dives but cannot hold on.

At lunch it is 78/2 with entertainment on the cards when they resume. For a while there is some, with Kanhai and Smith briskly adding 54. But the wicket starts showing signs of wear. Prasanna is difficult to get away. Bedi wheels away at Kanhai and suddenly shifts his line of flight. Tempted to drive at one which falls just a bit short of the stroke, Kanhai spoons it back to the bowler. That is the magnificent left-armer at his best.

A few minutes later, Smith is gone in the same way, hitting one back to Bedi. The last seven wickets crumble for just 33, the experience and skills of the two Indian spinners proving too much for the Warwickshire lower order. Bedi has 5/64, Prasanna 4/57. It mens victory for the Indians by an innings and three runs, with more than an hour and a half to spare. It is made more significant because Warwickshire are leading the Championship.

Wadekar and Adhikari sport wide smiles. It has been a special afternoon, especially after all the criticism about prolonging the innings in the morning.

Meanwhile, at Headingley, the Test match has ended a bit before the Indian tour game. It had been a rollercoaster of a chase. Pakistan, 231 to win, slumped to 25/2, then 65/4. Then, with Sadiq and Asif taking them to 160/4 they looked likely to coast to a win. But Asif was stumped off Gifford, Intikhab caught low down at slip off D'Oliveira, and at 187 Sadiq punched one back to the same bowler. Illingworth beckoned to Peter Lever and he ran in to knock over the last three wickets. Test and series clinched by the skin of their teeth, by a thin 25-run margin. John Woodcock's piece ran under the headline, 'Pakistan lose prize but share glory.'

The Indians left Edgbaston earlier than expected. The extra time allowed the team a leisurely three-hour drive to Cardiff. Farokh Engineer would join them there, Lancashire had released him for one match.

Warwickshire v Indians, Edgbaston – 10, 12, 13 July
Warwickshire 377 (Jameson 231, Smith 72*, Whitehouse 52) and 182 (Kanhai 59; Bedi 5-64, Prasanna 4-57) lost to **Indians** 562 (Sardesai 120, Abid 93, Viswanath 90, Wadekar 77; Blenkiron 5-100) by an innings and 3 runs.

21

FROM GYMKHANA TO WEMBLEY

AT EDGBASTON in 1932, C.K. Nayudu hammered Warwickshire to post 162 with six towering sixes. One of those hits, according to most accounts, cleared the embankment in the direction of the River Rea.

This enormous hit has generated the fable that Nayudu hit the ball from Warwickshire to Worcestershire. However, that has since been disproved by Michael Jones. The question is not whether the strike had taken the ball across the Rea. The problem is that the county border, which had been right there till 1891, had been shifted elsewhere. During the 1932 match the nearest point in Worcestershire was three miles away.

However, the exact position of county borders notwithstanding, Nayudu was a colossal hitter of a cricket ball. In fact, it is no exaggeration to say that it was Nayudu with his massive hits who propelled India into the Test world.

That was five and a half years before India played their first Test.

The MCC tour of 1926/27 had been sponsored by the Maharaja of Patiala. But that the Indians could play well enough to be taken seriously was demonstrated by Nayudu.

Hobbs, Sutcliffe, Rhodes, Woolley had all refused to tour. Fred Root, the Worcestershire professional, had accepted the invitation, but had been advised by his county management to rest during the winter. Skipper Arthur Gilligan, however, did manage to rope in Sandham, Astill, Wyatt, Geary and the star attraction in the form of Maurice Tate. On arrival, the captain explained that it was the strongest team that they could get together.

Tate captured 116 wickets at 13.78 on the tour, still a record for the most wickets in a first-class season outside England. He also scored 1,056 runs at 36.41 with two centuries. Enormously popular in India, he ended up in R.K. Narayan's *Swami and his Friends*.

When the side arrived at the Bombay Gymkhana to play the Hindus, they had won three and drawn nine games, dominating most of them. They piled up 363 in the first innings. On a green and lively wicket, C.K. Nayudu walked out to bat on the second morning with the score on 67/2. And his bat went berserk.

Unleashing some of the biggest hits seen in the land, many dispatched over the pavilion and out of the ground, he massacred the bowling. In 116 minutes, even as wickets fell at the other end, he amassed 153 with 14 fours and 11 sixes. As news spread across the city, office workers headed for the maidan in hordes to witness the devastating assault. Every tree and roof-top affording some sort of a view of the destruction was soon crowded with onlookers. The following day, a cartoon appeared in a local newspaper showing a group of spectators taking shelter from the shelling on the ledge of the University clock tower. The caption read: 'Don't hit us C.K., we are not playing.'

Gilligan noted, 'A really great batsman. His polished display of batsmanship was one of the best I have ever seen.' Two months later, on the manicured lawns of the Roshanara Club in Delhi, Gilligan sat with Patiala, English businessman Grant Govan, and Govan's Karachi-born Anglo-Indian employee Anthony de Mello in a meeting that laid the foundations of Indian cricket on the international scene. Gilligan urged the men to form an Indian Cricket Board. De Mello later wrote, 'A man so cricket-wise as Gilligan considered Indian cricket had reached a state in its development where it could challenge the world. Gilligan promised to state our case when he returned to Lord's.'

The BCCI was formed with Govan as president and de Mello as secretary. Gilligan kept his word. Two years later, India gained admittance as a full member of the Imperial Cricket Conference and made its Test debut at Lord's in 1932.

Did this new status reflect the contemporary British view of the Indians? Not exactly. Cricket reflecting society is a cliché and, like all cliches, it comes with its limitations.

The British attitude was encapsulated by the monarch himself. Speaking about Indian demands for self-government, King George V said, 'I suppose the real difficulty is the utter lack of courage, moral and political, among the natives.'

In 1928, just a year after Gilligan's team were in India, the writer Nirad C. Chaudhuri was told off for walking on the wrong side of Eden Gardens, the side reserved for Europeans. Reservation of separate amenities based on race was not legalised into an Act as in apartheid South Africa, but the unwritten rules were very much in evidence.

In 1926, Lord Birkenhead, the secretary of state for India, heard of the retainers of the Nizam of Hyderabad in London leering at inadequately dressed dancing girls. Fuming with rage, Birkenhead shot off a letter to Viceroy Irwin, 'Few things are more damaging to our prestige as a people than the exposure of the bodies of white women before Indians.'

Birkenhead did write frequent letters to Irwin, and not many of them were angry ones. Nor did many of them concern India matters at all. Rather, the discussions mostly involved cricket and tennis. When the conversation touched on cricket, it was not about Gilligan's team playing in India, but about that holy grail of the game – the Ashes.

In 1925, Birkenhead had said, "To me it is perfectly inconceivable that India will ever be fit for Dominion self-government."

It is true that Birkenhead was a Tory. However, British politicians with other leanings were not much different. The socialist Ramsay MacDonald, for instance, observed that parliamentary democracy could no more be transferred to India than ice in an Englishman's luggage. As we have seen from Pilger's question, by 1971 the British were quite proud of accomplishing yet another feat of human endeavour and innovation – transferring ice in their luggage.

In 1927, the 44-year-old Clement Attlee arrived in India – as a member of the Simon Commission set up to examine the possibility of granting self-rule to India. At that juncture, the future post-war prime minister of Britain did not know much about India. Nor was he enamoured by the prospect of spending months in a strange land away from his young family. Given these factors, perhaps we can take a lenient view of his abhorrence for the Indian nationalist leaders, especially Motilal Nehru. He summarily labelled Indian nationalism 'the illegitimate offspring of patriotism out of inferiority complex.'

By then Indian nationalist leaders had been clamouring for self-government for a while. The Montagu Declaration of eventual responsible government in 1917 had satisfied some, but frustrated others. The offered dyarchy of government functions – with the British retaining control over revenue, law and order, and the army – did not satisfy many.

Side by side with this came the infamous Anarchical and Revolutionary Crimes Act, also known as the Rowlatt Act, legalising a series of draconian measures, such as indefinite preventive detention, incarceration without trial and judicial review. As a result, a wave of nationalistic agitation hit the subcontinent. Amritsar, the Sikh holy city in Punjab, was particularly caught up, with looting, arson and wrecking of property. The British had been alarmed by the vandalism of churches and the assault on a female missionary.

On 13 April 1919, a huge crowd gathered for a meeting – a peaceful protest, but prohibited by the law. This was at Jallianwala Bagh, an enclosure near the Sikh Golden Temple. There was one small entrance and no exit from the enclosure, which meant nowhere to flee.

In one of the most infamous acts of massacre, General Reginald Dyer, officer of the newly constituted Indian Army, blocked the entrance with his Gurkha battalion and ordered his men to open fire on this ensemble of peaceful protesters: 1,650 rounds of ammunition were fired, the numbers killed vary in different accounts between 379 and 800.

This was followed by the implementation of martial law, with 108 Indians sentenced to death, public flogging and the shutting off of water and electricity supplies through the city. There was also serial bombing of neighbouring villages. Ritualistic humiliation included soldiers urinating into wells. Dyer also closed off the lane where the missionary had been attacked, enforcing crawl orders. This meant for two weeks residents had to crawl home through the gutter-filth of a street without sanitation.

All through Dyer believed that he was doing his duty. 'I thought it would be doing a jolly lot of good and they would realise that they were not to be wicked.'

Montagu did condemn Dyer's action as 'rule by terrorism, racial humiliation, subordination and frightfulness'. But Montagu being Jewish, anti-Semitic and anti-Indian feelings fused in parliament creating strong support for Dyer. Although Montagu won the vote, as many as 129 members of the Commons supported Dyer.

When Dyer was forced to resign, there was strong public support. Money was raised, almost like a sporting hero's testimonial. The conservative *Morning Post*, for example, persuaded their readers to part with £25,000 as a retirement gift for the sterling general. The mass murderer was also allowed to retire and receive his pension, without being subjected to anything in the nature of disciplinary action.

'I can no longer retain affection for a Government so evilly manned as it is nowadays,' wrote Mohandas Karamchand Gandhi in 1920. It was this incident, along with a spate of other immediate developments, that made Gandhi shift his stance. From negotiations with a sense of duty as a British subject, he changed to direct civil disobedience.

In the 1920s, Gandhian civil disobedience, structured on *satyagraha*, dealt a full-frontal blow to the British machinery through the brand new force of non-violence. For the first time, the entire land was swept by a common wave of nationalism.

Historical Monument of Folly

While the Civil Disobedience movement was in its full force, Edwin Lutyens was in the midst of his grand project, the Viceregal Palace in New Delhi.

Fusing European, Mughal and Hindu elements, he was constructing his masterpiece. There was 200,000 square feet of splendour, 285 rooms, 12 enclosed courtyards. Carpets for the three principal state-rooms were based on 16th-century Persian designs, woven by 500 weavers, using 7,000 miles of wool over two years. The Mughal garden had terraces, waterways, sunken courts, intersecting canals, fountains, paved alleys, lawn squares and geometrical groves of trees.

In 1922, when the Prince of Wales was visiting India, the British newspapers called the half-completed palace 'the Historical Monument of Folly'.

The structure was finally completed in 1929 – the conviction of staying on forever set in stone.

Back in Britain the supreme grandeur of the Empire continued to be viewed as a national accomplishment as the country went from the boom of post-war prosperity to the bust of the Great Depression through the 1920s. The British had not only won the Great War, the Empire had grown bigger and stronger.

'It was taken for granted that England was superior to other nations and the British Empire was the leading force for good in the world because it provided decent government to people who were not yet developed enough to govern themselves, training them for eventual self-government when they would become democracies like us,' recalls Bryan Magee in *Clouds of Glory*.

William Woodruff remembered his Blackburn schoolroom with 'a torn map of the world, most of it painted red. "The British Empire, our Empire," Mr Manners assured us.'

Of course, the war had been devastating. The born leaders were dead, among the 37,000 officers who were killed, many would have gone into politics and imperial administration. Other powers were definitely challenging their supremacy. The

Empire Exhibitions and Rummy Affairs

Through the 1920s, the common man in Britain remained somewhat distracted from the problems at home due to the sketchy knowledge of an Empire that was British and beyond anything ever witnessed in history.

Royal visits to the Empire were screened in newsreels. In 1920 the masses were shown *50,000 Miles with the Prince of Wales*, in 1921 *Across India with the Duke of Connaught* and *Tour of the Dominions by the Rt Hon L.S. Amery*.

Besides, it ensured that the Empire with its limitless expanse and possibilities remained in the consciousness of the populace through the Empire exhibitions.

A couple of years before Gilligan's tour, the new Wembley Stadium hosted the grandest of Imperial exhibitions. It ran from April 1924 to October 1925. From Canada to India, from Hong Kong to New Zealand, from Australia to Africa, the entire Empire was built in miniature across 220 acres, the buildings costing £12 million. The exhibits included reconstructions of buildings and landscapes, as well as actual native people from the distant corners, sometimes complete with animals. Rudyard Kipling chose the name of the streets – Dominion Way, Union Approach, Atlantic Slope. Ten thousand military bandsmen played in the Wembley Torchlight Tattoo, 10,000 voices and 500 instruments took part in mass concerts, 12,000 performers put up the Empire Pageant, including sections such as *The English Fleet in the Mediterranean* and *The Early Days of India*.

The exhibition was officially opened by the King, with a public broadcast over the *BBC* – the first such broadcast by a British monarch.

According to the *Official Guide for the British Empire Exhibition*, the purpose was to 'make the different races of the British Empire better known to each other, and to demonstrate to the people of Britain the almost illimitable possibilities of the Dominions, Colonies, and Dependencies overseas.'

'Everywhere the story is of progress, of the gradual overcoming of difficulties, of a victorious fight against ignorance, famine, flood and pestilence.'

With dissent fomenting in India on political issues of self-governance, the government of India was unable to participate in the exhibition. The British Empire Exhibition Commission purchased the Indian pavilion and leased space to individual merchants, thereby underscoring the image of India as an 'oriental bazaar' and not a developing economy worthy of full dominion status.

In the short story *The Rummy Affair of Old Biffy* in *Carry On, Jeeves,* the genius of P.G. Wodehouse captured every side of this extravaganza – the zealous ageing imperialist, the young man out for a good time, and the general attempt at propaganda. Sir Roderick Glossop describes the exhibition as 'the most supremely absorbing and educational collection of objects, both animate and inanimate, gathered from the four corners of the Empire, that has ever been assembled in England's history'. Bertie Wooster, on the other hand, is underwhelmed. 'Millions of people, no doubt, are so constituted that they scream with joy and excitement at the spectacle of a stuffed porcupine-fish or a glass jar of seeds from Western Australia – but not Bertram'.

Punch poked fun and Noel Coward satirised the exhibition as well. However, the idea of the Empire, as well as the unflattering image of the citizens of the far-flung colonies in comparison to the superior British people, was successfully embossed in the common British mind.

centre of financial power was shifting from London to New York. The British aristocracy were struggling to recapture the Edwardian days of pomp. Ancestral country houses were becoming liabilities.

As secretary of state for the colonies, Winston Churchill witnessed Egypt and India in revolt, 'on the edge of a blind and heedless plunge back into primordial chaos'. The whole future of the world, he said, 'seemed to be in a melting pot'. But the straitened circumstances of the country meant, 'the British Empire cannot become the policeman of the whole world.'

Many yearned to recapture the bright pre-war days. This gave rise to fables of the pristine pre-war era, smearing cricket forever with the fan-fiction of the Golden Age of cricket, promoted by the romanticising pen of Neville Cardus perennially dipped in Higher Truth, and the zealous cricket-evangelism of Plum Warner as editor of *The Cricketer*. In Warner's words, 'A Test match today is an imperial event.' In 1921, when Australian wicketkeeper Sammy Carter and manager Sydney Smith arrived in Cricklewood from Paris on an aeroplane – thus becoming the first ever members of a Test contingent to fly in – Smith addressed the Wanderer's Cricket Club dinner with the words, 'The visits of the cricket team act as Empire cement.'

It was now more than ever that cricket was given the aura of being 'beyond a game', a 'gentleman's endeavour', being 'all about fair-play and manliness, the epitome of Britishness'. Elements of this elaborate nonsense survive to this day, with many believing in some pristine gentlemanly virtue associated with a sport that could not be articulated even if one's life depended on it.

The lure of 'Amateur Ethos' and 'Gentleman Cricketer' was voiced by Lord Hawke in 1924, 'Pray God, no professional shall ever captain England.'

In 1926, in the summer before Gilligan took his men to India, England won the Ashes by virtue of an incredible partnership stitched together by the sublime duo of Hobbs and Sutcliffe on a sticky Oval wicket. Neither of the two ever got to captain England. In fact, the Saville Row suits worn by the dapper Sutcliffe were frowned upon by Cardus, who considered that the Yorkshireman was reaching above his status. In that Oval Test, the 43-year-old Hobbs, the 31-year-old Sutcliffe and the 48-year-old Wilfred Rhodes were led by the flamboyant 25-year-old amateur batsman Percy Chapman.

Indeed, as Gandhi had put it succinctly, a small island cannot colonise the whole world without first colonising its own people. To most of the British minds, the feudal system inside the country was as much a permanent feature as the Empire was outside.

22

VENKAT'S MATCH

THE WICKET at Sophia Gardens, Cardiff is not exactly one where Farokh Engineer will enjoy keeping to the Indian spinners after a long gap. Hence, it is Kirmani who shares the gloves with him. Wadekar bucks the trend by winning the toss, and Engineer enjoys himself in front of the wicket, coming in at No.6 and scoring 62.

Curiously, Glamorgan rest Don Shepherd, the veteran with more than 2,000 first-class wickets. Almost 44 and having bowled without much of a break for the past two decades, Shepherd can of course do with a bit of rest now and then, but it is surprising that the tour match is considered a good one for him to miss. Shepherd seldom lets go an opportunity to pit his skills against a touring side.

Skipper Tony Lewis, who will lead the England team in India during the 1972/73 winter, is unwell and often off the field.

Except for the Indian skipper every batsman gets runs, but no one goes on to make a big score. The pitch, with its colour of bleached straw, is easy enough, albeit with a tendency towards uneven pace. The ball skids through now and then. In the circumstances, the opening stand of 71 is quite a good one.

Gavaskar, dropped early, is caught in the covers off left-arm spinner Peter Walker. Wadekar and Baig both get out to the off-cutters bowled by Majid Khan.

Abid, batting unusually high at No.5, seems a bit overawed at the promotion. Viswanath, restrained by the double-paced nature of the wicket, cannot get the bowling away apart from a few scintillating square cuts. As Walker and Majid peg away, the duo score at less than two an over. Nevertheless, the stand of 89 is a healthy one. It is the little-used, left-arm wrist spin of Glamorgan's other international recruit, Roy Fredericks, that accounts for both of them. Viswanath mistimes a cut, Abid steps forward and is stumped.

Engineer pulls the West Indian twice to put him in his place and bats around a largely unproductive tail to remain unbeaten with 62. The total of 284 is a decent one, especially considering India are playing just four specialist batsmen. Wadekar thinks it is enough, given the uncertainty of the pitch.

* * *

The same day Woodcock reported that the possibility of a World Cup of cricket would come up for discussion when the International Cricket Conference met at Lord's the following week. 'The attractions of such a competition are abundant. Associate members such as Fiji, the Netherlands, and Ceylon, would be eligible to enter, and the early rounds could be played on a regional basis, after the style of the World Cup of football. The finals might take place every four years, in the different member countries, with the disadvantages of playing out of season being thus shared around,' he wrote.

Quite forward-thinking, really, when one reflects that the first three editions of the tournament, in 1975, 1979 and 1983, were played in England. In 1993, when it was confirmed that the World Cup was to be held on the subcontinent for the second time in eight and a half years, Christopher Martin-Jenkins lamented, 'There was a time, before money and politics entered the equation, when the community of cricket nations looked no further than the United Kingdom to stage the World Cup.'

While Martin-Jenkins had obviously overlooked the fact that the World Cup was a relatively new feature and had preferred autocratic hegemony to the level playing field of modernisation, even in 1993 it was a new and disconcerting experience for the

170

English not to have full control over the purse-strings and politics of the cricket-playing nations.

Of course, the ICC meeting the following week would also discuss the future cricket relations of member countries with South Africa while the policy of apartheid continued. The West Indies had asked that this should be brought up, and Woodcock warned that there could be an attempt by the non-white block to have Australia ostracised if they went ahead with their series against the Springboks later that year.

The risk of cholera in Calcutta and the persistent violence in Dacca would be brought up as well, given that the MCC were supposed to visit India and Pakistan during the winter of 1971/72.

In *The Birmingham Post,* it was reported that Roshan Lal Chadha, a 48-year-old clothes shop owner in Hyson Green, Nottingham, had teamed up with his friends, shopkeeper Baldev Singh and railway worker Guranditta Sharma. Together they had offered £100 to the first Indian batsman to make a century in the Test matches that summer.

The most interesting news item was, however, in the *Daily Mirror.* It reported that after the three-day look at the new Ugandan President Idi Amin in London, the diplomats had concluded that he was a 'thoroughly nice man'. He was 'gentle as a lamb' in conversation and did not bother about the sale of arms to South Africa, which so infuriated his deposed predecessor and some other African leaders. Besides, he was on his way to Scotland to catch up with old friends and check out the Royal Edinburgh Military Tattoo.

* * *

It is back to Bedi, Chandra and Venkat in Cardiff. The wicket does not offer much turn, but the dual-pace makes it complicated. The two-finger spinners use it masterfully.

In the morning, though, lackadaisical fielding sees Glamorgan seize the initiative through some majestic strokeplay from Majid. 'Majid (I refuse to be the only person in Cardiff to call him Khan) scored 78 in 100 minutes, blazing away with all his strokes after a quiet start,' writes Alan Gibson in *The Times*. There are glorious drives, elegant hooks and flashing cuts, and at 178/3, the hosts look to be thriving.

But finally Bedi sends down his arm-ball and the Pakistani is castled. All of a sudden the catching improves, the batsmen's luck runs out. Lewis is too ill to try to put bat to ball. The 17-year-old Llewellyn, who had a nasty knock on the head the previous day, is unable to bat. Bedi gets 3-66 and, once again, Venkat impresses with 6-76. Glamorgan are 203 all out, the last six wickets falling for 25.

The Indians go for quick runs, but three quick wickets check the flow. Majid sends back Baig, Fredericks yet again picks up a vital wicket, this time Gavaskar. Viswanath swings Walker into the hands of square leg. But the Indians continue to belt the ball. Wadekar times them sweetly in spite of the variable pace of the wicket, his cuts and drives finding gaps with ease. Engineer plays another vital hand of 28. But the star turn is by vice-captain Venkat. Promoted in the order to push the scoring along, he drives handsomely and even slams Walker over midwicket for six. Wadekar, too, strikes a six that clears the straight field and lands in the River Taff.

The captain is run out for 77, his deputy skies a catch at 57. India declare at 6.38pm, a tad late in the day perhaps. The spinners are on within two overs. Glamorgan end at 11/0.

* * *

The England 12 for the first Test at Lord's is announced that day. Illingworth, Amiss, Boycott, D'Oliveira, Edrich, Gifford, Hutton, Jameson, Knott, Luckhurst, Price and Snow.

Late at night news came through that US President Richard Nixon had accepted an invitation to visit China. Arrangements had been made during Kissinger's Peking visit during the previous weekend. Kissinger's trip in turn had been carefully facilitated by the Yahya government during the national security Adviser's sojourn in Pakistan in the midst of his round-the-world tour. Kissinger summed up the contribution of Pakistan with characteristically cold-blooded callousness, 'Yahya hasn't had such fun since the last Hindu massacre.'

* * *

On the final morning at Cardiff, Malcolm Nash, who has come in as the makeshift opener the previous evening, chances his arm. He has Engineer to thank, when he fails to stump him off Bedi and then grasses him off Venkat. Baig too misses a sitter and Wadekar's face becomes grim.

Lewis and Fredericks are both bowled by Bedi, but after 22 overs Glamorgan are 100/2, and the game hangs in balance. The target is 327.

At this stage, Majid drives one back to Venkat, and Nash's luck finally runs out. Yet, as Chandra is off the field with a sore finger, Bedi and Venkat find themselves stalled by a determined partnership between Alan Jones and Walker. Jones looks in fine form. He became a Test player during the previous summer's series against the Rest of the World. In 1972, The ICC will strip the matches of Test status and Jones will end his career without having played Test cricket, but at the moment he is officially a Test cricketer. At 185/4 at tea, and Glamorgan have batted themselves back into the game.

But at 198, Venkat has Walker caught. The following over sees Bedi strike twice. And soon it is all over, Jones the last man out, is caught at slip off Bedi. Bedi 6-93, Venkat 3 -97, both the spinners have nine wickets in the match. India win by 102 runs.

Three straight victories. No Indian team of the past have had anything close to such success. Back home in India, chairman of selectors Vijay Merchant can afford to smile.

Glamorgan v Indians, Sophia Gardens – 14, 15, 16 July
Indians 284 (Engineer 62*, Viswanath 52, Baig 47, Abid 46; Cordle 4-49) and 245-6 dec (Wadekar 73, Venkat 57) beat **Glamorgan** 203 (Majid 78; Venkat 6-76, Bedi 3-66) and 224 (Nash 75, Jones 55, Walker 44; Bedi 6-93, Venkat 3-97) by 102 runs.

23

TEA WITH TREASON AND
NAPOLEON BRANDY

MERCHANT'S SLIM, self-effacing autobiography tells the story of his asking for Gandhi's autograph in the same book that contained the signatures of 16 English cricketers who toured India in 1933/34. Gandhi had asked who those 16 were. When Merchant answered that they were English cricketers, the Mahatma scribbled his own below the cricketers as No.17.

Merchant had concluded that it was Gandhi's way of saying that he was opposed to British rule, but not the general British people – among them the cricketers.

In 1919, he went ahead with his movement of *satyagraha*, or truth-force, a civil resistance movement based on non-violence, truth, non-possession, control of desires, and a number of other principles of which the most crippling to the British was the idea of *Swadeshi* – the economic strategy of boycotting imported goods.

Perhaps he was not fully understood by all, perhaps he was a genius who was understood at different levels by people from different strata. But the impact of Gandhi was phenomenal. He was the first Indian leader to have a following all over India. Not only did the British run out of ideas to control him ... years later Martin Luther King Jr and Nelson Mandela were borrowing the ideas of *satyagraha*.

By the end of the 1920s, as the world struggled with the Great Depression, Gandhi set off from Ahmedabad to the Indian Ocean, his destination a village called Dandi. The salt monopoly was a long-standing issue, and with half the retail price of salt enriching the British coffers through taxes, Gandhi had devised a movement like no other.

Hind Swaraj

Having reached England almost at the same time as Ranji, Gandhi had come back with a law degree and tried his hand, rather unsuccessfully, at legal practice in India. In 1893, he had departed for Natal, to help settle a dispute between two Gujarati businessmen.

The one-year assignment became a completely different vocation lasting 21 years. By the time he left South Africa, having rehearsed his methods of activism for the Indians against the colonial, the Afrikaner and also the blacks, General Smuts commented, 'The saint has left our shores, I sincerely hope for ever.'

In 1909, travelling back from London to South Africa on SS *Kildonan Castle* Gandhi had written *Hind Swaraj*, his idea of Indian home rule documented in the form of a dialogue between a reader and an editor. He was not interested in the British leaving India only for the Indians to adopt British ways. His idea of freedom was rejecting Western civilisation altogether. To him, Indian independence was possible only through passive resistance, and that could be achieved through self-reliance. Self-reliance from the grassroots level, from the villages onwards. To Gandhi, the transformation of India into self-rule was not just political emancipation but a spiritual one. That meant refusal of all relations, including trade, with the British.

In a masterly application of *satyagraha*, he conceived the idea of publicly producing the salt himself. He announced his intention to do so in a skilful political letter to the viceroy Lord Irwin. Dressed in his white homespun, he walked 24 days, across 250 miles, starting with 78 people and ending with thousands. As he stopped and spoke in each village, the villagers kept joining the march.

The effect was staggering. The wave of *satyagraha* had shaken up the entire land. When he reached Dandi, newspapers across the world carried his photograph in that simple seaside village. All over India people started making salt, digging it out of the earth. In colleges and universities, professors led their entire classes to the seaside to collect salt. Not everyone was content with making salt following the Gandhian principle of non-violence, though. Soldiers were rebelling, there were riots, government salt depots were raided, newspapers were banned.

The confused British way of dealing with this entire situation was one of force. Around 100,000 Indian patriots were in prison by May 1931. 'I congratulate you on the new India you have created by your magic touch,' Jawaharlal Nehru wrote to Gandhi, the letter posted from his prison to the Mahatma's. More than that, the salt march brought India to the attention of world media. Global opinion rapidly turned against the British.

That was when Gandhi, released from jail, went up the viceregal steps to meet Lord Irwin. The same meeting that led Churchill to his famous lament about the 'seditious half-naked fakir'. Irwin had himself wondered whether to launch on a Gandhi-like fast to bring peace to India. The meeting was amicable, ending with Irwin saying, 'Good night, Mr Gandhi, goodnight, and my prayers go with you.'

By now Gandhi was a world figure.

When Don Bradman was leading his Invincibles in England, 1948, a letter had been dispatched with just the picture of his eyes denoting the recipient, with the address, 'Playing somewhere in England'. It had reached him. Gandhi had already achieved that sort of a universally recognisable persona in the early 1930s. Letters addressed to 'Gandhi, India' reached him every day, from everywhere.

By 1934, Cole Porter mangled the pronunciation of his name in *Anything Goes* to rhyme:

> *"You're the top, you're Mahatma Gandhi,*
> *You're the top! you're Napoleon brandy ..."*

When this half-naked fakir went to England later in 1931, to a round table conference convened by the Labour government, London street-urchins asked, 'Hey Gandhi, where's your trousers?' Churchill refused to meet him.

Others, however, had no such disinclination. From the ladies of the Lancashire cotton mills to the London Vegetarian Society, from Charlie Chaplin to Bernard Shaw, Gandhi met almost everyone.

Even King George V and Queen Mary hosted him for tea at Buckingham Palace. The King's first reaction had supposedly been 'What! Have this rebel fakir in the Palace?' But then he relented.

During the meeting, the King was supposedly, at least according to his private secretary, 'as is his custom, very nice to Mr Gandhi'. His majesty, however, also took the opportunity to let the curious little Indian man know that civil disobedience was a 'hopeless and stupid policy'. 'Remember Mr Gandhi, I can't have attacks on *my* Indian Empire.'

As Gandhi walked out of the palace, reporters asked him if he had felt properly dressed for the occasion in his loin-cloth and sandals. Gandhi's reply was, 'It was quite all right. The King had enough on for both of us.'

Four years after his meeting with Gandhi, the King and Queen celebrated their Silver Jubilee. The royal couple travelled together in an open carriage to a service in St Paul's cathedral. In front of them sat Bhupinder Singh, the Maharaja of Patiala, resplendent in his medallion-covered formal attire and decorated turban.

Gandhi's comment was not just a joke. It was steeped in the irony of how Ornamentalism triumphed over even the most fundamental tenets of human character. Dressed in gaudy regalia, a confirmed letcher, kidnapper and murderer was preferable to a half-naked great soul.

Mark Twain had summed it up in his 1905 story *The Czar's Soliloquy*: '[One] realises that without his clothes a man would be nothing at all; that the clothes do not merely make the man, the clothes are the man; that without them he is a cipher, a vacancy, a nobody, a nothing … There is no power without clothes.'

In 1927 Merle Johnson paraphrased the Twain quote as: 'Clothes make the man. Naked people have little or no influence on society.'

24

YET ANOTHER VENKAT TRIUMPH

DEAN PARK, Bournemouth, is the venue that resolves India's last few problems before the first Test.

India, resting Bedi and Chandra, go in with Venkat and Prasanna as the spinners. Other than them, there is the dicey medium-pace of Govindraj and Solkar. Barry Richards, one of the most exciting batsmen in the world and one who will never play Test cricket again, starts with two thunderous drives. But having got 10, he drives one back to Solkar and the left-armer grabs a blinder on his follow-through. The danger man has gone, and it is a small but significant landmark for India. One of their medium-paced all-rounders has finally got a wicket on the tour, in the last match before the first Test!

At the other end, Govindraj is also successful, but by now he probably knows that he is not getting into the team at Lord's. In any case, irrespective of the success for the medium-pacers, the two off-spinners are soon in action.

It seems that the wily Prasanna has peaked at the right moment. He is really impressive, especially when he lures the attacking West Indian Danny Livingstone into plopping up a catch. Venkat, for a change, looks rather off colour.

Yet again, Wadekar calls upon Gavaskar to bowl his leg-breaks. It works as well, with Sardesai taking a good catch at silly mid-on to get rid of Stephenson. Hampshire's innings ends when Gavaskar, called in for his second over, gets No.11 David White leg-before. Hampshire are 198 all out, Prasanna 3-37, Venkat 1-76. The sudden contrast in performances is a bit confusing for the team management.

Baig has scored 291 runs on the tour so far, at 29.10. It is perhaps his final chance to come good. But he manages just 4. Wadekar wisely sends Mankad in, leveraging the benefits of having three opening batsmen in the side. He is still there at the end of the day, unbeaten on 36, knowing that coming good at this juncture will cement his place in the Test side. Gavaskar falls just before the close, having scored his fourth half-century of the tour.

* * *

That same day Henry Kissinger met Lakshmi Kant Jha, the Indian ambassador to the USA. If war broke out, the Secretary of State warned, and if China became involved on Pakistan's side, 'we would be unable to help you against China.'

As the team rested on Sunday, *The Times* correspondent Peter Hazelhurst reported from Delhi that 10,000 guerrillas had just completed their training and were ready to move into the tense zone of East Pakistan. Another 15,000 would be ready in a couple of weeks.

Awk-Ward Bowling

The dropped slip catches make for an interesting sidelight. Earlier that summer the young Imran Khan had been told by a senior Pakistani player that if he ever snicked a ball in England he should not bother to look back. An English slip fielder never missed a catch.

Such beliefs were not uncommon. The English batsmen, with traditional English defence, never left a gap between bat and pad. One Pakistani youngster wondered, 'Will I be able to see the ball as it leaves Alan Ward's hand?'

And Ted Dexter lamented that the talent pool of England was not deep enough. Therefore, they had been forced to overlook Snow's lackadaisical approach towards fitness, Edrich's worst series of his career, Luckhurst's pair in the final Test, Amiss's first innings failure and a clutch of dropped slip catches, and Knott's unimpressive keeping.

* * *

On Monday morning it is slow going, as Mankad proceeds with understandable caution. His batting is solid, but unexciting. With Sardesai falling cheaply, he is joined at the wicket by Viswanath, the one Indian batsman radiating form. They put on 143, Viswanath by far the more exciting, his delicate strokes essayed with splendid timing.

The Karnataka batsman brings up his third hundred of the tour in 205 minutes, while Mankad labours to his first in 335. The rest of the batting does not amount to much. Indians are all out for 364, scored at a rather sedate pace.

The following morning sees a spirited first hour from Hampshire, as Barry Richards starts with a flurry of boundaries and then pulls Venkat for six. However, the aggression is not reined in. Soon he steps out, misses and the bails are whipped off.

There are some hefty blows. Lewis heaves Prasanna for six, and when Gavaskar is given the ball he is similarly dispatched by Gilliat. But in the end it turns out to be Venkat's day.

From half an hour after the start of the innings till he has Hampshire's last man caught by Baig, Venkat wheels away from the Lansdowne End. The length remains nagging. The batsmen attack, sometimes their hits come off, but ultimately they are outfoxed one by one. In the end, Venkat's figures read 36.3-13-93-9. The only other wicket is picked up by Solkar.

At the other end, Prasanna bowls 33 overs for 81 without luck or success. Too fast and too flat? One is prone to raise an eyebrow when this allegation is brought against Prasanna, the master of flight. However, that is what the English critics think of him that summer.

India get the runs without much hassle, other than the minor bump of Baig falling early yet again. There is plenty of time, and the Gavaskar-Wadekar duo ensure that no panic sets in. Venkat and Govindraj are sent out to throw their bats around, and both connect often enough to stay ahead of the clock. A handsome drive by Solkar ends the match in the 17th of the 20 mandatory overs, bringing up an unprecedented fourth consecutive victory as India go into the first Test.

The debate about the spinners in the side for the Lord's Test dies a natural death in Hampshire's second innings. Venkat's incredible effort puts an end to all that. The Indians have played eight matches on the tour. Bedi, Chandra and Prasanna have played five each. Venkat has played six. The overall figures put the debate beyond question.

	M	O	W	Ave
Bedi	5	267.2	32	20.53
Chandra	5	181.1	21	23.67
Venkat	6	291.5	41	18.95
Prasanna	5	232.2	15	36.13

'They just decided to drop me and then began to look for a reason for doing so,' Prasanna will complain later. However, he has not given 'them' too many reasons to pick him. Venkat has played one more match but has taken 26 more wickets at an average almost twice as good. The two other spinners have played the same number of matches as Prasanna. So, Prasanna's future lament, 'They just played me in every second game as they pleased,' will not make much sense either.

According to evidence and accounts before this tour, Prasanna had started to take his place in the side for granted. And as often happens in such cases, with the change of management a new captain brought in new plans and someone else responded. It took Prasanna too long to realise that he had to earn his place, the same as the others.

As far as the conundrum surrounding Gavaskar's opening partner is concerned, the final match decides that as well. Mankad's late success, coupled with the brace of single-digit scores by Baig, makes the decision obvious. Jayantilal has been unlucky to pick up an injury, but he has not quite made use of the chances he has been given early on.

	M	I	R	Ave
Baig	6	12	297	24.75
Mankad	5	8	310	44.29
Jayantilal	2	4	10	2.50

In a 2013 interview, Govindraj will tell me: 'Wadekar wanted men from Bombay.' Well, yes, both Baig and Jayantilal are from Hyderabad, the same as Govindraj. However, even here, the numbers back Wadekar.

As the captain himself put it, 'Our team picked itself.'

* * *

The day after the Hampshire game ended, senior Indian diplomat D.P. Dhar reached Moscow. In two long meetings with Andrei Gromynko, the Soviet minister of foreign affairs, the final touches were added to the forthcoming Indo-USSR treaty.

Hampshire v Indians, Bournemouth – 17, 18, 19 July
Hampshire 198 (Gilliat 50, Livingstone 44; Prasanna 3-37) and 271 (Gilliat 79, Lewis 71, Richards 45; Venkat 9-93) lost to **Indians** 364 (Viswanath 122, Mankad 109, Gavaskar 53; O'Sullivan 5-116, Worrell 4-102) and 106/5 (O'Sullivan 3-27) by five wickets.

25

FROM KIPLING TO GOLDING

THE ROSE Bowl, where Hampshire play now, is a magnificent venue with one major flaw. It is the only Test match ground in England completely in no-man's land. Getting in and out is a logistical nightmare. Unless, of course, one can squeeze into the Holiday Inn right next to the stadium, which announces itself with giant-sized stumps and ball. They have added a Hilton Hotel now, which constitutes one of the ends and houses the media centre. But given the pittance which freelancers earn, the five-star premises remain largely off-limits for journalists.

During the Test matches I have covered at Southampton, I have always stayed with Partha – my old school friend. The very same one with whom I used to return from school, scanning fellow passengers for transistor radios in our eternal quest to know the score. On some days we used to walk to a television store near the school where one small black and white screen would be beaming the live telecast. Craning our necks over the heads of people crowding around the window, we would try to catch a glimpse of the action.

Partha has been a consultant in diabetes and endocrinology at Portsmouth Hospitals NHS Trust since 2008. He was engaged there as the clinical director of diabetes when I visited England for the first time in 2011. On that occasion I was visiting not as a journalist but simply as a travelling cricket enthusiast. India were touring that summer, and after the World Cup triumph there had been an enormous build-up for the series. They performed disastrously, but Partha and I nevertheless travelled to watch the humiliations at Edgbaston and The Oval.

During the long train journeys, the two of us obviously had a lot to talk about. Cricket dominated the discussions, but we also spoke of the 15 or so years that we had not seen each other but for occasional friends and family get-togethers.

Oh, doctor, I'm in trouble

Physicians from the subcontinent had come in huge numbers in the early 1960s. Between 1960 and 1963, the then health minister Enoch Powell had, ironically in retrospect, overseen the immigration of 18,000 junior doctors. Nurses came in from Jamaica, Trinidad and Guiana even as the islands celebrated independence.

It had been a necessity. After the NHS had been established in 1948 with the grand goal of providing healthcare to every British citizen 'free at the point of access', the ambitions were somewhat waylaid with affluent British doctors reluctant to give up the time spent in lucrative private practice. By the early 1960s, the NHS was struggling with British doctors, stung by reduced pay and less than ideal working conditions, emigrating in numbers to the USA, Canada and Australia.

Even in the early 1960s, a survey in Manchester found that while outside the surgery the friendliness and respect often tended to vanish, the general British person was perfectly comfortable with being treated by a South Asian doctor.

In his early days as a junior doctor in Bournemouth, Partha had shared a chamber with Dr David Kerr, a senior English physician. They used to divide the patients between themselves. There had been the one time the senior partner had been miffed to find one patient too many on his roster than a fair division suggested. When informed by Partha that one of the patients had refused to be treated by a brown doctor, Dr Kerr had stormed into the waiting room and asked the man to get out.

'But I am sick.'

'Indeed, in more ways than one. Now, get out of my chamber.'

At the same time, a 2005 poll among British people had found that the doctor most would be comfortable in consulting was a 30-something South Asian female. Partha's experience was a rather isolated one.

'It's rare but I still get one or two patients, mainly from the older generation, who would like to be treated by "English" doctors,' Partha says today. 'Often we have to tell them that all the doctors available in the facility are South Asians and they have to make do with that.'

In 2016, he went on to become the national speciality advisor, diabetes, with NHS England. There were projects he kicked off, which often resulted in changes involving data and technology. Quite naturally, there was resistance. Process change, especially of the radical data-driven variety, is bound to come up against opposition. But in this case, a certain proportion of the resistance could be categorised into statements such as 'what makes you think you can tell us about our country?' and 'where you come from things are different'.

'I have also received emails telling me there is "irrefutable proof that British medical education is better than any other in the world". Only, the irrefutable proof has never been disclosed.' There was even one occasion when at an NHS meeting Partha, the lone Indian among a sea of white faces, was called 'Mowgli'.

When Covid-19 broke out, Partha played a major role in setting up a national diabetes advice line, focusing on the data around Covid-19 and mortality related to diabetes, developing guidelines for diabetics to deal with during the pandemic. In the 2021 New Year Honours list, Professor Partha Sarathi Kar was awarded an OBE for his services to people with diabetes.

While Partha, I and our classmates were caught up in cricket madness in the mid-1980s – the craze for the game reaching a frenzy during the 1987 World Cup hosted in the subcontinent – we ploughed through the curriculum of the Indian Certificate of Secondary Education (ICSE) Board exams coming up in early 1990. Modelled on the British curriculum, the coursework acquainted us with, among others, Dickens, Shakespeare, Wordsworth, Shelley, and in the senior classes, even Greene, Shaw and Golding.

During that frenetic season of 1987/88 – India suffered an unexpected loss in the Reliance Cup semi-final, Kapil Dev lost his captaincy, Vengsarkar led the side against the formidable West Indians – we were reading *The Merchant of Venice*, *A Tale of Two Cities*, a collection of poetry named *Panorama* and another collection of tales titled *A Treasury of Short Stories*.

One of the short stories was *Rikki-Tikki-Tavi*. We read it as a children's tale, an imaginary world of anthropomorphised birds, snakes, rats, with the hero in the form of a mongoose. There was not much scope for analysis, because the focus was on rushing through the matter and testing our memory.

Hence, we read without really registering the significance of Rikki-Tikki's mother carefully telling him 'what to do if ever he came across white men'. We did not question why the following bit had to be put in parentheses – 'he was an Englishman who had just moved into the bungalow'.

A few years before that we had, as a class, been taken to the theatre to watch the animated movie *Jungle Book*. Our teachers in the primary school had advised us to read the stories too. 'Rudyard Kipling was a great writer who lived in India and wrote many stories about the country. I think all of you will like *Kim*, in which a little boy like you is the hero.'

It was years later that I came to know that Kipling wrote these stories while sitting in his Vermont villa. I had never been too enamoured of him, mainly because of his blasphemous dismissal of cricketers as flannelled fools. But it did take me years to become aware of the underlying imperialistic jingoism and obvious racism that is now accepted as one of the primary ingredients of his works.

Sitting in the heartland of Bengal, we had been encouraged to read *The Jungle Book*, with the *bandar-log*, or the monkey people, so clearly a caricature of the English-educated Bengali babus. 'What the bandar-log think today the Jungle will think later,' was a direct adaptation of liberal Indian political leader Gopal Krishna Gokhale's quote, 'What Bengal thinks today India will think tomorrow.' In fact, the British preference for the martial races of the Rajputs and the Sikhs, and their eternal suspicion of the educated Indians, found their ways into the creation of Bagheera, Baloo, and the bandar-log. In the same way that Nag and Nagina demonstrate the shifty-eyed native villains, Chuchunder the untrustworthy native middle-man, Darzee the stupid, idol-worshipping native commoner, and Rikki-Tikki the loyal, brave, native warrior with fierce allegiance to the British master.

In *Kim*, the boy-hero is Irish, and justifies kicking Lala Dinanath's boy off the trunnions 'since the English held the Punjab and Kim was English'. From the beginning to the end of *Kim*, Kipling makes sure that we know there are the conquerors and the conquered. Indians are unsophisticated folk who think of guns as fire-breathing dragons and of museums as wonder houses. At school Kim is taught that one 'must never forget that one is a Sahib and that someday, when examinations are passed, one will command natives'.

When his teacher takes a jar, smashes it and tries to force Kim to believe that the pieces of the jar have reassembled, Kim refuses to believe him. 'Kim had been thinking in Hindi, but a tremor came on him, and with an effort like that of a swimmer before sharks who hurls himself half out of the water, his mind leaped up from a darkness that was swallowing it and took refuge in – the multiplication table in English.' That saves him. Kipling believed that the white man's mind was superior to the Indian's, that the syntax of the English language and the multiplication table were products of a rational and higher race.

Perhaps he was unaware that 'zero' had been an Indian concept.

There are way too many such examples in Kipling's works to list here. In the story *The Head of the District*, for instance, the passing away of an English sahib makes a babu travel to the KotKumharsen. The babu, Mr Grish Chunder De, a portly Bengali in English costume, induces the query, 'Has the Government gone mad to send a black Bengali dog to us?'

Incompetent and cowardly, he fails to rule effectively, and the district falls into violent chaos, before an English sahib returns to re-establish order.

When English professionals like Brockwell, Hearne and the others were busy earning their winter pay by turning out for Patiala's side in the late 1890s, Kipling was urging the Americans to take up the White Man's Burden by assuming colonial control in the Phillipines.

He was duly awarded the Nobel Prize for literature in 1907.

In 1911, he published *A History of England*. In it he explained, 'The prosperity of the West Indies, once our richest possessions, has largely declined since slavery was abolished in 1833. The population is mainly black … lazy, vicious, and incapable of any serious improvement, or of work except under compulsion. In such a climate a few bananas will sustain the life of a Negro quite sufficiently; why should he work to get more than this? He is quite happy and quite useless, and spends any extra wages which he may earn upon finery.'

Generations of English schoolchildren derived their sense of the black people from Kipling's text. Many of them were the white English people of 1971 who called Marylyn Neufville a n***** and asked her whether she lived in trees and existed on bananas and nuts. The book was still being recommended in the 1950s.

Much of Kipling's stuff cannot be overlooked, even with the fashionably comfortable justification of 'looking at it with the eyes of that era'.

In 1913, the Nobel Prize for literature was awarded to Rabindranath Tagore, the Bengali poet from the heartland of Kipling's bandar-log. He was the first non-white writer to win the prize and it would be 1968 before Yasunari Kawabata became the second. (In between, in 1953, the literature prize would be awarded to Winston Churchill for 'his mastery of historical and biographical description as well as for brilliant oratory in defending exalted human values'.)

Kipling did not seem very happy to share the exclusive platform of the Literature Nobel with a Bengali. That year, he wrote to his friend H. Rider Haggard (author of *King Solomon's Mines*, another famed novel full of implicit racism), 'Well, whose fault is it that the Babu is what he is? We did it. We began in Macaulay's time. We have worked without intermission to make this Caliban.'

Tagore was also awarded a knighthood in 1915, which he renounced after the Jallianwala Bagh massacre of 1919.

Coming back to Kipling, there are several quaint ironies that still survive with him.

Given his imperialistic jingoism and, especially, his description of the West Indian blacks, it seems incredible that one of the most popular sentences in cricket literature was derived by C.L.R. James who adapted Kipling's lament: 'What do they of England know who only England know?' *Beyond a Boundary* has often been considered the best book ever written about cricket (as Mayukh Ghosh says, frequently by people who have not read it). But most know of the sentence 'What do they of cricket know who only cricket know?' It is indeed surprising that a book eloquent with black activism had to derive its most celebrated phrase from the work of someone according to whom the blacks were 'lazy, vicious, and incapable of any serious improvement, or of work except under compulsion'.

But what is even more surprising is that even in the 1980s, in our Indian schools, we were still reading the Kipling stories and committing them to memory, blissfully unaware of the blatant racism therein.

As stated earlier, we also read Golding in later years. To a bunch of 16-year-olds *Lord of the Flies* was quite tedious. We did read Jack Merridew's words, 'We've got to have rules and obey them. After all, we're not savages. We're English, and the English are best at everything.' The bitter satire crafted by Golding escaped most of us, and our teachers failed to point it out.

Again, this was India in the late-1980s and early-1990s. The yoke of our past was everywhere even then.

26

FIVE IN FIRST SESSION

THE MORNING'S paper announced that the inquest jury had passed the verdict of murder on the arsonist who had set fire to the New Langham Hotel annexe in Bayswater in May. Wadekar was grateful to manager Adhikari yet again. Thanks to his negotiations, the Indian team were now housed in Kensington Close in Maida Vale. To think that they had checked into the same Bayswater hotel in the days leading up to their match against Middlesex.

There were plenty of news items that morning that now look at once interesting and curious to the modern reader.

Lord Walston, chairman of the Institute of Race Relations, observed that the past year had undone all the previous good in the effort to have immigrants and natives live in harmony with each other. The proposal for the 1970 South African cricket tour and the resulting chaos had not helped, the general election campaign had exaggerated problems and the proposal to sell arms to South Africa had been seen as a move towards a racialist foreign policy. Now there was the new Immigration Bill. 'The result of all those issues has encouraged the natives of this country to believe that it was once more respectable to look on immigrants both as people fundamentally different from themselves, and as a threat to their own wellbeing.'

In Canberra, the Springboks played the Capital Territories behind an 8ft barbed wire separator, protected by 600 policemen.

More than 1,000 protesters were kept out. Outside the venue, five aborigines put on authentic Springbok jerseys presented to them by Jim Boyce of the Australian Wallabies, who had refused to play the South Africans.

Those were colourful times.

However, Wadekar's attention was focused on the match preview by John Woodcock. *The Times* correspondent analysed that of the 124 wickets to have fallen to the tourists so far, 109 had been taken by the four spinners, and Abid and Solkar had captured four between them. The Indian captain, according to Woodcock, could perhaps seek reassurance from the fact that even as recently as in 1938 at Trent Bridge the Australian bowling had been opened by Bill O'Reilly partnering Ernie McCormick. Was there a case for playing four spinners and one supposed seamer?

'As recently as in 1938!' It was indeed just 33 years before that Don Bradman's 1938 Australians had toured. It lends us a proper perspective of the time.

As recently as 1938, Enoch Powell had travelled from England to Australia making about 20 stops on the way of which only one had not been under the British flag.

The following year, as recently as in 1939, at the outbreak of the Second World War, the viceroy Lord Linlithgow had announced on All India Radio that His Majesty's Government was at war with Germany and so was India. He had not bothered to ask even one Indian.

Wadekar's mind, though, was made up. The think tank – Adhikari, Venkat and the captain himself – had decided on the side. For the first time in his illustrious Test career, Prasanna would sit out a Test without doing so voluntarily, for example to pursue his engineering degree.

Having had his say about team composition Woodcock moved on to the topic of John Snow. Having missed the Pakistan series, the premier fast bowler was ready to have a go at the Indians.

Warnings about Snow were nothing new. On the eve of the team's departure the *Times Weekly* had already forecast inclement weather for the Indians, 'Beware of Snow! It may rain.'

* * *

As Wadekar walks through the Long Room for the toss, he looks confident enough. India have, after all, won four matches on the trot.

However, as Illingworth flips the coin against the dull, grey, misty sky, and his call turns out wrong, the Indian skipper is secretly relieved. Facing Snow and Price on that murky morning would have been a handful.

Hence the 14,000 who have turned up watch Boycott and Luckhurst take strike against the unheralded attack of Abid and Solkar are in for a rather nasty surprise.

Abid is nippy, rapping Luckhurst on the pad early on. Solkar moves it around in that warm, hazy atmosphere. Some of Abid's deliveries kick up at the Nursery End. After 35 hesitant minutes, Boycott prods at one that lifts just about enough to surprise him. Engineer holds the catch waist-high, three-quarters of the way to first slip. Boycott, having gone down with a stomach bug, has been declared fit only that morning. But the man who has hundreds in the past three Test matches, and has not had a single-digit score since August 1969, now trudges back for a measly 3 runs. It is 18/1.

Wadekar keeps the seamers on for exactly an hour. Fifteen overs are shared by the two and England are 32/1. Luckhurst and Edrich are both circumspect, wary. And now Chandra is brought on, with Venkat from the other end.

At 46, a googly from Chandra kicks up and Luckhurst stabs at it. Solkar at short leg throws himself forward to snap up his first superb catch of the series.

Amiss joins Edrich, and both of them push and prod for a while. At 56, Bedi is introduced. The ball is predictably tossed up outside off stump. Edrich has scored 648 runs during the Ashes win in Australia, and just 126 runs in nine Test innings since then. He drives at it. The snick flies to slip where Venkat juggles and catches it one-handed at the second attempt.

D'Oliveira is in, officially 36, but actually just a couple of months shy of 40. The manipulation is part of a story of incredible fortitude, drama, frustration and, finally, justice. If South Africa had been a normal country, he would have played against Vinoo Mankad and Subhas Gupte as a fantastic young talent. Here he is literally playing against the next generation, against Ashok Mankad and the others. He is still one of the best batsmen in England.

Wadekar immediately stations a leg slip for his paddle stroke. D'Oliveira gets a boundary. And then he stretches forward to Chandra. The googly takes the snick and then the pad. Solkar dives to his left and holds it one handed – 61/4. Knott walks in far earlier than he or anyone else expected.

The last over before lunch is bowled with seven men around the bat. England go into the break at 65/4. The members are still trying to wrap their heads around the score as the cricketers walk back through the Long Room.

* * *

A one-page advertisement paid for by several citizens declared that they were convinced that the addition of the UK, Norway, Denmark and Ireland to the EEC would serve the cause of democracy, world peace, economic advance and, above all, the interests of the British people. Prime Minister Mr Heath reiterated that 'the choice is clear, the prize is great and Britain must take it.'

On the other side of the world, on the eve of Nixon's impending visit, the Chinese government was accused of hatching a secret deal with Imperialism.

* * *

Twenty minutes after the break, Bedi floats one wider, slower. Amiss, after 53 painstaking minutes at the crease, drives at it. Engineer throws it up. Half the side is out for 71.

'I had taken the day off to go to the Test match,' says Chitta. Now in his seventies, he lives in Brixton after spending most of his life working as a chemist. However, in those days he had just got his first job with a plumbing firm. 'My Indian friends had laughed at me. Giving up a day's wages was not that easy. Plus, there was the price of the ticket. They thought I would see India bowled out by John Snow or the English batsmen would score mountains of runs. Everyone knew we had no pace attack.'

Captain Illingworth is batting way too early for his comfort. The bowling is way too complicated. He prods at Bedi and Gavaskar just about fails to scoop it up after diving forward at silly mid on. He plays back to a Chandra flipper that skids low, and umpire Fagg turns down the loudest of appeals. Standing close in, young Gavaskar is not impressed. The things he will later write in *Sunny Days* about the supposed impartiality and competence of English umpires will drip with sarcasm.

And then Knott enjoys a genuine piece of luck. He jabs at a Chandra googly, the ball flies off the splice of his bat, Solkar stretches out his right hand but just gets his fingers to it.

With this reprieve Knott starts to use his feet. He also uses his pads skilfully, using the 1970 law to good effect in countering the spin. Bedi is swung over midwicket for six.

Chandra has to be replaced now, his 20 consecutive overs bringing him 2/50. Venkat is on as Knott plays his fighting innings, cutting, driving, pulling. Bedi has to be rested too, after 24 overs on the trot which have got him 2/40. Abid is given another bowl as the partnership grows.

It is Venkat who gets Knott. With tea approaching, he makes an off-break take off and it goes off Knott's glove to Wadekar at backward short-leg. After a valiant innings of 67. Knott walks back having performed one of his many rescue acts. England are 167/6 at tea, Illingworth and Hutton at the wicket.

* * *

'I myself had no real expectation from the team,' Chitta says. He admits that after all these years memory can be a bit misleading. 'Those were uncertain times. The immigration laws were becoming complicated. It was unclear whether the wife of my cousin could come over or not. Sometimes we thought of our own future, although we did have permits. They were changing the rules so many times. What's more, I had relations across the border in modern-day Bangladesh. With the situation there, we kept expecting the worst. I guess I just wanted to go to the cricket to get away from all that tension.'

He pauses.

'Horrible things did happen to some folks I knew. Very horrible things.'

I change the topic. Did the Queen's visit have anything to do with his going to the stadium?

Chitta laughs. 'You know, I didn't even know she was going to be there. I had gone to the Nursery Ground and was looking at some guys at the nets. And suddenly there was applause. And then another. I went to one of the entrances to the stands, and saw her shaking hands with Bishan Bedi in his dark blue turban.'

* * *

Knott's innings has had its effect. The Indian performance flags a bit. They do not bowl or field badly, but the pressure has reduced, and the palpable expectation of a wicket off every ball is no longer there.

Wadekar declines the new ball when it becomes due. Bedi tosses one up and it curves away, taking Illingworth's edge and settling in Engineer's gloves – 183/7. 'Illingworth had a Job-like ability to find blessing in his suffering and he struggled through his discomfort to 33,' writes Arlott. It is just 33, but it has been a vital knock.

Hutton and Snow bat with a lot more ease now that the initial assistance for the spinners is less apparent. Snow attacks and Bedi keeps flighting the ball. 'Our spinners made the mistake of attempting to buy wickets, when they should have bowled tight against batsmen willing to chance their arm and luck,' Wadekar will write later. 'Bedi was one who believed in this theory and quite often he carried it too far.' Somehow, even as the team does better than any Indian team has done in England, this will develop to be a contentious issue between the captain and his ace left-arm spinner. Indian cricket is always complex.

It is Venkat, the spinner, who has no problems in keeping things flat and tight, who castles Hutton. The second new ball is taken at 238 and Abid sends down yet another good spell. He almost gets Snow, but Solkar puts down the sharpish chance at backward short leg. Snow remains unbeaten on 56, with Gifford showing admirable limpet-like qualities.

Having had England on the mat at 71/5, the score 252/8 looks a tad disappointing. 'They also averaged nearly 20 overs to the hour and it is a long time since that was done in a Test match in England,' writes Woodcock.

Apart from bowling their overs quickly – 97 of the 117 sent down by the three spinners – the Indians have provided the disconcerting evidence that even on the first day of a Test match their slow bowlers can be as effective as the English pace attack.

'Such sustained attacking spin bowling on true pitches has not been seen in this country since Ramadhin and Valentine,' writes Arlott.

* * *

'Did they get that many?' Chitta peers through his glasses as I pull up the end-of-play score on my laptop. 'I always thought we had bowled them out that afternoon. Memory is tricky. But, when I came back that day, I was a hero. The same people who had laughed at me for giving up a day's wage to watch cricket were the ones who were congratulating me. It seemed not Bedi or Chandra, I had taken the wickets myself. We had taken the first few wickets quickly. That had created quite a stir. We were not supposed to do well in England.'

Indians were not supposed to do well in England. It was almost an unwritten law. Beliefs that were hardwired through years of direct, systemic and subliminal nurture. Through reports of 'moral and material progress', 'War Cabinet meeting minutes' and Kipling.

England v India, 1st Test, Lord's – 22, 23, 24, 26, 27 July
England 252/8 (Knott 67, Snow 56*; Bedi 3-59)

27

HENTY IN MY SYSTEM

IT WAS not only Kipling who formed the curriculum, and minds, of those who passed through the hoops of British education.

The Royal Colonial Institute awarded prize money for essays on imperial topics submitted by schoolchildren and university students until 1928. Thereafter the prize continued in its new garb of the Royal Empire Society into the 1950s.

From the turn of the century, the British colonies and the British Indian Empire made it into the Education Code. In 1896, the Geographical Association recommended study of Empire geography in secondary books. In 1904, Colonial literature became a section of study in the library assistant's examination.

Soon history books became more and more Empire-oriented and simplified. Most followed the prototype of J.R. Seeley, the author of *The Expansion of England* – a selection that would chart the rise of the nation state, and present the British Empire as achieving the apotheosis of the state through the first great world political order. Imperial expansion was not only supposed to be historical teaching, but also moral. *The Expansion of England* was still in print in 1956.

Robert Roberts, who did his schooling in the years encompassing the Great War, wrote in *The Classic Slum*, 'Teachers, fed on Seeley's imperialist work, and often great readers of Kipling, spelled out patriotism among us with a fervour that with some edged on the religious.'

Her Majesty's Stationery Office Handbook of 1927 stated, 'History is for children pre-eminently an instrument for moral training. If the teacher made history live through the lives of individuals, children will learn naturally in how many different ways the patriot helped his country, and by what sort of actions nations and individuals have earned the gratitude of posterity.' The ideal heroes in the resulting books combined piety, adventure and military prowess in the tradition of Christian militarism of the 1860s and 1870s. However, they were studied far beyond the 1800s. The Cambridge University Press publications of 1911 contained 24 military figures out of 40 historical personalities, including Clive, Drake, Marlborough and Gordon. The ideas were still in vogue in 1949, when an Oxford junior series comprised of two texts, *Stories of Great People* and *Stories of Great Deeds*.

British history became a sequence of commercial and territorial wars through which world-wide dominion was achieved, and those who waged them became heroes of British expansion. Teachers were urged to teach the significance of the army and navy in the patriotic duty of defence. This tendency reached a peak when C.L.R. Fletcher teamed up with Kipling in 1911 to publish *A School History of England*. In this book, every prime minister was judged based on whether he increased or reduced spending on the armed forces. The objective was to drill home that if the younger generation did not prepare itself for defence the Empire would be lost.

The concept of supremacy over other races became embossed in these books and thereby the British psyche. Nelson's *The World and its People* (1907) described the African as an overgrown child, vain, self-indulgent, and fond of idleness. In Chambers' *Geographical Reader*, it was stated, 'Many of the Central African tribes are so savage as still to be cannibals.' Social Darwinism was yet another inevitable instrument of this sort of education system. As school children turned to do their 'one good deed per day' as Boy Scouts, in Baden-Powell's handbook they read how to read the character and level of intelligence of individuals from the racial traits visible in their faces – the African, the Jewish and the trustworthy English.

A Cambridge geographical reader, first published in 1920 and reprinted in 1924, stated, 'Notions of tropical abundance and the resulting tropical indolence abound. Africans in South Africa lapse into idleness, in East Africa they have no need for exertion, while all young people in Britain are taught the virtues of patriotism, no such feeling inspires the natives of India.'

This is in conflict with Attlee's otherwise obnoxious comment about Indian nationalism.

In 1924, *Principles and Methods of Teaching* suggested, 'Geography pupils should also be taught the concepts of development and undevelopment in the regions inhabited by civilised and uncivilised people.'

The partial telling of history continued down the decades. Muriel Masefield's *House of History – the Third Storey,* published in 1942, covered the Indian atrocities of the Mutiny in detail, while the horrific British retribution was passed off in a single phrase, 'After the Mutiny was quelled, the governor showed great mercy.'

In the 1950s, Masefield provided a number of suggestions for questions and class activities for her book. Her suggested essay topic was 'What has British rule in India done for its people?' She recommended Fitchett's *Tales of the Great Mutiny*, Strang's *Stories of Indian Mutiny*, Tennyson's *The Relief of Lucknow*, and Whittier's *The Pipes of Lucknow*, adding that some of them should be learnt by heart.

The Indian history post-mutiny in *An Introduction to English History* by G.W. Southgate consisted of the simple paragraph, 'Since the Mutiny India has been ruled by a line of Viceroys who have done much for the good of the people. India has been peaceful, and Indian peasants have been left to cultivate their little plots of land without having to fear that they would be slain and their homes burned by invaders.' Southgate's book was published in 1947, the year of India's independence. It was still being reprinted in 1969, and still being studied in 1971.

Like imperial history, imperial geography had not quite died out. Maps still marked the (erstwhile) Empire, the manuals for teaching methods, all these survived till the 1960s.

Apart from history and geography, from the 1880s until as late as the 1950s, the world view of several generations was shaped by Boy's Own stories, published in an extraordinary number of books and periodicals. Plenty of them are still found lying around in second-hand bookshops not necessarily antiquarian. Some even find reincarnation in modern day re-publication in shiny covers.

These were adventure stories combining elements of patriotism, military plots and racial themes. The most enduring of them all was *The Boy's Own Paper*, first published in January 1879, conceptualised by the Religious Tract Society. In 1885, it described its vision of the typical 'negro', 'The arm is two inches longer in proportion than that of a Caucasian, and the hands hang level with the kneecaps; the facial angle is seventy as against eighty three, the brain weighs thirty five as against forty five; the skull is much thicker ... there is no growth in intelligence once manhood is reached.'

The contributors included Conan Doyle, Jules Verne, R.M. Ballantyne, Baden-Powell and even W.G. Grace. The final edition of the magazine was published in early 1967.

With zealous propagandist authors such as G.A. Henty, Ballantyne, W.H.G. Kingston and others, the stories in such books and periodicals were essentially about the British lads going off in adventure to different corners of the Empire, demonstrating apathy for other races, indulgent respect for the martial communities and chiefs who collaborated with them, promoting the greater good and the expanse of the Empire through their code of morality-laced valour. Alongside these was the other major genre, popularising Imperialist war-mongering cult heroes with books such as *With Kitchener in Khartoum*.

'The condition of the negroes in Hayti [the contemporary spelling for Haiti] has fallen to the level of that of the savage African tribes ... unless some strong white power should occupy the island and enforce law and order,' wrote the prolific and popular novelist Henty in the preface to his book *A Roving Commission*. In it the average 'negro adult' just about matches the intelligence of a ten-year-old European child, Indians remain natives to be civilised by the white man. Henty was also severely antagonistic to Boers, Jews, even the French ... and even projected the British coal miners as villains.

All the Henty titles with their jingoism and racial stereotyping were still in print in 1955, and some were reprinted in the 1960s. Men who admitted to being influenced by the Henty stories included C.S. Forester, Henry Miller, Harold Macmillan, Lord Home, J. Paul Getty, A.J.P. Taylor and Field Marshal Lord Montgomery.

In 1963, the Bishop of London admitted in a speech to the House of Lords that there was still Henty in his system.

What the dickens?

Going beyond boys' stories and moving to imperialist fiction, Kipling led the way like a beacon but there were other luminaries. Hundreds of novels were written about the Mutiny. With very few exceptions all of them were accounts displaying extreme forms of polarisation of good (victorious) and evil (defeated).

The Mutiny, thus projected, saw Charles Dickens writing in a private letter to Emily de la Rue, 'You know faces, when they are not brown; you know common experiences when they are not under turbans; Look at the dogs – low, treacherous, murderous, tigerous villains.' Dickens called for the extermination of the Indian race and applauded the mutilation of the wretched Hindoo who were punished by being blown from English cannons.

As a boy I read Arthur Conan Doyle's *The Lost World*, marvelling at Professor Challenger and the world of the Ape Men. However, there were some confusing bits. When Gladys proclaims that she would rather marry a famous man, the inspired Malone responds, 'Why should you not? It is women like you who brace men up. Give me a chance, and see if I will take it! Besides, as you say, men ought to make their own chances, and not wait until they are given. Look at Clive – just a clerk, and he conquered India!'

It was confusing. Growing up in India, I knew Clive to be an unscrupulous villain who took over Bengal through a number of underhand deals and went back with untold riches acquired through greed and mismanagement. It resulted in one of the most calamitous famines in the land. And here was the great creator of Sherlock Holmes painting him as a hero worth emulating.

From *Thugee* to *Kim*, the examples in literature are plenty. It took quite a while for Forster and Orwell to balance the equation somewhat.

When British cavalry officer Francis Yeats-Brown's autobiography, *The Lives of a Bengal Lancer*, was made into a movie in 1935, it became a favourite of Adolf Hitler. He supposedly watched it three times. 'A handful of Britons holding a continent in thrall. That is how a superior race must behave.'

28

WADEKAR'S MASTERPIECE

DURING THE Second World War, M.A. Osmany had served the British Indian Army – first as a war-substantive lieutenant and temporary captain. Along the way he was promoted to platoon commander, battalion adjutant and battalion commander. He ended the war as a grade-two general staff officer. During the 1965 war against India, this East Bengali soldier had served the cause of Pakistan and later, before his retirement in 1967, had represented Pakistan at the Southeast Asia Treaty Organisation (SEATO) and the Central Treaty Organisation (CENTO) meetings as director of military operations.

Now, in July 1971, he was rebuilding the Bangladesh Liberation Forces, the *Mukti Bahini*. At the Tripura border of East Pakistan, he disclosed to the correspondent of *The Times* that East Bengal freedom fighters had killed between 15,000 and 20,000 West Pakistan troops. That was when the correspondent absolved him of any doubt regarding the high figures because, after all, he was an officer belonging very much to the old British Army tradition.

These words were printed in *The Times* on 23 July 1971. Kipling had been dead for just 35 years, but his perceptions and world-view were very much alive.

'*The Times* correspondent was only echoing the view that had become ingrained in British thinking over the course of two centuries, namely that the Indian cannot be relied upon to tell the truth,' says UCLA history professor Vinay Lal. 'Curzon was one of the more prominent exponents of this view, which he voiced, with absolute confidence and nonchalance, in a convocation address at the University of Calcutta. The British legal system in India assumed this as a matter of course.'

Recall Cecil Headlam and his evaluation of the lying Indian natives.

The Dewas Duo

In *Passage to India,* this same mindset is evident in the public-school-chiselled Ronny Heaslop.

It is interesting to note that E.M. Forster was employed as a private secretary to the Tukoji Rao III, the same Maharaja of Dewas who was the patron of Vijay Hazare. Forster's *The Hill of Devi* is set in Dewas.

Lal goes on to expound the reasons for this smug superciliousness. 'The British marvelled at the fact, as did everyone else, that what started out as a trading venture was eventually ruling over a vast country – and really with just a few thousand white men on the ground, so to speak. This circumstance alone was enough to encourage them to think that they were representatives of a civilization that had scaled the heights of human achievement. The British did think that they embodied a much higher standard of morality and ethical conduct.'

* * *

The English tail has had several months of vigorous training in stemming collapses. The saga continues on the second morning at Lord's.

In 1966, after Snow started his Test career by scoring eight runs in his first five Test innings, his father, the Rev Dr William Snow, promised him 10 shillings for each run he scored thereafter. That saw him get 59 from No.11 at The Oval against Hall, Griffith, Sobers and Gibbs. A week later he hammered 71 against Somerset. Those have so far remained his best scores in Test and first-class cricket respectively.

Today, with Gifford providing solid company, he goes past the Test mark and then the first-class. Sound, sensible defence, every now and then using his long legs to get to the pitch of the ball and driving down the ground. At 73, he is perhaps eyeing a hundred when Chandra's googly finds the inside edge of his bat. Abid holds a good tumbling catch at backward short leg; 61 added for the ninth wicket.

Even after that Price hangs around with Gifford for 25 minutes, before Bedi bowls the latter. It is a relief to see him walk back for 17. Chandra has hit him on the pads again and again, and appeal after appeal have come to nothing. After losing five wickets for 71, England have managed to score 304: Bedi 4-70, Chandra 3-110, Venkat 2-44. They have bowled 115 overs and three balls between them.

Now Snow and Price, a handful combination, come off their long run ups. The latter is nippy on this day, but Snow, perhaps still thinking about his long innings, is neither too quick, nor too tidy. But he strikes in his first over as Mankad fends uneasily at a short ball to be gobbled up by Gifford at short leg. Was the batsman distracted by a no-ball call from a spectator with a stentorian voice? It was a docile enough delivery to be pulled with time on one's hands.

In comes Wadekar, and Snow greets him with a bouncer. The Indian captain rocks back and hooks it for four.

Lunch is taken, Gavaskar looking circumspect, Wadekar fluent and aggressive.

Four years before, Wadekar walked out at Lord's in just his fourth Test. The pitch was lightning quick with J.T. Murray crouching way back. On a gloomy day with the sun absconding, John Snow, David Brown and Basil D'Oliveira made the ball move. Batsman after batsman snicked to the wicketkeeper, Murray ending up with six catches. Wadekar stood alone, apparently playing on a different surface, endowed with the ability to see the ball sooner than the others, getting into position with time to spare. With delectable timing and excellent wristwork, the left-hander scored 57 that day, out of a team score of 152. Some experts predicted that he was the next great batsman in the making.

Now, four years later, at 30, he has fallen way short of fulfilling those prophecies. In 26 Tests, his 1,515 runs have come at 32.23, with one solitary hundred.

Yet, from time to time he has produced glimpses of class. Today is one such day. At the other end, Gavaskar, soon to be recognised as one of the greatest batsmen in India, struggles against Snow and Price. And Wadekar produces strokes off the back foot of supreme quality, once again with plenty of time to play them.

At 29, Gavaskar falls after nearly 50 minutes of struggle. Price, looking the quicker and more impressive of the opening bowlers, swings them away with four men stationed in the slips. The little man nicks one.

The skies have darkened by the time Sardesai gets to the crease. After his recent success in the West Indies he gets determinedly behind the ball, remains careful, composed. Meanwhile, the captain seems wonderfully unconcerned about the dangers of quick bowling in murky light.

When Gifford comes on, he sweeps and pulls with élan. By the time India reach 50, Wadekar has already made 40. When he reaches his splendid half-century, India are on 66/2. A further 20 runs down the line, the light becomes too bad and the teams break for tea 25 minutes ahead of time.

* * *

On the same day, in Delhi, the Indian defence minister Jagjivan Ram told the Parliament that he had ordered the army and air force to attack any Pakistani aircraft which intruded into Indian airspace. Earlier that week, two Pakistani Mirage fighters had penetrated India's air defence system in Kashmir to make a low sweep over Srinagar airport. According to the defence minister, Pakistanis were preparing to open a diversionary front in West Pakistan because Yahya was feeling the impact of the increase in guerrilla activities in East Pakistan.

'Each day was nerve-racking,' remembers Chitta. 'I would have been much happier if I'd been at Lord's watching Wadekar bat. But I was not. I could not afford two days without wages. I remember trying to get as much action as possible on the radio. But at the same time, I had one ear on the news. They did not report all that was going on in the border, but we had to know.'

* * *

At 100, Illingworth comes on, bowling in tandem with Gifford. It slows things down, but what seems to bother Sardesai even more is the England captain's presence at silly point when Gifford bowls. It is perhaps an effort to disperse the close field that makes this man of near-infinite patience try to hit Gifford against the turn high to the leg. All he succeeds in doing is to get a feeble stroke on to his pads from where the ball loops up and then down into the hands of Illingworth. A two-hour knock for 28. India are 108/3.

With Viswanath joining him, Wadekar keeps stroking the ball with sublime timing. The Lord's pitch is showing signs of helping the spinners even more, and he knows India have to bat last. The skipper kills the spin with calm assurance, and keeps the scoreboard moving with deft placements. For 40 minutes, while Viswanath makes an unusually tense start, the Wadekar show goes on. But just when the clouds have cleared, and the sun first peeps through and smiles on Lord's, he is gone. The ball from Gifford bounces a bit more and it pops off his bat and pad into the hands of Illingworth at short leg. It has been a masterly innings of 85, but the Indian score is just 125.

Three hours and 12 minutes of exquisite strokeplay, with 11 boundaries to remember. One of the best innings of Wadekar's career. And just as he will end up doing six times in his eventual 71-innings Test career, he falls between 80 and 99.

Just over an hour is left in the day as Engineer comes in. By now the sun is shining brightly. It is a signal for the fastest period of scoring during the day. Viswanath, compact and neat, plays with plenty of responsibility tinged with elegance. Engineer, flamboyant and a trifle impetuous, goes about gathering runs in a more exciting, less assuring manner. The next 50 is raised at a run a minute.

Despite Gifford's success, perhaps England are feeling the absence of Underwood. After an hour and half of spin, Illingworth turns to pace again. Hutton runs in and Engineer slashes him to second slip where the England captain grabs him. His departure for 28 tilts the balance in favour of England. The score is 179/5 at the end of the day, Viswanath unbeaten on 24, alongside the scrappy Solkar.

* * *

On the other side of the Bangladesh border, suspicion was rife, directed at the Nixon-Kissinger-Yahya nexus. Fearing infiltration of American spies, the Indian government was on the verge of asking all foreign volunteers working in the refugee camps to leave the country.

England v India, 1st Test, Lord's – 22, 23, 24, 26, 27 July
England 304 (Snow 73, Knott 67; Bedi 4-70, Chandra 3-110)
India 179/5 (Wadekar 85).

29

LORDS, LADS AND LADIES

A YEAR before, the Lord's authorities had announced the arrival of 300 reels of barbed wire to safeguard the Test match scheduled to be played by South Africa later that summer. That was the extent to which the protests against the 1969/70 Springbok rugby team had put the cat among the pigeons.

The cost of protecting the grounds for play was proving to be enormous. To counter this, on 23 April, the MCC had launched 'The 1970 Cricket Fund' with a minimum target of £200,000. It was approved by the Cricket Council. The fund was launched at Lord's under the chairmanship of Lt Col Charles Newman, VC, and with a distinguished list of patrons including the Duke of Norfolk, Viscount Portal, Lord Wakefield, Judge Sir Carl Aarvold, Sir Peter Studd, M.J.C. Allom, Alec Bedser, Brian Close and Colin Cowdrey.

The Mecca of Cricket had been quite determined to ensure that the tour went ahead.

But it was not only the long-haired students who had been stirred into protest. A special meeting had been proposed by a 'rebellious group' within the MCC itself, headed by the former England captain, the Rev David Sheppard. Three motions had been proposed at the meeting. The members of the MCC would publicly regret their committee's handling of the matter leading up to the selection of the team for the 1968/69 South Africa tour from which D'Oliveira had been omitted at first. Second, no further tours to and from South Africa were to be undertaken until evidence was obtained of actual progress by South Africa towards non-racial cricket. Third, a special committee needed to be set up to examine such proposals as were submitted by the South African Cricket Association towards non-racial cricket.

The 26-year-old Mike Brearley had taken the incredibly bold step of seconding these proposals. Bold, because his cricket career had not yet taken off. Sheppard and his rebel group had been invited to a supposedly informal meeting at Church House in Westminster to discuss the points. When they arrived, they had been confronted with the full polish of the MCC brass, including ex-Prime Minister Sir Alec Douglas-Home, who had flown down from Scotland for the meeting.

The rebels lost the vote. According to Peter Hain, 'These votes were from typical cricket backwoodsmen who were opposed to any moves aimed at ending compromises with racialism in sport.'

The results of the voting (after counting the postal votes) were as follows:

Proposal 1: For 1,570 – Against 4,357
Proposal 2: For 1,214 – Against 4,644
Proposal 3: For 1,352 – Against 4,508
That was the scorecard of attitudes of the time.

The attitude towards condoning apartheid by 'not mixing politics with sports' was only one of the apparent features of inflexibility of the guardians of the game.

Five years after the 1971 Test match against India, the Lord's crowd saw Rachael Heyhoe Flint lead the England women against the Australians. It was quite an event for the members of the MCC to digest. One of them complained, 'I was quite shocked when I saw the women playing. Cricket is a game where concentration is very important and women are the greatest distraction a man can have around.' Another confessed, 'I was praying for rain. I couldn't believe this would happen in my lifetime.'

In fact, if Middlesex had not been beaten by Lancashire in the Gillette Cup, Lord's would not have been available for the ladies. Reflect. This is 1976 we are talking about. Just 45 years from the time of writing. Not quite Victorian times.

During the match, the players were allowed to use the dressing room and walk through the Long Room. But women spectators still could not enter the pavilion. And of course, the MCC did not allow women members.

In Heyhoe Flint's book *Fair Play – the Story of Women's Cricket*, there is the following verse by Heather Wheatley:

> *Parliament has ladies in both parties, Left and Right,*
> *They do not like bad language, so the men must be*
> *   polite,*
> *They all have had a vote, indeed, since 1923,*
> *But there are no lady members of the MCC.*
>
> *Women play their cricket with both credit and renown,*
> *They bat with skill and science and they bounce their*
> *   bumpers down,*
> *Their fielding is a pleasure, and as neat as it could be,*
> *But there are no lady members of the MCC.*
>
> *The day will come (or will it come?) – I hope that I'll*
> *   be there –*
> *When Lord's will see the ladies playing cricket on the square,*
> *The faces in the Tavern are a sight that I must see*
> *When the ladies win the toss against the MCC!*

In 1986, when the Indian women were touring England, skipper Diana Edulji was refused entry into the Lord's pavilion. She famously observed that MCC should change its name to MCP, the Male Chauvinistic Pigs that they were. It took 12 more years for common sense and basic decency to finally make their way past rigid Victorian mindsets into the Long Room. Women were finally allowed to enter the Lord's pavilion in 1998.

Edulji was not the only Indian cricketer to have been miffed by Lord's. In 1990, India and England were locked in one of the most memorable Test matches which saw Graham Gooch score 333 and 123, Mohammad Azharuddin hit one of his most magical hundreds, and, with nine wickets down, Kapil Dev get the 24 runs required to save the follow-on with four straight sixes off Eddie Hemmings. And competing headlines were made by Sunil Gavaskar, who turned down the invitation to become an honorary member of the MCC.

Gavaskar had retired three years earlier with the world record collection of Test runs and centuries. In an ironical coincidence, he had announced his decision during the bicentennial 'Test' at Lord's, after amassing a mammoth 188 in that high-scoring game between the MCC and the Rest of the World. However, he had been thoroughly disgusted by the offhand, sometimes rude, manner in which the Lord's staff had treated him, especially the notorious green-jacketed stewards.

It is not very difficult for anyone who has visited Lord's without an MCC tie dangling from his neck to empathise with Gavaskar. However, the complications of Indian cricket are so curious that this gesture of the great Indian batsman led another hero of our 1971 tale to react in a most peculiarly vehement manner.

Bishan Singh Bedi, the manager of the 1990 Indian side, stormed into the Lord's press box and distributed a statement saying how shocked he was at his former team-mate's behaviour, how Gavaskar had let down the Indian team and dishonoured Indians living in England. He added that he had been most delighted to have been made an MCC member.

It is difficult to understand how Bedi imagined he could speak for the Indians living in England. Later, even the tongue-tied Indian skipper Mohammad Azharuddin mumbled that the team had not been aware that they had been let down by Gavaskar. But two great cricketers, between whom relationships had become sour down the years, did make a lot of headlines that day. Gavaskar, with a finesse developed through years of opening the batting, shouldered arms to Bedi's awkward beamer.

That summer, the two of them turned out to play in the annual match at Tim Hudson's idyllic Cheshire ground. David Frith, leading the side that included the two, resisted mischievous suggestions to place them side by side at slip. Gavaskar did not make many runs, but had a great time bowling. One inside edge went to leg-slip where Bedi stuck out a desperate hand and managed to get his fingers to the ball as it sped past him. Thankfully, there was no exchange of words. They did not speak to each other throughout the entire match.

Gavaskar's disillusionment with the MCC was not a late development, though. His first autobiography, *Sunny Days,* was published in 1977 when he was still in his 20s. His first impression of Lord's is recorded in rather unequivocal terms, 'Quite frankly, I don't understand why cricketers are overawed by Lord's. The members are the stuffiest know-alls you can come across, and the ground is most uninspiring. It slopes from one end to the other. I shuddered to think of it as the Headquarters of Cricket.'

As my colleague Abhishek Mukherjee often says, *'Lord's is famous because it is famous.* It is neither the cradle of cricket, nor the oldest ground in England or elsewhere, nor the venue of the first Test match, nor even the venue of the first Test match in England.' It is certainly not the prettiest. Most of its claims to being the home of cricket are thrust upon the gullible cricket fan as gospel, and much like cricket's curious claims to being a gentleman's game and other gospels, this one is also seldom questioned.

A few years after Gavaskar's refusal, the MCC extended the invitation to him again. This time, fully aware that he had made his point, Gavaskar did accept. In 2003, he delivered the MCC Spirit of Cricket Cowdrey Lecture dressed in traditional Indian attire. It must have been quite a shock for that august institution. Bombarded with skirts for the first time in their history just five years before, they now had to deal with oriental pyjamas.

Yet, the tremendously complex endeavour of becoming an MCC member, involving a preposterously exorbitant financial investment alongside the complicated process of nomination, seconding by an MCC member from your part of the world, and

finally a waiting time that can last decades of completely ad hoc
and arbitrary decisions, is still an enormously coveted feather in
many a cricket-lover's cap.

Access to the Lord's pavilion, and the experience of watching
a match from the Long Room and elsewhere in the building, can
be experienced at much more reasonable expense by becoming a
member of Middlesex CCC and donning the mandatory jacket
and tie. As a Premier Member, one can walk to the Tavern Stand
and enjoy the game from the special hospitality box, with Angus
Fraser and Mike Gatting popping in from time to time to discuss
the game. On the way to the box, one has to pass two rooms –
among others – named after Sunil Gavaskar and Dilip Vengsarkar.

I have been stopped twice in front of these rooms while walking
to the Premier Member box by the green-jacketed stewards, and
somehow on both occasions the card proclaiming me as a Premier
Member did not make much of an impression. On both occasions,
I had to make my way to the Middlesex membership office to get
hold of membership secretary Julie Blakesley. She had to escort me
to the box, explaining to the stewards – yet again – that Premier
Members were allowed in those exclusive quarters.

Once on entering the MCC Museum, mainly to escape a
sudden shower, I was informed by an ancient green jacket – more
than a little brusquely – that Middlesex members had to pay the
entrance fee like anyone else. It is not the fee that I objected to,
but being unnecessarily informed about it when I was merely
taking shelter from the rain, as were a few others, and had made
no attempt to walk up the stairs to look at Denis Compton's knee
cap and the rest of the 'treasures' within. However, when I said
I would like to buy a DVD of the MCC tour to South Africa
in 1956/57 on display at the counter, and duly dished out £15, a
profound change came over the man. The erstwhile frowns and
barks metamorphosed into a toothy smile and little bobs of the
head which probably came close to curtseying.

Well, financial exchanges, albeit a whole lot more than £15, have
done a lot to change attitudes over the years as also Indo-English
relations, what with rich Indian investors on one hand and the IPL

on the other. Of course, there is no reason to believe these instances were linked to ethnicity or skin colour – although the example of Gavaskar, with 10,122 more Test runs than yours truly, being miffed by the same attitude, does lead to speculation. In a 2021 podcast, Farokh Engineer said in his characteristic unrestrained vein, 'We were all "bloody Indians" to them till a few years ago. Now once the IPL started, they … suddenly changed their tunes. India is a good country to go for a few months and do some television work, if not play and make money.' While Engineer is perhaps not quite the most reliable raconteur, his experience stretches from the late-1960s when he started playing for Lancashire to the present day when he has lived in England for several decades.

However, the boorishness of Lord's has been quite universal. While walking from the pavilion across the hallowed turf to the practice nets at the Nursery Ground, the champion Middlesex side had once heard an official MCC voice from the balcony telling them not to walk on the grass. It had led the future MCC President Mike Gatting to say, 'Stupid old fart.' Later, his team-mate Simon Hughes wrote, 'The MCC hierarchy is renowned for not wanting its beloved grass walked on. Ever, preferably.'

A lot has changed over the years. It is quite difficult to imagine even a Lord's steward with anything but a welcoming, reverential smile when confronted with a Tendulkar or a Kohli.

However, Lord's is symbolic. It perhaps represents the epitome of the lethargy with which English cricketing establishments react to change.

The progress at snail's pace is witnessed by Old Father Time, the weathervane presented by the architect of the old Grand Stand Sir Herbert Baker. The same Herbert Baker who teamed up with Lutyens in 1912 to design New Delhi. Father Time now stands atop the scorer's box on the Mound Stand, in the perpetual pose of removing the bails. He was damaged during the Blitz, and has been struck by lightning. But he continues to stand there.

Much like the trappings of Lord's.

In 1971, Lord's was still in the early stages of overcoming centuries of inertia.

30

GREATER WHEN DEAD

THE *DAILY Mirror* is vehement. 'Go-slow India put England –
and 21,000 cricket fans – through the torture Test.' The headline
blares, 'Only 134 in a Day'.

'Marathon performance by their youngest batsman Viswanath
and Solkar completely ruined England's plans of a quick victory,'
Ted Dexter writes in his article. He makes the mistake of calling
Viswanath the youngest batsman; Gavaskar was four months
younger. However, it is true that Viswanath bats for more than
four and a half hours for his 68. He is outdone by Solkar, who
spends more than five hours at the crease to end with 67.

In *The Guardian*, Arlott agrees that 'For Saturday's spectators,
watching a single day's play without context, this must have
seemed a funless cricket outing.'

In *The Observer*, Tony Pawson is understanding to an extent:
'In the context of the match, this determined battle for the
lead was understandable enough but it was a pity that the main
spectator day should again coincide with the dullest cricket.'

In *The Times*, Woodcock is more sympathetic. 'Half an hour
lost to rain, and it would be asking too much of the Indians to
think primarily of entertainment. They had a match to win, and
England in their attritional way, were making it as difficult as
they could for them.'

Of course, the Indians are aware they will have to bat last on
this wicket. Also, as captain Wadekar will later point out, 124

behind with half the side back in the pavilion, and only Abid to bat followed by a rather long tail, the batsmen can ill afford to take chances.

An early-morning shower notwithstanding, play starts on time. After the overnight batsmen have seen off eight overs from the spinners, Illingworth takes the new ball. Price charges in along his circuitous run up, and Solkar hooks his first ball for six.

However, excitement will not be the order of the day. Illingworth keeps bowling his pacemen in spite of the wicket showing considerable promise for the spinners. Snow, bowling from the Pavilion End, sends down a hostile spell, mainly targeting Viswanath with short deliveries. The little man ducks and weaves away. Twice Snow makes the ball cut back sharply down the slope, getting inside Viswanath's defence, but on both occasions the ball bounces over the stumps.

Gifford, when given a bowl, is flat and quick, in complete contradiction to being chosen ahead of Underwood due to his ability to flight. Viswanath, slow but untroubled, completes his half century. Solkar, looking far from comfortable, sticks around. By lunch India are 248/5, Viswanath 57, Solkar 34.

After the break, England look tired and bereft of ideas. Hutton and D'Oliveira are in operation, the conditions helping neither. The batting continues to be slow and sedate. India are within 37 runs of England's score when the light deteriorates, presaging a shower. And Viswanath cuts at a short and wide delivery from Hutton to be caught behind. Tony Pawson remembers W.G.'s warning, 'Mustn't cut, mustn't cut, too dangerous a shot.'

As Abid comes in, the umpires confer and decide that the light is too bad to continue. Viswanath must feel disappointed. The series rules specify no appeal can be made by the batsmen – it is the responsibility of the umpires to decide whether the light is fit for play.

The rain arrives after this, pelting down, and the match is held up for half an hour. Will the wicket be affected? Abid falls to Snow immediately on the resumption, but that has nothing to do with the pitch and everything to do with the impetuosity of his hook shot. Luckhurst has enough time to run in from mid-on to hold the skier at midwicket.

Tea is taken seven minutes early because of the rain. At 292/7, the first innings lead is still up for grabs.

After the break, the score crosses 300. And then Price softens Venkat with some lifters, and then gets him to waft at a short wide one. Hutton holds the catch at second slip.

At, 302/8, Bedi comes in to join Solkar. Three singles, the third a stolen run that almost results in a run out, and India have the lead for the first time in a Test in England since 1936.

After bowling flat most of the day, Gifford finally tosses the ball up. It turns prodigiously, beating Bedi and Knott and running away for byes. Bedi, seeking the aerial route, holes out to mid-on. Chandra enters with about half an hour left in the day.

The remaining period is curious. Solkar, well past his half-century, makes no attempt to go for big hits. He also refuses long singles to the deep. Chandra ends up facing 27 deliveries in that half hour. Nothing really happens, other than the light improving and Boycott looking increasingly uneasy at the thought of having to bat out the last few minutes.

He is spared the ordeal. When Solkar finally decides to go for a big one, there are just six minutes to stumps. The resulting snick is held at the wicket. India make 313, Gifford 4-84, a lead of nine.

* * *

In the *Sunday Mirror,* Ted Dexter warned that England must wake up to the Test truth. For too long India and Pakistan have been considered second-class powers in the world of cricket. During the whole of their careers, England's players have subconsciously believed themselves superior to any threat from that part of the world ... especially at home. 'These ingrained attitudes,' Dexter wrote, 'like prejudices of any kind live on in the background despite every conscious effort to shift them.'

However, the most entertaining cricketing article on that rest day came from the pungent pen of fiery Fred Trueman.

Former captain and MCC supremo Gubby Allen had recently selected an all-time England side to take on an all-time Australian side chosen by Don Bradman in a computer 'Test'. The man, who could walk into Lord's from his back garden, had chosen Larwood as his pace spearhead and had kept Trueman as the twelfth man.

'Gubby's gone up the creek,' screamed Trueman in *The People*. 'He's even got me carrying drinks. He's picked what he considers to be England's best-ever team for the "Test of the century" against Australia, the match to be played on a computer ... It's a pity he didn't let the computer pick the team as well, they don't get carried away by sentiment.' Fiery Fred had never had much time for the gentlemen of privilege who ran cricket of whom Allen was the very personification. Things had always been inflammable between them, strained beyond repair since Allen had asked him to land the ball on a handkerchief in a public net session at Headingley. It was always, as David Woodhouse put it, a titanic clash of snobbery and bolshiness.

Having criticised the omission of Wardle, Rhodes and Sutcliffe, and lamented that he made the effort of picking up 307 wickets instead of aiming for the batsman's head and picking up 78 like Larwood, he added, 'You become a much better player, it seems, when you are dead and buried. So I've got every chance of getting into the top eleven when they get around to picking the team for the Test of the Next Century.'

Prophetic words those and a sparkling analysis of rosy retrospection so rampant in cricket.

England v India, 1st Test, Lord's – 22, 23, 24, 26, 27 July
England 304 (Snow 73, Knott 67; Bedi 4-70, Chandra 3-110)
India 313 (Wadekar 85, Viswanath 68, Solkar 67; Gifford 4-84).

31

ASHES TO ASHES, END OF STORY

THE ONLY other occasion before Lord's 1971 when India had taken the first-innings lead in a Test in England had also been at Lord's 1936. Gubby Allen, then captain of England, had captured 5-35 as Vizzy's men had managed just 147. However, with Amar Singh spewing fire, England were bowled out for 134. Eventually, the hosts capitalised on a second innings Indian collapse to triumph by nine wickets.

The year before that Test had witnessed the Government of India Act, conceding responsible self-government for the provinces. This was an effort to divert Congress away from central government. There was also the chimera of a promise of eventual federation at all-India level, with the understanding that the princely states would be slow to accede and eventually veto the proposition.

The caveats notwithstanding it had been quite a significant step, especially given that just five years before Churchill had categorically stated that independence for India was not going to happen 'in any period that we can even remotely foresee'. No wonder Hoare, Simon and Halifax – the Conservative architects of the Act – were branded pygmies by the boisterous Churchill. In 1931, he had branded the Indian leaders men of straw.

Within another year, Congress had transformed itself from a mass movement into a political party. The general elections of 1936 and 1937 were held with an electorate of approximately 30 million people, including a proportion of women, and the Congress triumphed in 758 of the 1,500 seats, forming governments in seven provinces.

In 1919, there had been 1,177 Britons and 78 Indians in the Indian Civil Service. By 1939, the numbers would be 759 and 540 respectively. There had been a rapid decrease in the number of British applicants after the Great War.

Not that all this tampered with the imperial perceptions. Charing Cross Underground hosted an exhibition called 'Peeps at the Colonial Empire' in 1936; the Empire Exhibition in Glasgow went on as planned in 1938. The 1936 film *Rhodes of Africa* was specifically screened to urge emigration to Rhodesia.

Two years after that Indian visit to England, in the summer of 1938, Bradman took his men to England. By then Wally Hammond had managed to obtain private means of sustenance outside cricket. Assuming the status of an amateur, he thereby managed to become the captain of England. Australia went into the final Test 1-0 up, only to be confronted by the flattest of tracks at The Oval. Len Hutton batted for 14 hours and seven minutes to score 364.

In 1930, Bradman had set the world record by hitting 334 at Leeds. On their way back from the Bodyline tour of 1932/33, England had crossed the Tasman Sea. Against the hapless Kiwis, Hammond hit 227 at Christchurch and followed it up with 336 not out at Auckland. On going past the world record of his lifelong rival, Hammond had supposedly pumped his fists and cried, 'Yes!'

Thus, when Hutton batted at The Oval, Hammond's 336 stood as the world record.

On the morning that followed Hutton's epic score, *The Times* report read, 'England's young batsman Hutton, who is only 22 years old, has amassed the biggest individual score – 364 – ever made in the long history of games between England and Australia. D. Bradman, generally considered the greatest scoring force that the game has ever known, made 334 against England at Leeds in 1930, but this was yesterday surpassed by Hutton.'

The *Daily Mirror* spoke about, 'Leonard Hutton's achievement at the Oval when he broke Bradman's Test match record with a score of 364.'

The *Daily Herald* reported that 'Hutton's 364 beat Bradman's 334 at Leeds, 1930, the previous highest in an England-Australia Test; passed Hammond's 336 not out against New Zealand at Auckland in 1933 (formerly biggest innings in any Test).'

In *The Manchester Guardian*, Neville Cardus wrote. 'For seventy-five minutes this morning Hutton kept the great crowd on a reach of suspense, we were all waiting for him to beat Bradman's record of 334, the highest in a Test match between England and Australia.'

One can perhaps attribute it to the magic of traditional rivalry, but Test cricket as a contest did emerge a poor second to the Ashes. Also, in 1938 England and Australia were the strongest cricketing powers.

The alarming bit is that this attitude survived the Second World War, the rise of the West Indies and South Africa, and has survived even the decades through which England slipped down the rungs of cricketing powers and ended at in the bottom. In the 1980s every team was regularly hammered by the West Indies, through the 1990s England were repeatedly routed by Australia, and time and again by others. In the summer of 1999, after losing the home series to New Zealand, England slipped to the lowest rank in the *Wisden* Test Table. But the Ashes remained synonymous with Test cricket for quite a significant proportion of cricket followers.

It speaks quite eloquently about both the projected importance of the Ashes and the long slump into mediocrity of the England sides that the 2005 series win led the entire team to be honoured with MBEs.

In 1971 we saw Ted Dexter sagaciously warning England against taking India and Pakistan lightly in her own backyard. In 2020, Dexter's second autobiography was published, titled *85 Not Out*. In that, he writes of the tour to South Africa in 1964/65 with M.J.K. Smith's England side. He was 172 not out at stumps on the first day at the Wanderers, 'It was a perfect pitch with a flat outfield and as I walked out the next morning I thought I would never have a better chance of beating Len Hutton's score of 364.'

Seven seasons earlier, in 1957/58, Garry Sobers had scored 365 not out. Dexter's words suggest that going past Hutton's record for England was more important than getting the world record. That by then there existed a world of cricket records beyond England (and Australia, and by proxy in this case South Africa) still somehow eluded him in 2020.

In 2020/21, England visited India and lost the series 1-3 after winning the first Test. By then India was the top-ranked Test team according to the ICC. England's policy of rotating and resting their top players in Test matches rankled with many. Michael Vaughan became flustered enough to comment, 'If England continue to rotate players during the Ashes, it will be the death of Test cricket.' One wonders why rotating one's players against Australia spells the death of Test cricket, whereas the same rotation policy effected against the top-ranked team in the world does not really amount to the same fatal crime.

The Ashes of 2021/22, for all intents and purposes, became a third-place play-off. But only according to the points table of the World Test Championship. In many minds, such as that of Brad Hogg, it remains the only Test cricket there is.

Even today well-meaning elderly men in obscure cricket journals, experimenting with semi-sophisticated, statistical methods to compare players across eras, restrict their data to Anglo-Australian cricketers – thus eliminating seven of the top ten run-getters and six of the top-ten wicket-takers in Test cricket.

One can argue about the historical and temporal depth of the contest, the associated iconography, lore, legends and sentiments. However, this fixation with a two-dimensional cricket world hailing from the 19th century underlines how slowly certain aspects of the game change or simply refuse to change. Even as the game becomes global and moves away from these ivory towers.

When Wadekar's men toured in 1971, England had come back victorious from the quest for The Ashes in 1970/71. They would defend the urn in 1972. India and Pakistan were negligible annoyances, like the fillers to use up white space after meaty articles. Even as Dexter warned the England side against treating them as such, he himself could not quite rise from the Ashes in his own cricketing world-view.

The Indians arrive in London, having postponed their flight by two days after 17 June was deemed auspicious.

The opponents were formidable. Here is Ray Illingworth's Ashes-winning side of 1970/71 recording their Ashes song. According to David Frith it was a permanent if unmelodic souvenir of a historic win.

'As Gavaskar started to fall, I could hear the silence in the MCC Committee Room,' said Snow. The collision course at Lord's.

John Jameson is run out in the first innings at The Oval.

Leading by example. Wadekar strikes out in the first innings at The Oval.

Chandra gets Edrich: There have been others who have overcome disability to excel in cricket, but none converted his handicap into an asset like this leg-spinner.

The Elephant in the Stadium. Two-year-old Bella ensures that obstacles in the path to victory are overcome.

Drama on the final day. Knott, a thorn in the Indian side with the bat, now takes a blinder to dismiss Sardesai.

The winning boundary. With each retelling by Engineer, Abid's stroke gets streakier and finer. But Illingworth, Abid and Engineer himself look square of the wicket as the ball is about to be swallowed up by the crowd.

'We'll have a bloody riot on our hands if you don't go out there.' Wadekar and Chandra acknowledge cheers from a largely Indian crowd

The all-conquering heroes: their feat becomes more and more magical with every passing day.

The Jam Sahib of Nawanagar (Prince Rantjitsinhji) in his Uniform of Active Service, First World War. Princes were not allowed near the action, but their armies played a vital role.

This is what it felt like: the Indian fans celebrate.

George V with the day's bag of three tigers, after a hunt during the Durbar celebrations 1911. Hunting was a major attraction on Indian tours for cricketers as well.

Vijay Merchant with LP Jai. Both of them missed the 1932 tour because of the Hindu Gymkhana boycott. Merchant, one of the greatest batsmen of India, was the chairman of selectors in 1971.

Gandhi with Charlie Chaplin and Sarojini Naidu (standing) in London, 1931. Almost everyone was eager to meet the Mahatma, apart from the one who refused with bulldog tenacity.

3 February 1955: Queen Elizabeth II with the Commonwealth Prime Ministers at Buckingham Palace. Winston Churchill is to her right, and Jawaharlal Nehru second from left.

Refugees from Bangladesh arrive at Tripura in northeast India, during the Bangladesh War of Independence.

Times had changed since the half-naked fakir had so offended British sentiments. The Beatles and Mia Farrow flank 'the Sexy Sadie' Maharishi Mahesh Yogi.

'What the Indians need is a mass famine.' Richard Nixon, who voiced this opinion, sits with Mrs Indira Gandhi, whom he called 'the old witch'.

Less than a month after the Test match, the stadium is crowded again for Rock at The Oval and £15,000 is raised for the Bangladesh Relief Fund.

Not quite tigers, but Ian Botham goes shooting partridge during the 1981/82 tour.

Not as venomous as Anil Kumble: Robin Smith and Alec Stewart pose with a snake during the 1993 tour.

Joe Root and Virat Kohli with the series trophies ahead of the first Test match at Trent Bridge during the 2021 tour. The equations on and off the field have changed a lot down the years.

32

WAR DANCE OF DELIGHT

IT RAINS. And it rains again. In between, the players wait. The umpires, David Constant and Charlie Elliott, keep them waiting. The wait lasts several hours.

* * *

In India Mrs Gandhi protested against the suggestions of UN observers on both sides of the borders between East and West Bengal. Such a policy came across as an insult, tending to equate India with Pakistan, thereby suggesting that Delhi was partly responsible for the genocide in East Bengal.

* * *

The conditions are not really that unsuitable for cricket. The Indian spinners may find the ball too slippery. At the same time, it seems rather harsh for the spectators who have braved the elements as well as the rush hour.

It is just as well that the first showers started when Constant and Elliott were just about to walk out to the middle. The wicket remained covered through the couple of heavy downpours. The curious playing conditions stipulate that if even one ball has been bowled in the session, the pitch will remain exposed to the rain.

When play finally begins at 2.45, the Indian bowlers taste success immediately. In fact, even before all the persevering spectators have settled back in their seats, Luckhurst yorks himself trying to hit Solkar across the line. His middle stump is bent askew. The Indian medium-pacers have thus got an early breakthrough in each innings.

A slim lead of nine runs, but it takes England six tense overs to get past it. For a while, as gentle medium-pace is pinged at them, Boycott and Edrich pretend that they are weathering a Procter-Pollock storm. In the ninth over, spin is introduced in the form of Bedi. But strangely, medium-pace continues from the other end, perhaps in the hope of a repeat of Solkar's success. Edrich does most of the scoring. Boycott, his summer's average of 98 notwithstanding, finds it difficult to get them off the square.

By the time Chandra joins forces with Bedi, it is the 18th over. By now Boycott has settled down, and he pulls the leg-spinner disdainfully in the direction of Father Time; 50 up for England in 82 minutes, and the advantage has shifted. Venkat, introduced late, bowls a tight line. Tea is taken at 56/1.

In the second over after tea, Boycott decides to try to hit Venkat off his length. Twice the off-spinner pitches up, and twice he is dispatched to the pickets on the off side. And then the line is varied. The ball is pitched on leg and middle. Boycott tries to turn it. Off the bat and pad it goes to leg slip where Wadekar takes the catch: 65/2. It is as clear a dismissal as one can hope to see. Boycott, however, tarries and trudges off reluctantly only when umpire Constant raises his finger.

Amiss, young, eager and as yet unproven, comes in with the Indians scenting a chance. Chandra is difficult to get away. For 13 balls, he fails to get off the mark. Off the 14th, he desperately tries to. A push to cover point, where Solkar lurks, and he is halfway down the pitch. Edrich's 'No!' echoes around St John's Wood, but Amiss is still out of his crease when the throw comes zooming into Engineer's gloves for the bails to be dislodged; 70/3 and Amiss walks out of the England side for the time being.

D'Oliveira comes in, calm, assured, the man for crisis. Chandra troubles him early on, but soon he is essaying strokes with nonchalance. As Venkat strangles him with his tidy off-breaks, he takes a fair share of risks in playing some extravagant strokes. England add 47 at a run a minute, D'Oliveira scoring 30 of them. The man from the Cape is playing better than anyone else today, when suddenly he falls to a planned move. The Indians always have a man positioned for D'Oliveira's favourite paddle sweep. For Bedi the man is removed. The left-armer floats one outside the leg-stump, D'Oliveira immediately goes for the stroke. He attempts to hit it very fine, misses it and is bowled round his legs. This is a cruel form of dismissal; it makes a batsman look sillier than others.

'The pitch was what may now be called "characteristically English," writes Arlott in his *Guardian* report which the Indian myth-factory down the line will never read. 'Once that meant a lively green strip where the ball bounced at lively pace and moved off the seam. Now it is the slow turner which virtually shapes the game in this country, dictating the methods of bowlers, and in consequence, of batsmen.'

With 45 minutes left in the day, England are 117/4. Bedi in his flaming orange turban, Venkat with his luxurious hair flying everywhere, Chandra with his curiously fast action. They are queuing up to take the wickets. However, Edrich is joined by Knott and there can hardly ever have been a duo more prepared to scrap.

The bowling is blunted with some excellent common-sense cricket. Knott is all pluck and street-smarts. Edrich judges the line to perfection, head over the ball, watching it as closely as possible.

Minutes pass, a quarter of an hour, then another quarter, finally the third quarter. Almost. The two have all but seen out the 45 minutes. Bedi bowls the final over. Edrich 62, Knott 17, the score 145/4.

It comes down to the final ball. Bedi pitches it up. The left-handed Edrich pushes at it, a trifle tentatively. The ball takes the edge. Engineer thrusts out a glove, the ball pops up off it, the wicketkeeper catches it on his second attempt and emits a whoop of triumph. The Indians on the field break into a synchronised jig. 'A war dance of delight,' writes Peter Laker.

It is 145/5 at the end of the day. With that last ball, the balance has tilted slightly in India's favour. Quick wickets on the final morning and they can win the match. England's lead is just 136.

England v India, 1st Test, Lord's – 22, 23, 24, 26, 27 July
England 304 (Snow 73, Knott 67; Bedi 4-70, Chandra 3-110) and 145/5 (Edrich 62) **India** 313 (Wadekar 85, Viswanath 68, Solkar 67; Gifford 4-84).

33

SIMULTANEOUS EQUATIONS
OF SELF-RULE

THE INDIANS – or rather the All-India team – were not that overawed by Lord's where they were handing out a thrashing to the MCC in 1946. With play held up due to the timeless London showers, they huddled around a stretch of coir matting in the visitors' dressing room. Raosaheb Nimbalkar, the reserve wicketkeeper, turned his leg-breaks appreciably on the makeshift strip. 'I used to be a leg-spinner before I took to wicketkeeping,' he explained to whoever he could get to listen.

It was in that same match that Vijay Merchant defied the bitter cold with layers of sweaters, which hung heavy down to his wrists, and with a muffler stuck in front of his throat, defied moisture in the air and the absence of the sun with a mixture of technique and temperament and constructed a perfect innings of 148. Arlott wrote, 'An innings by Merchant grows: it sprouts no exotic blooms but its construction is perfect to the last detail.'

Arlott found it impossible not to like Merchant. 'His manners were polished to the last degree, his consideration for others impeccable – and he looks you in the face when he talks to you: his honesty is unmistakable – he speaks out the truth, but never crudely. His charm, like his cricket, has its roots in a tranquillity which runs deeper than the level of "temperament".'

At The Oval, in the third Test, Merchant was once again faced with November-like conditions, asphalt-grey sky and damp atmosphere. As Prime Minister Attlee watched the action with his wife, the Indian master countered the challenges with an innings of sublime precision, systematically putting the bad ball away while offering not a semblance of a chance to an attack including Alec Bedser and Alf Gover. He scored 128 in his final Test innings in England.

The Test coincided almost seamlessly with the Great Calcutta Killing of 1946. As mobs terrorised the streets, some 4,000 people from both the Hindu and the Muslim communities were massacred.

The team, still referred to as All-India, had arrived in batches, the first Test team to fly across continents.

The manager, Pankaj Gupta, arrived ahead of the rest. As he was met by the old friend of Indian cricket, Arthur Gilligan, at Bournemouth. Gupta expressed his concerns that the team's kit, sent by steamer from Bombay, might not arrive in time. When he was presented with 17 complimentary FA Cup Final tickets, he had to return them because the players had not yet arrived.

Captain Pataudi, Amarnath and Shute Banerjee flew in from Karachi on a BOAC Avro York plane, stopping in Cairo, and landing at Hurn Airport, near Bournemouth. Mushtaq Ali, C.S. Nayudu, Nimbalkar, Gul Mohammed and Sarwate flew 51 hours on an RAF Dakota flight from Karachi. Kardar, Sohoni and Shinde took another flight via Cairo.

The final batch of Hazare, Merchant, Mankad, Modi and Hindlekar arrived last by flying boat, Bill Ferguson meeting the tourists at Poole. Having landed late, this last group of cricketers was unable to attend the party given by the Indian high commissioner.

All of them had left behind a land in chaos.

India was on the brink of political emancipation, in the midst of one of the most sordid periods in the land's history.

Two and a half million Indian soldiers had fought for the Allies in the Second World War. But Lord Linlithgow's unilateral declaration that India was at war without consulting the Indian political leaders had made Nehru remark, 'There is something rotten when a foreigner, and a hated person at that, can plunge 400 million human beings into war without asking them.' Immediate transfer of power had been demanded, and it had been followed by the mass resignation of the Congress leaders.

Yet, the vacuum created by this mass-resignation, and subsequent jailing of the Congress leaders, had also seen the steep rise to power and prominence of the Muhammad Ali Jinnah-led Muslim League. While the Congress had refused to support the British war effort, the Muslim League had voiced their full allegiance. The British in India, struggling with the increasing nationalism, welcomed the differences coloured by religion. The Muslim League pushed for the idea they had conceived about 10 years before, that of a separate nation-state. The name was crafted out of the conceptualised parts: P for Punjab, A for Afghanistan, K for Kashmir, S for Sindh and TAN from Baluchistan. Pakistan remains the only nation to be born out of an acronym.

In March 1942, the Cripps Mission headed by the senior left-wing Labour Party minister Sir Stafford Cripps was dispatched to barter with the Indian leaders.

The Mahatma dismissed Sir Stafford Cripps and his offer of 'independence with the option of leaving the Commonwealth after the war'. He called it 'a post-dated cheque on a crashing bank'. His characteristic retaliation was through the Quit India Movement.

Churchill, for his part, voiced his reservations in private, dismissing Gandhi's hunger-strike 'antics' of February 1943 by saying, 'The old rascal has not the slightest intention of dying.' And in spite of the Cripps offer, in November 1943 the war-time prime minister said in a speech to the Lord Mayor of London's Luncheon at the Mansion House, 'We mean to hold our own. I have not become the King's First Minister in order to preside over the liquidation of the British Empire.'

There are quite a few reputed historians who claim, somewhat tenuously, that Churchill's opinions about India were personal. For example, the diary entry of his secretary John Colville, dated 23 February 1945, quotes Churchill as saying, 'Hindus are a foul race protected by their pollution from the doom that is their due. I wish Bert Harris could send some of his surplus bombers to destroy them.' Men like Ronald Hyam and others state that these were private thoughts, seldom voiced in public and even less seldom did they make their way into policies.

However, it is rather difficult to wash away his murky role in the Bengal Famine of 1943, even with the waves of hagiography that continue unabated. The British administration of India, like most administrations where the country itself comes way down in the list of priorities, saw plenty of famines. And India was not the only place where they occurred as Pax Britannia ruled supreme. Yet, the Bengal Famine was different. It was the only one not caused by drought. Three million people died, their deaths caused by the failure of policy rather than a failure of the monsoon.

There was enough to feed the region in spite of natural disasters and the fall of Burma into Japanese hands. Churchill's cabinet was repeatedly warned that the exhaustive use of Indian resources for the war effort would result in famine. Churchill's response was that the Bengalis were breeding like rabbits. The shortages, after all, could not be so bad if Mahatma Gandhi remained alive.

Churchill's close adviser, physicist Frederick Alexander Lindemann, Viscount Cherwell, advised that 'the Bengalis were a weak race and that over-breeding and eugenic unfitness were the basic reasons for scarcity.'

While rice continued to be exported from India to the rest of the Empire, boats carrying supplies to Bengal were stopped from reaching the coast to keep the resources from falling into the wrong hands if a Japanese invasion took place.

As a result of the policies, the number of people who died in the famine was many times more than the numbers killed during the religious riots that plagued the land as India toured in 1946.

By 1946, Attlee was prime minister. Churchill, according to the inimitable John (later Jan) Morris, 'was dismissed from office at the first chance, and went smouldering off to write his war memoirs and to complete his *A History of the English-Speaking People*.' In his account of the Second World War, published in 1950, the great man wrote, 'No great portion of the world population was so effectively protected from the horrors and perils of the World War as were the peoples of Hindustan. They were carried through the struggle on the shoulders of our small island.'

Just to reiterate, 2.5 million Indian soldiers fought for the Allies. Cardus is not the only lionised legend who considered the numbers on the scoreboard asinine if they contradicted his opinions.

The early 1940s saw plenty of contradictions in India as well. People died in millions in the eastern villages. Armies slaughtered each other around the world. In the cricket grounds, Hazare and Merchant broke each other's records in feats of marathon run-making. And the image of the British in India underwent ups and downs.

In 1943, even as the Japanese held on to Burma, the minister of labour and national service, Ernest Bevin, voiced that the same Burma could still be 'polished into an Empire gem'. That same year, Lord Linlithgow told journalist Durga Das that Indians would be ready for self-rule in 50 years. That was a large step down from the 500 predicted in the war cabinet meeting of 1917. In 26 years, moving from one world war to another, the projections had come down from 500 to 50. The proportion of error remained the same with mathematical precision, 40/500 scaled down to 4/50. There was perhaps a method in the Imperial madness.

However, the Viceroy did conjure up some concocted constants into this skewed equation of self-rule. He stated that the Indians would still require five or six million British men and women to come and live in India and teach them how to run a country.

Meanwhile, in relative silence, Digvijaysinhji, the heir of Ranji, was using the partial autonomy granted to the princely states to provide refuge to 1,000 orphaned Polish children, both Jewish and Catholic.

It needs to be noted that sanctuary of this sort was not allowed in the rest of India under British rule. A fairly large school was established for the children at Balachadi.

The Maharaja, who was called 'Our Bapu' by the Polish children, has a square named after him in Warsaw.

34

SNOW STORM

IF EVER there is a warning of things to come, Chandra supplies it early on that ominous morning. In his second over, Knott pulls a short ball, it strikes Solkar on the leg at bat-pad and is deflected fine. Wadekar, at leg-slip, sticks out his left hand and the man who specialises in being a stubborn lower-order thorn in the opposition flesh is gone for 24.

The next Chandra over sees Hutton beaten by the disconcerting pace and slight turn. The off stump is knocked back –153/7 and the Indians are sensing history, every movement on the field laced with anticipation.

Snow, fresh from his career-best effort in the first innings, joins Illingworth and looks confident enough. A few quick runs are all that are required to change the equation, and Snow is aware of that. Having moved to 9, he swings at Venkat. Chandra is in the thick of things again as the ball comes down into his hands at deep square leg: 174/8 and the end is in sight.

The end is prolonged by a couple of missed chances. With Gifford at the crease, Illingworth goes on the defensive, blocking ball after ball. Gifford, imitating his captain, pushes forward and snicks Venkat. Wadekar at slip reaches for it but cannot hold on. And then for once Solkar's incredible anticipation deserts him. Illingworth stretches forward and snicks the ball on to his pads. Solkar, moving in from short leg, makes a desperate attempt to hold it but fails. It would have lobbed right into his hands if he had stayed in his original position.

Five fielders crouch around the bat and the batsmen thrust their pads forward. A couple of appeals are turned down, and result in less than complimentary jottings ... first in young Gavaskar's memory and then his memoirs. At the end of the first hour, Illingworth has managed just 14 runs.

The skipper and Gifford frustrate the Indians for 45 minutes, adding just 15. Then Venkat floats one on the leg side. Illingworth's attempt to turn it around the corner is fatal. Wadekar flings himself in front to come up with a superb catch.

Price succumbs quickly enough, caught at slip; a fourth wicket for Venkat. The last five wickets have fallen for 38 on the final morning in an hour and a half. England are 193 all out. That leaves India 183 to win in four-and-a-half hours.

But those are four-and-a-half hours on paper, as long as one ignores the weather forecast. The pitch is playing as well as ever, but the light is turning murky and the predictions are gloomy, with rain in the air. Wadekar and Adhikari confer. And soon Gavaskar and Mankad walk in with a sense of purpose.

* * *

One needs to pause here and look at the decision to go for the runs. For the first 38 years in Test cricket, Indians were not known to be the most proactive bunch of cricketers. But time and again, while going for steep targets, they had punched well above their weight.

There had been one desperate attempt to get 548 at Manchester in 1959, when the debutant Abbas Ali Baig and the veteran Polly Umrigar had hammered hundreds. They had lost by a whopping 171 runs, but at 321/ 5, with the centurions at the crease, things had looked bright. Then there had been Pataudi's men chasing down 256 at the Brabourne in 1964, and the Jaisimha heroics taking them within striking distance of a 395-run target at Brisbane in early 1968. In contrast this target of 183 looked very moderate.

What made this a special chase was the strategic factoring in of the weather. Down the decades Indian cricketing folklore would make Pataudi the regal risk-taker, where Wadekar was an orthodox, defensive captain. It is the fourth innings at Lord's which debunks the myth. The instructions were clear, the batsmen were asked not to hang around, and after two quick wickets were lost it was Engineer who strode in at No.4, an astute move which underlined the positive approach.

When the umpire got too excited

The first major audacious chase by an Indian team had been in 1948/49 against the West Indians.

Set 361 to win at the Brabourne, Hazare and Modi had set it up by putting on 139 for the fourth wicket. Hazare was sixth out at 285 and the eighth wicket had gone down at 321. But Dattu Phadkar kept going for the runs. Stumps were drawn an over and a ball before scheduled close because of some confusion on the part of umpire Bapu Joshi. By then, India had reached 355/8.

That was not the only instance of Wadekar's quick thinking. At Port-of-Spain, when India lost their third wicket at 84 while chasing 125 to win, he had cannily promoted a free-stroking Abid ahead of himself and Solkar.

Projecting forward to 1985/86, we see a far more accomplished Indian team, which had recently won two major limited-overs tournaments and had more than the upper hand in the Test series against an inexperienced Australian team. At Melbourne, the vaunted Indian batting line-up was set 126 to win in two sessions, with very vocal predictions of rain. Kapil Dev and his think-tank decided to ignore the weather. The same Sunil Gavaskar, by then the world record-holder for runs and centuries, scored eight off 54 deliveries in an hour and eight minutes. Mohinder Amarnath stone-walled for 40 minutes to end with an unbeaten three. They crawled to 59/2 in 25 overs at tea when rain came pelting down to end the match. It took India another 33 years to win a series in Australia.

There are quite a few who defend the ploy of Kapil and his men, saying weather forecasts were notoriously untrustworthy in India in those days and they were not used to paying heed to them. That is nonsense. It was simply bad strategy.

In contrast, Wadekar, Adhikari and Venkat were far ahead of their times in the approach they adopted.

* * *

Gavaskar and Mankad come out looking for runs. The start is not really promising. Snow's second over has Mankad fishing outside off stump and Knott throws up the catch: 8/1.

The skipper walks in and essays a splendid straight drive off Snow. He looks all set to carry on from where he left off in the first innings. But with the score on 21, he mistimes a hook off Price and the ball is swallowed by Boycott at midwicket.

It is now 21/2. A time for caution? Instead the batting order is shuffled. Gavaskar is looking secure, playing the sheet-anchor. In comes Engineer, a neat move with dual benefit. The flamboyance will be used to power the chase along as the young man holds up the other end. Besides, Engineer's experience as an opening batsman will also help him against the ball that is still new as lunch draws near.

It is a calculated move, commended by Arlott in *The Guardian*, 'His batting is better suited to winning a game than saving it.' Engineer chances his arm, slicing his drives into the outfield, hooking with disdain. Price is hit like a bullet down the ground, and then pulled to midwicket. And in between the strokes, the two steal quick singles.

Price has been hit out of the attack, Hutton looks unimpressive, and the Indians are quickly into the forties. And now the infamous incident takes place.

Snow runs in, Engineer tries to turn him to leg and misses. The ball strikes the thigh and trickles away. The batsmen sprint for a short run.

According to Gavaskar, 'From the corner of my eye I saw Snow also setting off for the ball. I would have reached home safely as Snow had gone across to the other side on his follow through. However, I found to my surprise that he was level with me and with the ball nowhere near him, the hefty fast bowler gave me a violent shove which sent me sprawling.'

'The incident would have been adjudged a clear foul even in a Fourth Division football match,' writes Peter Laker in the *Daily Mirror.* 'An unceremonious and unmanly shoulder charge from behind that bowled over Indian opener Gavaskar like a shot rabbit. [It] could by no stretch of the imagination be confused with cricket strategy. Purely and simply, it was an exhibition of truculence of the type that would have provoked instant retaliation in a physical-contact sport like rugby or soccer.'

The difference in dimensions of the two men makes a severe impression on those who watch, and perhaps colours their reports. 'Gavaskar, a tiny fellow of 5ft 4in, was, metaphorically speaking, trampled on by 6ft-plus [Snow],' writes Laker.

What follows does not amuse the reporters either. Woodcock is scathing in his brevity. 'Nor was it with the best will in the world that Snow picked up Gavaskar's bat and returned it to him.'

Laker is of course more graphic in his denunciation. 'An ounce of common sense, a quick apology, a helping hand to the prostrate Gavaskar could have redeemed Snow. Instead, he retrieved the little Indian's bat, glared and tossed it across. Snow then turned on his heel and virtually shrugged off a caution from umpire David Constant as he prepared to bowl his next ball.'

This is perhaps stretching the facts a bit. Gavaskar will recount, 'Snow came and tossed the bat back to me. He did not fling it as reported in the newspapers.' Snow, whose recent Australian heroics have been tarnished by reports of misbehaviour, hostile bowling at tailenders, and arguments with umpires about intimidatory bowling, is not the most popular man at the moment.

Later Snow will write in his autobiography, 'The moment I made contact and Gavaskar started to fall, I could sense the shocked silence in the MCC committee room.'

Once the players emerge after the lunch interval he does apologise to Gavaskar, but apparently that is on being told to do so by TCCB secretary Billy Griffith and chairman of selectors Alec Bedser.

Here is Snow's version.

While walking into the dressing room, he sees Alec Bedser coming in from the players' balcony.

'Sorry about that, Big Al, it was a bit unfortunate, wasn't it?'

'You'll apologise, won't you?'

'Sure, just let me get my shirt off and wipe away the sweat.'

But then the door bursts open and in rushes a fuming Billy Griffith. 'That's the most disgusting thing I've ever seen on the field.' That is not the last of what he says and things are getting heated when Illingworth comes over and tells the secretary it will be better if he leaves the players to themselves.

In any case, by lunch the Indians have moved to 47/2 in just 11 overs. Engineer is blazing away, with 19 from 21 deliveries. Gavaskar is doing his bit as the sheet-anchor perfectly with 15 off 25. The chase is on, a race against the weather.

It is stepped up immediately after the break as spin is introduced. Gifford is walloped to the long-on fence by Engineer, who then cuts him for three. Gavaskar skips down and drives the left-armer through the covers and past mid-on for a couple of boundaries.

With Illingworth on from the other end, both the batsmen use their feet to bring off attractive strokes.

It is 87/2, with both the batsmen into their thirties, the stand has amounted to 66 in 50 minutes. And now Engineer charges down the wicket even as Gifford is still running in to bowl. The ball is deliberately shorter, and Knott whips off the bails. 'Engineer foolishly cast his wicket away,' Wadekar will write later. To be precise, that is what he will tell K.N. Prabhu. The wicketkeeper walks back for a 40-ball 35.

With dark clouds settling over the ground, the dismissal is perhaps the end of realistic chances of an Indian win. Viswanath joins Gavaskar, and the two little men continue at a trifle slower pace. Illingworth is hard to get away, but when the 100 is raised in the 23rd over there is still hope if the rains stay away.

There is encouragement from the Indian spectators. One fan assures, 'Don't worry, fellows, we've got a magician coming from Nottingham to keep the rain away.'

The momentum shifts with a dubious decision.

Viswanath sweeps Gifford and Amiss at backward short leg clutches at it. Indian accounts indicate there is doubt, but contradict each other. Sundar Rajan will write that umpire Constant raised his finger after a long while, although the ball seemed to have been caught on the half-volley. Gavaskar will recount, '[Viswanath was] caught in the leg-trap with the ball coming off his pads.' In any case, it is 101/4 and the 183-run target does not seem so trivial any more.

Seven runs later, Sardesai makes a mess of a straight ball from Illingworth. He tries to come forward, then goes back and essays a cut. The resulting chop deflects the ball on to the off stump. At 108/5, Solkar, the half-centurion of the first innings, walks out to join the persevering Gavaskar.

The opening batsman duly completes his half-century, notched up in exactly two hours off 92 balls. But three runs later, Gifford's delivery turns and bounces as if made of rubber. Off the shoulder of the bat it lobs to Edrich at gully. India are 114/6 and Gifford, with 3 for 31 from 11 overs, is looking increasingly likely to win the match for England. The Indians are struggling against canny field-placing and subtle tactics.

Solkar, having already demonstrated extraordinary tenacity in the first innings, shuts up shop. But England always have the other end to aim at. Abid Ali bats gallantly, defying the spinners for a considerable while, before swinging Illingworth into the hands of Snow at midwicket: 135/7.

Venkat follows a few minutes later, having scored all the seven runs of the partnership. He drives at Gifford and Hutton tumbles at second slip to hold the catch. It is 142/8, and by now the rain that India has been racing against is their only hope for survival.

There are three overs and three balls till tea. Solkar and Bedi hang on, adding just three in the process. Solkar, grim and determined, is unbeaten on 6 scored over an hour, consuming 54 balls. At tea it is 145/8. The importance of this resistance cannot be overstated. One more wicket and tea would have been delayed, and with Chandra the man to come in, the match could have been over in a flash.

Fifty overs have been bowled, 38 more runs are required, the hapless Chandra is padded up, the scoring has dried to a trickle. The advantage is heavily in favour of England.

However, even as the players leave the ground, a thin drizzle starts in its irritating manner. During the break, Bedser and Griffith make their way to the Indian dressing room, seek out Wadekar, Adhikari and Gavaskar, and apologise on behalf of Snow. 'Presumably, that is an end to the matter, although there remains much realism in the old army motto about one volunteer being worth ten repressed men,' writes Laker.

The common sense that Laker so deplored in Snow's reaction after the collision, is also absent in the English playing conditions. A drizzle will not hold up the game if it starts while the players are on the field. However, if it starts during the interval, the game has to be held up till it stops. Cricket has always struggled with rain rules, and England are to emerge as beneficiaries from one of the most ridiculous ever made ... during the World Cup semi-final 21 years down the line. But on this day, a similarly peculiar rule perhaps robs them of victory. The Engineer-Gavaskar partnership continued through a similar drizzle because the players were already on the ground. However, now the drizzle persists, and even as kids show how negligible the problem is by arranging impromptu games, the players have to stay indoors.

Half an hour from the scheduled close of play, it starts coming down in torrents and the Test is concluded as a draw.

The general verdict is that England have missed out on an exciting win. Wadekar disagrees, 'I had already consulted the weather bureau and ordered the batsmen to take a chance because rain was forecast in the afternoon. Otherwise we had all the time to score the 183.'

While some argue the odds were heavily in favour of England and two balls were all that would have taken them to clinch a win, some say that Bedi and Chandra could have assisted Solkar in making the runs.

Jim Swanton, with his magisterial air, declares that neither side deserved to win, 'England because their cricket was mediocre and India for throwing away a match they should have won hands down.'

Arlott, considerably more generous in spirit than his colleague, does point out, 'This match, even more than the third Test against Pakistan, has demonstrated the shift of power of world cricket.'

As Arlott steered clear of writing about the collision on the field, his colleague at *The Guardian*, Campbell Page, made the front page under the headline, 'Rain and Snow interrupt play.'

England v India, 1st Test, Lord's – 22, 23, 24, 26, 27 July
England 304 (Snow 73, Knott 67; Bedi 4-70, Chandra 3-110) and 191 (Edrich 62; Venkat 4-52) drew with **India** 313 (Wadekar 85, Viswanath 68, Solkar 67; Gifford 4-84) and 145/8 (Gavaskar 53; Gifford 4-43).

35

VINOO AND THE VERB

WITH ARLOTT eloquent in his praise of the Indian performance at Lord's, one can't help but wonder what his *Guardian* predecessor Neville Cardus would have made of the effort of Wadekar's men. But by the time the Indians visited, the charming painter of cricketing prose-fantasies was already in his eighties.

When the Queen had visited Lord's and met the Indian team of 1952, Cardus had declared with characteristic flamboyance, 'It was apt and delightful that Queen Elizabeth should have gone to Lord's on the day that saw an Indian cricketer bringing again to test-match the spirit of youth and adventure. This same match had begun gloomily and parsimoniously, not to say unchivalrously, by England's new captain Len Hutton, abetted by the amateur Simpson.'

Well, the details are a bit diluted by his fanciful dismissal of the professional captain – an oxymoron in the Cardusian world ruled by the MacLaren fantasy. India had batted first and scored 235, aided by Vinoo Mankad's 72 as an opener, with a straight six off Roly Jenkins. 'I know of no precedent of such a solecism during the first hour of a Test match,' Cardus had written. And what Hutton and Simpson had done was to put on 106 for the first wicket. Hutton, for all the contemporary frothing at the mouth about a professional finally leading England, had gone on to score 150, and England had totalled 537. Of course, it is now part of celebrated folklore that Mankad captured 5/196 in 73 overs.

On the morning of the Queen's visit, Mankad, unbeaten overnight on 86, had resumed his second innings. It was Monday, 23 June 1952, and not 'Monday, June 24th' as Cardus states in his essay. Besides, his innings was almost over by the time her majesty did get to visit Lord's. But a famous Cardus piece implies these signature blemishes. Mankad proceeded to add 211 with skipper Hazare, and was finally bowled by Jim Laker for 184. The target set by India remained a puny 77, and was overhauled with eight wickets to spare. Hutton, the professional captain, remained unbeaten with 39, denying Mankad (24-12-35-0 after being introduced in the third over) any further success beyond his already superhuman feats.

Cardus elaborated on his famous scoreboard quip, 'The secrets of cricket have so little to do with competition's values, averages and results that often I could wish for some other way than the score-board's of awarding the prize. India emerged from the Lord's Test match, thanks to Mankad and Hazare, on the side of the angels, as far as playing the game is concerned ... Personally, I would have given India the match on, say, aesthetic and spiritual points. And the crowd in the main would have been with me.'

I have a suspicion that based on the last day's play at Lord's, 1971, Cardus would have singled out Engineer for his dash, dazzle and chutzpah and would have been sufficiently appalled by the Illingworth innings of the morning to award the match to India in his exclusive judgment. Even more so perhaps because Engineer was a Lancashire regular.

Coming back to Mankad's feat of 1952, it was even more incredible because he had just joined the Indian team after an SOS call. He had been busy playing as a professional for Haslingden in the Lancashire League. He was obviously well known in England long before then. In 1946, he had scored 1,120 runs and captured 129 wickets, leading Arlott to write, 'He is a craftsman who lives in his craft so deeply that it becomes almost an art ... There are other comparable batsmen but bowlers of his class are few.'

By the time Cardus marked him out as an 'Indian cricketer bringing again to test-match the spirit of youth and adventure', Mankad was 35. He had made his mark long, long ago, in the pre-war days when Lionel Tennyson had brought his team along in 1937/38. In the victorious fourth unofficial 'Test', Mankad scored an unbeaten 113 from No.3 and picked up 3-18 and 3-55. He finished the series averaging 62.66 with the bat and 14.33 with the ball, leading Tennyson to remark that he would find a place in any World XI.

South African whitewash

Mankad was famous across the cricketing world, but for one monochrome section.

In 1956/57, Peter May's Englishmen visited South Africa and were engaged in an exciting series that ended 2-2. It was during this series that Trevor Bailey completed the rare double of 2,000 Test runs and 100 Test wickets. In *Pitch and Toss*, his account of the tour, South African batsman Roy McLean observed that the Essex all-rounder had now joined the ranks of Keith Miller and Wilfred Rhodes. 'Just imagine the difference in spectator value between a Keith Miller and a Trevor Bailey either as bowler or batsman.' He had never seen Rhodes, but added, 'I'm quite sure he could, despite [his Yorkshire] birth, never have been as dour as Bailey.'

At that particular point in time, Mankad had 2,084 runs and 158 wickets in Tests. But he did not feature in McLean's world of cricket. Perhaps he did not even know of him.

At the start of the 1950s, it was had been difficult to remain unaware of Vinoo Mankad. Yes, he had all those runs, and would go on to register the then highest score by an Indian batsman. He had all those wickets. Besides, Mankad had also added himself into the lexicon of cricket during the 1947/48 winter in Australia.

That was when he had run Bill Brown out in a tour match – after furnishing a warning – for backing up too far before the ball had been bowled. When Brown continued to rush out prematurely during the second Test at Sydney, Mankad ran him out again and eventually his name became a verb associated with that mode of dismissal. Hot and fiery debates raged for days – in homes, pubs, trams, trains and ferryboats. The newspaper offices were hit by an avalanche of letters.

While men like Bradman himself, Bill O'Reilly, Vic Richardson and Ray Robinson were solidly behind Mankad, a few like K.S. Duleepsinhji and Jack Fingleton thought otherwise. And while Mankad was roundly criticised in some of the letters to the editors, one missive pointedly asked, 'Would Brown have done this sort of thing against the Englishmen? I'll guarantee he wouldn't, because he knew he wouldn't have got away with it. Knowing the sportsmanship of this Indian team he imposes on it ... The only bad sportsmanship was shown by the batsman.'

The debate rages till this day.

Charlie Griffith was roundly booed by the Adelaide crowd when he ran out Ian Redpath, but once again found support in the unflinching O'Reilly.

When he dismissed Derek Randall in this manner, Ewen Chatfield was reminded by Ian Botham that he had once been hit by a bouncer and stopped breathing. 'You've already died on the pitch once.'

Kapil Dev warned Peter Kirsten before running him out, thus becoming the target of a torrent of abuse unleashed by the departing batsman. Kepler Wessels supposedly struck him on the shin with his bat. India's 1992/93 visit to South Africa being a diplomatic hot-potato of a tour, the footage of this incident was carefully removed under the supervision of Ali Bacher himself.

Jos Buttler, done in by Sachithra Senanayake during a 2014 ODI, was shocked when five years later Ravichandran Ashwin inflicted it on him in the IPL.

The most high-profile incident has probably been the 2016 Under-19 World Cup match in which West Indian captain Keemo Paul decided the match with a Mankad dismissal when Zimbabwe were three runs from victory.

Every such incident still polarises the cricket world. There are voices that still claim that it is against that curious esoteric concept called 'the spirit of the game'.

To me, it is as much against the spirit of cricket as a centre-forward anticipating a back pass from a callous defender and scoring past the goalkeeper is against the tenets of football. Somehow, none of the sentinels of this abstract concept of cricketing purity seem to mind batsmen cheating a part of a run.

However, the question is, did Mankad really start it all? Yes, he did bring off the first such dismissal in Test cricket. But, the mode of dismissal has been around almost since the days of cricketing antiquity.

According to the Association of Cricket Statisticians and Historians (ACS), the first such incident in first-class cricket occurred in 1835, effected by a round-arm fast bowler of Nottinghamshire called Thomas Barker. At the time of writing, the ACS lists 39 such instances in first-class cricket, 12 in the 18th century, 22 in the 19th and five in the past 20 years. If we equate 'Mankading' with the spirit of cricket, we have to conclude that there has not been much change in cricketing moral and spirit through the course of history.

The Nicholas Felix classic, *Felix on the Bat*, even has an illustration depicting this as a mode of dismissal. So, it had been in vogue before 1845.

However, the most telling evidence in terms of the acceptance of this manner of dismissal comes from a piece in the book *A History of Harrow School*. The said article is penned by Spencer Gore, old Harrovian and winner of the first Wimbledon singles title in 1877.

Gore describes the mode of dismissal in 1870 during the quintessential English fixture, Eton v Harrow at Lord's. An over-eager Harrow batsman, Conrad Wallroth, was run out in this fashion by the Eton captain. 'Harris … noticed that Wallroth, who was well set, was backing up too eagerly. He put himself on to bowl (quite rightly, to my mind), and, pretending to bowl, caught Wallroth tripping, and he paid the penalty.'

There was no warning and Gore seems quite appreciative of the opportunism shown by Harris.

The Harris of Eton in this tale is none other than our old friend who went on to become the captain of England, and later governor of Bombay, and, for all intents and purposes, ran English cricket for decades. Yes, Lord Harris himself.

All this was half a century before the 'spirit of cricket' claptrap shrouded the game with its sustained nonsense from the 1920s. That was the same decade that started with Johnny Douglas and Arthur Mailey each discovering that the other was tampering with the ball in the course of a Test match.

Less than ten years ago as I write, Vinoo's younger son Rahul Mankad was attending a formal luncheon during an India-Australia Test match at Melbourne. Paul Sheahan, then president of the Melbourne Cricket Club, introduced him as 'son of the notorious Mankad'.

No one points to the photograph on the back cover of the carefully airbrushed biography *Gubby Allen: A Man of Cricket* and observes that the author Jim Swanton and the subject Allen are sitting in the garden at Lord's named after the notorious Harris.

Yardsticks and attitudes.

Gandhi the lob bowler

Perhaps the most curious case of equating this mode of dismissal to something heinous occurs in an Ian Buruma novel.

Playing the Game is a very un-Buruma-like book by the Anglo-Dutch author who otherwise specialises in socio-political non-fiction. An unnamed writer researching Ranji's life in the 1980s comes across a hitherto unknown and unpublished letter in the royal archives of Nawanagar. The letter essentially forms the text of the novel.

The premise is interesting in the context of this book. The Prince of Wales, later King Edward VIII, was all set to visit Nawanagar as part of his 1921 tour of India. At the last moment, his plans were revised, and as a minor kingdom,

Nawanagar was dropped off the itinerary. In a petulant reaction, Ranji writes to – who else, but – C.B. Fry, asking his friend to judge his claims as someone who deserved to play host to the crown prince. Thereby he launches on an account of his life in fascinating detail – covering every aspect, cricketing, regal and otherwise.

There are lots of recognisable nuggets from Ranji's life that will delight an adherent of cricket history.

The most curious bit about the book is the portrayal of the schoolboy M.K. Gandhi as a lob bowler with a vicious break from the leg. Ranji comes across him during a match for Rajkumar College. In the tense climactic moments of the game the young Gandhi dismisses him by flicking off the bails at the non-striker's end as the young Ranji leaves his crease before the ball is bowled.

Later, Gandhi meets Ranji in London and the two watch cricket together. Ranji is fed up with Gandhi's pretentious and largely misguided commentary on the game.

As far as we know from historic archives, Gandhi never indulged in cricket. He was never a cricketer of either ability or note, and the accusation of 'Mankading' is rather far-fetched as far as poetic license goes. He did meet Ranji in London, but no account talks of their watching cricket together.

It may be that in his letter to Fry, Ranji wrote fictitious accounts of Gandhi's unscrupulous behaviour on the cricket field to underline that he was dead against whatever trouble the man was causing the British with his *satyagraha* nonsense in the early 1920s. However, if that had been the intention, Buruma does not clarify it in the novel.

What is clear, however, is that to the Anglophile Ranji, Gandhi is a troublemaker and thereby painted in negative shades. And the supposed dubious manner of dismissal is one of the dark marks that go on to constitute that negative character.

The satire achieved is sheer genius.

36

YOU CAN SEE THE MOON

SEVERE THUNDERSTORMS affect the extreme east of England overnight as the Indians reach Norwich. The first day of their match against Minor Counties at Lakenham is washed out. It is quite a merciful break for the entire team after the gruelling exertions of the first Test. Captain Wadekar has stayed behind in London for a short holiday from cricket.

Only one Indian sees action that day. It is Engineer who has gone back to Manchester. He has the misfortune to be dismissed hit wicket for two. Rain does hold up the Gillette Cup semi-final, more than an hour lost after lunch. But there is no system for reducing overs. Gloucestershire get 229 in their quota of 60. The scheduled close of play is at 7.30. By the time left-arm-spinning all-rounder David Hughes makes his way to the crease, the clock shows ten to nine with the match still in the balance, five overs and a few balls remaining.

Hughes goes up to umpire Arthur Jepson and complains about the non-existent light. The match can be completed the following morning. But 30,000 spectators are still huddled into Old Trafford. Jepson's answer supposedly is, 'You can see the moon. How far do you want to see?'

A disgruntled Hughes takes guard. The 56th over begins with Lancashire needing 25 off 30 balls. John Mortimore, the famed Gloucestershire off-spinner, runs in to bowl. Hughes launches into him to produce a brutally symmetrical output: 6-4-2-2-4-6. The scores are level. Lancashire win five balls later.

* * *

While England was drenched with rain, Prime Minister Edward Heath headed for the open seas, leading the British team in the 605-mile Admiral's Cup. Off the coast in Southsea, Heath stood on the 42ft craft designed by Sparkman and Stephens, the hull curved out of mahogany, part of his *Morning Cloud* fleet.

Lord Rosebery had won the Derby, A.J. Balfour had been a high-class golfer, Gladstone an exceptional shot. Alec Douglas Home had played for Eton against Harrow and had toured South America with the MCC. But Heath's rapid rise from a dinghy sailor to the captain of British ocean racing team was a cause of considerable surprise, some elation among the Tories and a lot of pejoratives from the opposition. With the Northern Ireland situation about to go haywire, the prime minister's adventures, eventually victorious, would continue to be viewed askance.

* * *

In comparison to the taxing overtime of Manchester and the sensation of the prime minister doing a Francis Drake, the Indian tour match is played in a picnic-like atmosphere. The home batsmen make merry against less than focused bowling, especially enjoying themselves against the medium pacers. Prasanna, continuing to have a miserable time in England, is down with a touch of flu. Bedi is rested. Venkat, leading the side, bowls his usual tight length. Chandra picks up three wickets. But captain Fred Millett manages to declare at a healthy 203/5.

By the end of the day, Gavaskar, Mankad and Baig have all scored runs, the Indians amassing 154/1.

* * *

On the following day, the news from home remained worrying, with friction along the East Pakistan border continuing to make international headlines.

In Britain, too, the situation was quite explosive. John Davies, secretary of state for trade and industry, announced that 6,000 men would lose their jobs as two of the three yards of the Upper

Clyde Shipbuilders would be liquidated. The resulting bedlam played out in parliament, in the Glasgow docks and in the streets of London.

* * *

At Norwich, Mankad remains sedate in his approach in spite of the ordinary bowling attack. He desperately wants some time in the middle. He is overtaken by Baig before both fall in quick succession. It is now Sardesai's turn to play a lethargic innings of 16. However, Solkar, with runs and confidence behind him, hammers five fours and two sixes in his unbeaten 44. Venkat calls them in after crossing 250.

Millett is rather late in declaring the second time around. Perhaps because he is busy enjoying himself, hitting a stroke-filled fifty as Gavaskar, Mankad, Sardesai all have a bowl. It leaves India 20 overs to get 151. There is no intention of going for the runs. Sent in as openers, Kirmani and Jayantilal block their way to 26 off 11 before the match is called off.

* * *

That week, Joan Baez performed at Stanford University and the University of Michigan. Her 'Song for Bangladesh' was inspired. It referred to the army's attack on the Dacca University campus during Operation Searchlight and questioned the international community's continued apathy in the face of massive abuses of human rights. The number of refugees in India numbered 7.23 million by the end of July.

* * *

That Sunday, both Ted Dexter and Fred Trueman focused on the new brand of one-day cricket in their respective columns.

Dexter, moved by the Hughes onslaught, suggested that the Lancashire hitter was ideal for the 'one-day Aussie Tests'. He pointed out, 'Cricket's latest love child may have taken as many years to fully mature as the normal baby takes months to be born. But the fully-fledged article which entertained a full house of

30,000 from 11am until 9pm need now have nothing to fear from those who still insist it is no more than an illegitimate form of something they sadly believe to be the real thing.' He contrasted the Lancashire-Gloucestershire match at Manchester with the two days of Test cricket that had produced 159 and 134 runs at Lord's. 'The currency of traditional cricket has been devalued.'

Dexter went on: 'That anyone with money to spend on a ticket gets better value from Gillette and Player League style matches than he can hope for from weighty and much vaunted five-day internationals. Next year there is direct choice available when England play Australia in three one-day Tests as well as the five normal ones. I suspect that fans will not be long in showing their preference.'

It was indeed a time of change. We see that the warnings about Test cricket being on its deathbed and non-traditional forms of the game taking over are also more than 50 years old.

Trueman echoed similar sentiments, although way more colourfully. 'Cricket has finally found a lifeline and the message should now be clear to everyone – even those men at Lord's who seem to have spent all their lives with their heads in the clouds. One-day matches are a winner and the more we see of them, the healthier the game will become.'

While the two men were penning their articles, with or without a ghost, the Indians were already back in London to take on Surrey at The Oval.

Minor Counties v Indians, Lakenham – 28, 29, 30 July
Minor Counties 203/5 dec (Maslin 61; Chandra 3-39) and 199/6 dec (Millett 50, Hunter 41) drew with **Indians** 252/3 dec (Baig 64, Mankad 63, Gavaskar 53, Solkar 44*) and 26/0.

37

COLONIAL CALCULUS

IN 1946, The Oval witnessed the Indians enjoying a few good days. On their first visit to the old ground, they lost their ninth wicket with the score on 205. Shute Banerjee, by no means a regular No.11 with two first-class centuries under his belt, walked out to join Chandu Sarwate. Sarwate himself, who would finish his career with a first-class average of 32 with 14 hundreds, was by no means a No.10 either. In that innings, Banerjee scored 121, Sarwate an unbeaten 124. They added 249, the only instance of numbers 10 and 11 both scoring hundreds. And then there was the Merchant hundred at The Oval during the third Test.

During a speech in a banquet at Lord's, Merchant expressed hope that the cabinet mission would succeed totally. Merchant was by now a senior statesman of the team. However, the side was led in the princely tradition by the Nawab of Pataudi, Iftikhar Ali Khan. After the 1934 season, Pataudi had played very little first-class cricket, only six matches in the intervening 11 years. In the 1945/46 season, he reappeared on the scene, scoring 7 and 1 in two innings, made himself available for India, and thereby became the captain of the first post-war Indian side.

That is not to say that Merchant would have been made the captain had Pataudi not resurfaced. He had spent his days from the start of the Second World War to the eve of the England tour scoring 5,003 runs at an unearthly average of 131.66 with

21 hundreds. However, there was every chance of the Maharaja of Patiala being made the skipper. Ornamentalism was difficult to displace.

Pataudi failed in the Tests, managing 55 runs at 11.00, but he was a classy enough batsman to score 981 runs at 46.71 on the tour, with four centuries.

A year earlier, on coming to power, Attlee had made it clear that the goal was to replace British by Indian rule within the five-year lifetime of the Labour government. The reasons had less to do with the Labour sympathy for the Indian cause and much more to do with simple economics.

They simply did not have the means – in currency, people or trust. In the Central Provinces for example, there were no troops, only 17 British ICS officials and 19 British police. The British soldiers were weary from the war and not really keen on staying in India. The recent defections to Subhas Bose's Indian National Army had shown that the loyalty of the Indian troops to Britain could no longer be taken for granted. The feeling was reinforced by the mutinies in the Royal Navy, especially in Bombay and Karachi. Viceroy Wavell was sending missives, 'We have no longer the resources, nor I think the necessary prestige and confidence in ourselves.'

The best six months

After the Indian tour of the summer, the MCC under Wally Hammond sailed to Australia to take on Don Bradman's men. Britain chugged along, victorious in the war but a country subjected to serious post-war rationing, focused on job security and housing. One of Hammond's promises to his men was 'the best six months of their lives' without the tethers of rationing. The English cricketers not only gorged themselves in Australia, they also had food packets sent home to their families.

Besides, India's economic importance had greatly reduced after the war. As Leo Amery expressed it to the Cabinet, 'In surrendering control from here, we should not be sacrificing anything that mattered.'

On top of that, there was a severe shortage of money. In July 1946, even as Hazare scored 244 not out against Yorkshire at Sheffield, John Maynard Keynes finally persuaded the American Congress to approve a $3.75 billion loan. A year earlier, when the Lend Lease agreed by the US in 1941 had ended, Keynes had described it as 'a financial Dunkirk.'

The Colonial Office was facing serious questions from Keynes, Aaron Emanuel, and other trained economists – a jarring experience for Imperialist mindsets brought up on fanciful illusions.

The die was cast. Lord Mountbatten of Burma – dashing, confident and handsome, cousin of the King himself – went up the steps of Lutyens' Palace, accompanied by his lovely wife Edwina. Soon he had insisted on and obtained plenipotentiary powers. He cabled, 'The only conclusion that I have been able to come to is that unless I act quickly I may well find the real beginnings of a civil war on my hands.'

His cousin was perhaps not so keenly aware of the situation. In his January 1947 speech, King George VI made no mention of Indian independence knocking on the door. Instead, he insisted that the Commonwealth and Empire had not been disrupted by the stress and peril of war.

In mid-February 1947, Fazal Mahmood bowled quickly and effectively for North Zone to capture 4-64 and 2-43 against South Zone at the Brabourne Stadium. For good measure, he hit an unbeaten 100 as well – his only first-class century. Captain Lala Amarnath was impressed. Soon Fazal would be on his way to join the Indian camp in Poona, preparing for the series in Australia.

The day after the match ended at the Brabourne, on 20 February 1947, Attlee stood up in the Commons to announce that Mountbatten would leave India in June 1948 and that was the deadline for independence. Seated in the Parliamentary Gallery that day was Enoch Powell, then a member of the Conservative Research Department. Less than a decade before he had marvelled at the expanse of the Empire. Now he was left in a state of shock. 'I walked the streets all that night. The world as I had known it was coming apart. Occasionally I say down in a doorway, my head in my hands.'

All that remained now was the task of drawing a couple of lines. A couple of lines through Punjab and Bengal that would determine what would remain India and what would become Pakistan. The person entrusted with slicing up the land in this way was a lawyer and king's counsel, who had never been east of Paris. Arriving in July, he had just about a month to mutilate the map of India.

It was hate at first sight. Sir Cyril Radcliffe, chairman of the Boundary Commission, did not enjoy India or Indians. He hated the experience so much that he sat cooped up in a house in the Viceregal estate, not even venturing out in Delhi, let alone going to the borders. His diary reveals that he detested every minute he spent in the land. He complained of the heat, the dust, the mosquitoes, his bouts of diarrhoea.

'He had commissioners, mostly Indian High Court judges, sitting simultaneously in Calcutta and Lahore. As he could not sit with both groups, he sat with neither,' summed up journalist and historian Brian Lapping.

The lines were nevertheless drawn, and Radcliffe hastened back to England. Beyond the reach of heat, dust, diarrhoea and mosquitoes, he insisted that the values of peace, order and justice were what British rule was all about. He declared the £3,000 fee because of the rather murky results of his hurried cartographic expedition. Nevertheless, he was awarded the Knight of the Grand Cross of the Order of the British Empire.

Some three decades later, sitting in the comfort of his country house in Warwickshire, he said he was still horrified by the results of his work.

What were the results? The hastily marked lines meant that during the course of the next four years, even as India gained independence and Pakistan came into being, 14.5 million people had to uproot their homes and lives, and set them up anew thousands of miles away. The Partition, a morbid chapter in the history of the subcontinent, led to massive riots, pillage, rape, absolute loss of property and the death of more than a million people.

Poor Fazal Mahmood turned up in Poona for the training camp, eyeing the tour of Australia with the Indian team. By the time it ended, communal violence was sweeping across the nation. Fazal's autobiography reports that while returning from Poona to Bombay, he was about to be lynched by rioters on the train when C.K. Nayudu stepped in, defending the young fast bowler with his trusted willow. According to an interview given in 2004, Fazal found out he could not go to Lahore via Delhi. He was warned that he would be killed if he did that. 'Another passenger gave me his ticket and that is how I could travel to Karachi.' Fazal could have become the first genuine fast bowler from India since Mohammad Nissar. Instead, he became the first of many fast-bowling greats produced by Pakistan.

The riots, killings and devastation in the aftermath of the transfer of power – along with a life expectancy of 31 and a 12 per cent literacy rate in lieu of the progress and improvement promised by Queen Victoria in 1858 – did not take long to be rationalised.

King George VI, no longer Emperor of India, sent his stilted greetings. But his mother Queen Mary noted in her journal, 'The first time Bertie wrote me a letter with the I for Emperor of India left out. Very sad.'

Mountbatten claimed it was a parting among friends. Many international newspapers reported Indian and Pakistani independence alongside photographs of Mountbatten and British officials applauding the raising of new flags. Mountbatten had all British flags removed in advance, thus avoiding embarrassing images of newly independent peoples cheering as they were pulled down.

In November 1947, on a visit to London, he pointed out that in all the trouble spots in India not more than 10 or 12 million people, or some 3 per cent of the population, could have been involved. The remaining 97 per cent were living in peace and quiet. In 1968, in the Nehru Memorial Lecture at Cambridge, Earl Mountbatten of Burma recounted, 'What I did in India in 1947 was one of the three most important events in the world in this century, equalled in significance only by the Russian revolution of 1917 and the Chinese Communist takeover of 1949.'

The British press, and eventually books, congratulated the government on a 'dignified transfer of power'. Hindus and Muslims were killing each other due to the Partition, but had they not always said that the Indian people would kill each other if the British left? When has one ever seen civilised Western societies killing each other, asked many British people while busy stubbing out the embers of the Second World War.

By the 1960s and 1970s, the withdrawal from the Empire had become mythologised into a particularly graceful and skilful British triumph. The spurious idea of the Commonwealth had now been extended to maintain a virtual façade of continuity.

In his 1954 book, *The Transfer of Power in India*, E.W.R. Lumby wrote, 'Britain can claim credit for the near miracle whereby the achievement of independence by India and Pakistan was effected without their departure from the Commonwealth … Time has shown that the Commonwealth membership of India and Pakistan is more than a constitutional device with a significance limited to the immediate situation. It is rather a phenomenon whose importance is unquestionably immense, though difficult to describe or assess.' Lumby's words curiously read like glorification of a batsman with a batting average of 28 by pointing at some vague, undisclosed beyond-the-numbers significance.

Even in 1989, talking to the historian Peter Hennessy, one close adviser of the Queen remarked, 'The Commonwealth is the most civilised method yet devised for the dismembering of an Empire.'

38

PLAY UP, PLAY THE GAME

UNDER THE iconic gasometers of The Oval, the Indians are seen in action on a Sunday for the first time on the tour.

The glory days of the 1950s, when Surrey won everything in sight, are long gone. There is no Peter May scoring tons of runs, no Bedser, Loader, Laker, Lock skittling out opponent after opponent. However, after sliding down to the bottom of the table in 1968, Surrey have made a rather remarkable recovery in the past two seasons. In the 1971 summer, they will end up winning the County Championship.

Skipper Micky Stewart is the link between the generations. The batting banks heavily on Edrich. Although not really the powerhouse of the old days, with Geoff Arnold, Bob Willis and Pat Pocock the bowling is decent. After this season, Willis will move to Warwickshire. Two Pakistanis, Younis Ahmed and Intikhab Alam, bolster the side. On this day, Younis hits 52, Intikhab 55. The highest score is Graham Roope's 60. According to Wadekar, who floors a sharp chance from him off Bedi, Roope is an excellent all-rounder in the making.

Prasanna, not yet fully fit after his flu, bowls all over the place. Younis lofts him for six; Roope, using his long reach to hit down the ground, thumps him for another.

It is a remarkable performance from Bedi on that easy-paced Oval wicket. Albeit helped by Surrey batsmen intent on quick scoring, his 7-111 from 37 overs is quite an effort. In contrast,

Prasanna goes for 89 in his 32 overs, wicketless until Pocock gives him the charge. Surrey's 269 is a decent, if not formidable, total.

With Gavaskar rested, it is Mankad and Jayantilal who open the innings and crawl their way to 28 in the one and a half hours that remain. The sparse Saturday afternoon crowd gathered at The Oval make their disgust apparent through prolonged slow clapping.

* * *

The good news for India came from elsewhere. At Hove, Snow had just run through the Middlesex innings with a devastating 5-34. Just after that, he received a call from Bedser informing him that he was being left out of the England side for the second Test. (Snow adds that Bedser told him that it was a direct order from above, and that his own answer was 'If you are sending messages one way you can send a message back. Tell them they can stuff themselves.')

In any case, Bedser issued a press release. 'Snow was not considered for this match for disciplinary reasons. My committee and I intend to ensure to the best of our ability that the game of cricket is conducted at all times in the right manner.'

Arlott did not seem happy with the development, 'His apology had been accepted by both Gavaskar and the Indian manager who described the matter as closed. Now, however, it seems that it is to be dragged on indefinitely so that what seemed no more than a storm in a teacup is to be allowed to boil over, to the damage of the English cricket team.'

He added, 'Snow is not by any means the first, and he is unlikely to be the last, fast bowler to burst out in anger or violence in word or action on a cricket field. Fast bowlers are fundamentally aggressive people, otherwise they would not be fast bowlers.'

Illingworth himself was rather miffed. A chapter in his 1980 autobiography is titled 'Big Bad John and Little Sunny'. In it he writes, 'It was just too daft for words for anyone to look upon it as a physical attack by one player on another. Snowy took a lot of good-natured stick about "picking on someone his own size", and in the normal course of a Test match evening he and Gavaskar were in the middle of a group of players with the light-hearted back-chat still going on. But we all reckoned without the reaction of officialdom.'

There was more cheery news for India from up north in Bradford. As bad light held up play in the John Players League match between Yorkshire and Essex, and everyone scrambled to see what that meant according to the rulebooks, Boycott hobbled out of the ground with a strained hamstring. The match was resumed and Essex went on to register an easy victory. Boycott did not take the field when on the following day Yorkshire resumed their Roses match against Lancashire at Sheffield.

That Sunday John Snow hit out at the English selectors. 'I would have thought it had finished there. I was wrong in my action. Nobody in the field at that time was shocked by it. Only, it appears, people sitting on the sidelines. Though I read suggestions I could be dropped, I am surprised and disappointed. I think it is ridiculous. I fail to understand what exactly is being proved over something that happened in a flash as the game reached a climax.'

Woodcock however, was, sanctimoniously dismissive of the fast bowler's reactions in an article underlining that the game should continue to mean in 'sporting terms' what it always has. That the title of the article was the Newboltian 'Play up and Play the Game' hinted at the steadfast Warner-Cardusian refusal to acknowledge the real past of the game filled to the brim with deviousness and skulduggery.

A similar history-oblivious view, laced with it's-not-cricket mythology, was offered by Michael Melford in *The Sunday Times*. 'It was the English who taught the Indians cricket. It would appear that now the Indians can give a lesson in cricket manners to the English.'

Snow sulked off and expressed himself in his curious attempts at verse that looked like poetry when viewed from a distance:

Standing on a still summer's day,
eye watching swallows

earth–hugging insect–chasing way,
wondering what to do,
knowing that it always happens
and now it's happened to you.

* * *

On the following morning, Mankad and Jayantilal bat unseparated for an hour and 20 minutes. They produce the highest opening stand for the Indians on the tour so far. Mankad, perhaps plagued by the barracking, opens up with a spate of boundaries before losing his wicket for 77. His place in the second Test is now secure.

Geoff Arnold, recalled to the England side after the axing of Snow, now proceeds to castle Wadekar and Sardesai in quick succession. He is loudly cheered by the Surrey supporters for his efforts. At the other end, Jayantilal's glacial approach continues. Perhaps smarting from a highest score of 9 in his previous six innings, he stonewalls his way to 50 in 205 minutes. A brief injection of intent sees him move at a faster pace to 84 before being run out – a knock that consumes 245 minutes and practically squeezes any chance of a result out of the equation.

By the end of the day, the Indians still trail by 12 runs with five wickets in hand. In the *Daily Telegraph* John Mason calls Jayantilal an enigma, while *The Times* leads with the headline 'Jayantilal in no hurry to get runs'.

* * *

That same Sunday afternoon, 27-year-old Mohiuddin Ahmed, a second secretary at the Pakistan High Commission in London, stood in front of 10,000 Bengalis in Trafalgar Square, said that he had decided to give up his job and offered his services to the Bangladesh mission in London. The previous year, Mohiuddin had helped arrange President Yahya Khan's stay at Claridge's.

Ahmed, who still had family in East Pakistan, refused to name his home town since he believed it could put his brother, sisters and father in danger.

At the same rally, British Labour MP John Stonehouse, who had visited the refugee camps in India, said that the situation in East Bengal was the worst man-made disaster since the Second World War.

'I sure heard of that,' says Chitta. 'Discussions were rife. A couple of friends even saw Mohiuddin Ahmed as he spoke at Trafalgar Square.'

Chitta smiles at my next question. 'You know, the normal British folks sort of stitched together the news reports and formed a picture of the problems. You cannot blame them. Very few of the Indians or Pakistanis or Bangladeshis back home had a realistic idea of what took place in England. Yes, some of them did say – we told you we would kill each other if you left. Not all, mind you.'

In New York, Abhulmaal Muhith, economic counsellor at the Pakistan embassy in Washington, dissociated himself from his government due to the situation in East Bengal.

And on that afternoon and that evening in the same Big Apple, Indian sitar maestro Ravi Shankar and Beatles guitarist George Harrison teamed up at Madison Square Garden for the Concert for Bangladesh. Held at 2:30pm and again at 8pm, the programme also featured Ringo Starr, Bob Dylan, Eric Clapton, Ali Akbar Khan, Billy Preston, Leon Russell and the band Badfinger.

Ravi Shankar and Ali Akbar Khan opened with a sitar-sarod duet called the *Bangla Dhun*. 'We are artistes. But through our music we would like you to feel the agony, pain and a lot of sad happenings in Bangladesh, and also refugees who have come to India.' George Harrison's closing composition was named *Bangladesh*.

The concert raised close to $250,000 and that sum went for relief work in East Pakistan through UNICEF.

* * *

The final day at The Oval is largely listless. India bat on to register 326/8 before declaring. And Surrey, with little left to play for, bat through the rest of the day.

Prasanna, regaining some form, bowls much better than in the first innings, and is rewarded as batsmen keep going for their strokes. Edrich is brilliantly caught off his bowling by Wadekar. But after that, there is mostly desultory cricket, with everyone but Viswanath and wicketkeeper Krishnamurthy merely turning their arms over.

Surrey end on 257/4, Prasanna picking up all the wickets. However, he has not done enough to dislodge one of the other three tweakers in the Indian side.

* * *

That same day, the Cricket Council decided that the MCC tour of India, Pakistan and Ceylon, slated for the winter of 1971/72, would have to be postponed given the volatile situation in that part of the world. The cricket authorities of the two warring countries, and also of Ceylon, would now be approached with the proposal to rearrange the tour for 1972/73.

At Folkestone, an Indian family was held on suspicion of being illegal immigrants for more than an hour as they got off the boat. The Jouhls, with family friend Jagir Singh, were returning to their home in Smethwick, Staffordshire, after a holiday in Switzerland.

In Washington, 15 East Pakistani Bengalis, including seven senior diplomats, resigned from the Pakistan embassy and the Pakistan mission to the United Nations. They all asked for political asylum in the United States

As the Indians left The Oval that evening, in *The Guardian*, Michael Parkin worked on a piece about how the Immigration Appeals Act harked back to the old British Raj. The discrepancies in the stories separately told by the husband and his alleged wife supposedly reminded the ex-district magistrates of British India of court cases over ownership of goats. 'Looked at in Western terms, it seems incredible that a man and wife should not be able to corroborate each other on such details, but the adjudicator at the appeal hearing is often dealing with an illiterate man from an Asian peasant culture in which timeless village life flows gently by with no need for such bureaucratic nonsense as birth and marriage certificates.'

Surrey v Indians, The Oval – 31 July, 1, 2 August
Surrey 269 (Roope 60, Intikhab 55, Younis 52; Bedi 7-111) and 257/4 (Storey 70*, Roope 56*, Stewart 45; Prasanna 4-69) drew with **Indians** 326/8 dec (Jayantilal 84, Mankad 77; Willis 3-75).

39

FOR GOD'S SAKE DON'T SEND ME

OF THE great Surrey side of the 1950s, men like May, Bedser and Loader, never toured India as cricketers. The teams sent to the country remained less than first-string for more than three decades after the Second World War. The spin-twins Lock and Laker, however, did visit the land; but like long-lost twins of Indian celluloid melodramas, their visits were separated by 11 years.

Laker never played a Test in India. He went there as part of the Commonwealth side of 1950/51. And Lock toured with Ted Dexter's side in 1961/62, already past his best and struggling after the second remodelling of his action.

By the time Laker visited, India had become a republic. Along with independence and Partition, India and Pakistan had become the first self-governing non-white dominions. According to the Indians, this allegiance to the British was a temporary measure before the constitution was drafted. The plan was to leave the Commonwealth once they became a republic. There was little intention of acknowledging the British King as some sort of a curious virtual head.

Most British politicians, on the other hand, were eager to see India in the Commonwealth. This had only partly to do with the continuing illusion of the Empire, although that idea persisted in the more Conservative minds still lost in the late Victorian era. Churchill, for example, suggested India could, in the style of republics in the Roman Empire, remain a republic within the Commonwealth and still accept the King. There were even suggestions that the King could be appointed as the president of India while the country was run by Nehru, the prime minister. However, even the much more realistic Attlee was of the opinion that it was of vital importance that India remained friendly. His idea was in the context of 'the very real threat of Communist encroachment in South-East Asia'. Attlee even went to the extent of stating that there was nothing inherently impossible in a republic forming part of a monarchy.

Six months into independence, the Mahatma was assassinated by a Hindu nationalist. The main grievance of Nathuram Godse and his ilk was that the father of the nation was overly sympathetic to the cause of the Muslims, especially during and after the Partition.

India staggered, as can be imagined, but Gandhi was already 78 and increasingly marginal on the Indian political scene. With Nehru at the helm and Vallabhbhai Patel as his deputy, steps were taken towards the establishment of a new nation. It was Patel, the Ironman of India as he was called, who was instrumental in absorbing the 675 princely states into the nation (some opting for Pakistan). When the incredibly powerful Nizam of Hyderabad held out, the Indian army marched in to force his hand in September 1948.

It was over the issue of the Commonwealth that Nehru and Patel did not see eye to eye. The political merit appealed to Nehru, while the cabinet severely opposed it. Meanwhile, in April 1949, the fourth Commonwealth Prime Ministers' Conference in London found a way for India to remain in the mix.

'While intending to be a republic India accepts the King as the symbol of the free association of independent member nations and as such the Head of the Commonwealth. But [while doing so], she will no longer owe allegiance to the Crown. The King would cease to have any constitutional function in India. He would cease to be King of India as he was under the Dominion constitution. Under the constitution being drafted the head of the State would be the president, who would replace Mr Rajagopalachari, the Governor-General appointed by the King in succession to Lord Mountbatten. The basis of the membership of the other Commonwealth countries remains unchanged.'

With this insufferable tinkering and badinage of words, it was made possible for India to remain within the Commonwealth.

Twenty-two yards and two yardsticks

It is interesting to look at what took place 11 years down the line.

On 31 May 1961, South Africa became a republic, and unlike India it severed its ties with the Commonwealth. The Afrikaner National Party had no intention of maintaining British ties.

According to Rule 5 of the ICC regulations, the membership of an organisation would cease if a country was no longer part of the British Commonwealth. There could no longer be official Test matches contested by the country. The same rule that had threatened India now reared its head against South Africa.

The South African Cricket Association requested a change in the ICC regulations. This was met with a resolution to defer the decision for a year. A vote was taken in which England, Australia and New Zealand were pitted against the non-white country boards – West Indies, India and Pakistan. The verdict was split along colour lines. The decision was to continue existing relations unofficially, the Test matches were to be decreed unofficial.

However, the white countries, Australia, England and New Zealand, continued to consider the representative matches played against South Africa as regular Test matches. C.O. Medworth of the *Natal Mercury* even condemned the cricket boards of West Indies, India, and Pakistan for 'allowing politics to encroach on the noble game of cricket'.

The ICC was monitoring Indian political developments closely. By leaving the Commonwealth, India was liable to be stripped of membership, thus losing their Test status. With Nehru ensuring membership in the Commonwealth, the danger was averted. On 26 January 1950, India became a republic. Dr Rajendra Prasad took oath as the first president. After being made a provisional member in the 1948 ICC conference, the country was reinstated as a full member when the committee met in June 1950.

There were other cricketing ripples that underlined just how important India's inclusion in the Commonwealth was from a diplomatic point of view.

The 1948 ICC meeting had also come up with another important conclusion. Post-war English cricket was giving cause for concern. Due to the loss of young lives during the conflict, a new generation of cricketers had been lost. Also, the post-war era was one of rationing, full employment and higher wages, none of these developments quite compatible with the pursuit of cricket as a sport. Mandatory national service was also a hurdle. MCC teams, which had done much to promote the game between the wars by touring multiple countries, were advised to engage in less frequent touring assignments.

What that meant was India was left with no tours to or from England for the next few years. In fact, a proposed tour of 1948/49 was cancelled, and the BCCI turned to former England and Lancashire wicketkeeper George Duckworth to arrange for the first Commonwealth team to visit India in 1949/50. It was a rather good side that turned up, with Frank Worrell, Bill Alley, Cec Pepper, George Tribe and others among them.

The following winter, Duckworth arranged for fellow wicketkeeper and ex-England star Les Ames to take a second Commonwealth side to India. This was an even better team. Apart from Ames, the side had men such as Worrell, Sonny Ramadhin, Bruce Dooland, Derek Shackleton, Harold Gimblett and, of course, Laker. Former Lancashire and England batsman Eddie Paynter, coaching in Bombay, helped the team out in a couple of matches.

However, when it was confirmed that India would remain in the Commonwealth, not only did the ICC push India to full-member status, they also fiddled around with their future tour schedules. Suddenly, India was to be visited by a touring MCC side on an official Test tour in 1951/52. And immediately after that, in the summer of 1952, India would play England in England. The two sides had not played any series longer than three Tests before this, and suddenly they were playing nine within the course of a few months.

Rebuff of the brown-sahibs

It is not only that England were eager to play India as a triumph of cricket-diplomacy. It was thoroughly reciprocated by the Indians.

In January 1951, Rashid Varachia, the secretary of the non-white South African Cricket Board of Control (SACBOC), visited India on an ambitious project. In Madras, he met Anthony de Mello, the president of the BCCI. The goal was to arrange an Indian tour to South Africa to play the non-white sides. The idea was to leverage the historic Indian connections to Natal and the scathing attacks on segregation and apartheid that the Indian politicians had constantly voiced. A non-white team playing non-white South African sides would not violate apartheid legislature and would provide incredible exposure to the non-white cricketers in that troubled land. SACBOC offered to cover all the expenses.

De Mello was non-committal. He said he would have to consult with the Indian government.

Varachia next approached K.R. Collector, the secretary of the Cricket Board of Pakistan.

Ultimately, neither of the proposed tours materialised. India was committed to the schedules mandated by the Imperial Cricket Conference, and SACBOC did not have membership in the official international body, which would have definitely complicated matters.

And while Pakistan was not bound by any such terms when Varachia approached them, they received Test status in 1952, which readjusted the priorities for them.

The enormity of the decision cannot be understated. To fit the Indian tour in, England pushed back the Ashes by a year. Lindsay Hassett's men arrived in England in 1953, a full five years after Don Bradman's Invincibles of 1948.

It was thus a republic into which Laker arrived to play in 1950/51. However, the fanfare, hospitality and even the people involved continued along the same lines as the pre-war tours. Perhaps what had changed – and that was a temporary change as far as India was concerned – was the difficulty in procuring alcohol in Bombay due to prohibition. Eddie Paynter's lemonade-shandy did not quite cut it as substitute.

While Lord Harris had entertained the English cricketers as governor of Bombay in 1893, he had not taken the field against them. It is somewhat of a surprise, given that 18 years later, at the age of 60, he had played for Kent against the 1911 All-India team and had managed to score 36. Perhaps the heat of Bombay and the weight of his portfolio had kept him from getting into his flannels.

Curiously, no such reservation held back the governor of Bombay in 1950, Raja Maharaj Singh. Hailing from the Kapurthala royal family, he had been educated at Harrow and Balliol College, Oxford and was called to the Bar by the Middle Temple in 1902. By the time he made his first-class debut against the Commonwealth team he was 72. He captained the Bombay Governor's XI and walked out to bat at No.9, by far the oldest player to play at this level, and by even more substantial distance the oldest debutant ever. With his aide-de-camp, the classy Indian Test batsman Rusi Modi, as his runner, the venerable batsman got off the mark by edging Laker for 3. He managed another single before Laker got him caught at slip. The 44-year difference between the ages of the batsman and bowler involved in a dismissal was another world record set by the brave old man on that day.

In the defence fund match of 1963/64, the 68-year-old C.K. Nayudu was dismissed by the 22-year-old Ajit Wadekar, thus bettering the incredible feat.

Raja Maharaj Singh took no further part in the game and the scorecard registered absent ill against his name in the second innings. The regal leadership in the match continued in the form of the Maharaja of Patiala.

The Maharaja of Patiala also entertained the visiting cricketers at his palace, just as he had done with many touring sides before. The players stayed at the guest house and were intrigued to see the Maharaja's side reinforced by Test cricketers such as Mushtaq Ali, Shute Banerjee and others. They were treated to an exhibition game of hockey on roller skates. They watched elephants pull the roller and were entertained by the spectacle of the Maharaja himself walking out to bat in his colourful turban.

Of course, there was hunting as well, with the players being taken on an all-night shoot in thick jungle country, riding in sturdy jeeps – although the bags were not as impressive as that of a Lionel Tennyson or a Prince of Wales.

Alongside the luxury and the banquets, there were sketchy hotels in the smaller towns, where monkeys ran in and out of rooms, birds nested in the fanlights and mosquitoes dive-bombed through the gaping holes in the mosquito-nets. There were long train rides, fraught somewhat with the anxiety produced by reports of recent attacks on travelling Europeans. There was even a kite that swooped down and picked up a huge rat from the good-length spot at Poona. In fact, the kites were so numerous that Ramadhin became quite adept with the catapult.

'On looking back,' writes Laker. 'This trip was a remarkable experience, but one I hope never to repeat.' Laker returned home early with sinus trouble.

It was a difficult tour for the Commonwealth side as far as some hotels and logistics were concerned. But at the same time, much of their travel was done by air while the Indian players had to make do with train journeys. The accommodation was also of a different standard. In Kanpur, for example, the visitors were put up in a comfortable private hotel, whereas the Indians stayed in a shabby guest house with bad food and inadequate blankets.

It was a country of contrasts, not something one got used to in a hurry if one had not been familiar. The efforts of the Indian administrators in providing way better facilities to the tourists did not really stop the familiar lament:

Send out the MCC to India,
Send out your bowlers and your batsmen,
Send out your gallant wicketkeepers,
And don't forget to take your spurs and spats.
Send out the boys of the MCC,
Who made old England free,
Send out Sir Pelham, Rait Kerr and Gubby Allen,
But for God's sake don't send me.

40

MOST SILENT DAY OF CRICKET

BOYCOTT'S HAMSTRING does not heal in time. With Snow already axed, it means England go into the second Test without their premier batsman and premier bowler. However, when the teams reach Old Trafford on the eve of the Test, the characteristic Manchester rain converts groundsman Bert Flack's traditional easy-paced wicket into a threatening one with a green tinge.

Arlott laments that England lack the killer touch, connecting that even on this wicket and without a pace attack of any sort, the Indians can end up a better attack because of their high-quality spinners. Others are more realistic. While Woodcock writes that the cold and wet conditions will be difficult for the Indians, his lament is the meagre interest in the Test while just the previous week the Gillette Cup semi-final has seen wild enthusiasm. Laker suggests that it will be 'idiotic' to predict anything other than an English victory, adding that any two of the trio of John Price, Peter Lever and Geoff Arnold will be sufficient to test the Indians in such seam-friendly conditions.

In the end, England go in with Price and the local lad Lever. Jameson, riding on his excellent form, comes in for Boycott. Fletcher replaces Amiss. The Indians have kept Prasanna and Jayantilal in their 13, based on their performances in the last match. According to Woodcock, 'Jayantilal is on the list after an infinitely tedious innings of 84 against Surrey.' But predictably they go in with an unchanged side.

Illingworth has some pondering to do on winning the toss. The sky is overcast, the cold biting and the wicket green. Should he let loose his trio of seamers? Or should he set forth his batsmen against a spin-based attack while gripping the ball is likely to be difficult?

He goes with the more conventional move. Abid's figures on the tour read 4-461 until now. In the first session he doubles his wicket count.

Jameson starts confidently enough, with a tad more caution than he generally shows in county matches. With Luckhurst rather sluggish, the Bombay-born man pulls ahead. But at 21 he slashes at a near long hop from Abid straight to Gavaskar at cover point. In the same over, Edrich offers a tentative bat and the ball swings just about enough to take the edge through to Engineer.

Fletcher falls in Abid's next over, playing across the line to a ball too full and struck plumb in front – 25/3.

At the other end, Solkar is giving nothing away. Luckhurst, who has crawled to 7, now nudges him down the leg side. At leg slip the ball goes at knee-height into Venkat's hands and out again. Solkar also beats D'Oliveira twice. The ball is wobbling around.

Solkar is taken off after 10 overs for 16. With Chandrasekhar on, D'Oliveira strikes the ball with obvious relief, getting a four and a three off the over. But off the first delivery of the next Abid over, he drives at an outswinger and Gavaskar holds him low down at second slip.

Peter Laker writes, 'This stubby gent with the Errol Flynn-type moustache and belaboured approach to the wicket whipped out England's first four batsmen for 15 runs in 67 balls.'

At lunch, England are still reeling on 53/4, Luckhurst having managed just 13 from 92 balls in the two hours. Abid 14-4-19-4.

That is reason enough to question the selection of the Indian side. According to Govindraj, 'The wicket in Manchester was absolutely green. Keith Miller, who was working in the media at that time, and wrote that if India did not play Govindraj on the Manchester wicket, they would never be able to produce fast bowlers. But the reliance on spinners was too great.'

According to Miller, hints have been dropped to make the Indians think in terms of such a move. But Govindraj is not even included in the 13. True, he has not done much on the tour to stake his claim, but with steady drizzle from the moment the train with the Indian cricketers pulled into Manchester Piccadilly, the thinking could have been a bit more proactive. All through the Test, the spinners will struggle with the slippery ball.

* * *

That day, in Rawalpindi, the Pakistan government published their own version of the events that had led to the virtual civil war. A white paper asserted that the nationalist Awami League in East Pakistan killed 100,000 men, women and children until the Pakistan army restored control.

In Delhi, the Indian economy felt the first real impact of seven million Bengali refugees when the Government asked parliament for a supplementary budget grant of £110 million to feed and accommodate the displaced persons.

* * *

It is Knott who breaks the shackles after lunch, hitting a couple of boundaries and overtaking Luckhurst in spite of a two-hour handicap. The conditions are easier, the ball older and Abid's magical powers of the morning seem on the wane. The score has reached 70. Luckhurst, having crawled to 16, now sweeps Venkat. The ball gains height fine on the leg side. Gavaskar scampers after it from backward short leg, but can only get his fingertips to it.

Abid is replaced by Bedi, the latter troubled by an upset stomach. Chandra errs in length once too often, pitching them too far up, quite a few resulting in full tosses. Slowly, Luckhurst starts to stroke the ball with confidence, while Knott thrives by sweeping, pulling and occasionally lofting the ball into the wide open spaces in the outfield.

Despite the relative acceleration, it is the 52nd over when the hundred comes up. The 6,000 people who sit scattered around the stands have very few reasons to make themselves heard.

Venkat, the most effective of the spinners, is brought back after seven overs from Bedi. With little help from the surface, he is pushing the balls through, keeping it tight. In the second over of his new spell, he bowls Knott with a well-concealed, tossed-up slower ball which hastens through between bat and pad. The gutsy wicketkeeper walks back for 41, having added 75 with Luckhurst.

With the England skipper at the wicket, Luckhurst produces a spate of boundaries, a square cut off Chandra getting him to his half-century.

The Indian leg-spinner thinks he has got Illingworth. At least all the Indians are convinced that he is caught at bat-pad by Solkar. However, umpire Tom Spencer thinks otherwise. 'This was the third time Illingworth had been given a second life by the umpires. I guess there are advantages of being an England captain in England,' Gavaskar will write in *Sunny Days*.

Chandra is not tight enough. His 18 overs till tea cost 53. Illingworth, having survived the scare, now slowly plays himself in. By the break Luckhurst is 71, the skipper 13, England 161/5.

After tea, Luckhurst does not stay long. After lifting Bedi for a boundary, he tries to bring off another lofted off-drive. The canny spinner holds it back. The sliced drive is skied to cover and Viswanath runs in from mid-off to hold a good catch: 168/6. The opener has consumed 215 balls for his 78, made over four-and-a-quarter hours.

Hutton drives hard a couple of times before Venkat beats him with his flight and anticipates well to move to his right to snap up the return catch.

Peter Lever joins his captain and play goes on in desultory fashion, the onus on survival. When 200 is raised, the spectators finally have something to cheer about and in the excitement some even run into the ground. This is followed by rain, bad light and a frustrating wait before the game resumes in the golden glow of the setting sun. As the Indian spinners struggle with the wet ball, Illingworth and Lever take the score to 219/7 by close of play. The captain unbeaten on 27, his partner 16. Illingworth's innings has used up 124 deliveries

'The most silent day's cricket I have ever seen,' writes Woodcock, 'And from England's point of view, one of the least distinguished.'

Arlott is a bit more generous, 'England pulled their innings ungracefully but determinedly from collapse to a semi respectable if uncertain uprightness.'

England v India, 2nd Test, Old Trafford – 5, 6, 7, 9, 10 August
England 219/7 (Luckhurst 78, Knott 41; Abid 4-35).

41

HOWARD AND HOWARD

TWENTY-ONE YEARS before India toured in 1971, Old Trafford had celebrated. The county had shared the top spot in the Championship table with Surrey. They had last won the Championship in 1934 and would not win again until 2011.

The captain during that 1950 season was Nigel Howard, a 25-year-old amateur, son of Major Rupert Howard. A major in the Royal Army Pay Corps, Rupert Howard had been the secretary of Lancashire since 1932 and had resigned his post at the end of 1950.

Nigel Howard was the only amateur who played regularly for Lancashire that season. In *The Manchester Guardian*, Denys Rowbotham had argued for a shift in attitude and the appointment of the seasoned professional Cyril Washbrook as captain. In the committee meeting, Donny Davies had argued Washbrook's cause. But, even in the post-war years not many were open to the idea. Howard was appointed captain by a 21-1 vote.

Not that surprising really. The previous year spectators at Lord's had been informed via loudspeaker that the scorecards had mistakenly printed 'F.J. Titmus' for 'Titmus, F.J.' – thereby committing the travesty of denoting a professional cricketer as an amateur. However, as the stalwart all-rounder later said, it was actually a sign of progress. They had after all come a long way from denoting the amateurs as Mr.

That season, Washbrook scored 1,526 runs at 42.38 with five hundreds. Howard got 930 at 23.84 with a highest of 79. But the latter led the side. Other than Washbrook, Geoff Edrich, Winston Place and Jack Ikin scored tons of runs, Roy Tattersall, Brian Statham, Malcolm Hilton and the others dismissed batsman after batsman. But it was Howard who flashed the victorious smile.

Each day on return from Old Trafford he sat with Major Howard and plotted the on-field strategy. As so often happens in cricket, we can never know for sure whether the father-son conversations had much to do with the county's eventual triumph. Amateur captaincy, and by extension the whole concept of captaincy in cricket, stands on such a fuzzy foothold.

With Freddie Brown planning to step down from England captaincy, it was Nigel Howard who led the Gentlemen against the Players at Lord's that summer. The Players, led by Denis Compton, won by 21 runs and Howard scored 1 and 0. But even before the season was over, he was appointed captain for the winter tour of India, Pakistan and Ceylon.

The Lancashire secretary, Major Rupert Howard's successor, was the young Londoner Geoffrey Howard. He was entrusted with managing the tour. *The Times* clarified, 'The two [captain and manager] are not related.'

It was not a trip many wanted to go on. The big names were absent. No Hutton, no Compton, no Bedser, no Washbrook, no Bailey, no Evans. Not one of the squad who had gone to Australia the previous season – apart from young Statham who had been sent down under as a reinforcement. Neither captain Howard nor vice-captain Donald Carr had ever come close to playing for England. There was a smattering of talent, with the classy Gloucestershire batsman Tom Graveney, Hutton's Yorkshire opening partner Frank Lowson, the cream of Lancashire bowling in Statham, Tattersall and Hilton. But ultimately it was way less than the best side.

For Geoffrey Howard it was rather less than a reward. Apart from the 16 players, there were two journalists who left from St Pancras Station for Tilbury Docks. There was no scorer, no baggageman, no masseur. As the train pulled away, MCC secretary Colonel Rait Kerr put his head into the first-class railway carriage and addressed the manager. 'Well, good luck, old boy. Rather you than me. I can't stand educated Indians.'

Less than 20 years before the Indian tour of 1971, the solid Kiplingesque traditions were as strong as ever.

Not that such an attitude was unexpected. Attlee's Labour government had established the welfare state, the NHS, committed to full employment, a mixed economy and recognition of trade unions, while juggling with a struggling pound. Now they had been voted out. With the Conservatives assuming power, at the age of 76 years and 330 days Churchill was back in the hot seat. With his solid Victorian world-view, he lamented Britain's decline as a great world power and was piqued with unwanted irritants such as the Malayan emergency and the Mau Mau rebellion. But his dreams rested on Britain's position in the triangulation point – cordiality with the United States, the continuing influence of Empire-Commonwealth and the European relationships.

Britain had lost India, and a few months later had given up Palestine. Burma, the rice bowl of the world, was also gone by 1948. However, complacency reigned supreme in all the places where the Union Jack fluttered away. As it did in Egypt, with 40,000 bored British soldiers stationed in Port Said. In 1951, a Royal Engineer found a report on his desk describing a traffic accident outside Cairo between a British army vehicle and a Rolls-Royce. 'Two wogs were inside, and their names were King Farouk and Ali Ismael.' When the officer admonished the driver, saying King Farouk should not be called a wog (once again Ornamentalism overriding racism), back came the retort: 'I asked them their names ... they were King Farouk and another wog called Ali Ismael.'

Of course, with such exemplary implementation of the values of peace, order and justice, the British government was aghast when, in October 1951, Egyptian Prime Minister Mustafa al-Nahhas announced unilateral abrogation of the 1936 Anglo-Egyptian Treaty and demanded British forces evacuate the Canal Zone. With the Middle East providing 70 per cent of the world's oil, this was obviously not playing the game in a gentlemanly

manner. Churchill thundered to his foreign secretary Anthony
Eden, 'Tell them if we have any more of their cheek we will set
the Jews on them and drive them into the gutter from which they
should have never emerged.'

The Egyptian situation would grow steadily worse as the
tour of Howard's men progressed. But since the end of the war,
a vision of a beneficent and regenerative Empire continued to
be presented through the BBC. At Christmas 1947 and again
in 1948, the Empire broadcasts had been soothing. The 1947
broadcast was read by Lawrence Olivier, to background music by
Benjamin Britten. In 1948, Robert Donat was heard on the radio.
King Solomon's Mines had hit the screens in 1950, *Kim* and *Soldiers
Three* in 1951. The Imperial Institute had mounted an exhibition
titled *Focus on Colonial Progress* as part of the Festival of Britain
in 1951. As many as 147,885 people attended the films screened
by the Imperial Institute.

Rait Kerr's reservations notwithstanding, Geoffrey Howard
would have been hard pressed to get by in India without the help
of Narayan Karmaker, the Indian board's liaison officer, and a
sterling representative of the educated Indians. The manager
enjoyed himself, absorbing the strange land, visiting Gandhi's
bungalow, the Golden Temple in Amritsar, climbing to Mussoorie
from Dehra Dun. 'The people were so delighted to see you. The
history was fascinating.'

Many of the players followed George Duckworth's advice to
Tom Graveney, 'Eat eggs and chips, because they've got to cook it.
Drink as much whisky as you can, because it kills the bugs. And
if you want to score any runs, don't get hit on the pads.' However,
there were some who could not abide by these rules and enjoy the
tour. Foremost among them was the captain.

The presence of monkeys, vultures and lizards was rather
upsetting. At Poona, Jaiko the Monkey, a local favourite, held
up play for a while. At Nagpur a cobra wriggled into the ground.
Nigel Howard kept worrying about his health. In his letters home,
the manager further confided, 'I was rather unsuccessfully trying
last night to persuade Nigel that true civilisation did not depend

on plumbing, wireless and motor cars!' It is rare for an English manager to echo near-Gandhian philosophy. The captain thought he was putting on an act.

India could have won the first Test had they not scored too slowly, Merchant and Hazare intent on breaking each other's record for the highest Test score by an Indian batsman. The second and third Tests were drawn with painstakingly defensive cricket. At Kanpur, India misread the pitch. The went in with two leg-spinners while Tattersall made the difference, and England took a 1-0 lead. And finally, at Madras, Mankad's 12-wicket haul and centuries by Polly Umrigar and Pankaj Roy saw them achieve their first ever win in Test cricket.

It had taken 25 Test matches and 20 years (albeit with a 10-year-gap in between), and had come against a rather ordinary side. But at long last Indian cricket had notched up a mark in the wins column.

That final Test at Madras was a gloomy affair with the news that King George VI had died. Rait Kerr called from Lord's asking the side to wear black armbands, and if possible not to play the following day. That remained the only communication between the MCC and the team during the tour. Some of the Indian cricketers sympathised, even telling the English cricketers that they had lost because they were mourning the monarch.

In spite of the troubles with the occasional fly, lizard and monkey – and a floating corpse as the team was out boating on the river – the visiting cricketers enjoyed much of the hospitality that marked every cricket tour to the land. Even as they marvelled at the squalor of the poor in the streets, the banquets were lavish and the entertainment extravagant. Many of their journeys were by air, although the air-conditioned compartments during their long train journeys were earmarked for the amateurs only.

At Hyderabad, they were entertained by the Nizam, no longer an independent ruler but still one of the richest men in the world. His exalted highness was dubbed his exhausted highness by the English cricketers on account of his incredible number of wives. It was at Hyderabad that they went on a shoot. Don

Brennan, the Yorkshire wicketkeeper, bagged a panther with his first shot.

Thus, many of the traditions – princes, hunts, banquets, second-string sides and monkeys running off with breakfast – continued during the 1951/52 tour.

Incidentally, 21 years down the line, after losing their first home series to India, England would once again send a less-than-full strength side to play in India, led by yet another debutant in Tony Lewis.

That same winter of 1951/52 saw India's first general election under universal adult suffrage. It involved an electorate of 176 million, unprecedented in the entire world. The newly independent nation moved straight to a one-person-one-vote system rather than phasing it in as their Western and, in most views, more advanced counterparts, who had for so long excluded the rights of the working class and women.

Mother India

The case of women makes for interesting reading. After years of the suffragette movement, that incidentally included the burning down of the pavilion at the Tunbridge Wells cricket ground, the United Kingdom finally permitted women over 30 to vote in 1920. The vote was opened to all adult women in 1928. Other European countries followed different timelines and in Switzerland women had to wait till February 1971. In contrast, India opened the polls to all adult women from the beginning. By the time Switzerland saw women voting, Indira Gandhi had been the prime minister for several years.

However, at the same time, in 1951 as many as 2.8 million women had to be struck from the electoral rolls because they were registered not by their own names but as X's mother or Y's wife.

The turnout was 45.7 per cent. It involved 224,000 polling booths, two million steel ballot boxes made of 82,000 tonnes of steel, 16,500 clerks appointed on six-month contracts, 380,000 reams of paper, 56,000 presiding officers, 280,000 helpers and 224,000 policemen.

What is more, in 1951, nurtured as the nation was for 200 years by the benevolence of British rule, 85 per cent of the population earmarked to use their voting rights could not read or write. Hence pictorial signs for political parties evolved as an inseparable part of the election process.

But the elections did take place. The Congress Party swept into power, winning 364 of the 489 seats. Jawaharlal Nehru became the first democratically elected prime minister; he would remain in office till his death in 1964.

42

AS DRY AS OLD TRAFFORD

THE NEWS of the imminent Delhi visit of Andrei Gromyko, the Soviet foreign minister, put the cat among anxious pigeons. This could only mean that the clouds of war that had closed in were about to release their ominous contents. Senior Indian diplomat D.P. Dhar visiting Moscow was equally intriguing for the many nations that watched from ringside. Especially the Nixon-Kissinger faction. Did Dhar carry a shopping list for arms? Or was he just looking for assurances of support? Or was it both?

* * *

At Old Trafford there are not too many such difficult questions posed by the Indian bowlers. Bedi, Chandra and Venkat try their best with a slippery ball, while Illingworth and Lever calmly add to their scores. There is one streaky boundary from llingworth's edge past a diving Wadekar off Venkat. But otherwise there is no alarm.

After 10 innocuous overs, Abid is brought back, warming up for the new ball. Illingworth swings his first delivery over fine leg for six.

With the conditions nowhere near as helpful as on the previous morning, the Indian new-ball duo are once again toothless . Lever milks the runs, Illingworth is way more positive today.

By the time lunch provides a welcome break for the Indians, and the threatening skies hint at additional respite, Illingworth is 97, Lever 65 and England are cruising along at 355/6.

It is a relief for the Indians when the gloom gives way to a strong drizzle and play is held up for almost an hour after the break. With the conditions wet and miserable, Wadekar goes back to his seamers on resumption. With a brace off Solkar, Illingworth completes his second Test hundred, a knock of immense value in the most critical of circumstances.

In 1936, at this very ground Walter Robins and Hedley Verity added 138 against India for the eighth wicket. Illingworth and Lever better that by 30 before the former drives at Venkat, hits the ground with a thud and the ball is caught by Gavaskar at slip. Perhaps not sure whether he has hit the ball into the ground, Illingworth waits for the decision. Engineer, rather uncharitably, informs him that the umpire has *finally* given him out.

As it starts raining again, tea is taken 18 minutes ahead of schedule with England on 380/8.

As rain holds up the resumption by a few minutes, the news comes in that BCCI President A.N. Ghose has voiced displeasure at the MCC's suggestion of putting off the 1971/72 tour by a year. 'I feel the tour must go on as normal conditions prevail in India.'

Once again it is the tale of a wet ball after a break. Wadekar calls on his seamers, and Solkar gets Gifford to edge to the keeper; 384/9, and Price walks in with Lever on 86.

Keen to rotate the strike and help Lever along to his hundred, Price pushes Abid to midwicket and takes off. Lever sends him back, and the No.11 tries to turn and slips in mid-pitch. Solkar is there, moving quickly, picking it up and sending in the return. Lever, having hardly made a mistake all day, remains unbeaten on 88. But 386 is a huge score considering that on the first morning England were 41/4.

It has been one of the more dismal performances by the spinners for a long time: Bedi 1-72, Chandra 0-90, only Venkat managing decent figures of 3-89.

Gavaskar and Mankad walk out in a rather tension-charged atmosphere, and see off the four overs bowled by the English bowlers before a storm harsher than the earlier ones brings a quick end to the proceedings. Given that they are eight without loss, the headline in *The Times* is rather premature, 'Languid Indians help England towards emphatic victory.' In Manchester at least, one should always keep the weather in mind.

England v India, 2nd Test, Old Trafford – 5, 6, 7, 9, 10 August
England 386 (Illingworth 107, Lever 88, Luckhurst 78, Knott 41; Abid 4-64, Venkat 3-89) **India** 8/0.

43

CROWN 11 – COLONIES 0

IT WAS supposedly at the bar at Old Trafford that Fred Trueman walked in, saw Adhikari and remarked, 'Hello, colonel, I'm pleased to see you've got your colour back.' There are multiple versions of the story, one told by as imaginative a narrator as Dickie Bird. The tour on which this meeting took place is also uncertain. Bird and some others say it was 1974 when Adhikari and Wadekar combined once again, this time with disastrous results. Some maintain it was said during the Old Trafford Test of the 1971 tour. There are naturally Indian parables in which, stung by the remark, Adhikari manages the team with a vengeance, inspiring the first Test win. Trueman himself denied the tale.

However, even today people recall the scary bowling of the Yorkshireman during the 1952 tour. The plight of the Indian batsmen, characterised by Umrigar and Adhikari, became folklore. Adhikari was struck on the mouth. The fiery Trueman charged in to bowl to Umrigar, one of the premier Indian batsmen ... the batsman moved towards square leg ... debutant Tony Lock quipped from leg-slip, 'I say, Polly, do you mind going back to your crease? I can't see the bowler.'

Umrigar scored 43 runs in the four Tests at an average of 6.14. Three times he was bowled by Trueman while backing away. Umrigar retired 10 years later as the then highest run-getter for India, with the most hundreds as well. A sterling career of 59 Tests amounting to 3,931 runs at 42.22 with 12 centuries. However, he never recovered from that dent in his reputation.

After that tour, Umrigar was remembered as an excellent batsman but for his weakness against genuine pace.

Ten years down the line, in his final series and penultimate Test, Umrigar faced West Indies at Port-of-Spain. He bowled 56 overs of off-breaks and cutters, capturing 5/107, Hunte and Kanhai among his victims. Then as India batted against a rampaging Wes Hall, he came in at 25/4 and struck 56. India followed on, and Umrigar batted four hours for a magnificent unbeaten 172 against Hall, Stayers, Gibbs, Worrell, Sobers and Rodriguez. As the hosts chased down a small target, he sent down 16 overs for 17 runs.

Was he suspect against fast bowling? Port-of-Spain is not really the fastest wicket in the world, but facing Hall and Stayers in their prime could be a handful. Yet, the impression had already been made. And it had been made in England. That is well-nigh impossible to unmake.

Mihir Bose argues in *A History of Indian Cricket* that Umrigar, very successful in the tour matches of 1952, was not really intimidated by fast bowling but by the image of Trueman – the wild fast bowler with a mane of unruly hair, staring him down and letting four-letter words fly. That may be true or partly true. What remains undeniable is that Umrigar's performance in Port-of-Spain in 1962 was at least as good as Mankad's heroics at Lord's in 1952. Yet, there was no Cardus, no Swanton, no Arlott writing odes to his deeds in the West Indies. Queen's Park Oval may be a way more picturesque ground, but it is far, far away from the Home of Cricket that Lord's insists on being.

So much of cricket history is skewed by the chroniclers and the setting, that more often than not cricketing perceptions end up lopsided.

To return to Umrigar, that 1962 West Indian tour was not the first one in which he set the islands on fire. Immediately following the 1952 visit to England, India toured the Caribbean in 1952/53.

It had not only been a pioneering tour in the cricketing sense. It had seen a reunion of a people. In Guiana and Trinidad, for the indentured Indian labourers who had settled down a century before, the arrival of cricketers from the land of their forefathers was an epochal event. It was history being made in all poignancy on the sporting field and beyond. The people of Indian origin in the West Indies were ecstatic, many of them emotional. A large percentage of them spoke an old version of Hindi and observed the same religious festivals and rituals as the visiting cricketers. In fact, they were perhaps a bit more committed in their observance because of the protected pocket in which the culture had been preserved for more than a century.

The Indian cricketers became madly popular in these communities and beyond. They not only had common roots, they came from a country that had been freed from white men. Many of the East Indians in Guiana and Trinidad ended up cheering for the visitors. An East India XI even took the field against the visitors.

And the Indian side played delightful cricket. The West Indians, with their three Ws, Ramadhin and Valentine, Gomez, Rae and Stollmeyer, were already a superb side. The Indians fought hard and the series ended 1-0 in favour of the hosts with four draws. Subhash Gupte took 27 wickets at 29, delighting one and all with his classy leg-spin. One such delighted spectator was Carol Goberdhan, a Trinidad girl of Indian ancestry. Gupte, perhaps the greatest leg-spinner produced by India, would marry her in 1957 and settle down in Trinidad in the early 1960s.

Throughout the tour the Indian fielding was a revelation. A decade down the line the credit for creating a culture of good fielding would be bestowed on Pataudi. However, on that tour men such as Gadkari, Gaekwad, Umrigar, Apte and Ghorpade prowled and chased in the outfield, cut off rasping strokes and sent in quick, fast returns.

And Polly Umrigar hit two hundreds in the Tests, amassing 560 runs at 62.22. Not many remember that. This incredible story of the Indian tour of West Indies 1952/53 also remains very sketchily remembered.

The centre of attraction of the cricket world at that moment was, of course, England. Lindsay Hassett's Australian side was about to arrive for the 1953 Ashes. There was the associated magical aura lent by the Coronation. With all this about to take place, the focus was not really on an off-beat Indian visit to West Indies.

Even historians of West Indian cricket such as Michael Manley or Tony Cozier do not dwell on this incredible social interaction of two people with common roots. Much like the 1921 visit of the Natal Indians to India, this tour has fallen off the annals of cricket history.

In *Beyond a Boundary*, his cricket-linked political fantasy, C.L.R. James did not really consider this experience of the Indian community in the Caribbean important enough to eclipse the considerable number of pages on Thackeray, Hughes and Arnold.

Chronicles of cricket, be they history or fantasy, can be very skewed due to partial retelling.

A banana-boat-ride away from Guiana and Trinidad, on 2 June 1953, the streets of London remained frenzied with excitement. Many had spent the previous night on the pavements to ensure they had a proper view of the Coronation procession. The rain could not dampen the mood as the young Queen waved to the massive gathering on her way to Westminster Abbey.

The Coronation was televised, from 10am to 11.30 at night. At the beginning of 1953, fewer than two million UK homes had a television. By Coronation Day, an additional 526,000 sets had been sold.

Serendipitously, on the same day, the magnificent news came through that Edmund Hillary and Tenzing Norgay had conquered the highest peak in the world. The Everest expedition, a Commonwealth venture – the mountain was scaled by a beekeeper from New Zealand and an Indian Sherpa guide of Nepali origin – was splashed in the papers as a 'British triumph'. 'Colonel John Hunt, a serving officer of the King's Royal Rifle Corps, led the British team of thirteen,' announced *The Guardian*. The three flags placed on the summit were of the United Nations, Nepal's unique non-quadrilateral national flag and the Union Jack. Between the three ensigns was a just-visible Indian tricolour.

Under the headline 'Symbol of British Endurance', *The Times* compared the expedition to Drake's voyage around the world and reported that Sidney Holland, the prime minister of New Zealand, in London for the Coronation, had hailed Hillary for becoming the 'the first Britisher to conquer the hitherto unconquerable Everest'. The *Daily Express* screamed, 'Be proud of Britain on this day,' adding that 'the old, defiant heart of the race remained unchanged.'

There was indeed a British hand in the Indian flag finding an obscure place on the summit. Prior to Partition, Tenzing Norgay had lived in Chitral, a princely state in the skirts of the Hindu Kush on the Pakistan side of the border between the Northern Areas and Afghanistan. He happened to be one of the seven million non-Muslims who had opted to leave Pakistan and make the journey into India. If he had not done so, there could have been a Pakistan flag out there. Sir Cyril Radcliffe's handiwork was omnipresent.

The rest of the 'British' claims remain somewhat curious.

On being crowned, the Queen told her subjects that like her Tudor forbear she ruled a country that was 'great in spirit and well endowed with men who were ready to encompass the earth … rich in material resources and richer still in the enterprise and courage of its peoples.'

The Coronation was celebrated across the globe, from Canada to Hong Kong, from Australia to South Africa. On the hottest evening of the year, five Commonwealth high commissioners in Delhi gave a reception attended by 1,200 guests, including the president of India. A 31-gun salute celebrated the event at noon in Karachi.

For the ceremony itself there was a gathering of international glitterati. From Nehru to Menzies, from the Prince of the Netherlands to the Sultan of Zanzibar … everyone was present to watch the archbishop proclaim Elizabeth Queen.

There was a difference, though. King George VI had been 'by the Grace of God of the United Kingdom of Great Britain and Northern Ireland and of the British Dominions beyond the Sea,

King, Defender of the Faith, Emperor of India.' His daughter was merely 'of the United Kingdom of Great Britain and Northern Ireland and of Her Other Realms and Territories, Queen, Head of Commonwealth, Defender of the Faith.'

Amidst all the fanfare of the season, Hutton's men provided the icing by winning the Ashes, the first time they had done so since Bodyline. The Coronation Ashes – four drawn Tests with a result in the fifth – have been recounted often enough in glorious terms. The pictures of Hutton on the balcony of The Oval, half-smoked cigarette in the fingers of one hand, acknowledging cheers with the other; the famed duo of Compton and Edrich running in through the throng of spectators after the winning hit; Brian Johnston's simple, emotion-tinged commentary, 'Is that the Ashes? Yes, England have won the Ashes.' … all these are images embossed in cricketing recollections.

These often give the impression that it was a dramatic series. Far from it. Two Tests were washed out by rain, one was spoilt in the end by amateur cricketer Trevor Bailey's negative bowling down the leg side; the decider was not really the most exciting of Test matches. The series had its moments, such as Willie Watson and Bailey saving the Lord's Test with a limpet-like display at the crease. But, once again, the literature and memories that survive – both padded to a great degree due to the majestic backdrop – underline the Anglo-Australian skew in the chronicling of cricket.

Eleven full-length books have been written about the 1953 Ashes. Rex Alston, John Arlott, Trevor Bailey, Sid Barnes, Norman Cutler, Jack Fingleton, Bruce Harris, Keith Miller with Dick Whitington, Jim Swanton, Peter West, Peter Wynne-Thomas with Peter Griffiths … all queued up to pen their accounts. Perhaps more will be written down the line.

Not one book has been written about the 1952/53 Indian tour of West Indies.

Again, both were five-Test series, which ended 1-0 in favour of the hosts.

In 1953, the first time since 1904, the Gentlemen won both the fixtures against the Players. Less than a year later, Oxford medical student Roger Bannister created history at the Iffley Road Track by breaking the four-minute mile barrier, completing the distance in 3:59.4. According to the historian Dominic Sandbrook, 'It seemed as though the old Corinthian character had been successfully revived.'

44

ANTIPATHY AND THE BARBER

LESS THAN a month before, at Headingley, Pakistan were 201/7, with 28 more to get, when Illingworth brought an end to a 14-over spell by Gifford and tossed the ball to Peter Lever. Having been taken off after just two overs, Lever ran in and picked up the last three wickets in a nine-ball spell. Illingworth and Gifford combined to bowl 60 overs in that innings, but the three overs and three balls by Lever proved match-winning. Curiously, he was dropped from the team for the next Test, at Lord's against the Indians.

Back in the side at Old Trafford, Lever already has the unbeaten 88 under his belt. Now he proceeds to enjoy his second successive day of success, which leads Ted Dexter to call him Peter the Great in his Sunday report.

Bowling with the wind behind him, he keeps the ball just short of a good length and swings it away, allowing the probing willows of the Indian batsmen to do the rest. At the other end, Price starts to make the ball fly. Gavaskar mistimes a hook terribly, and it flies over the third slip. Mankad looks anything but comfortable. The task before the Indians looks ominous.

A crisp on-driven boundary off Lever underlines the class of Gavaskar, but in the Lancashire bowler's following over Mankad nibbles at an outswinger. Knott flies across and clutches it with an outstretched right glove in front of the slips, and completes his 100th Test dismissal.

With Wadekar in, Price keeps buzzing short deliveries around his head, trying to induce the compulsive hook. But the skipper desists, bats on with an impassive air, happy with the occasional glances and nudges for singles. Meanwhile, Gavaskar is looking in control. Cautious against Price, when Hutton is brought on he essays a rasping square drive. He strikes another valuable blow for India when Gifford tries to stop his hook at backward square leg and breaks his thumb. 'My hand went numb as I fielded that ball,' the spinner says. 'I thought I had a bruise, but as life returned it became very painful. That looks to be it for the rest of the season.' A left-arm spinner cannot operate with a broken left thumb.

However, Illingworth is not too inconvenienced. The wicket demands pace, Price and Lever are kept on most of the day from the Stretford End, while Hutton and D'Oliveira generally do a good job of moving the ball from the other. The skipper himself does not bowl until after lunch.

The score has crossed 50, the first hour seen off, and the Indians are breathing more easily when Hutton gets Wadekar with a ball that moves away. England are on top once again. Sardesai looks a pale shadow of his glorious West Indian days as he scratches around, looking distinctly uncomfortable when Price is brought back and the length shortened again. Gavaskar is still going on nicely, clipping D'Oliveira to leg, driving Hutton through the covers. It is a tense morning, but at 72/2 the score does not look too bad when the players came off for lunch. Gavaskar, having done the bulk of the scoring, is on 45.

It is Illingworth who starts off after lunch, and Gavaskar straight drives him twice to get to his half-century. It has been a commendable knock, weathering the early barrage. However, the little man soon runs into problems as Price makes the ball fly from the other end, causing it to rear and leave the batsman. Gavaskar is beaten twice, rendered scoreless for a while, and then one ball rears up and moves away. The opening batsman leans back desperately to avoid it, but the bat is held high and the ball kisses it as it flies to Knott. Gavaskar out for 57, India 90/3.

The other little man of the Indian team takes Gavaskar's place, but scoring runs continue to be difficult. After a tense half-hour, Viswanath neatly places Lever for four to bring up the hundred. But in that same over the Lancastrian gets one to come back at great pace and sends Sardesai's off stump cartwheeling. In his next over, Viswanath is yorked. India stand at 104/5 in the 53rd over, a tale of morose struggle and a looming threat of following-on.

Once again the lower order comes to the rescue in the form of Solkar and Engineer. Having watched Solkar stonewall his way to safety at Lord's, many fear a similar approach in so desperate a situation. However, at Lord's it was an unpredictable pitch. Here, on a seaming but truer surface, it is Solkar who takes the initiative. Timing the ball sweetly from the start, he outscores Engineer, who holds his attacking instincts in check. Dropped off Price on 6, the flamboyant wicketkeeper is content to play second fiddle. Solkar's excellent driving through the off, against both Lever and Price, leads Dexter to wonder why he bats as low as No.7 in this shaky Indian line-up. He also goes on to suggest that Wadekar can open with Gavaskar, with Solkar coming in at No.3.

By tea, Solkar has stroked his way to 30, Engineer is on 17 and India look a lot healthier, but by no means out of danger, at 153/5.

It is Lever who strikes again after the break, but not in the unplayable manner that has seen him dismiss Sardesai and Viswanath. Engineer unleashes a fierce cut and Edrich holds on to the ball at gully. It is 163/6, and a run later, a leg-cutter from D'Oliveira removes the off bail of Abid. At 164/7, the target of 187 to avoid the follow-on is still 23 runs away with only the tail to come.

Venkat plays and misses against Lever in the most tantalising way as Illingworth crowds him with close catchers. Lever and D'Oliveira continue asking probing questions. Solkar slows down considerably. He plays 16 dot balls on 37, once almost offering a return catch to D'Oliveira.

It is Venkat who provides the excitement, driving Lever for a boundary through the covers and hooking him for a brace. A

D'Oliveira no-ball takes the score past the follow-on mark. The dressing room can relax.

Lower-order resilience

The double-barrelled success of the Indian team in 1971 has a lot to do with lower-order resilience. The following table shows the partnerships for the different wickets managed by the side on the tours to the West Indies and England. The healthy contributions from the lower half were often more prolific than the efforts of the frontline batsmen. The 6th and 7th wicket partnerships in particular, were far more productive than most of the top-order stands.

Wicket	Partnership Runs	Ave	100	50
1	477	34.07	1	3
2	424	30.28	1	0
3	764	54.57	2	4
4	442	36.83	0	2
5	347	28.91	1	3
6	530	48.18	1	3
7	391	39.10	1	1
8	232	23.20	0	0
9	191	21.22	1	0
10	113	12.55	0	1

The lynchpin for these rearguard efforts was Solkar, whose 392 runs at 39.20 over the two series were as vital as his 14 catches in the eight Tests.

In relief, Venkat drives Dolly for three and then hooks Lever for four. The latter vents his frustration by coming round the wicket and angling it across. Venkat gets a touch to Knott. It is a fifth wicket for Lever after his unbeaten 88. Dexter's epithet is justified.

The following over sees Solkar getting to his fifty with a four and a brace off D'Oliveira. The sizeable portion of Indians in the crowd bursts into applause, a few of them running on to the ground. Perhaps it affects Solkar, who pushes at the next one defensively. The ball, a leg-cutter to the leftie, goes off the edge low to the second slip where Hutton makes the chance look simpler than it is.

It is 200/9, by now Lever has tired and the toils of the day seem to have taken a lot out of the England bowlers. As Bedi and Chandra, not the most distinguished last-wicket pair, come together, the bowling does not seem to trouble them. They stick around for seven more overs, Bedi even growing confident enough to change his pads. With the final delivery of the day, Price, running in with the new ball, plucks out Bedi's middle stump. A huge lead of 174, but England have to bat again. As Woodcock writes, 'India have time on their side.'

* * *

On the rest day, the papers were full of praise for Gavaskar and Solkar. In *The Daily Telegraph*, Swanton marked Solkar out as 'a stroke-player of class'. Would he remember it as an example of 'As I said at the time?' One wonders.

John Warr, on the other hand, marvelled at the perfect balance of Gavaskar, his getting into line with a still head and minimum of fuss, and playing the ball very late.

In his weekly column in the *Sunday Mirror*, Dexter wondered at the Snow business, which had seen no charge, no trial but 'what a sentence'. 'Snow stands convicted of offending against a moral code where the dividing line between what is acceptable and what is not is a matter of opinion rather than a matter of fact.'

Dexter described the unruly mob of curls sported by Snow, contrasting them to chairman of selectors Alec Bedser who wore his hair short. 'Often there is no way of bridging the generation gap which divides them, there is no denying the instant antipathy between men of different convictions when giving instructions to their barbers ... but there is still, for my likes, all too much of the headmaster Bedser ticking off the schoolboy Snow, a situation that does less than justice to the maturity of both parties.'

Why, oh why, did Dexter not stick to this sort of a turn of phrase instead of penning those ghastly mystery novels with Clifford Makins a few years later?

The Sunday papers were also full of news of the opposition leader Harold Wilson vacillating about his position regarding British entry into the Common Market. That was, of course, a feature of the entire summer, as well as that entire year and many years before and after.

The right-wing Monday Club, set up in the 1960s to oppose decolonisation, issued a statement insisting, 'the so-called British Asians are no more and no less British than any Indian in the bazaars of Bombay. They had no connection with Britain either by blood or residence.' Buckinghamshire South MP Ronald Bell added, 'They should go back to their own country.'

England v India, 2nd Test, Old Trafford – 5, 6, 7, 9, 10 August
England 386 (Illingworth 107, Lever 88, Luckhurst 78, Knott 41; Abid 4-64, Venkat 3-89) **India** 212 (Gavaskar 57, Solkar 50; Lever 5-70).

45

TIMED OUT

IN APRIL 1970, just weeks before that election, Gallup found that just 19 per cent of the voters supported British entry into the EEC. More than 50 per cent rejected the idea of even holding talks. Of course, the business leaders thought differently, and so did Edward Heath, who became the prime minster two months later. But the issue remained a divisive factor ... and as we can see in 2022, it has remained so with knobs on.

Sir Roy Denman earned the wrath of many a British minister for championing the European cause. This British and Brussels diplomat, who negotiated the details of Britain's eventual entry into the EEC in 1973, later reflected on this resistance in his 1996 book *Missed Chances: Britain and Europe in the Twentieth Century*. According to Denman, memories of the war were to blame. 'Britain had won the war, the continentals had not. Those who had fought Britain were wicked; those who had not were incompetent, for otherwise they would not have been defeated ... For a great power to abandon its world role, the leadership of the Commonwealth, and its favoured position with the United States in order to throw in its lot with a bombed out, defeated rabble south of the Channel seemed to the British unthinkable.'

Alliance with the 'continentals' was a rather far-fetched conception – in both popular opinion and much of parliament. On D-Day in 1944, after the greatest amphibious assault in history to liberate Europe, Churchill supposedly said to General de Gaulle,

'Each time we have to choose between Europe and the open sea, we shall choose the open sea.'

The idea was that the British had defeated the evil Nazis and their axis 'alone'. The 'alone' bit was aided by soldiers joining in their millions from all across the Dominions and the corners of the Empire, but they were all 'British' just like Edmund Hillary and Tenzing Norgay. With a Churchillian sleight of mind and tongue, those millions could be considered as belonging to countries that had been carried through the war by the 'little island'.

Besides, the decisive role in the defeat of Germany had been played by the Red Army. Seven-eighths of all the fighting in which the Germans were engaged between 1939 and 1945 took place on the Eastern Front; 16,825,000 Russian people died in the war, more than 15 per cent of the country's population. However, those encounters had the same fate in Churchill's *A History of the English-Speaking Peoples* as non-Ashes cricket and statistical rigour have in the annals of the game's romanticised memory.

The Allies were, of course, further aided by the entry of the United States. But then the Americans were linked through a common stock, language and the *special relationship* between Churchill and Roosevelt.

For a lot of British people, it was their pluck that had kept the Nazis at bay, while the feeble French and other European countries had crumbled in front of the Luftwaffe. This was depicted by the famous David Low cartoon of the Tommy standing on the white cliffs of Dover, shaking his fists at the oncoming German bombers. (To be fair, there were balanced views as well. A *Punch* cartoon by Fougasse was published in July 1940 which showed two soldiers looking out at the sea. One says, 'So our poor Empire is alone in the world.' The other replies, 'Aye, we are. The whole five hundred million of us.'

With the French falling to the Nazis, a Thames boatman had triumphantly shouted to a group of MPs, 'No more bloody allies!' And George VI had echoed the plebeian sentiments when he told his mother that he was pleased 'now that we have no allies to pamper'.

Ten years down the line, the Queen Mother continued to refer to the Germans as 'the Huns'. This must have charmed Prince Philip. His maternal grandfather, Prince Louis of Battenberg, had adopted the Anglicised version of his last name after becoming a naturalised British citizen, owing to anti-German sentiment in the United Kingdom at that time. Both grandfather Louis and Philip himself served in the Royal Navy. But when Phillip's relatives visited, the Queen Mother instructed her staff unequivocally, 'You certainly don't curtsey to Germans.'

Had Britain entered into an alliance with Europe in the mid-1950s, they would have come in as a major economic and military superpower. By 1967, when Wilson finally applied for membership, the nation was already staggering from the 1966 sterling crisis. By 1970, Britain's share of world exports had collapsed from 26 per cent in 1950 to a mere 11 per cent. Germany, France and Italy all led them in terms of GDP.

The England football team was routed 3-6 by Hungary at Wembley in 1953, but in the packed stadium the fans kept singing, *'If it wasn't for the English, you'd be Krauts.'* When Chelsea were invited to participate in the inaugural edition of the European Cup in 1955/56, the Football League asked them not to take part. As far as the authorities were concerned, the real things were the First Division and the FA Cup.

The back-to-back Ashes series wins of 1953 and 1954/55 were vindication of English dominance, but that they happened under Len Hutton continued to peeve some traditionalists. When the coup they envisaged by promoting the claims of David Sheppard did not materialise, pens such as Swanton's found flaws with almost everything the professional captain did in Australia.

However, the class structure was not just limited to cricket. It was not only the Test team that habitually played with ten and a half men with an amateur captain at the helm, and not only cricket was fettered with anachronisms such as Gentlemen v Players fixtures. Much of British consciousness was governed by the same principles. One simple illustration is that of manufacturing industry and engineering. The management was far less technically and professionally competent than their continental counterparts, with the propertied classes making the major decisions. It was in the 1950s that Britain's auto industry turned down the possibility of manufacturing Volkswagens, because the privileged minds thought they would not sell. Once the war-devastated continental factories were re-equipped, the antiquated British auto industry went into a slump.

Gentlemen and Players in fiction

By 1937, Sir Buckstone Abbott was already struggling and trying to sell off his ancestral pile, Walsingford Hall, to a wealthy princess in *Summer Moonshine*.

By 1953, P.G. Wodehouse had gone further, with Lord Towcester intent on selling his country house and even Bertie Wooster was summarily dispatched to a school for a course in fending for oneself in *Ring for Jeeves*.

Novels like *Lucky Jim* by Kingsley Amis heralded the lower middle-class challenge in the world with profound irreverence for the upper classes.

Those were the years when Britain refused the Schuman Plan. 'I cannot conceive that Britain would be an ordinary member of a Federal Union limited to Europe in any period which can at present be foreseen,' said Churchill in 1950. He reiterated the statement on his return to power in 1951. According to Denman, part of it was because of 'an Anglo-Saxon suspicion of imposing an ambitious paper schemes dreamed up by clever foreigners'. Churchill's successor Anthony Eden was no more eager.

In 1955 the Benelux governments formally proposed that the foreign ministers of the Six would meet at Messina and consider a Benelux memorandum with suggestions for a general Common Market. When a senior Quai d'Orsay official phoned London requesting the possibility of British attendance, he was simply told that Messina was 'a devilish awkward place to expect a minister to get to'.

That was late 1955.

46

LITTLE MAN, LONG SPELL

ILLINGWORTH IS every bit the practical, hard-boiled Yorkshireman. When talking to the press on the rest day, he refuses to read much into England's strong position. 'A lead of 174 sounds marvellous, but it wouldn't be so hot if our second innings became 20/3.' He is thinking in terms of a big target. 'I can't possibly think in terms of leaving India 300 in their last dig, because they could get 'em. With a target like that, no further rain and a wicket that would get slower and slower, you have to back them every time.'

The skipper also hints at the way they will go about getting the runs. 'If we can add 200 or so in less than four hours, that's fine. But if that happens it won't be because we carve them up in the first hour.' Besides, there is the Gifford-factor. 'We've now lost Gifford and therefore, assuming the ball starts to turn, the pretty useful opportunity of exploiting the rough. India have two frontline left-handers in Wadekar and Solkar and it needs a left-armer like Gifford to put them on the spot in these circumstances.'

When play starts on the cloudy Monday, the England batsmen do not throw their bats. But there is a definite plan as they progress.

From the first over, it is clear that the magical movement generated by Abid on the first morning has been a bizarre anomaly. But he does produce a half-chance, which curiously jeopardises the Indian cause. In Abid's second over, Jameson cuts hard and it flies low towards gully. Solkar stretches out his left hand. He cannot hold it, and if Solkar cannot none of the Indians can. However, the attempt sees him bruise his hand, and the Indians are left with just one of their two military-medium bowlers.

Wadekar makes the sign, and Gavaskar warms up. All of 5ft 4in, he runs in with the three-overs-old ball. Innocuous, gentle, medium-pacers with a hint of inswing. The England openers milk him without urgency, giving a bit too much weight to the newness of the ball. At the other end, Abid runs in from a great distance before unleashing friendly medium-pacers. The two keep on bowling together until the 25th over when Solkar returns after repairs and takes over from Gavaskar. Except for Chandra sending down the last over of the morning session, the three formidable spinners do fielding duty till lunch. It is nothing to do with the conditions or the pitch. Wadekar just cannot afford men bowling off three paces, getting through their overs quickly.

Is Govindraj missed one wonders? Even if his effectiveness with the greenish tinge on the wicket is debated, no one can possibly question the length of his run-up.

Hence Gavaskar bowls on. Before this innings, he has bowled three overs in his entire Test career, two of them in the first innings of this very match. Earlier on this tour, he was used as a very occasional leg-spinner. And now he sends down 11 consecutive overs of medium-pace. Luckhurst is content to bide his time, Jameson looks more enterprising. The latter's approach is refreshing; there is no hint of caution due to the grand occasion of a Test debut. He scores faster than Luckhurst. But even he does not really capitalise on rather club-class bowling.

Luckhurst seems to be indecisive about his approach, whether to treat this as a venture of enterprise or a regular Test innings. So much so he often takes a few steps forward, considering a run, and then calls off the deal as fraught with risk. Some thrilling singles are run, but Jameson is often confused about his partner's intentions. In the end it leads to fatal results. Luckhurst plays Abid to square leg and jogs forward. It takes Jameson a while to realise these are tentative steps. When he turns to get back to his crease, the debutant slips. Viswanath's slow lob of a throw hits the wicket. England lose their first wicket at 44. It is the 17th over, and more than an hour's play has already taken place.

The arrival of Edrich does not change things much. He takes 10 balls to get off the mark, and after the 21st over England have still not reached 50. Gavaskar has bowled nine overs, conceding just 11. And then finally the shackles come off. Edrich drives Gavaskar for four. Nine runs are taken off his following over. Wadekar takes Gavaskar off after the longest spell he will ever bowl in his 125-Test career. Solkar is back on and medium-pace continues.

It serves its purpose in allowing just 30 overs before lunch. England are 89/1.

* * *

From early dawn on that same day, the disastrous Operation Demetrius was being implemented in Northern Ireland.

British troops sealed off streets across the province, and snatched a total of 342 men in raids, virtually kidnapping them to various makeshift camps, the Long Kesh airbase and HMS *Maidstone* being the most infamous. A few had links with the IRA, but many did not. The intelligence of the Royal Ulster Constabulary, on which the troops had acted, was extremely faulty.

The decision to reintroduce the policy of imprisonment without trial had been taken four days before during a discussion between Prime Minister Brian Faulkner, head of the Unionist government, and Edward Heath. The 'five techniques' methods of interrogation, taught to local forces by specially trained personnel who made the trip to Northern Ireland specifically for the purpose, were dehumanising, and, by various accounts, either bordered on or were euphemisms for torture. According to some accounts, families were terrorised and even beaten during the arrests.

In the immediate aftermath, a surge of violence swept through the country, especially in Belfast. Between 9 and 11 August, 20 civilians, two members of the Provisional IRA and two members of the British army were killed. As many as 17 civilians were killed by the British army, 11 Catholic civilians were shot dead in the Ballymurphy housing estate in West Belfast. As violence raged, Protestant families fled the Ardoyne district in North Belfast, 200 or so burning their homes as they fled, 'lest they fall into Catholic hands'. Some 7,000 people, most of them Catholics, were left homeless, with refugee camps set up for the Catholics south of the border.

Troubles with a capital 't'

The troubles in Northern Ireland, without the capitalisation of the 't', have raged from the time of the Plantation of Ulster in the 17th century. They lasted till the peace talks in the late 20th century. Catholic versus Protestant, Republican against Unionist, they raged through the rise of Republicanism, Home Rule and the civil rights movements, the growth of Sinn Féin and thereafter of the opposition, the DUP.

The emergence of a structured subversive organisation with IRA aggression from the late 1960s turned the conflicts into militarism and capitalised the 't' of Troubles. The Ballymurphy riots of West Belfast in April 1970 was a definitive end to the idea of British efforts to win Catholic hearts and minds. The escalation to The Long War was drastic. By late 1970, according to some accounts, the British government adopted a 'lance and boil' policy, escalating the level of violence to the point where the IRA would overstretch and expose itself with counter-blows. By June 1971, the Conservative home secretary Reginald Maulding announced that the British government was 'at war with the IRA'.

The major flare-up of August 1971 was just one of many. The Troubles would rage on from the late-1960s to the late-1990s.

The afternoon session sees a distinct change in the attitude of the England batsmen. Venkat and Abid bowl, and both the batsmen shed their pre-lunch inhibitions to go looking for runs. Towards the end of the first hour, Abid has tired and is being struck to the boundary by both Luckhurst and Edrich. After a marathon spell of 22 overs, he is taken off and replaced by Gavaskar. Edrich promptly dispatches the part-timer to the fence with a drive and a cut. Having completed his half-century, Edrich is looking increasingly threatening.

Wadekar has kept the ball away from Bedi for three hours – perhaps worried as much by the incredible speed with which he finishes his overs as by his tendency to flight the ball regardless of the situation. Now, he finally turns to the left-armer. In his second over, Bedi bowls Edrich as the batsman tried to sweep: 167/2.

But Luckhurst has by now fully changed gears. With Bedi offering air, something Wadekar distinctly disapproves of at this stage, he jumps out of his crease and hoists him back over his head for a four and a straight six. The captain takes his left-arm spinner off.

Abid is given the ball once again, and Luckhurst launches into a pull for four. And when Solkar comes on, he slams him in a similar way to square leg and brings up his fifth hundred for England, his first in fourteen months. Having come into the Test with scores of 0, 0, 30 and 1, he has been under pressure. However, after crawling to 19 in 63 balls, he has scored the next 82 in 105, which signals a roaring return to form.

He is dismissed in rather curious circumstances. The ball from Solkar is down the leg side and Luckhurst misses the attempted sweep. Engineer, standing up to the gentle medium-pace, collects it and notices the batsman's foot is on the line. Luckhurst is apparently not aware of it, the Indian stumper flicks off the bails and appeals at leisure.

At 212/3, and England pushing for a declaration, is an ideal moment for D'Oliveira to come in. He starts by skying a catch towards mid-on. Ashok Mankad reacts late, tries to reach the ball and dives in futile desperation. He misses. With Fletcher striking two pleasant boundaries off Solkar in the next over, D'Oliveira celebrates with a blistering cameo, driving Venkat high and straight for two sixes.

England go in to tea at 245/3, having hauled their scoring rate up to a run a minute. The lead is 419 and there is little doubt that the declaration will be made during the break.

Could they have got the runs a bit quicker? After all, 66 overs have been bowled and only one ball from Venkat has landed on the rough, jumped and turned. Elsewhere the bowling has been as benign as could be. Twelve of the overs have been sent down by Gavaskar, and England have taken only 37 off them. Even factoring in the scoring patterns of the era, it seems that the runs could have been gathered a little faster. India have, however, done everything possible to slow things down, bowling their medium-pacers and even non-bowlers with a sizeable run-up, taking their time over drinks on a cool, sun-less day.

Perhaps the top order makes it a bit complicated for England. Jameson, on debut, has been refreshingly free in his approach. But Luckhurst and Edrich have struggled for runs ever since the Australian tour of 1970/71. Fletcher has just been recalled and his batting average is 24 in his previous 12 Tests. Perhaps a promotion of the free-stroking D'Oliveira or the tactic of sending in Knott to keep the scorers busy may have speeded things along.

In normal circumstances, the match is set up perfectly for the final blows by the bowlers, but there is a race against the weather and the venue is Manchester.

* * *

In New Delhi, the Soviet minister of foreign affairs Andrei Gromyko and the Indian defence minister Swaran Singh signed a treaty of 'Peace, Friendship and Cooperation'. Valid for 20 years, it was aimed at 'expanding and consolidating the existing relationship of sincere friendship'. Ambassador D.P. Dhar's negotiations had borne fruit, aided by the Nixon-Kissinger obstinacy. Kissinger's veiled warning to L.K. Jha had been instrumental in the impassioned Indian wooing of the Russians.

Addressing a huge public rally at India Gate, Indira Gandhi reiterated that as a poor nation themselves, Indians had to bank on unity to help the people of Bangladesh.

* * *

Gavaskar and Mankad walk out with India needing to bat out four sessions to save the Test.

Six years before, John Price came back from South Africa with eight wickets at 52 apiece from the four Tests. Since then, Snow had taken on the role of the spearhead, Ken Higgs and David Brown did fine jobs through the remainder of the Sixties, with Jeff Jones chipping in now and then. Things looked bleak for the Middlesex bowler by the end of the decade. With the arrival of Bob Willis during the 1970/71 Ashes, he believed his Test career to be over.

But with all the uncertainty around Snow, he suddenly found himself bowling against the Pakistanis at Lord's. And now, at 34, he is charging in off his round-the-corner run-up, making the Indian batsmen hop. This is not the first time Price has troubled the Indians. In 1963/64, he bowled an excellent spell on the first day at Eden Gardens, Calcutta.

Mankad turns him for three, is missed in the slips off Lever. And then he cannot bring his bat down in time to meet a scorching Price delivery. The off stump goes flying and India are one down.

Price continues at a terrific pace, Wadekar negotiates him with caution, Gavaskar with composure. The skipper drives Lever for four, steers Price for another. And then there is another express Price delivery, Wadekar's bat comes down late, and his off stump is torn out of the ground. At 22/2, defeat is staring India in the face.

In four more overs of watchful circumspection, Sardesai and Gavaskar try to steady the ship. And then Price runs in for his seventh over. Sardesai pushes a single. Gavaskar essays a neat deflection for two. Price sends down a bouncer, the little man swivels and hooks him for six.

Price has tired. Seven overs have earned him 2-24. With Hutton on at the other end, Lever replaces him. Twice in succession, Gavaskar drives him through the on side, finding the fence on both occasions.

Hutton runs in and after Sardesai has rotated the strike, Gavaskar leans into his drive and sends him through the covers for four. The 50 is up and Gavaskar has 20 off the last 11 deliveries. 'Little Master', notes Woodcock.

And then suddenly he is gone. Hutton moves one away off the pitch and with the spate of strokes behind him Gavaskar drives at it. The ball is feathered and Knott throws it up – 50/3, and what promised to be a brilliant gem ends in a miniature of 24.

Viswanath and Sardesai survive the remaining tense moments of the day. Neither is comfortable, either against Hutton or Lever or during the final three-over burst by Price. Even D'Oliveira is negotiated with uncertainty. However, under gloomy skies, they hold on. It is 65/3 in 27 overs of struggle when the clock shows 6:33pm and the players come off.

'Illy's vultures are waiting for the kill,' writes Laker with ominous foreboding, before adding the caveat, 'Only the weather can save India now.'

'India will save the second Test only if the weather helps them,' agrees Woodcock.

'Only the weather or exceptional resistance by the remaining batsmen can prevent [England] beating India in the second Test,' writes Arlott.

The Weather is always a factor at Manchester. Even during Jim Laker's Test of 1956, grey skies and persistent rain allowed Australia a glimpse of hope.

England v India, 2nd Test, Old Trafford – 5, 6, 7, 9, 10 August England 386 (Illingworth 107, Lever 88, Luckhurst 78, Knott 41; Abid 4-64, Venkat 3-89) and 245/3 dec (Luckhurst 101, Edrich 59) **India** 212 (Gavaskar 57, Solkar 50; Lever 5-70) and 65/3.

47

OLD TRAFFORD AND EDEN

'I WAS drinking a cup of tea in the pavilion when [Don Bradman] returned from inspecting [the Old Trafford Test pitch in 1956],' Jim Laker writes. '"What do you think of the track?" I queried. "It's nice and flat, isn't it?" Bradman joked and then more seriously, "It's just what our fellows have been waiting for. They will get a packet of runs here."' Laker ended the match with 9-37 and 10-53, Australia got rather less than a packet, to be precise 84 and 205. But with the third and fourth days being washed out, they did glimpse an opportunity to draw the Test before Laker snuffed that out that on the final afternoon.

Two years before Laker's feat, Old Trafford had hosted Yorkshire in the County Championship's Battle of the Roses. Lancashire had been destroyed by an innings and 38 runs. Johnny Wardle 9-25 in the first innings, Bob Appleyard 7-33 in the second. That was the year Appleyard had come back to cricket after having half his left lung removed. He had made his Test debut at Trent Bridge and removed four Pakistan top-order batsmen with his first 27 deliveries, finishing with 5-51. He went to Australia in 1954/55, while Laker was left behind. Stand-in captain for that Nottingham Test, David Sheppard, often wondered, 'Had Bob stayed fit, would Jim have got back in the England side?'

Appleyard playing cricket at all in 1954 was itself a miracle of medical science. In 1952, at the Leeds General Infirmary, thoracic surgeon Geoffrey Wooler had informed him, 'You have a tuberculin infection, but it's nothing we cannot cope with ... I may have to do a little surgery.'

In 1952, medical science had just about learnt how to treat tuberculosis surgically. Wooler removed the upper lobe of the left lung completely. Luckily the lower lobe was saved. Appleyard came out with a reduced lung capacity, but a heart full of hope. A scar from the armpit to the waist would remind him of the primitive needlework performed to stitch him up after the operation. But he managed to play 117 first-class matches after that, picking up 496 more wickets. That included 31 wickets at 17.87 in nine Tests.

At the other extreme of the medical landscape of the time was a simple surgical procedure gone disastrously wrong, which perhaps changed the course of world history, at least the history of Britain and the Middle East.

The year following Appleyard's operation, in April 1953, the Deputy Prime Minister Anthony Eden went under the knife at a London clinic. It was supposed to be a simple gall-bladder operation. The surgeon's knife slipped and the biliary duct was cut. Eden had to be operated upon twice more, the third procedure lasting eight hours, before his life could be saved. His health never recovered.

Eden took over as the prime minister in April 1955 after Churchill stood down because of poor health. He himself resigned on health grounds in January 1957. In between he wrestled with the problems of Suez, ending with a humiliation of the sort that at least some historians equate with the end of the Empire for good.

On 26 July 1956, the Test match at Old Trafford commenced after that curious conversation between Laker and Bradman. That same day Nasser nationalised, or more accurately de-internationalised, the Suez Canal Company in which the British government held about 44 per cent of the shares. Eden had already become testy about the situation in the Middle East and had started seeing Nasser as a personal adversary. Later that month, he was already discussing the possibility of military action with his chiefs of staff. Jingoistic press reports fuelled the fumes. The *Mirror* reminded readers of the sad ends of Mussolini and Hitler.

The war-memories were still fresh. In an old soldiers' reunion, it was said, 'Politicians don't know ... that the only way to deal with [the Orientals] is to kick their backsides.'

In late October, British and French bombers swept down on the Egyptian coast, destroying 260 Egyptian planes within 24 hours. They did so in alliance with Israel and with the support of white cricketing cronies South Africa, Australia and New Zealand. No other country stood by them, nor did the UN. Until that moment, the United States had been trying to defuse the tensions. Eisenhower was less than amused at being pre-empted.

Three days later the UN General Assembly met for the first time in an emergency session and approved an American resolution calling for a ceasefire over Suez.

Eden had been goaded into action by his own misjudgment of the situation caused to a great extent by his health problems, which made him tired, irritable and impatient. It did not take him long to realise his blunder. However, the bugles of war were greeted with festive fanfare by the Conservative press. With the British on the verge of going on the offensive, the *Daily Sketch* blared, 'Let Crybabies Howl! It's GREAT Britain Again.'

Post-war rationing had ended, employment was at its peak. As would be famously voiced the following year, the majority of British people had never had it so good. There was the familiar rumble of British guns overseas. Britain indeed seemed to be great again!

Only, that was the biggest and briefest of illusions. Fifty years before, it could have resulted in an imperial triumph. But sentiments were in favour of Egypt, not only across the world but even among younger people at home. Anti-war demonstrations took place in Trafalgar Square, Labour firebrand Aneurin Bevan spoke out eloquently against the old-fashioned imperialist manoeuvres. Families argued over the topic, in general the younger generation were against the war, while the older ones supported it. It is captured in John Osborne's play *The Entertainer*. When young Jean tells her grandfather that she has attended an anti-war rally in Trafalgar Square, the 70-year-old retorts, 'I should think you want your bloody head read.' Even the Queen confessed she was 'having the most awful time' making up her mind about the issue. And while the Conservative press continued in their jingoistic swagger, publications such as *The Economist, The Observer, The Spectator* and others opposed military action.

Even attempts to pass the aggression off as 'strengthening the weakest point in the line against Communism' did not fool anyone. Ultimately, it boiled down to money. The depletion of the British gold and dollar reserves played a major role, along with the canal blocking British access to Middle Eastern oil. American assistance to ensure a loan from the International Monetary Fund was guaranteed only if a ceasefire was agreed. The Americans even vetoed the British proposal of staying on in Egypt as part of the UN peacekeeping forces. Egypt soon started expelling British, French and Israeli residents. By the end of the year, British troops had left Egypt, and Eden, on his doctors' advice, had left for complete rest in Jamaica. By January 1957 he had handed his resignation in to the Queen.

Eden's successor, Harold Macmillan, later said, 'He was trained to win the Derby in 1938, unfortunately he was not let out of the starting stalls until 1955.' The change of times could not have been summed up in a crisper manner.

Eden himself wrote in a memorandum: 'Surely we must review our world position and our domestic capacity more searchingly in the light of the Suez experience, which has not so much changed our fortunes as revealed realities.'

Not only had the tradition of imperial attitudes become palpably unsuccessful and increasingly a target of mockery, the sham of parity with the United States as a major world power was now exposed as a futile pretence.

48

MIND YOUR LANGUAGE

'LATE THAT night, the tattoo of raindrops on the window awnings was sweet music to my ears,' recounts Ajit Wadekar (as told to K.N. Prabhu) in his autobiography.

Reaching the ground in the morning, the captains emerge beside the playing arena as the relentless Manchester rains continue. Illingworth spends an hour and a half, periodically casting morose glances at Old Trafford's saturated acres. Shortly before the early lunch, he sighs and sits down to play poker with the boys. Some of the Indians join in. The cards are dealt out as the rains continue to splash across the arena.

England v India, 2nd Test – Old Trafford, 5, 6, 7, 9, 10 August
England 386 (Illingworth 107, Lever 88, Luckhurst 78, Knott 41; Abid 4-64, Venkat 3-89) and 245/3 dec (Luckhurst 101, Edrich 59) drew with **India** 212 (Gavaskar 57, Solkar 50; Lever 5-70) and 65/3.

* * *

Back home in Delhi, Gromyko chose his words very carefully as he spoke to Mrs Gandhi. 'Moscow believes the Pak military will not succeed in keeping down the people of East Pakistan for long and the rule is doomed. It is not for us to prejudge whether East Pakistan should be separate from West Pakistan or one with it. You may rest assured that in regard to the refugees we shall always support your position.'

That same day the Indian prime minister dispatched a message to the heads of government, 'The Government and people of India are greatly perturbed by the reported statement of President Yahya Khan that he is going to start secret military trial of Mujibur Rahman without affording him any foreign legal assistance.' She urged all the recipients of the message to exercise their influence on Yahya.

* * *

At Lord's there was scope for debate about the probable outcome if the weather had not intervened. There is no such quandary in the second Test. The Indians have been saved, Wadekar admits it, as will Gavaskar in his book.

But, as quite often mentioned in the course of the last few pages, rain in Manchester has never been a surprise. Persistent downpours washed out even the first day of Test cricket at Old Trafford, way back in 1884. Six years down the line, Manchester's full potential for precipitation was realised, resulting in first ever Test to be washed out without a ball being bowled.

In 1938, the Ashes Test between Don Bradman's Australians and Wally Hammond's England met with the same fate. In Alfred Hitchcock's *The Lady Vanishes,* Charters and Caldicott ride through the mysterious adventure discussing Hammond and Grimmett with the help of spoons and salt-shakers, and fantasising about the forthcoming Test match at Manchester. When they reach London, they are informed by newspaper headlines that the Test has been abandoned. The movie was released on 1 November 1938.

In 1954, on their first tour to the country, Pakistan were 0-1 down in the series. At Old Trafford, after the second day had been washed out, England totalled 359 and dismissed Pakistan for 90. At the end of the third day, Pakistan were 25/4 in the second innings. The rains then rolled in again and the remaining two days saw the England players waiting with frustration, while the Pakistanis sat in front of the pavilion singing supposed monsoon-inducing songs.

That 1954 Old Trafford Test led Cardus to rant, 'In my opinion, a mistake was made by those authorities who decided that the time was now ripe for Test matches between Pakistan and England. To say the plain truth, the Pakistan team would scarcely hold its own in the county cricket championship against Yorkshire, Nottinghamshire, Middlesex or Northamptonshire, not even in a fine summer.'

Keeping up with the Cardusian

After his laudatory sentiments about India in 1952, it seems Cardus was being surprisingly uncharitable towards the underdog. Pakistan had indeed lost to Yorkshire, but they had beaten Nottinghamshire on that tour, after forcing them to follow on; they had held their own against Northamptonshire in a draw. And even though they had not played Middlesex, they had beaten Lancashire and drawn against Glamorgan, and had the better of a drawn encounter against Derbyshire – both Glamorgan and Derbyshire finished above Middlesex in the County Championship that year.

All these tour matches had taken place well before Cardus penned his scathing words. But then he had never been a stickler for facts.

At The Oval, Fazal Mahmood captured 6-53 and 6-46, and Pakistan squared their first series in England by beating the hosts by 24 runs.

While the Pakistan cricket team was putting Higher Truth in its proper place, in India a major restructuring of the country was being carried out. Modernisation and industrialisation were being handled through rolled-out five-year plans, and a clear centre-state division of power was put in place. At the same time there was the need for logical reorganisation of the provinces that had been left in the wake of the colonial past.

Through the years of the Raj, the provincial boundaries had been dictated by administrative convenience. It had created several cultural and linguistic anomalies. Madras and Bombay, two principal provinces, were multilingual. At the same time, the large populace of Oriya and Telugu speakers had been split into two or three provinces. Erstwhile independent states such as Mysore and Hyderabad were now large and free-standing, and with the absorption of the princely states into the country, small principalities had been hurriedly cobbled together into administrative structures such as Madhya Bharat. It was this linguistic divide that made many an expert predict the balkanisation of the country, especially after the horrendous experiences of Partition.

In December 1953, the states reorganisation commission was set up. By September 1955, spending a shade longer on the job of drawing lines on the map than Sir Cyril Radcliffe, the commission submitted its report. The implementation saw the country divided into 14 states on the basis of language. The southern states of Kerala, Mysore (now Karnataka) and Tamil Nadu were set up for people speaking Malayalam, Kannada and Tamil respectively. The fourth state, Andhra, had already been formed in 1953, and it was merged with the Telugu-speaking regions of Hyderabad to form Andhra Pradesh. Even in this century, the Telengana movement led to the bifurcation of Andhra Pradesh into two states. Telengana, created in 2014, is essentially composed of the Telugu-speaking parts of the erstwhile princely state of Hyderabad.

The massive Bombay state remained bi-lingual with Marathi and Gujarati speakers until 1960, when it split into Maharashtra and Gujarat.

Additionally, some small states, historically governed by a chief commissioner or a lieutenant-governor appointed by the president of India, were made into Union Territories.

In 1966, the other great state of Punjab was split into the Punjabi-speaking Punjab and two Hindi-speaking states, Haryana and Himachal Pradesh.

Sikkim, traditionally a kingdom ruled by the Chogyal Buddhist priest-kings, remained a protectorate till 1975 before becoming an Indian state.

This was neither an easy solution nor a permanent one. Andhra Pradesh was obtained after a Gandhian fast that went on literally to death. The boundaries of the northern Hindi-speaking belt have been drawn and redrawn several times. Secessionist tendencies have not been infrequent.

The north-eastern states, especially Nagaland through its troubled history, have been subjected to rather ruthless military repression, brutality and a significant amount of discrimination, often manifestations of the sort of dictatorial government policies India proudly dissociates itself from.

However, with these exceptions, linguistic reorganisation can be viewed as one of the success stories in the long run.

By the time I was in school and geography lessons were being rammed into our heads, the number of states stood at 21, and the number of union territories nine. While they were still being rammed into our heads, the number of states became 24. At present, there are 28 states and eight union territories.

It makes a curious historical case when one looks at the cricket teams that participate in the national tournament, namely the Ranji Trophy. Thirty-eight teams currently take part, loosely based on states. However, some of the old pre-reorganisation sides still play in the tournament and are way too powerful in prowess and historical context to be rendered defunct. After all Bombay, now Mumbai, have won the title a whopping 42 times, Delhi seven times and Hyderabad twice. Mumbai, therefore, continue to play although there is a separate state team of Maharashtra. In the political sense, Mumbai is the capital of the state of Maharashtra. Delhi, the capital of India, is politically administered as the National Capital Territory. Hyderabad, name inherited from the princely state, co-existed for several decades with Andhra Pradesh while the latter fielded a separate state side called Andhra. When the state of Telengana came into existence, the Hyderabad side, for all intents and purposes, became the Telengana team, while their name remained the same. It would be unthinkable to think of the Ranji Trophy without Mumbai, Delhi and Hyderabad.

On the other hand, there are several teams that have become defunct with the reorganisation. These include former provinces and princely states. Central Provinces and Berar, Northern India, Sindh, Southern Punjab, Western India, North West Frontier Province, Northern Punjab, Eastern Punjab, Madhya Bharat, Travancore-Cochin are provinces that are no longer in the map, nor in the tournament tables.

Nawanagar, the famed small state ruled by Ranji, the King of a Great Game, became Kathiawar, and later Saurashtra. The Saurashtra side still plays, alongside Baroda – yet another erstwhile princely state – although both lie within the political state of Gujarat, which has its own team.

States such as Holkar and Patiala had once taken part in their full princely pomp. Holkar, with Mushtaq Ali and the great C.K. Nayudu, continued until 1954/55, going on for several years after merging with Madhya Bharat. Patiala, being Patiala, continued until 1959, once teaming up with Eastern Punjab States Union.

A complete list of Ranji Trophy sides with their various manifestations and bifurcations can be found in the appendix.

While linguistic reorganisation was relatively successful, the question of a national language was far more complicated. Tussles over an official language, especially the dispute over Hindi being forced upon the southern states of the Dravidian tongue, led to outcries, problems, movements, riots and also killings. It was not till 1967 that a sort of dynamic equilibrium was found in a virtually indefinite policy of multilingualism.

Language remains a complex issue in India. There is no national language. According to the constitution, 'The official language of the Union shall be Hindi in Devanagari script.' The discourses in the Indian parliament take place in Hindi or in English. English is used as an official language, and is considered the primary language by many of the educated urban populace.

The states have the liberty to legally specify their own official language. The constitution recognises 22 regional languages. In several states, English is listed as one of the official languages. Three states in the North-East – Meghalaya, Nagaland and

Arunachal Pradesh – list English as the only official language. About a third list Hindi. The state of Sikkim lists Nepali, another foreign tongue, as one of its four official languages. The Union Territory of Puducherry (formerly a French territory) lists French alongside Tamil and English.

In all there are approximately 19,500 mother tongues in India, including 121 major languages spoken by more than 10,000 people.

There have been Indian cricket teams with two players able to converse with each other only in English. Sometimes they don't have any language in common. At the same time, there have been teams with pairs of cricketers able to converse in four or five languages.

While writing the book *Sachin and Azhar at Cape Town*, my co-author Abhishek Mukherjee and I communicated with the former Indian cricketer Dodda Ganesh. We spoke in English, a language in which Ganesh is reasonably articulate by now. When he had walked out to bat on his Test debut at Cape Town in January 1997, captain Sachin Tendulkar was at the other end in the midst of his blistering 169. Allan Donald charged in and beat Ganesh all ends up, but the tailender survived. Donald, who had taken plenty of stick all day, let out a mouthful. Tendulkar had to inform the fast bowler that the Indian No.11 did not even speak Hindi, let alone English, so unless Donald was prepared to swear in Kannada he was wasting his breath. Luckily, that team had several members from Karnataka. But for the other players to speak to Ganesh would have required an interpreter.

Many of the Indian languages have extraordinary heritage, in the field of literature, drama and film. Many did so even when Thomas Babington Macaulay summarily dismissed the entire body of Eastern languages without knowing any of them. From Thiruvalluvar to Kalidasa, the examples are plenty. The film industry does not necessarily mean commercial Bollywood. There are masterpieces abundantly sprinkled among the millions of films, alongside a huge number of rather shambolic productions, made in regional languages. The Telugu film industry, for instance, makes more movies in a year than most European countries do.

There are three songs that vie for the status of the national song in India. None of them are in Hindi. The official national anthem, 'Jana Gana Mana', was penned by Tagore in Sadhu Bangla, a classical, heavily Sanskritised Bengali. 'Vande Mataram', the verse adopted as the national song in 1937 by the Congress Working Committee, was written by another Bengali, Bankimchandra Chattopadhyay, and is in Sanskrit. The one accepted widely as the national song, with lyrics that most of the masses understand, is 'Saare Jahan Se Achchha Hindustan Hamara'. Curiously, this is written in Urdu, the national language of Pakistan, and penned by Iqbal, who became the national poet of Pakistan. To add to the complexity, when the new nation of Bangladesh was born, they adopted 'Amar Sonar Bangla' as their national anthem, yet another song composed by Tagore in spoken Bengali. (In fact, 'Sri Lanka Matha', the national anthem of Sri Lanka, is also heavily influenced by Tagore.)

India is that complex, without scope for simplification. Languages are windows into the heart and soul of the nation. A lack of knowledge of at least some of the languages makes it difficult to glimpse the culture, the nuances, the underlying meaning of expressions, the interpretations of events. This skein of multilingual and multicultural heritage that runs through the country is a defining hallmark of Indianness. Most of us grow up learning three languages in three different scripts, if not more. Yet, we may struggle to understand the culture and sentiments of someone from a distinctly different part of India.

There are plenty of good works on Indian – and subcontinental – cricket penned by authors primarily from England and Australia. And there are plenty of not-so-great works as well, written using the traditional James Mill method, trying to make sense of the country, culture and cricket with Macaulayan or Radcliffian levels of insights.

The language barrier is an important issue. It is not impossible to write excellently about a country without knowing the language, or, in this case, the languages. Otherwise only a tiny fraction of travel books would have been penned. But, such an endeavour is fraught with perils of errors and superficiality, often both. There are able names that stutter and stumble into these pitfalls.

In the modern day there are very few gargantuan embarrassments of cultural ignorance of the *Thousand Miles Through India and Burma* variety (unless we take social media into account). But unfamiliarity with language and fuzzy understanding of culture do induce the tendency to draw the cloak of existent or non-existent style and perception over the palpable lack of substance.

This is not an attempt to discourage the excellent writers penning their accounts of cricket in that part of the world, but perhaps a helpful finger pointing at probable problems.

The reason for making this particular point is more an effort to show up the negative space – the illogical contrast.

Quite a few Indian, Pakistani and Sri Lankan authors grow up following the educational and schooling models set up during the British era. They get to know Shakespeare and Shaw, Dickens and, well, Kipling. The ones devoted to literature mostly end up devouring Conan Doyle, Wodehouse, Maugham, Orwell and others. Often, if schooled in a Christian institution, of which there are many, they develop a reasonable familiarity with Christianity, and thereby its denominations, and the Bible. In Don Bosco School, for instance, I had to grapple with [expurgated versions of] both the Old and New Testaments as part of my curriculum. With adequate travel, these writers from the subcontinent should be in a very good position to understand, interpret and chronicle the cricket and society of England or Australia from an outsider's viewpoint. In fact, given the respective familiarity with the languages of each other, they are at a distinct advantage over the English and Australian authors trying to write books about the cricket and culture of the subcontinent.

Yet, to quote from *Sachin and Azhar at Cape Town,* 'except for Vasant Raiji on Trumper, and Mihir Bose on Keith Miller, it is very difficult to think of books on white cricket by non-white writers that have been acknowledged by the ivory towers of cricket writing. Non-white writers are generally acknowledged if they stick to non-white cricket. In other words, they remain beyond a boundary.' Or in the corner of the foreign field where they belong. The defined swim-lanes of cricket history.

Deep extra cover

In *Apartheid: A Point to Cover* – my book on cricket in apartheid South Africa leading to the Stop The Seventy Tour (STST) movement – I deliberately covered official post-war Test cricket played by South Africa in a lot of detail. This was parallel to the descriptions of the stark history of discrimination.

The idea was to demonstrate how excellent cricket went on in all pomp and excitement even as a huge proportion of the population lived under near-inhuman subjugation. I also wanted to show how fantastic cricketers from the underprivileged communities tried to carry on playing the game in a parallel circuit, and could not dream of making it to the highest level of the game.

In his review for *The Cricketer*, David Frith was charitable enough to say that he found the early history of South African cricket fascinating in the book. Simon Sweetman was very perceptive in his brief analysis in *The Cricket Statistician*, 'Read carefully, [the book] may answer the question, "Why did people think it right to disrupt the tour?" which seems to be one that many people still wrestle with.' That was precisely what I had set out to answer.

However, one gentleman, who himself had penned a book on STST, wondered, 'I cannot understand why Arun, siding with the downtrodden such as D'Oliveira, yet devotes so much loving attention to the whites-only SA Test matches.'

Quasi-professional nit-picking or otherwise, there is that very palpable tendency to keep cricket-writing colour segregated, the segregation with semi-permeable boundaries allowing one privileged colour to seep through to the other side. [This has not been the only such instance at defining boundaries]

The James Mills of the cricketing world are still writing histories of cricket as it is played in 'godawful places'. There is far too much of the tendency to control how history should be written, in what shades, and how to keep the subject matter both familiar and antiseptic for 'wholesome reading'. If we toe that line, much of the history of cricket and society will remain untold. And taking the knee will remain a superfluous modern fad.

As explained in the prologue, this book is written with a complete disregard for such archaic stipulations and sentiments.

49

HAWKE-LAND

THE IRA threatens a gun war in Britain, and rain continues to chase the Indians. Gavaskar takes a well-deserved break, and Mankad sits out the game against Yorkshire. Hence, when play begins an hour late at Headingley and stand-in captain Don Wilson asks them to bat, Baig and Jayantilal walk out in a bid to regain their touch against a probing Yorkshire attack spearheaded by Richard Hutton and Chris Old. Neither of the out-of-form openers manages to create an impression. They add 34, but that is aided by a series of streaky strokes through the slips.

The luck does not last. Having scored 14, Jayantilal pushes at Hutton with his bat 'like a billiard cue' and is caught in the slips. His painstaking 80-odd in the previous outing has not really heralded a return to form. Baig plays across the line and is bowled. Sardesai spends a long, unconvincing period at the crease before losing his stumps for just 1.

All the Indian batsmen, Viswanath included, play tentatively, expecting the ball to move around. The canny Wilson holds himself back, finally bowling his left-arm spin rather late in the day and quickly picks up three wickets.

That India reach 145 is mainly thanks to Wadekar. Distinctly bolder than the rest of his men, the skipper leans forward and drives with class. There are nine fours in his 59, most of them delectably struck. He looks good for a lot more when he drives at one from Hutton and the edge is held at slip by Phil Sharpe.

It is indeed a welcome return to runs for the Indian captain. After his spectacular 85 in the Lord's Test, he has managed just 29 in four innings.

By the end of the day Leadbeater and Lumb have taken the hosts to 46 without loss.

Meanwhile, Gifford is ruled out of the third Test. 'It seems obvious that Underwood should return to what had seemed to be his established place,' writes Arlott.

* * *

By the end of the day, the body count in Ulster had increased to 23. Lieutenant-General Sir Harry Tuzo, General Officer Commanding Northern Ireland, saw no early end to the killings.

And while the secret trial of Mujib began in West Pakistan, a spokesman for the banned Awami party announced that a large number of West Pakistan hostages captured by East Bengal guerrillas would be killed if their leader was harmed in any way.

* * *

Richard Lumb is a 21-year-old colt plucked from the second eleven. This is just his second first-class match. On the second day, as the sun shines briefly, he bats with calm assurance against Bedi, Prasanna and Venkat to score an unbeaten 57 in front of the 3,000 people scattered around the stands. That is before the rain comes down and does not stop for the next one and a half days.

Within another couple of years, Lumb will become a regular in the Yorkshire side. His best summer will be 1979, with 1,465 runs including five hundreds. The following year, a son Michael will be born in Johannesburg to his South African wife. Thirty-three years later, Michael Lumb will hit 106 against the West Indies, becoming the oldest cricketer to hit a century on ODI debut.

The Richard Lumb of 1971, as he flogs the Indian bowlers, cannot possibly have imagined that his son will go on to sign a deal worth £30,000 to play for Rajasthan Royals in 2010.

Yorkshire are 137/3 when the match is stopped, the three spinners having picked up a wicket each. The county has won four of their previous eight encounters against the touring Indians and are well placed in this game when it is called off.

* * *

From the troubled refugee camps along the border with East Pakistan, the news was not encouraging. Dr Nevin Scrimshaw, head of the nutrition department at MIT and accompanying Senator Edward Kennedy on his tour of the refugee areas, said that hundreds of emaciated children were in danger of dying within days because of the conditions. Kennedy had already said that the refugee problem was 'one of the greatest tragedies of our times', caused by a systematic campaign of terror with genocidal consequences. He added that there had been efforts by the Nixon administration 'to whitewash one of the greatest nightmares of modern times'.

The newspapers were flooded with letters voicing grave concern over the situation in both faraway East Pakistan and nearby Ulster. One letter was from M.T. Williams, QC, Labour and Cooperative MP for Warrington, who had appeared for Mujib's defence in the tribunal set up for his previous trial before the Supreme Court in Dacca. Mr Williams was greatly disturbed that the trial was being held in secret with none but Pakistani lawyers and said that this should be considered illegal. He urged both the British government and the UN to express concern in the matter.

* * *

The remaining day is spent in trying to get some practice at the nets whenever the rain stops. As they play a cat-and-mouse game with the elements, an immigrant from Punjab takes delight in describing the proceedings in Hindi over the loudspeaker.

Boycott has come down to the ground, too, although he is not playing in the match. His hamstring has not quite healed, but he wants to get as much practice as possible. The Yorkshireman even manages to coax some of the Indian bowlers to bowl to him.

In the afternoon the players attend a reception given by Indian students at Leeds University before they set off for Nottingham.

Yorkshire v Indians, Headingley – 11, 12, 13 August
Indians 145 (Wadekar 59; Old 3-33, Wilson 3-12) drew with **Yorkshire** 137/3 (Lumb 57*, Leadbeater 40).

50

WINDS OF CHANGE

THE COAL-MINING towns of Nottinghamshire had given cricket the pace of Harold Larwood and Bill Voce, and were thus intricately linked to the Bodyline controversy. It was in one such town named Eastwood that another famous and, eventually controversial, son of the county was born in 1885.

His father was barely literate, but David Herbert Lawrence went on to become one of the leading literary figures in the English language. He passed away at 44, having completed his final novel, *Lady Chatterley's Lover*, a couple of years earlier.

The book was published privately in Italy in 1928 and in France in 1929. A heavily censored version was released in the USA in 1928 and banned for obscenity. The full unexpurgated version of the novel was published for the first time in Britain on 16 August 1960 by Penguin.

The result was the *Regina v Penguin Books* trial at the Old Bailey, the publishers charged under the Obscene Publications Act of 1959. The trial began on 21 October 1960 and lasted six days. The less-than-ideal viewing arrangements did not deter people from crowding into the Old Bailey every day, the seats only available to those who arrived ridiculously early. Not only London, not only Britain … the whole world was gripped by the drama of the trial.

'[Is this] a book you would … wish your wife or your servants to read?' the prosecutor asked the jury. He was Mervyn

Griffith-Jones, veteran of Eton, Trinity Hall (Cambridge) and the Coldstream Guards. The question underlined exactly why the trial was a contest between the old and the new worlds. A world steeped in stuffiness, chauvinism and class distinction, against everything that underlined progress. It led Bernard Levin to write, '[It was] a circus so hilarious, fascinating, tense and satisfying that none who sat through all its six days will ever forget them ... The Sixties began with an attempt to stop the decade entirely and replace it with an earlier one.'

Appropriately the man who represented Penguin was Gerald Gardiner, a founder member of the Campaign for Nuclear Disarmament. His 35 expert witnesses included E.M. Forster, Rebecca West and the Bishop of Woolwich, John Robinson.

Griffith-Jones attacked Lawrence's uses of the word 'womb' and 'bowels', attacked Constance Chatterley for committing adultery, a crime all the more serious since she was 'morally obliged to behave in a manner befitting her class'. He attacked the long-deceased Lawrence himself, because he had run away with his friend's wife. In the end he claimed Constance and her lover were guilty of 'buggery', and unbridled sex was the cause of the recent rise in crime in Britain.

The Bishop stood up calmly after this diatribe and said, 'I think ... Lawrence is trying to ... portray the sex relationship as something essentially sacred ... as in a real sense an act of holy communion.' Asked whether it was a book that Christians ought to read, he responded, 'Yes, I think it is.'

It took the jury just three hours to return a verdict acquitting Penguin Books of all charges. Two hundred thousand copies were made available almost immediately for 3s 6d. In the next two years, Penguin sold 3.3 million copies of the book. In new editions, a note was added that said the trial was not just a legal tussle but a conflict of generation and class.

Kenneth Tynan summarised in *The Observer*, '[The real battle had been] between Lawrence's England and Sir Clifford Chatterley's England ... between freedom and control.' Barbara Barr, the stepdaughter of Lawrence, put it succinctly, 'I feel as if a window has been opened and fresh air has been blown right through England.'

The winds of change had been mentioned in Prime Minister Harold Macmillan's famous speech in Cape Town in early 1960. Although he was referring to the African continent, Macmillan knew very well that the symbolism was as appropriate, albeit in different contexts, in Britain.

In 1957, when he had taken over from Anthony Eden, there were still 45 countries under the governance of the Colonial Office.

During his administration, one by one they left the imperial shadow. Ghana, Malaya, Cyprus, Nigeria, Sierra Leone, Tanganyika, Western Samoa, Jamaica, Trinidad and Tobago, Uganda, Zanzibar and Kenya all achieved independence. The Empire was officially a thing of the past.

As Britain coasted through a wave of consumerism, with record players, cameras, vacuum cleaners, television sets and new settees in thousands of home, with packed beaches on sunny days and a general air of contentment, Macmillan and his colleagues at the helm realised that the Empire too had to yield to the winds of change.

The call-ups for National Service thus ended by 1960. By May 1963, the last young man 'maintaining peace by keeping nationalistic troublemakers in line' had left the armed forces. In 1964, a speech in Canada by Macmillan's successor, Sir Alec Douglas-Home, accepted that colonisation was nearly at an end and positive co-existence had emerged.

The windows of the Long Room of Lord's were, as ever, closed to the winds of change.

In the glorious warm summer of 1959, India, under yet another prince Datta Gaekwad, were being clinically thrashed 5-0. At Old Trafford, Colin Cowdrey refused to enforce the follow-on as the tourists trailed in the first innings by 282 runs. 'Would the Saturday crowd have enjoyed watching India struggle?' he publicly wondered. Cowdrey also suggested that the Test matches be reduced to four days to give India a chance.

During the same summer, while wage earners by now often made more than salaried staff, the Duke of Norfolk's MCC committee voted that *the distinctive status of the amateur was not obsolete, was of great value to the game and should be preserved.* According to Diana Rait Kerr, this was 'not ... for the sake of the old school tie, but with a sincere desire to regain and preserve the unfettered spirit of high adventure, which, since the Golden Age, had been the amateur's priceless contribution to cricket'.

In September 1962, at the North Marine Ground, Scarborough, Ken Barrington hit exactly 100 and Tony Lock, Fred Trueman and Brian Close shared the bowling honours as the Players defeated the Gentlemen by seven wickets. That winter, the archaic amateur status was finally abolished. *Wisden* editor Norman Preston protested that 'cricket was in danger of losing the spirit of freedom and gaiety which the best amateurs brought to the game'. The fact that in the immediate past Trevor Bailey and Denis Compton had been respectively an amateur and a professional had perhaps escaped the *Wisden* editor's notice.

However, Ted Dexter had already admitted that he made a good deal more from cricket than from business. Swanton lamented the passing of an era, but Michael Melford blandly commented that what was being abolished was a form of legalised deceit.

Thus, the tradition of Gentlemen-Players matches ended after 274 encounters. The Players held a 125-68 advantage, with 80 draws and one tie.

Change was taking place across many spheres, but often quite slowly. Several young minds were still being formed around the idea of a Greater Britain. As David Cannadine recalls, 'My sister's first doll was named Queenie after the queen of Tonga, one of the overseas celebrities of the coronation. [The British expedition conquering Mount Everest] was a Henty-like adventure story that was regularly retold throughout the 1950s, especially to my generation of schoolchildren. Then in 1961, the Queen paid a state visit to India, a kind of post-imperial durbar complete with elephant processions and tiger shoots. At my primary school we made a map to trace this royal progress. My primary school also possessed a large world map, on which the British Empire was coloured red, as in those days it invariably was. It was … years out of date, which meant the empire as it had existed at its territorial zenith between the First and Second World Wars. It was an extraordinary vista of early dominion for a Birmingham boy of nine or ten to behold.'

This was 1961 … the 1971 Indian tour of England was just 10 years away.

It is curious but *Lady Chatterley's Lover* came up in court in India as well. In 1964, Ranjit Udeshi of Bombay was prosecuted under Section 292 of the Indian Penal Code for selling an unexpurgated copy of the book. In the Supreme Court of India, Chief Justice Hidayatullah invoked the 1868 Hicklin test to determine when a book can be regarded as obscene. The court upheld the conviction.

Just like the result of the trial in Britain had been a symbolic reflection of the times, so was it in India.

The first few years after 1947 had seen the newly independent nation take rapid steps in drafting a constitution, becoming a republic, organising the first elections, reorganising states according to language, putting an article in the constitution in an effort to eradicate untouchability, and taking a major role in Asian relations. With Gandhi and Patel both dead, Nehru was unfettered in his liberal leadership, playing a leading role in the Bandung Conference and the Non-Aligned Movement (NAM). Indeed, there were representatives from 29 anti-imperialist and recently independent states from Africa and Asia in Indonesia for the conference, but it was Nehru, accompanied by the daughter Indira Gandhi, who set the pace. Nehru's Five Principles of Peaceful Coexistence, fleshed out into twelve, were adopted in the final communique and incorporated into the NAM charter.

At the same time, Nehru himself chaired the National Planning Commission, which rolled out the second five-year plan in 1956. Concrete was everywhere. Excellent engineering colleges were set up, steel mills popped up and hydroelectric dam projects were kicked off.

However, by the mid-1960s, the outlook had changed from optimism to frustration. The GNP had increased from 1950 but not anywhere close to the optimistic predictions. Bureaucratic blockages had produced a virtually unnavigable system of license raj, more or less crippling the private sector and basic industries. Agricultural growth failed to keep pace with the increase in population, leading to the necessity of huge quantities of cereal imports from the United States.

Frost in the tropics

Robert Frost was not really a household name in India in those days, and in our British-modelled education system dominated by Wordsworth, Coleridge, Keats and Shelley, there remained just about enough space for a couple of Americans to tag along – generally Longfellow and Whitman.

But Frost seems to have been a favourite amongst the Nehru family. When a year after Indira Gandhi became prime minister, she quoted the poet's *How Hard It Is to Keep From Being King, When It's in You and in the Situation*. To a friend she wrote that she felt exactly like the man who did not want to be king and drew his hand away when offered the kingdom by his father. To his son Rajiv Gandhi, she wrote, 'To be king is within the situation and within me.'

And because of the Nehru connection we all grew up reading *Stopping by the Woods on a Snowy Evening* as part of our curriculum.

Besides, the Sino-Indian friendship, the 'Hindi-Chini-Bhai-Bhai' slogan, took a rather major hit with the Chinese taking over Tibet. The Dalai Lama fled to India, along with thousands of other refugees. Besides, the bone of contention remained the Aksai Chin region towards the north of Kashmir.

The eventual Chinese march across the McMahon Line was less of a war and more of a walkover – a humiliation in which Assam looked under threat and bombing raids were anticipated in Calcutta. The Chinese withdrew, announcing a unilateral ceasefire, keeping their hold on Aksai Chin, and Indian self-esteem suffered a huge blow.

It is often said that Nehru never recovered from this shock. In 1964 he suffered a stroke. As he lay dying, there lay by his bedside a book of poems by Robert Frost. The open page showed *Stopping by the Woods on a Snowy Evening*. The last four lines were underlined:

> *The woods are lovely dark and deep*
> *But I have promises to keep*
> *And miles to go before I sleep*
> *And miles to go before I sleep.*

51

CHANDRA SHOW

THE BULLETS continue to rain in Belfast; Julian Francis, coordinator of the Oxfam Relief Operation in Calcutta, says that malnutrition is worse than in Biafra; a crowd of West Indians protest in Acton High Street about alleged racial prejudice involved in attempted arson at one of their clubs; Indira Gandhi is universally hailed as a magician for engineering the signature of Andrei Gromyko on to the treaty ... and at Trent Bridge the Indians twiddle their thumbs as rain washes out the first day's play.

So many legends will be stitched together about the 1971 tour that the patchwork of fables will make it difficult to detect the underlying pattern of actual events. So it may read somewhat curiously here, but one of the men fighting to keep his place in the third Test is Chandra. In the two Tests so far, he has struggled, managing just five wickets at an expensive 53, and labouring nearly 21 overs for each wicket. In fact. Chandra finds himself at the bottom of the bowling averages, after Solkar and Abid.

Indian bowlers after two Tests

	Wickets	Ave	Strike Rate
Venkat	9	27.00	73.2
Bedi	8	25.50	85.8
Solkar	3	33.00	88.0
Abid	5	43.40	99.2
Chandra	5	53.00	124.8

Not that Prasanna has really been on fire, but it is always difficult to keep the most experienced bowler on the bench, especially in an Indian side. Prasanna's 124 wickets weigh in heavily against Chandra's collection of 67 at a not-earth-shattering 32.94.

Hence, perhaps both are on tenterhooks as the rains do not allow any cricket on Saturday.

* * *

On the Sunday, as the visitors enjoyed a day of rest, India celebrated the 24th anniversary of independence.

Her father had made the famous 'Tryst with Destiny' speech in 1947. 'At the stroke of the midnight hour, when the world sleeps, India will awake to life and freedom,' he had said. Now, 24 years later, Mrs Gandhi's speech from the ramparts of the Red Fort stressed that India's policy was peace but declared that the country was prepared to face effectively any military challenge from any country. The prime minister reiterated that events in Bangladesh culminating in the influx of more than seven million refugees constituted the greatest challenge faced by free India. 'The Indian government was not threatening anybody or even using strong language. The threats had come from others but, if translated into action, these would receive a fitting reply.'

The tension was mounting, with Pakistani saboteurs blowing up two Indian trains as they passed over the mined culverts between the towns of Silchar and Karimganj in the border district of Cachar in Assam. One of the trains had been carrying food to East Bengali refugees in Tripura.

* * *

On Monday morning the rain continues, preventing play before the second hour. As bored spectators leaf through *The Times*, they come across a half-page advertisement on page three. 'Wake Up World: Please act immediately to stop camera trial,' it announces, with the picture of Mujib underneath. 'Secure release of the President of the People's Republic of Bangladesh.' When play does start, much before grappling with the question of spinners, the

Indians are faced with the continuing problem with their opening combination. Garry Sobers is resting, and the Brian Bolus-led Nottinghamshire are hardly a tough proposition. Especially on a soft and easy-paced wicket with ordinary medium-pace on offer. Yet, Gavaskar is out swishing outside the off stump for just 7 and Mankad produces a painstaking 22 in more than an hour and a half in another desperate bid to find some form.

It is Wadekar whose batting produces the excitement yet again. Fluent and confident, he drives with customary elegance and looks untroubled. With off-spinner Bob White put on to bowl, the Indian skipper strikes him for three sweetly-timed boundaries in an over. It looks as if his touch has been well and truly recaptured at Leeds.

However, the other experienced batsman, Sardesai, continues to struggle. Playing and missing with embarrassing regularity, it is not until after tea that he manages a couple of fluent drives on both sides of the wicket.

Wadekar 49, Sardesai 57 not out, Viswanath treading on his stumps for 12, Solkar and Abid run out in going for quick runs. India declare at 168/6 to infuse some life into a potentially dead match. Almost incredibly it is the medium-pacers who rattle the Nottinghamshire batting.

Two wickets to Abid Ali, two to Govindraj, one run out. Nottinghamshire are 39/5 at close of the second day.

With a day of the three-day match lost to rain, the follow-on can be enforced with a 100-run lead. And due to the quick strikes by the medium-pacers, it looks a possibility.

* * *

That same day, on completing his five-day fact-finding tour of the refugee camps, Senator Edward Kennedy declared that he was convinced that genocide had taken place in East Bengal.

* * *

The third day at Trent Bridge sees plenty of excitement injected through spirited declarations. Abid gets rid of Bolus early in the day to reduce the hosts to 40/6 and the follow-on looks a real possibility. However, aided by Mike Taylor, Nottinghamshire get to 69 with seven wickets down. Immediately Bolus declares, throwing India the challenge of going for a win. With the seamers proving such a success in the brief 27.3-over innings, there are just three overs bowled by the spinners, all of them by Chandra who finishes with 1-7. It cannot have amused Prasanna much.

Gavaskar falls early again, but this time Mankad is more confident. Playing all the bowlers with composure, he looks tidy in defence and times his drives well. Wadekar, Sardesai and Viswanath all play fluent knocks at the other end, and at lunch India are 104/3. They bat on for half an hour after the break, Mankad completing his half-century, Viswanath sweetly stroking his way to 38. When White bowls the latter, Wadekar calls his men in with the score reading 145/4.

An hour and fifty minutes remain alongside 20 mandatory overs, and the target is 245. Govindraj and Abid run in again, but they cannot repeat their success. Within a dozen overs, Bolus and Frost knock off 50 runs.

Hence, Wadekar calls on his two spinners. And Chandra strikes almost immediately, trapping Bolus plumb lbw. Before tea he also bowls Smedley. At the break the score is 75/2.

After the interval, it is Prasanna from one end, Chandra from the other. Both bowl their hearts out. No easy run is on offer, the strikes continue to be dealt from that one end. Chandra removes Bielby and White to make it 94/4 as the mandatory overs start.

In the second of the 20 overs, Chandra has White caught by Solkar to make it 97/5. Frost has batted all along with admirable pluck, but now, in the next Chandra over, he pushes one tamely back to the bowler – 100/6, with 16 overs to go. It does seem that for the very first time India can win against Nottinghamshire.

However, Mike Taylor proves stubborn yet again, and Peter Plummer sticks around. The hosts play out the last few overs to finish on 115/6.

Chandra has 6-34 in the second innings, and his place in the Test side is secure. Prasanna has bowled 18 overs for 18 runs without a wicket, and the final opportunity to clinch a spot in the eleven has come and gone. Wadekar and Adhikari are not in favour of including him. They are not convinced of his fitness – he has needed medical attention during his spell. Besides, a fourth spinner makes the tail way too long for a side that has been rescued by the late order so many times.

At the other end of the order, Mankad has once again come good on the eve of the Test match, ensuring that India will go through the series with an unchanged side.

On the English front, with Boycott's fitness still in doubt, the seasoned Somerset batsman Roy Virgin is summoned as a backup. Of course, Jameson will start as the replacement if Boycott does not recover in time, but Virgin is included in the squad.

Curiously, in his end-of-the-tour piece in *The Cricketer*, K.N. Prabhu will write that Virgin was one of the six English batsmen to impress him on the tour, the others being Denness, Fletcher, Jameson, Luckhurst and M.J.K. Smith. This is curious because the summer of 1970 will remain the only English season in which Virgin will manage an average over 40, and he will finish his 20-year career with a first-class average of 29.87. Of all those named by Prabhu, Fletcher will come closest to a Test average of 40 but will still fall short with 39.90. On the tour Prabhu has seen, among others, Boycott, Amiss, Edrich and D'Oliveira, cricketers of distinctly better pedigree and with end-of-career records that will underline how good they are.

It makes one aware of the limitations of judgment based on data-blind visual impressions in cricket.

On the bowling front, Snow is recalled as a possible deputy for Lever who is suffering from Whitlow, a gesture to indicate that his offence at Lord's is forgotten.

Nottinghamshire v Indians, Trent Bridge – 14, 16, 17 August Indians 168/6 dec (Sardesai 57, Wadekar 49) and 145/4 dec. (Mankad 50*) drew with **Nottinghamshire** 69/7 dec (Abid 3-23) and 115/6 (Frost 50; Chandra 6-34).

52

CLASS APART

AT THE Oval, some nine years earlier, England had trounced Pakistan by 10 wickets to win the 1962 series 4-0. *Wisden* had gushed, 'The match proved a triumph for the three England amateur batsmen, Sheppard, Cowdrey and Dexter.'

Indeed it did. Cowdrey scored 182, Dexter 172 with five sixes. Sheppard, taking time off from his church duties, got 57. Barrington did score an unbeaten 50, but he was of course not an amateur by a long shot.

When All-Time English XIs are discussed, Barrington, averaging 58.67 for his 6,806 runs, is generally ignored, while May (4,537 at 46.77), Dexter (4.502 at 47.89) and even Cowdrey (7,624 at 44.06) are pitchforked into the discussion if not into the final team. Amateur status carries its aura even today.

However, that was the last time England played with a side split as amateurs and professionals before the ridiculous distinction was abolished in November 1962. So, although they lost their final encounter against the Players, the Gentlemen cricketers did have a triumphant swansong in Test cricket.

The amateur-professional divide had permeated out of the cricket grounds and social strata into the tussle for the top seat in Britain. The Eton-Balliol-educated son-in-law of a duke Harold Macmillan had started to look more and more antiquated with his Edwardian air and courtly manner. Plagued by the Vassall affair and the Profumo scandal, the prime minister used his benign surgery for prostate problems as an opportunity to resign. The man who was chosen by the Conservative party to replace him till the next scheduled elections was even more anachronistic. Although the 14th Earl of Home disclaimed his peerage and took office as simply Sir Alec Douglas-Home, he exuded the make-believe aura of privileged amateur leadership and everything that was archaic about the system.

His opponent was the Labour leader Harold Wilson, who promised to forge a new Britain in the 'white heat' of scientific revolution. Asked which class he belonged to, Wilson replied, 'Well, someone who started at elementary school in Yorkshire and became an Oxford don – where do you put him in this class spectrum? I think these phrases are becoming more and more meaningless.'

The Earl of Home claimed he wanted to keep Britain in the first XI, as one of the *four* opening batsmen. In trying to mix geopolitical and cricketing metaphors, he went one opener beyond England's 1970/71 ploy of Boycott, Luckhurst and Edrich. Even Tory supporters said that he reminded them of 1912. But using his own cricketing metaphor, Wilson was cautious in his optimism, 'I was given *Test Match Special* [actually *Test Match* Surprise] by Jack Hobbs for my eighth birthday. It was about a cricketing peer, Lord Ravensdale. He gets attacked by the press, but goes on to make 51 in the second innings and to take 5 for 50.' He was right to be cautious, because the Conservatives made a surprising recovery in the popularity charts and Labour only managed to win by a slim margin.

Changes were taking place in the game, with the limited-overs tournaments about to stretch across the landscape of English summers. However, when the MCC visited India once on each side of the abolition, the attitude towards such *insignificant* tours remained frozen in time.

While the choice of the 26-year-old Ted Dexter as captain for the 1961/62 tour was definitely a step-up from Nigel Howard ten years before, the composition of the squad remained less than the cream. May had retired; none of Cowdrey, Edrich, Subba Row, Trueman, Statham, Close or Flavell wanted to go. In the absence of May and Cowdrey, Dexter was given the job.

The first sight that greeted the cricketers was once again squalor and poverty. The saga of long journeys and not-so-luxurious hotels continued, alongside dreadful misadventures with food, recurring stomach ailments and endless social engagements.

The eating problems were by now anticipated. Unilever had offered to send out consignments of food, but the MCC did not want to upset their Indian hosts and declined. Allsopp's brewery sent out a quantity of beer to every Test centre, but could not deliver in Bombay because Maharashtra was a dry state.

There were accidental visits to kitchens with primitive set-ups which shocked the players. There were unpleasant discoveries of room attendants filling carafes of supposedly boiled water directly from taps.

The team was overjoyed when Peter Richardson's wife, a BOAC air-hostess, arranged access to Speedbird House, the lodgings of BOAC aircrew, where they could finally get regular drinks.

At the same time, at the Great Eastern Hotel in Calcutta, a special lunch was laid out for the cricketers on Christmas Day. The Maharaja of Cooch Behar entertained them that evening at the Tollygunge Club.

This other attraction of an Indian tour – that of being entertained by the Maharajas – had become sidelined by 1962. But Dexter did get invited by the Maharajakumar of Vizianagaram to his family estate in Benares. Vizzy presented him with a lavish gift of a tiger skin, complete with a fearsome head.

Dexter also enjoyed the hospitality of his Sussex colleague, the 'titular ruler of Pataudi and Bhopal'. M.A.K. Pataudi had just recovered from the accident that cost him almost total vision in one eye. He made his debut in this series, and scored a hundred in the final Test at Madras. In the next series in the West Indies, Nari Contractor would suffer a near fatal injury and Pataudi would be made captain.

There is a story about a fan asking Pataudi when he had decided that he could play Test cricket in spite of the damage to this eye. The witty Nawab's instant answer had been, 'When

I saw the England bowling line-up.' The light-heartedness notwithstanding, the comment does underline the quality of the team sent by the MCC. They had some depth in the spin department, with the veteran Tony Lock and the industrious David Allen. But they were no match for the Indian spinners in their home conditions. Powered by strong performances from the likes of Vijay Manjrekar, Chandu Borde and Salim Durani, India won the series 2-0.

In the final Test at Madras, England surrendered to Durani's spin to lose by 128 runs. The same Test witnessed the tragedy of a spectator dying of a heart attack in the stands on the third day. Disappointed by the English performance, veteran journalist Berry Sarbadhikari reported, 'The cricket fans of Madras have arranged for a hearse, following all the rules and rituals. They probably want to convey that English cricket has died.' This beautifully constructed paragraph raking over the ashes did not quite get the attention it deserved.

It was also a series in which persistent complaints about umpiring were heard. According to the writer Mark Peel, in the fourth Test at Calcutta, umpire Habib-ur-Rahman Ibrahim Choudhury not only upheld a number of questionable appeals by the Indian bowlers, but also raised his cap when he walked in with the crowd of 80,000 giving him an ovation.

According to Dexter: 'I felt that for what was in effect an "A" team tour, we hadn't done badly, and almost all of the new caps went on to become important members of England sides over the next decade. This clearly demonstrated the value of "A" tours, which I insisted on sending out regularly later in my administrative career.'

The successful series for India also saw the curtain fall on one of the greatest cricketers produced by the country. During the Delhi Test, ace Indian leg-spinner Subhas Gupte shared a room with the batsman A.G. Kripal Singh at the Imperial Hotel. The latter, smitten by the hotel receptionist, called her to ask for a date. Perhaps there were calls after a firm 'No', perhaps not. The details are hazy. The girl complained to the manager of the Indian team, the matter escalated and both Gupte and Kripal were suspended. Kripal for trying to set up a date, Gupte apparently for being the room-mate of a man trying to set up a date.

He did not play for India again. Mihir Bose summed it up, 'India's first great spinner ended his career because he happened to share a room with a man who wanted a drink with a girl.'

That was one year after Penguin had won the case of *Lady Chatterley's Lover*. In the 1960s, there was as great a cultural gap between India and the West as the world would ever witness.

When two years later Dexter was asked whether he would be interested in another tour of India, he refused. 'The last Indian tour had been tough, and in the end, not hugely rewarding.'

While the 1961/62 tour had been a combined India-Pakistan-Ceylon affair, the 1963/64 trip was a short one of eight weeks focused on India alone. But even the shorter duration was no enticement for many. Apart from Dexter, the ones who dropped out were Trueman, Statham, Illingworth and, initially, Cowdrey. The captaincy was handed over to another former amateur cricketer, M.J.K. Smith.

The abolition of amateur status had done little for the outlook of the MCC selection committee. Barrington had by then played 45 Tests for his 3,454 runs at 52.33, and on the previous tour had been extraordinarily popular with the Indian crowds. However, Smith, with his Oxford credentials and former amateur status, was obviously a more comforting choice at the helm. These credentials outweighed his 22 Tests till then, with 1,090 runs at 32.05. There was no comparison between Smith and Barrington as cricketers, but the contrasts between their roots and background were plenty. Very few Australian teams would have thought twice before appointing Barrington as skipper. But England was different. The British electorate could opt for a self-made Harold Wilson ahead of the aristocratic anachronism Sir Alec Douglas-Home, but no such sentiments reached the inner sanctum where Gubby Allen held court. In fact, in 1966, Sir Alec would become the president of the MCC.

Smith, of course, was an able captain and did quite a good job in his 25 Tests as skipper. However, one can definitely detect the currents of old-world considerations flowing through the decision-making process.

This time Saccone and Speed, wine and spirits merchants, shipped out hard liquor and tinned provisions to the team with the help of the British High Commission. The increase in internal flights made travel from venue to venue less strenuous. However, the players did face problems, such as dust on their plates and cutlery, and a swimming pool where they found dead animals and rotting vegetation.

Holy Cowdrey

On the second day of the Calcutta Test, England crawled to 149/3 after dismissing India early in the morning for 241. Cowdrey was the primary culprit, batting nearly three hours to remain unbeaten on 41 at stumps.

A frustrated Sankari Prasad Basu later wrote the following in his Bengali cricket book *Not Out:* 'Mr Cowdrey, I am sure you remember 1959, when India lost all five Tests in England. Showing great qualities of mercy you asked for the number of days to be reduced for Tests featuring India, because one-sided matches were no fun at all. At Old Trafford, as captain, you refused to enforce follow-on. When people asked probing questions about your sporting spirit, you answered, "Will the Saturday crowd enjoy India batting for survival?" O Mr Cowdrey who cares so much about the pleasure of the crowds, I ask you ... Granted today is not a Saturday but Thursday. But 50,000 people have gathered, bunking schools, colleges, offices, and have spent their money, to watch you play. Standing there like corpses on the ground, what pleasure have you provided the Indian crowd?'

As the tour progressed, disaster struck in the forms of Asian flu and stomach disorders. Only ten men seemed fit for the second Test at Bombay and Henry Blofeld, then a young reporter for *The Guardian,* was informed by the England manager David

Clark that he would be playing unless one of the casualties made a recovery.

Not that the press contingent was immune to stomach ailments. Michael Melford reported one morning that he had been 'to the loo 12 times, but I am not claiming a world record because I was wind-assisted'.

Blofeld did not make his Test debut, thanks to Micky Stewart discharging himself from hospital. He threw up while fielding on the first day and had to be admitted yet again, leaving England a man short. The visitors somehow drew the Test, Titmus batting at an unusually high No.5 and scoring 84 not out over five hours. That was the Test in which Bapu Nadkarni bowled 131 consecutive dot balls. And for the second successive Test, Pat audi generously asked Kripal Singh to field for England as a substitute. Kripal did do some interesting things during those two tours.

The cricket in the series was rather insipid and defensive in spite of a couple of enterprising hundreds by Budhi Kunderan and debutant Hanumant Singh. With Cowdrey and Peter Parfitt coming in as reinforcements, England managed to draw 0-0.

Of course, England were helped by the curious decision of Pataudi to insert the opposition on the most benign of tracks in the fifth Test at Kanpur. Having done so, he opened the bowling with Jaisimha and Durani. After four draws, Pataudi was keen to do something different. Smith responded by suggesting that he would declare at the end of the first day at 271/2 if Pataudi agreed to do the same on the second day. The amateur strain perhaps? I am led to speculate that had it been 1946 and had the senior Pataudi been at the helm, perhaps his regal prerogative would have allowed him to accept the challenge. But this was 1964, India had been independent for 17 years, a republic for 14, and the princely states had been absorbed into the republic for 16. Pataudi Jr decided to toe the democratic line and consult the Indian board. The officials of a country hemmed in by bureaucracy and licence raj found the proposal a bit too dynamic. As a result England totalled 559 and after following on India saved the Test due to a remarkably patient hundred from No.3 by Nadkarni

The Maharaja element was totally absent this time. However, almost three decades after his unfortunate stint as captain of the Indian side, Vizzy created potentially combustible diplomatic headlines. He got into a tiff with the noted correspondent E.M. Wellings over the seating arrangements in the press box. Wellings, not the most amiable of characters, threw his typewriter at the Maharajakumar's ample midriff.

Vizzy had put up a sponsored marquee during the Test match where English journalists were invited for lunch and tea. Of course, due to the showdown, Wellings could hardly go there. So Ian Todd, a young reporter for the *Daily Mirror*, got him some bananas.

The matter escalated to higher and higher echelons of the administration, and finally Paul Gore-Booth, the British High Commissioner in India, had to intervene. There was also a 'stiff letter' from Gubby Allen on behalf of the MCC committee accusing Wellings of misconduct. Nothing came of it. The MCC seriously considered sacking Wellings from the club, but in the end did not go through with it. According to Blofeld, 'Not for the first time he got away with a disgraceful piece of behaviour which, I am afraid, was typical of the man.'

But this was an exception. Overall there were very few incidents, the players were treated to lavish hospitality. Gubby Allen, who had travelled to India, reciprocated by treating the hosts to caviar and smoked salmon flown in from home.

M.J.K. Smith's side did suffer from flu and stomach problems, but perhaps the tact of the captain and manager allowed them to focus on the cricket without too many complaints.

The problems with facilities, food and logistics would continue well into the 1990s. Even in 1997/98 Shane Warne would have cans of baked beans shipped all the way from Australia.

With the economy opening up and the subcontinent becoming the epicentre of cricket, from the turn of the century India rapidly became the most coveted of cricketing destinations. The hospitality and facilities that the cricketers come across now in the hotels and elsewhere are unmatched anywhere in the world.

And then there has been the phenomenon of the Indian Premier League. Times have changed by leaps and bounds.

But during most of the second half of the 20th century, India meant poverty, squalor, hunger, heat, dust, noise and millions of people. Underdeveloped, chaotic, a curious melange of impossible contradictions.

53

355 IN A DAY

EDRICH WAKES up on the eve of the Oval Test with lumbago. 'He wouldn't have had a cat in hell's chance of playing if the match had started today,' says Alec Bedser. Meanwhile, Old Trafford hero Peter Lever keeps his finger's crossed, as much as he can that is, following the lancing of a painful Whitlow on the third finger of his bowling hand.

Somerset's Roy Virgin is ready to take strike at No.3 if required. At 31, he is not really the young talent about to burst out on the cricketing scene. He had an immensely successful 1970 summer, scoring 2,223 runs at 47.29.

As for the bowling, Snow is perhaps the most high-profile backup in history. Perhaps the Indian camp is as fervent as Lever himself in wishing that his finger heals quick.

The Indian team management do include Prasanna in the 12. Chandra's fantastic performance in the second innings of the Nottinghamshire game makes it clear that none of the three spinners will be asked to make way for the most experienced tweaker in the side. However, Arlott speculates on whether Prasanna will be played instead of a batsman. After all, Solkar, Abid Ali and Engineer are all competent with the bat and Venkat has shown some ability as well. 'At his best [Prasanna] is worth a team place instead of a batsman if India are prepared to attack,' he writes.

Woodcock wonders if the comparable tightness of Prasanna's bowling will make the Indians nod in his favour rather than Chandra. But what Woodcock desperately wants is a result. Rain has played havoc in two Tests and India has had 'great good luck in being saved from two probable defeats'. It is a pity, according to Woodcock, that an extra day has not been set aside to ensure a result at The Oval.

* * *

The sporting world in Britain was shocked with George Best being sent off by referee Norman Burtenshaw as Manchester United played Chelsea at Stamford Bridge. In Glasgow Green, 50,000 protesters marched against the Clyde shipyard closures.

Along the Irish border, the army and the IRA were engaged in a game of death.

On the other blazing border, six Britons and two Americans who crossed into East Pakistan with relief supplies and without visas were sent back into India by Pakistani troops.

* * *

Even as Woodcock and Arlott are guarded in their predictions, Laker is confident that the odds are 3-1 in favour of England in the decider. 'In view of the thundery weather forecast, the professional all-round efficiency of home-bred cricketers could transform this decisive match into a one-horse race.'

In the end Lever sits out nursing his finger, while Edrich does make a recovery to be included in the final XI. It perhaps seems a blessing for him when Illingworth wins the toss for the third time in the series and the fifth consecutive time in Tests. England bat. Edrich is perhaps further relieved when he sees the first ball from Abid Ali bounce twice on its way to Engineer. One can expect at least an hour of uneventful batting against the purported new-ball attack on this sluggish surface. However, the southpaw is pressed into action as early as the tenth ball.

For the third time in the series, Solkar gets Luckhurst. The second ball sent down by the left-armer is an innocuous half-volley outside off stump. Luckhurst flashes at it uncharacteristically and misses. The next ball is almost a replica. The batsman flashes again, and this time his nick is held by Gavaskar at second slip.

The batsman's three Test innings at The Oval have thus far got him one solitary run.

Edrich plays and misses against Solkar several times, but is as unflappably professional as ever. At the other end Jameson hits the ball with amazing power. The first bowler to suffer is Abid, as the opener twice pummels him past cover point. Abid has to be taken off before the hour is up and Gavaskar comes on for one over. It is 37/1 at the end of the first hour, Jameson 26.

It is the start of the second hour that witnesses a distinct change in approach. In Bedi's second over Jameson strides down the wicket and dispatches him over the straight field on to a member's lap.

Wadekar introduces Chandra, and Jameson responds by pulling him to the boundary twice. And then he jumps out to Bedi again, cracking him hard and high, and it lands in the fifth row of the pavilion. According to Peter Wilson in the *Daily Mirror*, 'It had the effect of one of the stuffier rooms of Madame Tussauds being brought to life.'

Wadekar speaks to Bedi, asking him to restrict his flight and peg his attack in line with the off stump. This interaction remains a bone of contention between the captain and his star spinner for decades to come.

Jameson, with his thickset build, his rather unathletic movements, and the resounding thump with which he hits the balls is bringing back fond memories of the unfortunate Colin Milburn. By now Edrich is looking fluent as well. The outfield is fast, the pitch easy-paced, and it looks like a long day of leather-chasing for the Indians. Bedi makes way for Venkat and at the other end an unimpressive Chandra is replaced by Bedi. By lunch, Jameson is on 54, Edrich 33 and England are on a formidable 97/1.

The signs seem ominous after lunch. Venkat, the only bowler who has managed to check the flow of runs, sends down a relatively indifferent over. Twice Edrich dispatches him to the fence. The partnership is worth a hundred, and in quick time. England look like running away with the match on the first day.

But Bedi is still giving it air, and Edrich is not quite at ease against him. The tantalising loop is always a threat. At 41, Edrich pushes forward and there is a noise. Engineer throws the ball up. Umpire Dusty Rhodes seems to be in doubt, before his finger starts to go up. Edrich shows no sign of agreeing with the verdict, but he has to turn and make his way back to the pavilion. Nelson has struck; 111/2.

Fletcher is not really the right man to come in at this juncture. Four days ago, he turned out in the John Player League against Leicestershire at Grace Road and scored a painstaking 32. Here his tentative pushing and prodding undo much of the momentum built up by Jameson and Edrich. Jameson tries to continue in the same vein, pulling Venkat and driving Bedi for boundaries. But slowly caution creeps into his batting as well.

After 20 uncertain minutes, Fletcher flashes at Bedi and Gavaskar holds his second catch of the day. The Essex man trudges back for one. At 135/3, the Indians are clawing their way back.

D'Oliveira, the new man, starts out looking distinctly uncomfortable against Bedi. Eventually, in a bid to get off the mark and away from strike, he pushes to cover point and calls. Perhaps the batsmen have overlooked Wadekar's left-handedness. The Indian captain moves quickly and the throw beats the desperate Jameson. It is a close decision but it goes in favour of the Indians. The Warwickshire batsman is dismissed in the most unfortunate manner after a thrilling innings of 82. England are now in trouble at 139/4.

Three overs later, they slump even further. D'Oliveira, apparently perturbed at his role in Jameson's dismissal, hits Chandra uppishly to mid-on and Mankad pockets the catch. It is 143/5, and the tables have turned.

Of course, they still have to contend with the skipper and the stumper, two of the most obdurate lower middle-order batsmen. Illingworth and Knott put on 32, the former dour, determined, but eager to belt anything loose, the latter pugnacious, cheeky and a fighter to the core.

The captain falls in the most uncharacteristic fashion. Always good with dispatching the long hop, he now takes his eyes off the ball as Chandra pitches awfully short. He misses by a long way and is bowled – 175/6, and the game has shifted India's way.

And now it swings back. Knott takes charge almost immediately, thrusting his broad pads forward, upsetting the bowling plans. Frequently he brings out the sweep, going down on his knees, aiming between midwicket and long leg. Resorting to the straight bat, he dispatches Bedi over long-on for six. If they pitch short, he cuts quite delicately and pulls with élan.

At the other end, Hutton starts tentatively but is soon playing with confidence mingled with urgency. He is driving with pluck and nonchalance, and soon Bedi, in consultation with Wadekar, is filling up the cover area with the quicker fielders.

With Solkar prowling that zone, there ensues a fascinating duel. Knott pushes a bit on either side and sprints, the great fielder swoops down and sends in his returns. The cheeky stumper wins the first round, with one stolen single after another adding to the score.

The two men put on 51 in half an hour before the tea interval. After the break, the strokes flow from both ends as the sun shines on The Oval. Knott continues to sweep and cut. And Hutton starts dominating the spinners.

It is difficult to dissociate what the reporters see and write from what actually happens, such is the power of the famous Hutton name. Here is Peter Wilson again. 'Thirty-three years ago, when I saw one Hutton make 364 at The Oval, I never dreamt I'd see another consolidating England's Test prospects beyond conceivable hope of defeat. Yet that's what Richard's 81 did and his cover drives were reminiscences in willow.' So caught up is the chronicler in his throes of nostalgia, that the result is a foregone conclusion.

Arlott recounts the drives essayed in the 'handsome fashion of his family'. Woodcock says his cover drives did justice to a famous name. Even Wadekar, ghosted by Prabhu, writes, 'Some of his off-drives proclaimed his lineage.'

We can perhaps conclude that the drives played by the younger Hutton are laced with class, even though perhaps a bit of the sheen is reflected from the name on the scoreboard rather than the strokes themselves.

Knott falls when in sight of a very well-deserved century. With the partnership becoming increasingly worrisome, Wadekar takes the new ball in the 87th over. Knott promptly hits Abid for back-to-back boundaries to move to 90. Solkar runs in and sends down a wide. The following ball to Knott is a well-disguised slower delivery. The drive is essayed early and the ball pops back into the safe hands of the bowler. A valiant innings comes to an end and along with it a partnership of 103. It is 278/6.

The breakthrough is achieved, India are wary of Snow. But the fast man is not able to repeat his Lord's heroics with the bat. Solkar gets him to snick one and it is 284/7.

How many basking in the glory of the great Oval win years later will remember Solkar as the highest wicket-taker in the first innings?

If the Indians think the end is in sight it turns out to be premature. Underwood, making a comeback to the England side, proves a solid ally for Hutton. The latter changes gear to become even more aggressive. As the 10,000 spectators sit enjoying the sun, the two bat briskly to add 58 in quick time. With drives off Abid and Solkar, Hutton gets to his half-century and keeps going. When Bedi returns, he strikes him for two consecutive boundaries as well.

With Underwood managing to send both Bedi and Chandra to the fence, it starts to become really frustrating for the Indians. Having dismissed half the side for less than 150, they have the familiar experience of England recovering through their lower order and the game slipping away. When Hutton leans forward and drives Venkat through the off side, the score speeds over 350 and the bowlers seem bereft of ideas.

And now, ten minutes from the scheduled close of play, Venkat's tossed up delivery lands on Solkar's boot-mark, turns sharply to beat Hutton's forward stroke and strikes the stumps.

A fantastic knock of 81 comes to an end, the third well-deserved hundred of the day that remains unscored. But one wonders whether the boot-mark, encouraging bite and spin, is a pleasant sight for Underwood watching from the non-striker's end.

When Underwood turns Venkat into the hands of Wadekar at the stroke of stumps, the England innings ends at a rather imposing 355. The Indian shoulders show signs of drooping as they come off the field. Solkar 3-28 from 15 overs, and one wonders if he should have bowled more. Chandra 2-76 from 24 has been less than devastating, Venkat has bowled well in patches for his 2-63 from 20.4 overs. It is Bedi with 2-120 from his 36 who has been really expensive.

England v India, 3rd Test, The Oval – 19, 20, 21, 23, 24 August England 355 (Knott 90, Jameson 82, Hutton 81, Edrich 41; Solkar 3-28).

54

OLD AND NEW

FORTY-SEVEN YEARS down the line, in 2018, The Oval was witness to an incredible Glamorgan win over hosts Surrey in the T20 Vitality Blast. Set 195 to win, without two main players, Joe Burns and Colin Ingram, Glamorgan overhauled the target with six balls to spare. Later, chief coach, the former England off-spinner Robert Croft, tweeted that the side had been motivated by a quote he had scrawled on the dressing-room whiteboard. 'The pessimist sees the difficulty in every opportunity; an optimist sees the opportunity in every difficulty.' Along with the hashtag #Glammydressingroomwallinsurrey, Croft tweeted the picture of the board with the line, 'Thanks, Mr Churchill.' The quote, it was explained, was attributed to 'the late Prime Minister and war-time leader.'

In January 1965, the former prime minister and war-time leader passed away at the age of 90. On television, the then prime minister Harold Wilson addressed the British people, 'Tonight our nation mourns the loss of the greatest man any of us has ever known.'

The many questions that arise about the method and accuracy of Wilson's comparative scale of greatness are not really relevant here. As Churchill's body lay for three days at Westminster Hall before the state funeral, 320,000 waited for four hours or more to pay their respects to the fallen leader.

An estimated audience of 25 million watched the funeral live on television.

Several decades later, in his autobiography *Paddington Boy*, David Frith wrote, 'The death of Winston Churchill in January 1965 was not so much a shock (he was 90), but it was the removal from our living ranks of a major symbolic foundation-stone.'

It was indeed a symbolic break with the past. Churchill had left 10 Downing Street for the final time in 1955. Since then, there had been the Suez crisis and cascading decolonisation. Nyasaland and Northern Rhodesia had just been removed from an uneasy portfolio. Imperial glory and gunboat diplomacy were passé.

To add to the symbolisation of changing times, in October the same year four young men from Liverpool with curious hairdos trotted up the steps of the Buckingham Palace to receive their MBEs. 'How long have you been together as a band?' the Queen asked. Ringo Starr and Paul McCartney supposedly answered, 'We've been together now for 40 years and it don't seem a day too much.'

It was a new era of the youth, of rock and roll, of free love and chemical high, of Aldermaston marches, of Flower Power, of peace and protest. It was also the era of supermarkets, the washing machine, the colour television revolution … the fastest-growing organisation of the decade was the Consumers' Association.

Britain was no longer an important world power. However, George Orwell's gloomy prediction of a cold and unimportant island where everyone had to work hard and live mainly on herrings and potatoes had not come true. London was a swinging city, the capital of modernity and fun-loving hedonism, the fun funnelled by youth expenditure that reached £800 million a year.

In the heady summer of 1966, the Barclaycard, the first British credit card, was launched in June, and a month later, at Wembley Stadium, Bobby Moore wiped his dirty hands on the velvet cover at the front of the royal box, so as not to soil the Queen's lily-white gloves before he raised the World Cup.

But on the other hand, the grandiose National Plan projecting 25 per cent economic growth between 1964 and 1970 did not get anywhere. While growth and prosperity seemed comforting enough in absolute terms, when mapped against the countries across the Channel there was a sudden and distinct feeling of inferiority. Between 1965 and 1966 the crisis with the pound became acute enough for the government to invoke the special relationship clause with Lyndon Johnson's administration. Wilson's secret agreement with Johnson was to desist the withdrawal of British presence 'east of Suez'. The phrase was of course borrowed from Kipling's *Mandalay,* in which the writer spoke of 'sending forth the best ye breed, To serve your captives' need, To wait in heavy harness, On fluttered folk and wild – Your new-caught, sullen peoples, Half devil and half child.'

Johnson also demanded active British involvement in the Vietnam War. Wilson refused, but that was not immediately apparent. Enoch Powell complained that Britain was behaving like an American satellite. Gerald Scarfe's cover for *Private Eye* mercilessly lampooned the Wilson-Johnson alliance.

The day after Bobby Moore held the world in his hands at Wembley, the Colonial Office ceased to exist. The following month, as the bitter confrontation between the British and Indonesian troops in Borneo came to an end, new questions were raised about the continuance of a military presence east of Suez. Five years after the government had announced their intention keeping a permanent British garrison in Aden, the forces had to withdraw in 1967.

In his 1971 account titled *The Labour Government,* Wilson admitted that hanging on to the east of Suez had been his worst mistake, and it had taken a lot of hard facts to convert him.

John Lennon would return his MBE medal in 1969 to protest against Britain's support of America in Vietnam, alongside his protests against 'Britain's involvement in the Nigeria-Biafra thing and against *Cold Turkey* slipping down the charts'.

Moreover, when Britain applied for membership of the EEC in 1967 for the second time, the application was summarily rejected. It had been just 12 years since they had hung up on the Quay d'Orsay official, saying Messina was 'a devilish awkward place to expect a minister to get to'. Quite a few things had changed in the interim.

Things had changed in quite a few spheres. While the very presence in London of a half-naked fakir called Mahatma Gandhi had driven Churchill to apoplexy, now a hairy Indian mystic known simply as the Maharishi Mahesh Yogi checked into the Waldorf Hotel. Indeed, in the words of Bernard Levin, 'teachers, prophets, sibyls, oracles, mystagogues, avatars, haruspices and mullahs roamed the land, gathering flocks about them as easily as holy men in nineteenth-century Russia, and any philosophy, from Zen Buddhism to macrobiotics and from violence as an end in itself to total inactivity as an end in itself, could be sure of a respectful hearing and a group of adherents.'

Among the disciples of the Maharishi were the four recent MBEs, the Beatles, who followed him back to Hrishikesh in India. Their pledge of eternal allegiance with his god-man lasted somewhat less than eternity, varying between ten days and seven weeks. One of the principal grievances was the sexual advances the Maharishi made towards Mia Farrow. Lennon promptly wrote the song *Sexy Sadie* and the whole alliance was being dismissed as a 'public mistake'. They were not totally disenchanted by the East, though. In 1970, George Harrison was singing *My Sweet Lord* with 'Hare Krishna' chants in the background.

So, was it a new emerging society in Britain? To some degree it was. To a great extent it was not. While there was enlightened liberalisation in view, it did not quite trickle down to one and all. Most of Britain remained conservative and old-fashioned. There remained complicated contrasts.

For example, the contraceptive pill was marketed from 1963, but was made available to single women only from 1967. There was a call for a moral clean-up of television in view of violence, sex and bad language. Home Secretary James Callaghan called for a halt in the rising tide for permissiveness. Even in 1970, women comprised only 28 per cent of university students.

Apart from the complicated racial problems with immigration becoming a major political issue, there were also cultural factors which gave racial innuendos and direct vilification a great degree of respectability. Alf Garnett of the immensely popular television series *Till Death Us Do Part* poured out his venom at the left-wingers, 'darkies' and the 'wogs', insisting 'the bloody coons' should be sent back to 'their own countries'. His fantasies included experimenting with genetics and creating a breed of small darkies to do household jobs. Peter Worsley wrote in the *Financial Times* that Alf was 'the rampaging, howling embodiment of all the most vulgar and odious prejudices that slop about in the bilges of the national mind ... hidden hates, irrational fears, suppressed loyalties [that] stand in the way of our slow stumble towards a more civilised society.' However, both *Till Death Us Do Part* and Alf Garnett remained extremely popular through the second half of the Sixties and first half of the Seventies. To be fair, sitcom writer Johnny Speight intended Garnett to be a satirical character. He was calling out those prevailing attitudes and was rather dismayed that many people missed the satire. He later created the left-wing equivalent of Garnett in another show named from wedding vows – *For Richer ... For Poorer.*

There was racial violence in pockets, especially with the rise of the skinheads in urban working-class areas. In April 1970, a Pakistani porter called Tosir Ali was stabbed to death a few days after a skinhead rampage in the East End of London.

Thankfully, in spite of the politicisation, none of this could become rampantly part of legislation other than the controversial immigration bills. That is how D'Oliveira ultimately emerged at The Oval in 1968 where his innings of 158 put the cat among the milk-white pigeons of Vorster-land. That same year Kingsley Amis published *I Want It Now*, in which systemic prejudices were heard through one of the characters, 'London! You-all have got all these coloured people coming in all the time from the Caribbean and India and Pakistan ... and you-all are not doing one damn thing about it.'

A few months before D'Oliveira's class act, Mick Jagger explained to an interviewer that immigration was going to break up British society. For the benefit of those less informed in such matters, this great expert on community relations summarised, 'Because they are different and they do act differently and they

don't live the same, not even if they were born here they don't ...
and it breaks up the society.'

The clash of the two schools of thought was in palpable
evidence as the young long-haired brigade against sporting ties
with apartheid South Africa took on the establishment in the
1969/70 season, holding demonstrations and direct-action protests
in every match contested by the visiting Springbok rugby team.
They were up against the establishment and their supporters,
generally men who were older, with the cosy comfort of shared
camaraderie with the South Africans often cloaked in the self-
righteous robes of being on the same sides in a common war that
the younger generation had not seen.

When, under immense political pressure and threats of
disruption, the cricket tour of 1970 was cancelled, the conservative
reaction was scathing. The home affairs spokesman Quintin Hogg
called it 'a classical illustration of the inability of this government
to preserve freedom in this country or to maintain law and order'.
Enoch Powell compared it to the loss of the *'Prince of Wales'* and
the *'Repulse* ... beneath the waters of the Gulf of Siam.' Jack
Bailey, of the MCC, believed that 'the rule of threatened mob
violence had won the day.'

To this day there are those who wrestle with the question why
politics needs to be mixed with sport.

55

ABANDONED GAMES

IN THE *Daily Mirror* Laker declares, 'Thanks to the most brilliant piece of improvisation seen on a cricket field this summer, England are poised to hammer India out of sight in this decisive Oval Test.'

When, three hours before the scheduled start of play, the irritating showers begin, and continue steadily till mid-afternoon, the chances of another weather-driven stalemate seem to be on the cards. With the outfield soggy, the umpires have to call off play for the day and Woodcock grows frustrated. 'Only one of the six Test matches this summer was not affected by rain. If the authorities are reluctant to introduce time-limited (he surely meant time-unlimited) Test matches there is no earthly reason why a sixth day should not be set aside to be used in the event of thunder, lightning, rain or riots,' he writes. He adds the caveat, 'There is, of course, still plenty of time for England to win at The Oval.'

Premature? Yes, but hindsight is always a handy weapon for mockery. Laker and Woodcock have been fascinated, like most English fans on that day, by the resilience of the unheralded men of English batting: the explosive hitting of Jameson and then the rearguard recovery by Knott and Hutton.

Knott's batting in the series has been an asset. The wicketkeeper now has nearly 1,500 runs in Test cricket at an average of 38. More importantly, his value as a player in crisis situations is already established and will continue through his career. The hundreds against Lillee and Walker at Adelaide and against Holding, Roberts and Daniel at Headingley will come later. But already his 101 and 96 at Auckland earlier in 1971, walking out with the innings in jeopardy on both occasions, have showed his mastery against swing. The 116 after coming in at 127/5 at Birmingham against Pakistan has been another superb innings under pressure, this time against spin.

It is unfortunate that he has had to wait till 1971 to get his first Test hundred. He should have got one in Karachi two years before, but was stranded on 96 when the match had to be abandoned. And although riots were the reason, one doubts Knott would have wanted an extra day to complete his hundred had one been available according to the Woodcock prescription.

That had been when the MCC had hastily arranged a Test series in Pakistan to compensate for the cancelled 1968/69 tour of South Africa. After all the intrigue involving D'Oliveira, Vorster, Cowdrey, Cartwright, Gubby Allen, Billy Griffith and the rest of them, the Pakistan tour as a replacement represented a jump from the frying pan to an actual fire. It was as close as a touring Test side would get to warfare before the Sri Lanka team bus would be shot at by terrorists in the same country 40 years later.

Ayub Khan was still at the helm of the disturbed dictatorship. A former president of the Pakistan Cricket Board, he was plagued by the power struggle between Bhutto and Mujib. At the same time Nixon was already eager for a strategic alliance with Pakistan. The special relationships and the support for the pound ensured Britain was onboard in the sport of the diplomatic dark arts. While the MCC looked for a proper winter assignment for the contracted players after the cancellation of the South African trip, the Foreign Office encouraged them to send the players off to Pakistan. The itinerary included a Test in the combustible East Pakistan capital of Dacca.

Karachi was under curfew from dusk to dawn, even as the players reached the country. Horror stories, including a tangible death toll, reached the team daily as they went about apprehensively from tour game to tour game

The conditions proved too much, even for the perennial amiability of Colin Cowdrey. When the MCC side was forced to get up at 5.30am and fly in to Lyallpur to play the Central Zone immediately after their match against the BCCP XI at Bahawalpur, he refused to take the field without having his tea. 'No English side has ever started a game of cricket without having a cup of tea,' he announced. As Saeed Ahmed waited for the toss, and the crowd grew impatient, Cowdrey refused to go in until they had been served tea and had partaken of it at leisure.

With student protests for democracy a very tangible threat, Ayub Khan personally ordered the Tests to be cut from five days to four.

The second Test at Dacca was held while the East Pakistan capital was besieged by rioters and the police and military had pulled out of the city. The English players wanted to leave but were informed that their coach would not make it to the airport if they did. The cocktail party with the British Deputy High Commissioner Ray Fox on the eve of the Test match had to be cut short. Another group of representatives from the British and European community had rushed in to meet Fox. They needed to discuss plans for evacuation.

The third Test at Karachi was extended to five days because the series was still undecided. England batted for over two days and were 502/7 on the third morning. Milburn and Graveney hit hundreds, Knott was unbeaten on 96. But at that juncture demonstrators among the crowd rushed into the ground.

Cowdrey's men had had enough. The Test was abandoned, and they took the flight home that night.

A couple of years later, a Micky Stewart-led International XI were engaged in a match at Dacca just a few weeks before Operation Searchlight. The BCCP XI were eight down in their second innings and not ahead by too many when the interruptions occurred. Stewart recalls, 'The ground had concrete terracing all around it and there wasn't much of a crowd. We went out after lunch with a substitute fielder, a West Pakistani, and I put him down on the boundary at deep square leg. Don Shepherd was bowling and, when I looked round from my position at short leg, I saw the lad was only ten yards from me.'

Stewart asked what he was doing so close to the wicket the answer was, 'They're throwing stones at me.'

Stewart asked Gifford to go down there.

'Swap with him? You're joking. I'm not going down there.'

And as they spoke, the terraces became aflame with fire. This was followed by the unnerving sight of a large group running out from the pavilion towards the pitch. Stewart discovered that they were all students.

'Captain Stewart, there's no danger to you or your players. But we wish the game to be abandoned. We're protesting because Bhutto has called off a meeting with our leader.'

Groomed in the Surrey school of the 1950s, Stewart had other things on mind. 'Can't you just wait till we get these two wickets and knock off the runs?'

No, they wanted the match abandoned.

Sarfraz Nawaz, one of the batsmen, recalled asking a soldier to fire at the crowd before the Pakistan team were lynched. The soldier responded by turning the muzzle of the gun towards him.

So off they trooped to the pavilion. As they waited in the dressing room, shots were heard from not far away. Finally, they were escorted by a high-ranking army officer and driven away to an army camp in a military vehicle. As they drove away, they saw several dead bodies.

When they were escorted back to the hotel, they ran into an airline pilot who agreed to fly them out at midnight. As they took off, several local people sat between the seats in the aisles.

The Pakistani cricketers were flown out a day later after a tense night under curfew and after Intikhab Alam had sought help from senior army officer Brigadier Haider. In fact, the Pakistani board had selected two teams for the third match. One if the players made it back to Lahore, one if they did not.

Student rebellions played a special role in the struggle for liberation and the eventual emergence of the new nation of Bangladesh.

More than 20 countries across the globe witnessed student rebellions in 1968, across America, Europe (West and East), Latin America, Africa and all over Asia.

There are plenty of books that try to explain this with the Western-centric view of the coming of age of a generation that had grown up after the war, without the fetters of air raids, thrift and fear of their parents. There was the new-found security of post-war governments, with social welfare systems to cushion the blows of economic hardship. Free medical care, free education and subsidised housing encouraged a sense of wellbeing and a belief that opportunities abounded. The older generation's aspirations, limited by peace and social security, were too limiting for the baby boomers who complained of the 'disgusting economic miracle' and superficiality of affluence ... whose quest for happiness led to weird hairstyles, rock and roll, coffee-houses, skiffle bands, Marlon Brando, James Dean, the angst of Holden Caulfield, and a surge of idealism. There were protests against the Bomb, the Vietnam War, and support for the Black Power movement. Television in every home gave them a common world view, a transistor radio in every room gave them individual, youthful and rebellious music.

Of course, much of that is true ... but much of that was also limited to Western Europe and North America. Student protests rang out as loud from countries of lesser press and privilege, such as Uruguay, Mexico, Brazil, Japan, Poland, Czechoslovakia ... and both West and East Pakistan.

On Christmas Day 1968, a demonstration of 10,000 students and 20,000 workers surged through Rawalpindi demanding a people's government and the resignation of Ayub Khan.

A couple of weeks later, the student groups of East Pakistan came together to form the Student Action Committee (SAC). A heavily politically attuned organisation, the SAC advanced an 11-point programme, demanding, among other reforms, full autonomy for East Pakistan within a federal constitution. They established 17 January 1969 as Demands Day, leading to the first coordinated general strike throughout Pakistan with massive demonstrations in Dacca and Rawalpindi.

The protest in East Pakistan was one of the most successful student movements, eventually playing a pivotal role in the birth of a new nation. Unfortunately, not much of it is found amongst the truckloads of available literature on student rebellions of 1968.

The Ashes and cricket are not the only topics that are subject to skewed historic retelling.

56

HEAVY OUTFIELD

IT IS a gloomy Saturday morning. Cars have to keep their sidelights on. Not many miles away from London, they have to use their windscreen wipers. The gloom seems to reflect the conditions in Belfast, where blasts keep hitting shops in the city and the IRA threatens the families of army personnel.

But Ted Warn, the Oval groundsman, and his men are up to it. Three years ago, they managed, albeit with the help of the crowd who had come down to the ground with every kind of rag they could find, to make sure England had enough time to take the last five Australian wickets ... even though the ground had resembled a swimming pool. Now, in spite of the incessant rain and the dullness of the weather, they manage to get play under way just 15 minutes after the scheduled start.

Snow and Price charge in but find their threat killed by the pitch.

Not that it seems to help Gavaskar and Mankad in any way. They remain cautious, slow. In the third over, Mankad glances Snow to the boundary. In the ninth, Gavaskar cuts a rising Snow delivery past gully for four. Otherwise, both find it difficult. Ducking into one of Snow's attempted bouncers, Gavaskar is caught in a tangle, the ball passing him too close for comfort, brushing him and breaking the gold chain around his neck. Illingworth picks up the broken ornament from short leg, 'You mustn't wear gold in a Test, lad.' One wonders if Illingworth would have given the same advice to a Wes Hall charging at the batsman with his famous crucifix swinging around his neck.

It is watchful cricket on an unhelpful surface. When Price, relying on pace rather than off the pitch, bowls Mankad with a full inswinger, the score reads 17/1 in the tenth over. Mankad, already the recipient of sarcastic clapping on reaching double figures, walks back for 11 as his middle-stump lies in the distance.

Four runs later, a black Labrador runs on to the field, sniffing Snow's foot marks with curiosity and looking at the stumps with meditative ominousness. Umpire Elliott is having none of such pitch invasions, and the Metropolitan Police springs into action. The intruder is chased, apprehended and removed from the scene. The interruption does not have much positive effect on Gavaskar, whose fear of dogs has become almost as legendary as the man himself. 'Those who know me are aware that I am mortally scared of dogs, and this one had come and stood so close to me that I was literally shivering. I tried to make a supremely nonchalant gesture of looking the other way. In no way do I ascribe this incident for my dismissal because it was a good ball that got me.'

Snow's next delivery is fast and full, and moves in from the leg. The opener cannot get his bat down in time and yet again the middle stump goes for a walk. With Gavaskar back for 6 after almost 50 minutes of struggle. India are in trouble at 21/2.

Wadekar and Sardesai, the most experienced batsmen in the side, steady the ship. Wadekar hooks Snow once and glances the bowler fine. Neither stroke reaches the boundary, with the outfield rendered sluggish by the rain. Sardesai cuts Snow for four, drives Price for another, and gathers his runs with neat deflections. Soon Snow, Price and Hutton look less than threatening and India recover to 58/2 at lunch.

It is not until the 34th over, with the clock showing 2.40 in the afternoon, that Illingworth introduces spin. He comes on from the Pavilion End. In the following over, Underwood runs in from the Vauxhall End. The Indians are already past 70. Before that, Hutton and D'Oliveira have bowled whenever Snow and Price have been given a break. Is it a mistake?

The pacemen operating on a sluggish surface against seasoned batsmen caught in a crisis have made for less than riveting cricket. Now, with the introduction of the slower bowlers, it becomes thrilling. The ball turns appreciably, Wadekar snicks Underwood past slip, while Sardesai turns Illingworth dangerously between Knott and Edrich at leg slip. Wadekar follows it up with a streaky cut past gully.

Things become especially interesting when Sardesai takes strike to Illingworth. The England captain sticks to his line outside the off stump, and Sardesai keeps playing the drive through the covers, against the spin. As Wadekar cuts and sweeps Underwood, Sardesai's aggressive intent is a revelation. Overtaking his skipper after lunch, he moves briskly to his fifty. A half-chance off Underwood when on 39 is the only blemish and otherwise his risk-taking has come off. A delicate late-cut off Underwood follows, and it would have been four but for the heaviness of the outfield.

At 114/2, things are starting to look bright for India when the penchant for driving against the spin brings about Sardesai's downfall. Illingworth cannily keeps to the same line, bowling into Solkar's foot marks, and this time Sardesai's drive is beaten and the ball goes through bat and pad to peg the stumps back. A classic off-spinner's dismissal.

Almost immediately Wadekar is dropped off Underwood and then creams the bowler for a boundary. And then Viswanath under-edges another off-break from the foot marks and on to his stumps. At 118/4, all the dismissed batsmen have been bowled.

Wadekar puts an end to this monotony of dismissals. Having batted nearly three hours for his 48, he essays a half-hearted cut at a ball from Illingworth that turns appreciably. The snick flies off Knott's glove and Hutton flings himself to his left to come up with a spectacular catch.

India are 125/5 and Illingworth has 3-18 from 13.2 overs.

It is time for yet another Indian rearguard recovery. They have two excellent men in the middle to essay one. And there is a rather strange move by Illingworth which seems to help them along.

Solkar and Engineer take them to tea with the scoreboard reading 139/5, aided by three innocuous overs from Hutton who has replaced Underwood. And after the break Illingworth persists with Hutton while the Kent man loiters in the outfield. Solkar and Engineer wisely milk him for runs. Six ineffectual overs cost 22. At the other end, Illingworth is tiring from his long spell. By the time Underwood is brought back, both the batsmen are well set.

Engineer is the first to break free. He entertains the 8,000-strong crowd with his unconventional leg-side strokes. The Indian stumper repeatedly comes down the pitch to counter Illingworth's spin. With Solkar a willing partner, he runs like a hare between the wickets. Solkar himself drives and pulls with panache. The latter's continuous success in crisis situations leads Woodcock to wonder – with some degree of hyperbole – whether he is the best Indian all-rounder since Vinoo Mankad. Yes, it is not exactly a highly competitive field, and Solkar does bowl in two different styles. But while his batting average has climbed to the mid-30s and his fielding is perhaps the best in the world, his bowling average hovers in the high 40s, with 15 wickets from his 13 Tests. With the likes of Dattu Phadkar, Chandu Borde and Bapu Nadkarni around, alongside the crowd favourite Salim Durani, it is an unusually tall claim.

The Solkar-Engineer association has an effect similar to the Knott-Hutton partnership of the first day. On the verge of knocking the Indians over – even the follow-on did not look out of the question at one stage – the bowlers are held up by some smart counterattacking. The score moves along a tad slower than it should have because of the outfield. It is quite revealing that the half-century by a batsman as flamboyant as Engineer does not contain a single boundary. Too many strokes just do not reach the fence. On as many as five occasions, Engineer strikes the ball to the wide expanses in the country and runs three.

The score reads 222 when a wicket falls against the run of play. D'Oliveira is brought on to send down his gentle swingers. Solkar dabs at one and Fletcher snaps up a left-handed slip catch of pure reflex.

Eight runs later, an erratic and apparently useless Snow bouncer climbs high enough to be ignored even while standing upright. Engineer, who has gathered his 59 runs with solid common sense, now plays a silly flat-batted smash. The ball goes towering up and comes down into the skipper's hands at mid-on. 'Not for him a quiet finish with an eye on Monday morning,' writes Michael Melford in *The Sunday Telegraph*. The batsman is already walking before Illingworth holds it. The applause that greets his return underlines the entertainment value of his innings, even though he has failed to find the fence.

With Abid and Venkat playing out the remaining overs, India end the day at 234/7, still 121 behind England. The late dismissals of Solkar and Engineer are rued in the dressing room.

Arlott infers that with two days left it remains a race against time for England to force a result. Woodcock reflects on the similarity of the situation to the Test at Old Trafford, and adds that Illingworth must look for an early declaration. Given the position of the match, Dexter expects the England captain to force a win.

* * *

On the day of rest, a bomb blast blew open the gates of a prison in Belfast. Back home the Indian Board insisted that the winter's tour of the MCC should go on.

And in New Delhi, the prime minister, Mrs Indira Gandhi, attempted to soothe the fears of the press contingent regarding speculation about a government attempt to control the press by diffusing newspaper ownership.

England v India, 3rd Test, The Oval – 19, 20, 21, 23, 24 August
England 355 (Knott 90, Jameson 82, Hutton 81, Edrich 41; Solkar 3-28) **India** 234/7 (Engineer 59, Sardesai 54, Wadekar 48, Solkar 44; Illingworth 3-49).

57

INDIA OF INDIRA

THINGS HAD not been easy for the Indian prime minister since she had occupied the hot seat.

Lal Bahadur Shastri had not had the chance to fulfil either the few optimistic and the many pessimistic prophecies in the aftermath of Nehru's death. The 1965 war with Pakistan had just ended, with both sides claiming emphatic victory. John Frazer had painted a picture for Western eyes in *Reader's Digest,* 'Vultures hung over corpses on the Grand Trunk Road, the immortal highway of Kipling's *Kim.*' And within hours of signing the Tashkent agreement that ended the war, Shastri died from a massive heart attack.

Indira Gandhi, pitchforked into power, had to fight her first election in 1967. She won it with ease, but not without factions of opposition. There were rival parties that had captured power in some states, including the communists in Kerala and West Bengal. Her party itself was divided with plenty of dissent, involving caste, ideology, religion, ethnicity and language. The patriots with considerable education and a social conscience, who had historically been attracted to join the party, had started to steer clear of both the Congress Party and politics in general in India. Bureaucracy was rampant, middlemen were calling the shots, politics was a murky domain.

International observers were gloomy in their predictions. Even before the election, Sol W. Sanders claimed 'India: A Huge

Country on the Verge of Collapse' in the *US News and World Report*. He thought it possible that the breakdown of law and order would be so complete that the army would take power, as had happened in Pakistan and Burma. 'Collapse of the present regime in India [look at the term "regime" once again, as opposed to "administration"] would add a grim new element to the job the US has taken on in Vietnam – the effort to ensure political stability and economic strength in Asia.' While we can perhaps dismiss the Sanders report as typical typecasting of the East without any effort at understanding the country, a far more experienced India-hand among journalists, Neville Maxwell of the London *Times*, was equally despondent in his analysis and predictions. In a series titled 'India's Disintegrating Democracy', he wrote about a corrupt administration, a governing party that had lost public confidence, of impending crisis, the fraying fabric of the nation which pointed to the formation of sub-nations, threatening famine and symptoms of imminent army-backed dictatorship.

Even commentators from other parts of the world, from South African Ronald Segal to the voice from the Caribbean V.S. Naipaul, echoed the sentiments. 'Indian poverty is unique,' wrote Segal. 'It is unique in its depths which seem incapable of supporting life at all, unique in its blatancy for it is everywhere, in city and village, not concealed, not isolated, but everywhere … unique in its magnitude … unique in the quality of its submission, which registers a kind of glazed pride.'

The prophecies of doomsday did not come to pass, but there was no denying that the country was a shambles. Over half the Indians earned less than a living wage and most went hungry. There had been a succession of poor harvests, and with the increase in defence spending due to the wars with China and Pakistan, the rupee had been devalued by half. A huge food aid package of PL 480 wheat was negotiated with the United States. While there is definitely a case for the alleviation of famines after the end of the British Raj, countless people starved in Bihar in 1966/67. The historian John Keay also argues that part of the riddance of the famines had to do with Partition relieving New Delhi of the responsibility for East Pakistan and eventually Bangladesh.

To deal with the situation, the prime minister developed a rather dictatorial streak. The nationalisation of banks and insurance companies was one of her ways of addressing the economic problems, and this was done by relieving her finance minister Morarji Desai of his portfolio. Another measure was to deprive the ex-rulers of the princely states of their 'privy purses', something that affected the then Indian captain.

That was not the only thing that plagued Mansur Ali Khan Pataudi. He was battling loss of form and increasingly unsuccessful team performances against Australia and New Zealand at home. Bungling by the ground staff, much of it deliberate, was the only way that the Kiwis under Graham Dowling were prevented from winning the Hyderabad Test, played at captain Pataudi's home ground, and thereby the series. Bill Lawry's men battled pathetic hotels, inedible food, riots, heat and dust, ended up undernourished and sick, lost weight, but still managed to win the series 3-1.

According to Keith Stackpole, the first ride to the hotel set the tone, 'You could see the mouths of the blokes drop. You could see them thinking, "What's happening here?" It was close to midnight, there was hardly any light, and it was pelting with rain. Yet I could see people sleeping in the street.'

Sometimes they had to drag their kits through streets filled with beggars. And then there was the question of food. After a hunt for bread in the hotel, Brian Taber informed the team, 'If you want to eat another meal in this place, don't go down and look at the kitchen.'

Garth McKenzie shed six kilograms and felt lethargic. Alan Connolly came down with bronchial pneumonia. Apart from the food and health issues, there were riots and crowd trouble, something faced by the West Indians three years earlier. When the team flew to Johannesburg for their series against South Africa, an ill-planned twin tour from hell, the commentator Alan McGilvray was shocked, 'They looked haggard. Their eyes seemed to be standing out of their heads and some of them looked positively yellow.'

However, it should be added that the Australian administrators were as much to blame as Indian infrastructure. Late in the tour, when they finally got booked into a decent hotel, the players realised that there were quality establishments in the country but their board had not put them up in many of them.

No England side toured India between 1963/64 and 1972/73, but the experience of Lawry's men, and the West Indians before them, did not paint a flattering image of the country around the cricketing world

The common Indian man – cricketer or otherwise – looked at the world from beneath the layers of an inferiority complex borne out of squalor, mismanagement and poverty. The differences were too stark.

Vinay Lal of the UCLA said, 'While I would not wish to undermine the achievement involved in universal franchise, democracy in India had largely been reduced to an electoral exercise. The poor do not care what kind of political system they get since the question of where they will get their next meal is paramount.'

Even if the hunger and deprivation of poverty were ignored, the difference between the middle classes of Britain and India was mind-bogglingly huge. While the British middle class during the late-1960s was busy spending holidays in coastal Spanish towns, driving cars to work, and equipping their homes with televisions, refrigerators, vacuum cleaners and washing machines, the parameters for the Indian middle class were considerably different.

Even affluent upper-middle class homes often did not have running water. In the posh Flora Fountain, for example, Bombay municipality supplied water once in the morning and once in the evening. Buckets were filled when water was available and mugs were used for the purposes of washing, bathing and cooking.

A car was the privilege of the reasonably rich, and even then it did not cover all in that category. By 1970, every county cricketer in England was driving to matches. In contrast, only about half-a-dozen of the wealthier men in the Indian squad to England in 1971 – Baig, Engineer, Sardesai, Wadekar, Bedi and Prasanna – had their own cars. Most Indians, including cricketers, used government-run transport and private buses, where the signs suggested space for 36 or so passengers, while four times that many actually crammed in. On the backs of the seats of these buses, and on the walls, one saw one of those inimitable Indianisms in English that announced: 'No Eve-teasing'. This meant 'no molestation allowed' ... a warning against the perverts who groped women as the passengers swayed along the way with the lurching of the bus, fused into one unsavoury mass of humanity.

Import tariffs, queues for necessities, endless waits for telephones, the corruption-laced waiting time for licences to carry out business ... it was a depressing, closed system with an envious fascination for everything that was foreign. An imported car granted a social status almost worth the enormous surcharges paid to get it into the country. People craved *Vilaity* goods because they were so difficult to obtain (the term was the root for the much-used Blighty).

It was in such times that Mihir Bose, the future author of *A History of Indian Cricket,* migrated to London. He travelled with £800 sewn into his underpants because the Form P, approved by a Reserve Bank of India signatory and necessary to obtain an airline ticket, allowed a maximum of £2.

A look at garishly nationalistic Bollywood movies such as *Purab Aur Paschim* (1970) makes it clear that the common man, with limited international exposure, had a peculiar mix of fascination, envy and also a reasonable amount of hatred for the West, especially Britain. Until at least the mid-1990s, the non-resident Indians portrayed in Bollywood movies remained either evil or buffoons or both. Misconceptions about India abounded in Britain. There was a fully reciprocal set of misconceptions about Britain and the rest of the Western world in India. The difference was that while the skewed outlook was heavily mixed with imperialist superiority in case of the British, it was a case of the hangover of colonial inferiority for the Indians.

In late 1970, Indira Gandhi took her opponents unaware by announcing a snap election in 1971 – to use another quaint Indian-English term, *preponed* by a year. With her *garibi hatao* (remove poverty) slogan she romped through, winning by as great a margin with her divided party as her father had won with an undivided Congress in 1962.

As she continued to rush through the takeover of the banks, insurance and coal industries, and abolishing privy purses, she dealt with the situation in Bangladesh and the associated refugee problem in India with the same assertive aggression.

Few things can more strikingly invoke conceptions of greatness of a country than the drums of war. The Indian team had won in the West Indies just as the conflict with Pakistan was reaching a tipping point. And the country was simmering with increasing jingoism as Wadekar's men took on England at The Oval.

58

THE DAY OF THE MIRACLE

LATER WOODCOCK will estimate the odds as 33/1 against India at the start of the fourth day. The idea for Illingworth's men is to quickly wrap the innings up before setting out for some quick runs to declare with enough time to force a win.

The plans go awry from the outset. The skipper's own success on Saturday afternoon is not enough for him to discard the traditional formula of starting with pace, regardless of the lack of pace in the wicket. Hence Snow and Price start off with some unimpressive overs. The two Indian batsmen comfortably negotiate the pace, Abid glancing and driving Price for two boundaries while taking 11 off his two overs.

Hence, by the time the England captain starts wheeling down his stuff in the fifth over, Abid and Venkat have already got their eye in. An edged boundary from Venkat off Snow has also brought up the 250.

Even Illingworth, bowling in tandem with Snow seems less than threatening. Venkat slams a boundary off the faster man and then both batsmen slog fours to get 13 valuable runs in one Illingworth over. The runs are not only flowing, they are doing so quickly. Underwood replaces Snow and Illingworth tightens his line.

The pair have added 48 – 44 in the morning – when Illingworth hits Solkar's foot marks again. Abid is beaten on the front foot and it strikes timber. A valuable knock of 26 comes to an end.

The dismissal seems to tamper with Venkat's composure. His batting becomes less orderly, more like a tailender. A hoicked boundary off Illingworth and then a wild swing attempted off Underwood and he is leg-before for 24. An over later, Bedi drives Illingworth high, and D'Oliveira comes forward from long-on to hold the catch.

India, all out 284, trail by 71. Illingworth has figures of 34.3-12-70-5. Yes, the pitch is aiding spinners, and the three Indian tweakers are waiting to have a go. However, there is also the consideration that India will have to bat last with Illingworth already proving difficult to survive against.

At 12:45 on this pleasant afternoon, Luckhurst and Jameson walk out with consolidation the primary goal.

First, there is the mild new-ball attack in action again, and the openers go about the first few overs with unhurried composure. It is again Jameson who takes the initiative, slamming a boundary off Solkar to announce his intentions.

That is enough for Wadekar. Six overs of bland medium-pace have produced 16 runs. Venkat is now introduced from the Pavilion End, and from the Vauxhall End Chandra comes on. The idea is perhaps to get a few more overs in by lunch even as the batsmen settle. Or it is perhaps a ploy to exploit the turn. Whatever it is it bears fruit, initially in the most unexpected manner.

Chandra is in his second over. Luckhurst drives the second ball straight back. The bowler puts his hand down in an attempt to field. The resulting deflection crashes into the stumps. Jameson is out of his ground. He shakes his head as he walks back, run out for the third time in four Test innings, the first man to be run out in both innings of a Test match in England. It remains unique in England even today: 23/1.

A single to Luckhurst, a couple of defensive pushes by Edrich. That is the over for Chandra. Venkat wheels in and Luckhurst plays out a maiden as befits a professional English batsman with lunch approaching.

Chandra begins his next over. Dot ball, dot ball. He turns to bowl the third delivery. Mid-step, he hears Sardesai from mid-off,

'Mill Reef'. The name of the Derby-winning thoroughbred, the most appropriate code for the faster one.

Chandra whips it through. Edrich's bat is still completing its back lift as the ball crashes into the stumps. 'In the manner of Doug Wright, a wrist spinner of similar method and pace,' writes Arlott. It is 24/2.

Fletcher is the new man, walking in when no batsman wants to, with just a minute or two left before lunch, eager fieldsmen circling around him. Chandra's next delivery is a perfectly pitched googly. The tentative prod just manages to find the edge, Solkar puts in the dive, rolls on the pitch and comes up with the catch. At lunch, England are 24/3. The tables have turned. From looking for a quick declaration, the focus is now to digest the shocks and play for survival.

'At Port of Spain, Durani had claimed Sobers and Lloyd to put us on the road to victory. At The Oval, the moment Chandra [dismissed] Edrich and Fletcher, off successive balls, I sensed that the game would be ours,' Wadekar will write later, helped along by oodles of hindsight. However, it will not be a stretch to say that the Indians go in to lunch with victory coming into the equation for the first time.

Bella is already there in the outfield as D'Oliveira and Luckhurst walk in. On resumption, D'Oliveira is hemmed in by fielders. Chandra is on a hat-trick and the match is there for the taking. The experienced campaigner smothers the spin of the first ball. However, he jabs at the next, sending it head high at an angle to Sardesai at slip.

'I made a mistake, I neglected fielding early in my career,' Sardesai will always be ready to admit. An easy enough catch for a more agile fielder. The Bombay batsman makes an effort that looks valiant, but D'Oliveira gets a life and three runs. In the process Sardesai injures his hand as well, and Jayantilal jogs on as substitute.

Wadekar keeps Venkat on at the other end, using him to choke the runs. And choke he does. Three runs result from the next five overs, Dolly escaping once again as he pushes forward to Chandra and the catch is too sharp for even Solkar's lightning reflexes.

Luckhurst remains defiant, but passive. D'Oliveira tries dispersing the fielders with calm aggression ... 'in truth less assured than he looked' according to Arlott. He does manage to hit Chandra for two boundaries, but then chances his arm once too often. Trying to loft Venkat, he skies to mid-on where Jayantilal judges the catch well. At 49/4, Knott is walking out to attempt another of his rescuing acts.

Knott. A man most difficult to dislodge. The Indians have seen too much of him already. They will try anything to send him back. At any rate, Solkar does. He knows while taking guard Knott marks his spot with a bail lifted from the stumps. Solkar comes up with an idea. He asks Wadekar if it this is within the laws. The captain replies that as long as he puts things back in time for the game to restart there will be no problem.

So, as Knott approaches the crease, Solkar moves from short leg and pockets the bails. Knott reaches the crease, looks for the bails and is confused when he does not see them. He proceeds to ask for his guard and mark it with his bat as most batsmen do. Once he is done, Solkar replaces the bails.

Does this prank disturb Knott? One cannot say for sure. But he does not last long. A few pushed singles see Luckhurst hog the strike and gingerly negotiate the double-spin attack. And then a ball from Venkat pops up just enough to strike the bat a bit too close to the handle, and Solkar flings himself full-length to take a miraculous catch.

Solkar stretched out on the ground, Engineer about to exult, Venkat leaning back prior to throwing his arms up, a young Gavaskar airborne in excitement at slip. This remains one of the famous moments in cricket captured on camera.

Knott, due a failure according to Arlott, walks back for a solitary run. England are 54/5 and India know they are on the verge of making history. Venkat has not only played the role of a stock bowler, he has also dismissed the man who has a track record of being a real thorn in the flesh.

But England bat deep. Illingworth is in, not the man to surrender without a fight. There are plenty of moments of alarm as he bats, but he hangs on. Luckhurst is never too comfortable but keeps going. For over after over, Wadekar keeps bowling Chandra and Venkat. In the outfield, under his tangerine turban, Bedi looks vexed. He has not had a bowl yet.

And now it is time for Chandra's second magic wave. A slower ball deceives Illingworth as he goes through with his drive. Chandra holds the return catch: 65/6. The distressed captain is walking back, the last of the all-rounders crosses him on the way.

Hutton has scored 81 in the first innings. Yet, two overs later, Luckhurst refuses a long single to third man. It must make for curious viewing from the press box, given that two days ago writers kept finding genetic links in Hutton's batting to tie him with his great father. Even more so because Luckhurst edges his attempted cut off Chandra's next ball and Venkat at slip holds a good catch. A fighting 33 over almost two hours for the opener – 72/7.

Four balls later, Snow drives straight back and Chandra catches him low down; 72/8, just 146 ahead, and five for the leg-spinner.

The question now is whether England can get to three figures. They try hard. Underwood proves to be a stubborn tailender for the second time in the match, even squeezing out a couple of boundaries off Chandra. Hutton, always able with the bat, carries on. For nine overs, they hold the Indian spinners at bay, adding 24 in the process. After 36 overs on the trot, the bowling is changed. For the first time Wadekar calls on Bedi to give Chandra a rest. Underwood gets down on his knees and sweeps him high on the leg side. Mankad runs in from the deep and holds the catch. It is 96/9.

In the next Venkat over, Price drives him into the outfield to runs three and the hosts reach three figures. That is the last scoring stroke. It is just that one over for Bedi. Wadekar summons Chandra again. His first ball, a top-spinner, is too good for the England No.11. The home team are blown away for 101 in just two and a half hours, Chandra 18.1-3-38-6, one of the greatest spells in the history of Test cricket. This was later recognised by

Wisden as the spell of the century by an Indian cricketer, ahead of Anil Kumble's 10-74 in 1999.

It is time for tea. The match has been turned on its head in the course of a session and a bit.

England's score is their lowest at home since Bradman's Invincibles skittled them out for 52 on this very ground in 1948.

The target is 173. As Gavaskar and Mankad go out the second time, life comes to a standstill on that Bombay evening, with men huddled around transistor radios.

But it is not going to be handed on a platter. Snow charges in. In his second over Gavaskar does not offer a shot and is trapped leg-before. There are some interesting versions of this dismissal.

According to Arlott, 'Gavaskar played no stroke at a ball he thought to be passing down the leg side: it proved to be a late outswinger and he was plainly and dejectedly lbw.'

According to Sunder Rajan, 'The batsman offered no stroke to one that appeared to have been pitched on the off stump.'

According to Gavaskar's own rather churlish version in *Sunny Days*, 'I was given out leg-before to a ball from Snow which clearly pitched outside the leg stump and to which I offered no stroke. But then you don't question an English umpire's decision, do you? They are supposed to be the best in the world. However, I earned the distinction of getting out for a duck for the first time.'

So much for eyewitness accounts. The ball could have pitched anywhere, but the decision seems to lean two to one in favour of being fair ... and Snow seems to have had the upper hand over Gavaskar. What is palpable, however, is the disenchantment with the myth of English fair play that Gavaskar, with his post-independence birth, has clearly come to abhor. The autobiography will be penned when Gavaskar, never the embodiment of political correctness, is just 27, and the words perhaps read a bit sharply in retrospect.

Wadekar enters with his calm reassurance. The English bowlers are running in with zeal and effort, the fielding is keen and sharp. Mankad, without a Test innings of substance behind him, is playing straight and solid, intent on survival. Runs seem to be a distant afterthought. The captain, with the same degree of meticulous care, changes this and goes about the business of collecting some. The onslaught of Snow and Price lasts 10 overs, and India progress to 21/1, Wadekar 12, Mankad 6.

Underwood is introduced in the 11th over, Illingworth comes on in the 12th. Mankad spends 17 balls on 6, twelve more on 8, and fourteen on 11. He does not get further than that, lunging to drive Underwood and edging it to slip where Hutton parries it with his left hand and clings on to the rebound as if his life depends on it. Mankad has lasted 74 balls for 11, and that is his highest score in the series. But the 78 minutes he has spent at the crease are invaluable, by the time he is dismissed Wadekar is settled on 21. The score reads 37/2, not the most reassuring when chasing a tricky target. But with the back-in-form Sardesai walking out, the two most experienced heads are together at the crease, and the dressing room is relatively relaxed.

Mankad takes his performance in the series with characteristic good humour. Once he has showered, he remarks, 'At least now I can go back and tell them what the English spinners were like.' He asks how much he had scored. Learning that it is just 11, he says, 'A pity the Tests are over. I was just getting into my stride and by the fifth Test I would surely have scored 25.'

A few minutes later the Englishmen are sure they have got Wadekar. The skipper tries to swing Underwood and the ball lobs behind the wicketkeeper where Edrich runs around to catch it. However, umpire Elliott decides that there is enough doubt whether there has been a touch. Having survived the scare, Wadekar pulls Underwood for four and then brings up the fifty with a square cut.

Sardesai continues his first-innings ploy of stepping out and driving Illingworth against the spin. He shows considerable skill in coming down the wicket to Underwood's brisk pace as well whenever the Kent spinner gives it a bit more air. Towards the end of the day, Illingworth puts D'Oliveira on for a few overs and switches Underwood's end. It almost works, with the left-armer getting a snick from Sardesai, which is put down.

By the end of the day Wadekar has progressed to a serene 45, Sardesai is 13 and India 76/2. Just 97 remain to be scored.

'If India become the first country since South Africa in 1965 to take a series off England they will light fires from Cape Comorin to the Himalayas,' writes Woodcock.

Deformity of Destruction

Len Hutton enjoyed years of sustained brilliance after having his arm shortened due to a gym accident during the Second World War, and Denis Compton returned to Test cricket after having his knee cap removed. Fred Titmus bowled for England after losing three toes in a boat accident. Pataudi enjoyed a long career after losing most of his vision in one eye.

Yet, Chandra was unique. He was perhaps the only one to turn his handicap into his lethal weapon. The thinness of his arm resulted in unique flexibility, helping him produce extra bite in his top-spinner. With time, he developed a near classical loop, and started turning his leg-breaks more often. However, for most of his career, he sent down top-spinners and googlies, at close to medium-pace, often unplayable off the pitch.

The closest parallel is perhaps Bert Ironmonger, who captured 74 Test wickets at an exceptional average of 14 with his left-arm slow bowling after losing most of his left forefinger in a childhood accident. The stub which flicked the ball undoubtedly gave rise to the unique nip in his deliveries.

Laker is a bit more scathing on the home team, 'The combination which has come through 26 Tests and seven series without defeat failed because of their own dismal batting errors.' He adds that although there is nothing impossible in captain Illingworth's book, he does need a touch of Houdini to save himself from defeat. Peter Wilson uncharitably brands the English performance 'ridiculous.'

Well, the English batsmen have not batted extraordinarily well, but it would have required more than extraordinary batting to withstand Chandra's devastating spell that afternoon.

A less partisan Arlott is keener on explaining to his readers how the polio-deformed, withered and weakened right arm of Chandra is capable of producing such unplayable spin, while he picks up and throws with his left.

In light of the batting disaster, the news of Boycott hammering the Leicestershire attack to score 151 does not really cheer the English camp.

England v India, 3rd Test, The Oval – 19, 20, 21, 23, 24 August England 355 (Knott 90, Jameson 82, Hutton 81, Edrich 41; Solkar 3-28) and 101 (Chandra 6-38) **India** 284 (Engineer 59, Sardesai 54, Wadekar 48, Solkar 44; Illingworth 5-70) and 76/2 (Wadekar 45*).

59

I WAS THERE

IN 2017, James Mettyear recalled his experiences as a 13-year-old. 'On the Tuesday, as I travelled on the dusty train up from the coast to the smoke with my sandwiches in my army surplus gas-mask case and my "emergency money" in my pocket, I listened intently to men in linen jackets and regimental ties talk bullishly of England polishing off the "little" Indians. "They've never won a Test here, you know, and that's after 19 attempts." "Snow'll do for them – they don't like the quick stuff." "We'll be back home in time for early supper, you'll see."

'I knew enough to fear that this blithe dismissal of the tourists' chances was shallow-rooted in the tired ground of imperial entitlement and Fred Trueman, rather than the way things were now.'

Rob Faversham of Rochester was five years older. 'I must confess that there were misgivings but I sincerely believed that we could not lose. Well, it took a while but the process started on that day. You can imagine what it was like for me to sit at Lord's in 1986 and watch the Indians clinically outplay us. Nowadays I wonder why it does not happen more often.'

Yet, that day was more than the shock of a defeat. 'I must tell you I did not know what to make of that elephant in that strange headgear. I saw it on the fourth afternoon, as Luckhurst and D'Oliveira walked out to bat with the innings tottering. I was sitting in what is now the Bedser Stand, and the elephant was right in front of me. I made the connection soon enough. Must be some Indian tradition, I thought to myself, but even then I thought they had gone overboard. I mean, just imagine someone trying to pull off that sort of thing at Lord's.'

Rob pauses and adds with a twinkle in his eye. 'Well, now that I think about it years later, instead of that oriental headgear if the elephant had a bacon-and-egg tie around her neck, she would have walked into the pavilion of Lord's, no questions asked. The age of some of those stewards, I doubt whether they would be able to squint and make out what the tie was wrapped around.'

Asif Siraj was there as well. 'I had not followed the game that Monday. As far as I recall India were in a pretty bad position and the talk on the rest day was whether there would be enough time for England to win. Of course, we had other things on our minds. Mujib's trial was going on in what was for all intents and purposes a kangaroo court. Several of us had our relations stranded in East Pakistan. But when we looked at the evening news and found that Chandrasekhar had turned the game on its head, we had to go there to watch it. Some of us made a mad rush for tickets. We were rooting for India, in many more ways than one. Really rooting for them. So much depended on India.'

'I had to be there, didn't I?' says Chitta Majumdar. 'I was mocked, even shouted at by some, for missing a day's pay in the hope of seeing a miracle at Lord's. And what did I do? I missed another day's pay, believing fully that the miracle was going to take place this time. Tebbit schebbit. I wanted India to win. India meant so much to us. And boy, am I not pleased that I was there that day. Yes, I lost the day's pay. To add to it, there was the cost of transportation and ticket. I could barely afford it. But that was peanuts to pay for what remains the greatest day of my life.'

It remains the greatest day in the life for the now 73-year-old Sarabjeet Singh Saini, who had made the trip from Birmingham. In a curious Anglo-Punjabi-accented Hindi he says, 'You know what? I had attended the first day of India's match against Warwickshire, and all I had seen was Jameson clouting sixes and our bowlers being taken to the cleaners (*dho dala tha*). And I spent the next two days licking my wounds. I did not even go to the ground, which was literally next door, and suddenly I found out Bedi and Prasanna had bowled India to a win. Imagine that. Now when the news of Chandra taking all the wickets came filtering in, I started making arrangements. I would not miss out the second time. *Goro ko harane ka maza hi kuchh aur tha. Ab to yeh log hamesha haraten hain, tab baat alag tha.'* (It used to be especially satisfying to defeat the white folks. Now they lose all the time, but then it was different.)

Mark Pemberton had been there too, as a 21-year-old mathematics student and a serious club cricketer. 'It was quite unbelievable, the noise, the people, the elephant in the outfield. In the stereotypical ideas, the elephant was so very Indian. And as far as I remember it was an Asian elephant, underlining the Indian connection. I expected them to pull it off. It must have been like playing at home for them. More importantly, I knew the balance was loaded in their favour. There were guys who said that four years ago they had been thrashed 3-0, but there were many differences. The batsmen scoring runs against them had been Boycott, Barrington, Graveney and D'Oliveira. Four years down the line, Barrington was the manager, Graveney had retired, Dolly was getting old. And Boycott played just one Test in that series. True, these same spinners had been thrashed in 1967. But that meant all of them had been in England and knew how to bowl. Besides, they had the first half of the season in 1967, when it is colder and difficult for the spinners. This time they had the second half, and the wickets had been almost curated for them. I am not making excuses, mind you. But I knew they had the advantage.'

Mark, a pure numbers man, predictably recalled the score better than the others.

For Prakash Chandrasekharan, on the other hand, the score was a mystery, although the memories are unforgettable. 'I was just nine. I had no idea what was going on. So much enthusiasm in a cricket match was new to me. I had gone with my grandfather, who kept telling me how he had watched India beat Britain at Wembley in 1948 in the hockey final of the summer Olympics. That was the first time India and Britain had faced off in hockey and they had won 4-0, thus winning the gold medal. I remember *tatta* telling me all about Balbir Singh scoring his brace of goals, how incredible it felt watching the Indian side overcome the British on the field less than a year from independence. Strangely that is what I remember more than what happened at the cricket. I do remember Knott catching Sardesai and the general reaction after Abid's final stroke. But that is about all. It's more the people, the noise, the crowd on the ground after it was all over ... those are the things I still remember. That and Balbir Singh's heroics that I kept hearing about. I don't remember any of the strokes played by Engineer or Viswanath but know that Balbir Singh converted a penalty corner to make it 3-0.'

The most poignant memory is, perhaps understandably, not visual. Says Ramesh Chirpad of present-day Mumbai, 'We chaps born in the Fifties ate, drank and slept cricket. My parents used to give me a rupee as bus and train fare to go to Ramakrishna Mission and read the Bhagavad Gita. Instead, I would travel on footboard in bus and train, get down at Dadar station, cross over to platform one, and wait under the huge clock. A few minutes before the train bound for Churchgate arrived, the tall figure would arrive, clean-shaven, immaculately dressed in cricket cream flannels. I would follow him diligently into the train and stand next to him. Someone would hand over the day's *Times of India*, with the sports page showing his photo and describing his exploits with the ball. And he would politely smile, and wink at me. Bapu Nadkarni knew that I was a most diligent fan.

'I would follow him daily during the Times Shield Tournament. He would ruffle my hair with a smile and I would be on top of the world. I would shadow him into the pavilion tent of ACC and sit in one corner admiring Polly Umrigar, Dilip Sardesai, and others. Year after year. Once in a while we used to be lucky enough to see them in a Ranji game. But whenever they went overseas the news that came through was of nothing but disappointment. This time it was different.'

Says Pramathanath Sastry who listened to the BBC Commentary as a teenager in Hyderabad, 'We were in a neighbour's house, ten boys around the radio, the girls further away, the mothers very amused at this palpable excitement. I remember the room, the friends, the aunties, the ups and downs in our emotions more than the words we heard in the broadcast. In any case there was lots of static. That radio had valves. It took a while to unscramble it in our minds. We could not quite believe it when it was over.'

Chirpad continues about his experiences in Bombay that afternoon. 'I remember a large group from our community assembling well in advance, huddling around a big, old-fashioned radiogram in the home of one of the uncles. I was older by then and joined in the discussion among the elders once in a while. The younger kids talked amongst themselves, waiting expectantly for the action to start. Some of them could not follow the English commentary, and we had to paraphrase the events more or less after every ball. I recall the elders of the locality discussing the situation in Bangladesh, about the poor Bengalis, how India had the moral duty to step in more strongly. Those days it was rare to find people universally agreeing about a political issue. That is true even today in India. But that was one issue which had total consensus.

'And then the discussion stopped as the BBC commentary started. We listened rapt for hours as the drama unfolded, the batsmen fighting the bowlers and the reception fighting the static. And when Abid hit those winning runs most of us were out on the streets, dancing with joy.'

Dilip Vengsarkar would make his way into serious cricket five years later. In 1971, he was a 15-year-old schoolboy. He says, 'We huddled around a radio, willing India to get the runs. And then Ajit Wadekar was run out. We started praying ... and kept praying till the last run was scored.' Fifteen years later, Vengsarkar would play a leading role in the 1986 triumph in England. 'By then we knew that it could be done. We had been shown that it could be done.'

60

CLIMAX

'THERE WAS a splendid attendance with, appropriately on the Hindu festival of Ganesh, more turbans and saris than any English cricket ground ever before,' writes Arlott.

The Indians in the stands, the elephant in the outfield and the buzz of anticipation in the air. The feeling of playing at home is further enhanced when Wadekar, facing the first ball of the day, finds Illingworth running in off his few paces rather than Snow off his many. Calmly, he bats out a maiden. But behind the façade of calmness there is plenty of anxiety. It is apparent from what happens next.

As Underwood runs in from the Vauxhall End, Sardesai cuts the first ball fine. It is Wadekar's call. He hesitates, changes his mind, and dashes down. By then D'Oliveira has moved quickly to short third man and sent in a flat return into Knott's gloves. Wadekar is short of his ground. A disastrous start. The captain looks at the umpire's raised finger, tucks his bat under his armpit and walks off the ground. A neat innings of 45 has done much to put India on course. However, there could not have been a worse start to the day.

Little Viswanath walks in, on a pair. Illingworth hems him in with close fieldsmen. For Viswanath, he has Underwood bowling to four men close on the off side and a short leg. When it is Sardesai, he takes just one close-in fielder away and places him at cover. For several overs, the two Indian batsmen bat just to protect their wickets. Three singles and a two, that is all they manage in the first nine overs. India have inched to 81/3.

It is when D'Oliveira comes on in place of Underwood that a ball beats Knott and results in four byes. Other than that, the scoreboard does not really move. Underwood's end is changed. Illingworth wants him to try and hit the spot that helped Chandra so much the previous afternoon. He gives it more air than he normally does. Viswanath pushes at him, it lobs over Edrich at slip for two runs. In the next Underwood over, Viswanath edges again, through the slip and gully, at a very catchable height. It is chased down, and the batsmen run three. Viswanath has 6 off 34 deliveries, five of those runs off the edge.

At the other end, Sardesai has moved to 18 off 90 balls. He now drives D'Oliveira. After a long time the ball goes to the outfield off the middle of the bat. Three more runs are added. The scoring continues at snail's pace, the pressure is unrelenting. Ian Woolridge writes in the *Daily Mail* that the Indians were like a sepoy unit with England 'conceding singles as unwillingly as some Douglas Fairbanks retreating inch by inch to the cliff edge'.

A Viswanath sweep off Underwood sees the batsmen run another three and the hundred is up. And then at mid-day, after more than an hour's play, Sardesai drives Underwood straight for the first boundary of the morning.

At 108/3, slowly and surely the match is slipping away from England even though their grip remains as tight as ever. Illingworth bowls another over himself and brings on Snow to replace Underwood.

'It was a desperately slow pitch, Snow might as well have bowled a poached egg as a bouncer,' Woodcock writes. Snow sends down six intelligent overs that produce just six runs, Sardesai playing out three maidens. At the other end, Illingworth is giving nothing away. His 25 overs have so far cost just 26. But importantly for India, the wickets column in the captain's analysis still reads zero.

Snow is taken off. Underwood, rested and ready, is handed the ball again. Sardesai drives him to the boundary to take his score to 40. And then he leans forward defensively. The ball turns just a shade. And the dipping edge is snapped up almost from the bat by the extraordinary Knott. The incredible Kent pair have struck. Sardesai's mammoth vigil is over. Forty from 156 balls, over two hours and forty minutes. India are 124/4. The crucial 48-run partnership was constructed over 35 overs.

And now in walks Solkar, the man England have struggled to get out all summer. Underwood and Illingworth continue, and Viswanath's onus on survival remains unchanged. Solkar does not show much inclination to push the score along either. The runs come in occasional, infrequent singles. The idea is that if they stay there long enough the target will be achieved.

Ten more are added in eight overs, when Solkar drives Underwood. A bit uppish and the bowler sticks out his left hand. The result is a spectacular return catch: 134/5. Still 39 runs to get. Making runs has seemed a backbreaking task all morning. Underwood has 3-51 from 29.4 overs. Viswanath has shown a predilection for the forward defensive push and little more. He has inched to 25 from 130 deliveries. Engineer is walking in, the last of the genuine batsmen. Later Illingworth will say that he still believed England could win it if they made short work of the Indian wicketkeeper.

The nerves are all taut with tension. In the dressing room, Wadekar lies down, refusing to watch the game. Abid, padded up, prefers to play cards with Gavaskar and a couple of others. But the ears prick up with every bit of action in the middle.

Engineer, however, is immensely experienced. There is no sign of tension or tentativeness as he plays the ball according to merit. In the final over before lunch, he cuts and drives Underwood for a pair of braces and suddenly India require just 27 more as they go into the break. Viswanath has made 29 in two hours, few of them from the middle of his bat.

Illingworth is exhausted. He has sent down 36 overs and conceded just 40, but the wickets column still remains blank. The new leg-before rule has been magnificently exploited by the Indian batsmen. You cannot be given out struck on the pads outside the off-stump if you are playing a stroke. Later Illingworth will say that he hit the pads two or three times each over. It is frustrating. Underwood has done an excellent job, but he is not the ideal bowler for this wicket where the slower you are through the air, the more turn you extract. He has tried to give them more air and sent them down slower, but has not managed to sustain this manner of bowling for more than a couple of overs.

As the Indian batsmen go in, some fans shout canny advice, not putting anything beyond the English think-tank, 'Don't eat the fish and chips they give you. Eat a good plate of curry and rice.'

As the players re-emerge, a group of Parsi fans shout their advice to Engineer, 'Farokh, steady, steady … Remember you are playing for India, not Lancashire.' There are some West Indians among them as well, offering sagacious pointers of a completely different sort, 'Hit them over the top, maan.'

Viswanath takes strike, and plays out yet another maiden. It is the following over by Underwood in which Engineer's natural flamboyance takes the upper hand. Two attacking strokes, not really risky but with the shroud of caution taken off. One goes for a couple and the other races to the off-side boundary. Illingworth perhaps realises the game is over; 150 up.

According to Sunder Rajan, 'India progressed towards their target in leaps and bounds, with Engineer doing the bulk of the scoring.' It is only half-true, with Engineer indeed the one doing most of the scoring. The runs keep coming at a glacial trickle. The Indians are in no hurry.

At 159, Illingworth concedes the inevitability of an Indian win. He takes himself off and hands the ball to Luckhurst. The opener does toss up his left-arm spinners more than his illustrious Kent team-mate and purchases some turn as well. Engineer cuts him for four, and in the next over straight drives Underwood for another. It is 170/5, and a considerable proportion of the crowd, most of them Indians, hover around the perimeter, eager to run on as soon as the winning runs are hit.

And now Viswanath, having batted nearly three hours without a rash stroke, essays an awful cross-batted swipe at

Luckhurst. Up goes the ball and comes down safely into Knott's gloves. 'The dark masses gathering like vultures around the boundary were temporarily foiled by Viswanath's departure at 170,' writes Laker.

Three runs to win, the clock shows 2.40pm. Abid lays down his cards, puts on his gloves and walks out to bat. 'Don't do anything silly,' Engineer advises. Abid nods gravely, takes guard and charges out at the first ball like one of the posed photographs of a Golden Age hero. He manages to pop the ball up perilously near a close-in fieldsman.

With a sheepish glance at Engineer, he plays the next two balls watchfully. And then Luckhurst pitches short. Abid cuts it away past the infield. A good enough stroke. With each retelling of Engineer down the years the cut will get streakier and finer. 'I had made all those runs but Abid came in and played a streaky edge through the slips and was swept off his feet by the crowd,' is the general Engineer version. The picture snapped at the end of the stroke, however, shows him, along with the fielders and the batsman, looking perfectly square of the wicket.

'The ball was promptly swallowed up by a mad charge of a predominantly Indian crowd,' writes Laker.

Campbell Page is more graphic: 'What follows is like one of Eisenstein's crowd scenes. While the ball is still 50 yards from the boundary, massed Indians leap the barrier and charge. The English team sprint for the pavilion. The umpires gather up the stumps before they are lost to the marauders. Hot on the heels of the shock troops, a little Indian girl not more than 5-years-old lifts her even smaller brother over the fence, takes his hand, and drags him to where the action is. In no time the Indian batsmen are being swept towards the pavilion on the shoulders of the crowd.'

'Invasion of the field by the Indians of London,' pens Woodcock. Only not all of them are from London. Not all of them are Indian either. James Mettyear, Rob Faversham, Mark Pemberton are only some of the many Englishmen who are there that day.

'Then it was all happiness, pride, garlands, sweets, and a hint of nostalgia,' writes Arlott.

Keith Miller notes it down as 'the most touching moment in cricket I can remember.'

Towards the final stages of the chase, Wadekar fell asleep in the rear of the dressing room. It is there that England manager Ken Barrington finds him as he walks in to congratulate the winning captain.

Barrington nudges the skipper awake and lets him know the good news. 'I always knew we'd win,' Wadekar remarks.

The unscheduled nap perhaps makes him a bit late to appear on the pavilion balcony. 'We'll have a bloody riot on our hands if you don't go out there,' coaxes Barrington.

A huge crowd waits in front. And when he does come out and waves, a huge cheer erupts. The cheers are heard again when Chandra appears smiling beside him.

And perhaps for the first time on the tour, the public saw Wadekar's face break into a smile. Clive Taylor of *The Sun* captured the moment, 'Old Stone Face stood in front of the balcony and smiled. He might never stop smiling for the rest of his life.'

In India, buses are stopped as fans stream onboard to inform passengers of the result. Sweets go around homes, housing complexes, compounds, colonies (a term for a cluster of apartments, not the erstwhile British pastime) and neighbourhoods. Crackers go off well into the night. There is joy, there is disbelief and there is celebration.

Speeches follow from the Surrey president Maurice Allom, the Indian high commissioner, Illingworth and Wadekar.

The England captain is generous in his praise, 'On the strength of their performances against the West Indies and England, India have proved themselves to be a world-class side.' However, he has some rather harsh words for his own men, 'We deserved to lose because we batted very, very badly on Monday. Full marks to Chandrasekhar. He proved he was an accomplished and positive spinner – but nobody will ever convince me that this was a 101 wicket. In most cases Chandra didn't get us out. We did it for him.'

He has an interesting take on the effect of limited-overs matches as well. 'How can you expect anything else if your middle-order men are sent in to slog out ten or fifteen overs every Sunday? The result is that the country's foremost batsmen are openers – but if you try to fit them in lower down you put them at a mental disadvantage.'

Intriguing indeed. At that moment England have several opening batsmen in the form of Boycott, Edrich, Luckhurst, Jameson and Amiss. The skipper obviously has some unpleasant things to say about the slow turners prepared for the Tests throughout the summer.

The win is also a 'prestige lever' for the Indian board and the politicians back home to demand that the Cricket Council's proposal to postpone the winter's tour by a year be overturned. Wadekar echoes the thoughts, 'We would love the chance this winter to prove that this was no flash in the pan. I think we are good enough to beat you again.'

Ravi Tikkoo, chairman of Globtik Tankers, hands out special prizes: £1,500 to the Indians as the winning team, £250 to the Indians for the faster bowling rate, £250 to England for the faster scoring rate, £250 to Chandra as the Indian player to give the most enjoyment and £250 to Knott as the English player in the same category.

The English cricketers join in with champagne for the celebrations. Plans are made to have an Indian dinner hosted by the high commissioner at a fashionable restaurant. The fare will eventually include the innovatively named – if somewhat contrived – dishes such as Wadekar Cutlet, Gavaskar Curry, Bedi Pulao and Chandrasekhar Soup.

Some Pakistani cricketers join the celebrations in the dressing room. Zaheer Abbas is there, a guest of Abid Ali. And then there are the Surrey professionals Intikhab Alam and Younis Ahmed. They tell their Indian counterparts how happy they are at the triumph. As indeed a lot of them are.

And during the celebrations a voice floats in from the crowd, 'Indira Gandhi is flying over tonight to give everyone a kiss.'

The prime minister does not quite fly in. She contents herself with a telegram to the captain, 'The country is thrilled to hear of your exciting victory. Congratulations to you and your team.' She ends with a somewhat vacuous cliché, 'You played cricket as it should be played.'

She does understand the importance of the victory.

England v India, 3rd Test, The Oval – 19, 20, 21, 23, 24 August
England 355 (Knott 90, Jameson 82, Hutton 81, Edrich 41; Solkar 3-28) and 101 (Chandra 6-38) lost to **India** 284 (Engineer 59, Sardesai 54, Wadekar 48, Solkar 44; Illingworth 5-70) and 174/6 (Wadekar 45, Sardesai 40; Underwood 3-72) by 4 wickets.

61

CONQUERING HEROES
AND THE HEROINE

IN FACT, the Air India flight from London to Bombay was diverted to New Delhi to enable the prime minister to meet the returning cricketers. Palam Airport was decorated with festoons and banners as people gathered in hordes to catch a glimpse of the all-conquering heroes. Some danced *bhangra* in typically Punjabi fashion. As they walked out to a royal reception, some members of the Indian team joined in to the music and beats.

The felicitation took place at Feroz Shah Kotla, with the Education Minister Siddhartha Shankar Ray presiding. That evening Mrs Gandhi received the players at her Teen Murti Bhavan residence, congratulating each member of the side individually. She spent a fair amount of time with Wadekar, discussing the arrangements for matches in aid of the Bangladesh Fund. That winter four matches were played for this purpose at Calcutta, Delhi and Bombay between the victorious Indian team and a Rest of India side.

The following morning, the team flew to Santa Cruz Airport, Bombay, in a 737 Boeing Garuda. They touched down to huge cheers and the blowing of conches. The police band played 'Hail to the Conquering Hero' as Wadekar led his men down the gangway.

More than one-and-a-half million people turned up to watch the motorcade as it covered the 20-kilometre route from Wankhede to the Cricket Club of India (CCI). As the players stood waving, they were showered with rose petals and colourful bursts of *gulal*. As they passed the blind school at Worli, the convoy paused as the students garlanded the stars whose sparkle they could not see.

'Our cricket reflected the new resurgent spirit in the country,' wrote Wadekar.

As *The Times of India* noted, "Glorious to be living at this hour and to be an Indian, Days, months, years will pass, but our cricket team's magnificent triumph over England in England will remain unforgettable."

Indeed, the triumph has remained unforgettable.

* * *

The cricketers end the tour on a high.

They are in a bit of a bother against Sussex at Hove, but some resolute batting by the ever-reliable Solkar sees them to a respectable score in the first innings and a dour innings by Jayantilal, followed by the most irreverent hitting by Govindraj, helps them hold out for a draw. The Indian recruit Uday Joshi captures five second-innings wickets but cannot quite force the result.

Solkar's 90 from No.4 is quite significant given talks are on about his re-joining Sussex in 1972. Ultimately, the return does not materialise.

Sussex v Indians, Hove – 25, 26, 27 August
Indians 220 (Solkar 90; Greig 4-78) and 276/7 (Jayantilal 57, Gavaskar 40, Govindraj 40*; Joshi 5-107) drew with **Sussex** 386 (Buss 140, Greenidge 62; Prasanna 5-137, Bedi 3-105).

* * *

On the second day of the Sussex match the final decision was taken, and the MCC postponed the winter's tour of India, Pakistan and Ceylon by a year. A pity really, given the high spirits of the Indian side and the way they had made the world sit up and take notice.

Arlott had voiced the opinion that the Indian spinners were arguably the strongest attacking force in world cricket, supported by the most sophisticated, enthusiastic and effectively deployed fielding ever produced by an Indian side in this country. An editorial in *The Daily Telegraph* was no less flattering, 'Too often it seems that our players need to be helped by conditions of wicket or weather in order to thrive. Against this, the Indians have shown themselves to be men for all seasons.'

A bit far-fetched that, given spinning tracks at Lord's and The Oval and their rain-aided escape on the seamer's wicket of Old Trafford. One could understand the disappointment fuelling the editorial, but it was quite a stretch to say that England needed favourable wicket or weather to win. They had won their last series in Australia, the West Indies, New Zealand and South Africa, and drawn in Pakistan. They had lost in India in 1961/62, but that had essentially been an England A side.

But there was a lot of truth in what Don Bradman said, 'The important thing is that India have been able to gather a team capable of winning a Test series in England. Their win has shown a considerable advance in their ability.'

Yes, a pity that the winter's tour was cancelled. But, then, it was not as if the MCC were left with a lot of choice in the matter. On that same day Indira Gandhi spoke to the secretary-general of the World Peace Council, saying, 'The struggle in Bangladesh is between 75 million people on the one side and the vindictive, cruel and autocratic military regime of Islamabad on the other. The people of Bangladesh are united in the fight for their just demands. How can we fail to take note of [the threat of war]?'

The issue was well and truly global now. On that very same day, prompted by a humanitarian appeal issued by 29 leading Latin American intellectuals, including Victoria Ocampo and Jorge Luis Borges, the Latin American Parliament at Caracas adopted a resolution calling on Pakistan to desist from further violation of human rights.

* * *

At Taunton, the veteran Tom Cartwright dismisses the first five batsmen to have the visitors in some trouble at 158/5. However, this is followed by a superb partnership between the Indian opening bowlers with bats in their hands: Solkar 113, Abid 102 not out.

When Somerset bat, Sardesai drops Close at 9. The veteran slams a century. As the match peters out into a draw, Wadekar enjoys himself in the second innings to hit 74.

Somerset v Indians, Taunton – 28, 29, 30 August
Indians 349 (Solkar 113, Abid 102*; Cartwright 5-79) and 162/5 dec (Wadekar 74; Cartwright 3-42) drew with **Somerset** 226/4 dec (Close 103*, Virgin 47) and 127/2 (Robinson 52*, Close 43*).

At Worcester, Gavaskar and Wadekar hit big hundreds as both of them complete their respective thousand runs on the tour. A young Pakistani lad with spots on his face sprays it all over the place, bowling 16 wayward overs and conceding 73 without any success. While batting he scores a duck and 15.

It is difficult to imagine that down the years he will become not only the greatest cricketer produced by Pakistan, but also a sex symbol and eventually the prime minister of the country.

Worcestershire v Indians, New Road – 1, 2, 3 September
Indians 383/3 dec (Gavaskar 194, Wadekar 150) and 150/8 dec (Viswanath 53; Wilkinson 3-48, Griffith 3-58) drew with **Worcestershire** 248 (Parker 91, Wilkinson 48; Venkat 4-60) and 250/5 (Ormond 76, Yardley 104*; Abid 3-64).

Finally at Scarborough, in a match played in a festive atmosphere, Tony Lewis leads T.N. Pearce's XI and declares at 357/3 and 199/3 to set a target of 251 in four hours.

It is Ashok Mankad, carrying the bat for an unbeaten 154, that allows India to respond with 306. In the final innings Gavaskar hits four sixes and 10 fours in a scintillating 128 as India win by five wickets with half an hour to spare.

The triumphant series is completed on a winning note.

TN Pearce's XI v Indians, Scarborough – 4, 6, 7 September
TN Pearce's XI 357/3 dec (Virgin 176, Bolus 75, Fletcher 67*)
and 199/3 dec (Bolus 106*, Parfitt 63) lost to **India** 306 (Mankad
154*, Solkar 79; Hobbs 5-94) and 252/5 (Gavaskar 128; Hobbs
4-64) by five wickets.

* * *

Less than a month after the decisive Test match, on 18 September,
more than 35,000 people thronged into The Oval on a sunny
late afternoon. They stood inside the historic ground, under
the famous gasometer, as the stage set up at the Vauxhall End
hosted performances by The Who, The Faces, Atomic Rooster,
Eugene Wallace, America, Mott the Hoople, Quintessence,
Lindisfarne, Grease Band and Cochise. In keeping with the
venue, The Who's roadies wore cricket gear. Roisterer Keith
Moon appeared on stage brandishing a cricket bat, which he
used as drumstick for the first number. The bat was then thrown
into the audience, much to the consternation of Jeff Dexter, the
master of ceremonies, who had borrowed it from Surrey as part
of his on-stage costume.

The event raised £15,000 for the Bangladesh relief fund.

Ten days later Indira Gandhi spoke at the luncheon given by
A.N. Kosygin, chairman of the USSR Council of Ministers, in
Moscow. 'Indian history will remember 1971 as an eventful year.
We are certainly at a momentous juncture. From March until
now, there have been many important developments. At the year's
beginning, our economy had just regained its élan after eight
troubled years. Our general elections, held in March, brought
greater clarity to the national scene and gave a firmer direction
to our political life.

'We were all set to launch the second phase of our national
development during which the promise of equality and freedom
from want could come closer to reality. Our parliament had
been in session for just a week and the representatives of the

nation were still shaking one another's hands when beyond our borders there occurred events which have created incalculable difficulties for us.'

During this Moscow visit, she refused to negotiate with any Soviet leader lesser than the general secretary of the Communist Party Leonid Brezhnev.

Having spent the first few years as prime minister fighting hostile opposition and factions in her own party, and battling against her own inexperience, her victory in the 1971 elections had launched a new, confident phase of premiership. She led the country brilliantly during the Bangladesh crisis, right up to the war in December 1971. She harmonised the military, political and diplomatic wings of India with exceptional skill, building national consensus before any major move, keeping in touch with the opposition leaders.

Many of these sterling facets that one saw in her during those months would become palpably absent during the years that followed, especially the dark years of the Emergency.

She dealt with the refugee situation with aplomb, making sure that they did not mix and mingle with the people from West Bengal – wfrom whom they were indistinguishable – hence disappearing into the slums without returning where they came from.

And in late October she went on a 21-day tour of foreign countries, to Belgium, Austria, West Germany, France, Britain and the United States, defending the Indian position and showcasing the plight of the Bangladeshis.

'Our fear,' said Sir Alec Douglas-Home, 'is that there would be war.'

'We won't start it,' was Indira Gandhi's laconic reply.

'No government could have shown restraint like the Indians despite such tremendous provocation and threat to our safety and stability,' she told the BBC. When the interviewer, much as in every country during her visits, harped on 'restraint', she shot back, 'When Hitler was on the rampage, why didn't you say, "Let's have peace with Germany and let the Jews die?"'

She knew international opinion was behind her, even as Nixon and Kissinger poured forth four-letter words to discuss her and her country. She used it to the fullest.

Home truths

A day after Indira Gandhi's speech in Moscow, Douglas-Home met Swaran Singh during the UN session in New York, leading to a remarkable exchange. When Sir Alec expressed concern about guerrilla operations, Singh frankly said, 'One has to accept the existence of the freedom fighters, one simply cannot wish them away.'

Sir Alec was one of the torch-bearers of a long tradition of wishing away such men, or branding them terrorists. By no means was he the last of them.

On 3 December the war began with a Pakistan offensive. On 6 December Mrs Gandhi announced her recognition of an independent Bangladesh to a wildly cheering Parliament. By 16 December it was over, with an overwhelming victory for the Indians. Never since the Second World War has such a large-scale surrender taken place.

Shujauddin Butt, the left-arm spinner who played 19 Tests for Pakistan between 1954 and 1962, was an army officer captured during the war. He spent 18 months as a prisoner-of-war in India.

The country was delirious with joy and jingoism. They were victorious, a major power in the area, and most importantly they held the moral high ground in the conflict. Indira Gandhi was hailed as the personification of Durga, the goddess with multiple arms, each bearing invincible weapons. She was literally worshipped, often as the reincarnation of *Shakti* or female energy. *The Economist* described her as The Empress of India, a title hitherto used only for Queen Victoria.

In 1972, before leaving for Stockholm to address the first UN conference on the environment, Indira Gandhi read Alvin Toffler's *Future Shock* from cover to cover. This was mentioned in a snippet in *The Times of India*. All major bookshops in Delhi and Bombay witnessed near-stampedes as every single copy of the book was sold out. A quarter of a century later, as I walked under the colonnaded verandas of the Oberoi Grand along the Jawaharlal Nehru Road, Calcutta, I came across authentic bookshops and street hawkers selling pirated copies of the book.

By then Indira Gandhi had been lionised and vilified several times over, criticised and lauded to the extremes, jailed, made prime minister yet again, assassinated and mourned. Very seldom was she unbiasedly analysed.

But copies of *Future Shock* were still sold. Not too many knew what it was about. Yet most people bought it, and the general consensus was it was a very important book.

The war was a complex issue, like any war. And it worked the miracle of unifying a country as diverse, as divided by language, culture, religion, climate, food and landscape as India.

The triumph over England in England was a small but important piece in the jigsaw that led to the growth of national confidence and identity, the emergence from decades of inferiority complex.

Indira Gandhi was aware of that. And therefore, she made time for the team in spite of several battles – domestic, international and at the East Pakistan border – that kept her busy, and often sleepless.

Much as Indira Gandhi was lionised as a leader after the war, the members of the winning side became figures of worship. In Indian cricketing folklore, some became the greatest batsman ever, taming the greatest of bowlers with magical bats. Some became the greatest spinners ever, successful on every surface, performances never bettered before or since.

Not one of those conclusions can be defended with data. But just like beliefs lacing the divine, the very mention of evaluating demi-gods with numbers is revolting to most.

People thronged around while some of the stars did their shopping, for *darshan* – a typical Indian concept of sighting a noble soul that builds one's own spiritual capital.

They had achieved what had seemed impossible, a victorious conquest across seven seas, across *kala pani,* in a privileged nation with every facility denied in an impoverished, third-world country under the yoke of corruption and a struggle for the basic necessities of life. A victory over the conquerors whose superiority had been taken as much for granted as their own inferiority.

Years later, I was working as a freelance cricket journalist for a website. The editor, a print journalism veteran, was making use of my slightly non-trivial statistical methods for evaluating the performances of different cricketers from different eras with a great degree of relish. In fact, he had published my pieces with Mann-Whitney analysis for non-parametric data, t-test for comparing ratios and even one using the Kaplan-Meier method of survival analysis for a better estimate of average score. Not that he understood much of it, but statistical articles always got 'eyeballs'. For days he had wanted me to produce an iconoclastic piece on Bradman by pointing out chinks in his record. I had to inform him that apart from his record on wet wickets, one could not really find flaws with The Don. It is difficult to average 99.94 with visible chinks.

At this juncture I wrote a 10,000-word biography of Sunil Gavaskar for his upcoming birthday. While lauding his technique, consistency and acknowledging him to be the first true world-class batsman produced by India, I did add that some of the legends associated with him were not quite accurate. The major point demonstrated was that contrary to popular belief, his record against the famed four-pronged West Indian bowling attack was just about good rather than outstanding. While his overall average against them was 67 with 13 hundreds, most of those runs came against depleted sides during a period of rebuilding in 1971 or the Packer era. When the actual famed four-pronged pace attack bowled to him, his average dropped to 40, and he had three hundreds, two in rained-off matches, with a fair share of failures in between. Similarly, while he had played Imran excellently, he had generally failed against bowlers such as Hadlee and Lillee.

My editor exploded. 'Sometimes, just sometimes, numbers don't tell you the actual story,' he vented in an email. Thus, after blissfully entertaining Mann-Whitney and Kaplan-Meier, he stumbled on basic long division.

I stood my ground, and because I was working for less than peanuts, the argument could not be concluded with a wave of a superior's prerogative. To his considerable credit, my editor thought about it and grudgingly agreed that the figures were accurate, while reiterating that his 'respect for the idol' would remain the same. He added that he had been an ardent fan of Gavaskar for the past 40 years and had written a poem about him during the early 1970s.

We agreed not to make changes other than superficial ones, carry the statistics, and to even send the article to Gavaskar himself. Unlike most of his fans, Gavaskar himself did not have any problems with the piece. His only comments were that it was a bit too long for him to read at one go, and that there was a very minor factual error in the second paragraph. 'But, it is just like missing a ball outside off-stump and carrying on batting,' he wrote.

The man is a lot more grounded than his fans.

Just like my editor, who ran my account of the Oval triumph with the headline 'The Day India Ended England's Home Rule', this particular editor's dilemma with statistics underlined the fixation that many have with the icons of 1971. I have run into many fans, and even cricket scribes, who are shocked when I say that the numbers very starkly indicate Indian spinners were not quite the best of all time. Many counter such analyses with questions such as: 'Who are these people? Never heard of Blythe, Trumble, Wardle and Tayfield.'

Yes, there are myths about the 1970s icons. Myths that cannot be stripped away. There is a magic surrounding them. Magic that has already cast its irreversible spell.

But there were reasons for myths to develop.

As the writer Mircea Eliade explained, hagiographies of celebrated figures transform them into near-gods and their sagas into myths. Myth describes how, in primeval times, a god or near-god created a phenomenon. Outright gods are credited with creating natural phenomena, culture heroes with social phenomena. A myth honours its subject's establishing something in the physical or social world, that continues to this day.

The team of 1971 are cultural heroes, creating the social phenomenon of defeating the erstwhile conquerors in their land.

62

EPILOGUE: THE LAST 50 YEARS

NO ILLINGWORTH, no Snow, no Boycott, no Edrich. One can argue that Edrich was omitted after failing to reach 50 even once in his five Ashes Tests of the 1972 summer. However, the rest opted out in the time-honoured manner. It was Tony Lewis who led England in India in 1972-73, emulating Nigel Howard of the 1951-52 tour by captaining his country on debut. The defeat at home had not really changed much in that respect. England lost the series 1-2.

It was not until 1976/77 that a full-strength English side actually visited the country. Tony Greig was a canny enough captain to know that having the crowd on their side was of utmost importance in such a strange, excitable land. He planted his long legs down the wicket and neutralised the spin, asked Derek Randall to turn cartwheels to entertain the crowd, fell out with rival skipper Bedi over the latter's allegations of Vaseline abuse, used his blond locks and charisma to win over the masses. He blew kisses to the ladies in the ground, famously rode on the back of a scooter, befriended the press with a heady mix of charm and flattery. It was his magical tour in 1976/77, when he was idolised by millions, and numerous Indian children born during the tour were given the nickname 'Tony'. In Robin Marlar's memorable phrase, he became the 'Clive of Cricket', and the normally partisan fans did not really mind when England took the series 3-1.

The England tour of 1976/77 was during the final dark days of the Emergency into which Indira Gandhi's government had plunged the nation. By then the heydays of the 1971 war had given way to some of the most oppressive shows of near-dictatorial rule in India, with fundamental rights all but abolished.

Down the years, the visits of the England teams remained eventful in plenty of ways.

The 1981/82 tour was in jeopardy even before the cricketers boarded the flight. The fact that Boycott and Geoff Cook had been in South Africa in the recent past miffed Mrs Gandhi enough to raise ominous signs of cancellation. The Indian government announced that Boycott and Cook were unacceptable as members of the side and once again the cricket world was on the brink of a division along colour lines.

The Indian stance on apartheid had always been unwavering. In 1974 they had forfeited the Davis Cup final after coming up against South Africa in the title round. In fact, with Garry Sobers visiting Rhodesia and spending time with Ian Smith, the 1971 tour of the West Indies had also come on the brink of cancellation before the island governments stepped in to negotiate.

The diplomatic manoeuvring that kicked off to save the 1981/82 series was made complicated by Boycott holidaying in Hong Kong. Eventually both the cricketers declared their repugnance for apartheid. The prime minister was placated and the tour was allowed to proceed. There was a major hiccup early on when Boycott made a characteristically tactless remark about South Africa to an Indian journalist, and as a result received his first major dressing down by the England tour management. It would not be the last.

The series saw some of the most colossally boring cricket of all time, with Boycott and Tavare putting sluggish glaciers to shame with their lethargic batting, and being matched block by block by Gavaskar and Vengsarkar.

Away from cricket, they did experience some of the old world attractions of an Indian tour. They played West Zone in the Moti Bagh – Pearl Garden – the personal ground of the Maharaja of

Baroda. The cricketers were entertained by dancing girls and also the Maharaja's collection of crocodiles – 'both at an appropriate distance', Scyld Berry assures us.

Boycott achieved his ambition of going past the record Test aggregate of runs amassed by Sobers. Mission thus accomplished, he opened the batting at Calcutta, complained of feeling listless and let John Lever field in his place. On the final day of the Test, with his team-mates sweating it out on the field, he went off to the Tollygunge Club to play golf. Confronted by an angry captain Keith Fletcher and manager Raman Subba Row, he claimed that the doctor had prescribed fresh air and that was the only place in Calcutta where he could get some.

Boycott was sent home and never played for England again, but even in his final rejoinder there was a barb about the pollution in India. He was already 10 at the time of the Great Smog of London, but perhaps never came down south from his Yorkshire home.

Boycott did go further south after the tour. After all his declared repugnance for apartheid, he departed with the likes of Gooch, Underwood and others to South Africa on the first of the rebel tours. He also played a leading role when the tour was being arranged with cloak-and-dagger secrecy.

Dark Knights

The Boycott attitude towards the problems of colour and racism makes for interesting analysis. In 2017, disgruntled at being overlooked for a knighthood, he went on record saying, 'Mine's been turned down twice. I'd better black my face.' The underlying connotation was that people like Garry Sobers, Viv Richards and Curtly Ambrose had been knighted because they were black.

There was widespread condemnation. While some maintained it was a comment from the 'dark ages', Edgbaston's Labour MP Preet Gill was a tad more direct, 'Let's call it what it is, it is irresponsible, it is racism.' It led Boycott to admit that the comment had been wrong.

Three years later, Boycott received his knighthood. His words were taken seriously ... one does wonder whether that applies to his apology or his original comment.

In 2017, *Test Match Special* carried out an 'on-air prank' on the former England cricketer, with Jonathan Agnew reading out a fake ICC release in the most serious fashion, insisting that Boycott's number of first-class hundreds had been reduced by one. While the prank itself was carefully constructed and a successful one, and it is always gratifying to put one over on the outspoken Boycott, the premise chosen was frankly rather controversial. Agnew read out that further to the request of the South African government, the ICC had now considered the question of downgrading the status of all statistics from the series between England and the Rest of the World in 1970, the series having been contested against the spirit of the Gleneagles Agreement. That meant one century was supposedly deducted from Boycott's first-class career, and the 100th hundred that he famously brought up in an Ashes Test would now be considered the 99th.

Knowing Boycott, and given the sensitivity of the issue of apartheid and the Gleneagles Agreement, this was opening the door for some serious faux pas on live radio. In particular, the trivialisation of a colossal cause for humanity – and the apparent ignorance of the commentators gathered on the occasion about the same – makes one wonder when the world will actually start understanding the history of racism.

To the many who thought it was incredibly funny and perfectly harmless, I would like to ask if bringing up a similar prank based on the Holocaust or deaths on 9/11 would have been acceptable.

The Indian visit in 1982 coincided with the Falklands conflict – considered by many as the last of the British colonial wars. The manner in which imperial history creeps into modern times is rather disconcerting.

However, far more dramatic were the English tours to India.

In 1984/85, the country was in the grip of cricket fever. Kapil Dev's men had won the World Cup in 1983 and the game had become immensely popular across the nation.

At the same time, Indira Gandhi, in her third term as prime minister, had ordered the army to storm the Golden Temple – the Sikh shrine at Amritsar – to flush out the secessionist terrorists. The casualties had been heavy, damage to the holy shrine extensive and a veritable arsenal had been confiscated.

The English team reached India in the early hours of 31 October 1984. On that same morning, as the prime minister stepped out of her official residence and walked along the pathway connecting her house with the adjoining bungalow that served as the prime minister's office. A fence ran through the complex, broken by a wicker gate. Mrs Gandhi had just reached this gate when her veteran Sikh bodyguard, sub-inspector Beant Singh, shot her in the abdomen with his revolver. As she collapsed on the concrete path, Sikh constable Satwant Singh emptied his Sten gun into her.

Years later, Mike Gatting sits in the Middlesex Premier Members' box at Lord's and tells me, 'We had arrived late, at around three o'clock in the morning. I came down at around nine o'clock in the morning, got out of the lift and heard people talking about it. And I said, "That cannot have happened." There was a 13-day mourning period, and so we went down to Sri Lanka for preparation, and then it did not seem to stop raining. After that, one day we were just about to go for practice when all of a sudden there was a huge explosion in the naval yard. It was just about half a mile from our hotel. The Tamil Tigers had blown up half the yard.'

As the English cricketers sojourned in the strife-ridden Colombo, across India anti-Sikh riots broke out, resulting in the worst spate of killing since Partition. In many Sikh quarters, there were suspicions that the riots were organised in a calculated attempt to use the assassination to suppress any secessionist tendency by the community.

Gatting continues, 'We came back to Bombay, and went to meet the deputy commissioner [Percy Norris] who was retiring in three months. The following morning our practice was delayed. We asked, "Why's that?" They said, "The bloke you went to visit yesterday evening has been assassinated."'

There were thoughts about returning home. The Indian board secretary Judge Kanmandikar promised 'complete and fool-proof security', which was dismissed as ludicrous by the *Guardian* correspondent Matthew Engel. However, when investigations revealed that the Norris assassination had roots in the Middle East or even Ireland, and had little to do with India, fears receded a bit.

As Gatting put it: 'They had assassinated Indira Gandhi, they had assassinated the British deputy high commissioner. What about the cricketers? It would make a great international ripple. There was a bit of talk about leaving. In the end we decided to knuckle down and carry on, and I am glad that we did.'

Indeed, they won the series 2-1, the last time that they would win in India until 2012/13.

The England team was supposed to tour in 1988/89. The TCCB selected a 16-member side and named Graham Gooch captain. Alongside him, they named Allan Lamb, John Emburey, Kim Barnett, Phil Newport and Graham Dilley. Gooch and these five all had South African links. This not only underlined the rather lenient and ad-hoc attitude that prevailed in England on the South African question, it was also as good as waving a red rag at an anti-apartheid bull such as the Indian government. Within days of the announcement of the team, it was declared that India would deny visas to those six members.

While the Indian government expressed disappointment that Gooch had never apologised for the rebel tour, the objection was somewhat curious because the Essex batsman had played in the Reliance Cup the previous winter. However, the response of the chairman of selectors Peter May was, 'We don't pick teams for political reasons,' harking back to the days of the D'Oliveira affair and the enormous resistance to supposedly mixing 'politics and sport'.

Nevertheless, it was Gooch who led England when they arrived in 1992/93. By then, Indira Gandhi's son and successor as prime minister, Rajiv Gandhi, had also been assassinated by a suicide bomber of the Tamil Tigers. It was one of the repercussions of the Indian involvement in the Sri Lankan civil war, with the deployment of their own peace-keeping force – in itself an illustration of the predilection to play the role of a major power in Southeast Asia. This dichotomy continues in India … squalor and poverty, corruption and bureaucracy remain virtually unchanged, but at the same time the status as an emerging nation, economic epicentre and a nuclear power are zealously maintained.

Runs, Ruins and Royalty

The complaints about pollution were given a curious twist by royalty. In 1983, the West Indians were playing in India and at the same time Queen Elizabeth was on a state visit. Between the Ahmedabad and Bombay Tests, Sunil Gavaskar went over to Delhi at the invitation of the British ambassador to attend a cocktail party and meet the Queen and Prince Philip.

When the Prince heard that the next Test was in Bombay, he quipped, 'Stay there for 15 minutes. After that the smog of Bombay will exhaust the fast bowlers.' Gavaskar writes in *Runs 'n Ruins:* 'It was on the tip of my tongue to tell him that Manchester was no better but then good sense prevailed and I just let the remark about my home-town pass. There are certain balls you just don't hit. And this was one such.'

The tour was conducted under the looming shadow of the Ayodhya temple-Babri Masjid destruction and the resulting riots. The first match at Ahmedabad, a hotbed of communal tensions, had to be cancelled. The first ODI was also called off, and replaced with a seventh game at another venue.

But the humiliation of a 3-0 'brown-wash' could hardly be attributed to the issues with security. Indeed, chief selector Ted Dexter tried to take a leaf out Boycott's 1981/82 book and blame the defeat in the Calcutta Test on pollution, only to be put in his place by the Indian forest and environment minister Kamal Nath, 'In view of Mr Dexter's unease I've decided to commission a report into the effect of pollution levels on the trajectories of Indian spinners.'

Pollution was not the only factor quoted to justify England's dismal performance. Dexter and the selectors also found a lot to complain about in the attitude of the English cricketers, including their unkempt appearance and a supposedly objectionable sprouting of facial hair.

In reality, England were up against a new breed of Indian cricketers. The country had just given in to the pressures of the IMF and embraced an open-market economy. The BCCI had also suddenly realised they had been sitting on a potential goldmine in the form of broadcast rights. The board had found the launchpad which, within a very few years, would make them the strongest financial power in world cricket. And the new generation of cricketers turned out to be less overawed by foreign names, redrawing the limits of possibility.

Anil Kumble – whom manager Keith Fletcher had scouted in South Africa and had dismissed saying, 'I didn't see him turn a single ball from leg to off' – captured 21 wickets. Variously Mohammad Azharuddin, Sachin Tendulkar and Vinod Kambli plundered mountains of runs off the English bowlers. The selection policy of dropping 35-year-old David Gower – while playing 40-year-old John Emburey, handing the captaincy to 39-year-old Graham Gooch and bolstering the middle-order with another 35-year-old in Mike Gatting – did not really pay off either. More so with Gooch and Gatting indulging in a plate of Chinese prawns ahead of the second Test.

It did not help that there was an ongoing strike of Indian Airlines pilots. That resulted in some long train journeys, harking back to the 1950s. On other occasions pilots were brought out of retirement and some were hired from Uzbekistan. Dermot Reeve writes in *Winning Ways*, 'One flight into Delhi was particularly hair-raising. We came to a juddering stop just 40 yards from a fence and the co-pilot gasped over the intercom: "Oh, it's only through the grace of God that we have landed safely, we've had total hydraulic failure.'"

Reeve, who came in as the replacement for Gower, was out playing the sweep shot. When he queried the decision of the umpire he was told to stop complaining and play straight. In six ODIs, Reeve managed 68 runs and captured one wicket. Perhaps a more important role was played by his mother, who took on the responsibilities of the official England scorer after Clem Driver was taken ill.

And poor Richard Blakey. Seven runs in his four Test innings, falling to Kumble three times. Throughout the flight back home he kept muttering 'Anil Kumble', padding the name with an expletive or two on either side. Kumble did not threaten physical injury like Trueman, but the scars suffered by Blakey were perhaps rather good approximations of the marks left on Umrigar's psyche.

That was perhaps the last time complaints over food and transport were heard from English teams in India. The opening of the economy, the commercial arrangements around the 1996 World Cup, along with the proliferation of satellite television in the land, soon made the country the financial powerhouse of the cricket world. The triumph in the inaugural T20I World Cup in 2007 and the subsequent launch of the Indian Premier League transformed India into the place every cricketer wanted to be. The facilities, including hotel accommodation, food and travel, were by now world class, and the enticing IPL contracts too mouthwatering.

Besides, by the early 2000s the Indian team had become one of the strongest in the world. Their batting line-up was the envy of every side in the world, and at home their bowlers were more often than not unplayable. The days of sending second-string sides were long gone. By 2001-02, Ashley Giles was being lauded for managing to keep Tendulkar quiet – after the maestro had amassed 88, 103 and 90 in his three Test outings. Heaps of praise were being poured on Nasser Hussain, including some suggestions of knighthood, for managing to lose the series just 0-1.

The shadow of unrest, however, continued to dog the visits. The 2001/02 series was conducted during the ongoing 'war against terror', with officials from the ECB visiting India before the tour to review the security arrangements. While most of the originally selected team did travel, Robert Croft and Andy Caddick decided to stay at home because their families would be worried about their security. The opening match was switched from the Bombay Gymkhana ground to the Wankhede Stadium because the former lacked perimeter fencing.

The team played their last ODI on 3 February 2002 and left for home. The infamous Gujarat riots kicked off on 27 February.

The most poignant visit was the 2008/09 tour of Kevin Pietersen's team. The English cricketers stayed in the Taj Palace Hotel in Mumbai as they played two games against a Mumbai Cricket Association XI. Following that, they travelled across the country playing an ODI series. They were engaged in an ODI at Cuttack when 10 members of Lashkar-e-Taiba, an Islamist terrorist group, carried out a series of synchronised attacks across Mumbai, with the Taj Hotel experiencing six explosions and becoming the venue of a massive gun battle involving a terrorist takeover and more than 200 hostages.

The English cricketers flew home, returned to Abu Dhabi to attend a training camp, and thereafter made their way back to India. The first Test was shifted from Ahmedabad to Chennai. In an emotional match after the terrorist attack, India rode a blitzkrieg 83 by Sehwag and a serene unbeaten 103 by Tendulkar to chase down 387 in the final innings.

Examples of England continuing their tours under duress should not necessarily be concluded as evidence of changing attitudes. To their credit, the history of English cricketers continuing tours in the midst of political turmoil are plenty. Right from 1895/96, when Lord Hawke played cards with the English prisoners in the Johannesburg prison during the Jameson Raid, to Colin Cowdrey plodding on with the Pakistan Tests in spite of civil and military unrest, to David Gower's men carrying on after Indira Gandhi's assassination, the Newboltian tenet of playing up and playing the game has been historically strong and unflinching.

Yet, the reasons why men like May and Trueman opted out of tours in the 1950s are a huge contrast to the reasons which made Caddick and Croft say no in 2001.

England were awfully slow in getting off the mark in the IPL. Criticism of the degenerate format and evil money-grabbing franchises tarnishing the illusory halo around the pristine game were plenty in the first few years. And then they trickled in, and now they queue up. England captain Joe Root does not hide his disappointment at being ignored.

This is another wind of change that has taken a while to blow through the jammed windows of the Long Room, but it ended up doing its share of ruffling ancient feathers.

By 2014, the Indians were once again playing five-Test series in England, for the first time since 1959. Yes, they are a very good team as I write.

The bowling attack is better than anything ever possessed by the country. They lead 2-1 in the unfinished series of 2021, a series that was supposedly a piece in the intricate structure that forms preparation for the next Ashes for England.

But more importantly cricket is a lucrative commodity. The cricket-mad Indians, with the incredible population figures, constitute by some distance the game's biggest market. In fact, once the Indian figures are jotted down, the rest of the world looks like a few extras.

What about the sentiments that prevailed in the pre-1971 days? Do we still come across them?

Yes, we do. They resurface from time to time in various guises. We come across Michael Vaughan, the former England captain, flagrantly dismissing the spinning tracks of the subcontinent as 'bad for cricket' with complete disdain for facts and figures, which show that the green strips on English grounds produce even shorter Test matches. The English definitions of proper cricket are still forced on the world, with dusty turning wickets symbolic of the underdeveloped subcontinent, while grassy carpets masquerading as pitches are taken to be delightful reflections of the idyllic village green.

Similarly, Brad Hogg insists that the Ashes ignite public interest far more effectively than any World Test Championship.

There are similar varieties of condescension that survive in pockets, which still consider the Ashes to be the be-all and end-all of cricket. The English and Australian chroniclers still dominate the cricketing world view.

The anachronistic deadweight of the Anglo-Australian veto power was removed from the game in 1993, but there remains a massive inertial residue of self-bestowed privilege as exclusive sentinels of things cricketing. Perception of the present is often skewed as a result and history is too often subject to being cherry-picked.

And time and again we come across revelations about discrimination that still continues in dressing rooms, clubs, counties, first-class and international sides.

Some of the balance has been addressed, some of it remains to be addressed, some will perhaps never be addressed. In a curious historical equation, the retelling of history is a function of the former history itself.

The face of the Indian team has also changed down the years. In the late 1970s, Karsan Ghavri used to bowl to English batsmen all day only to find them looking through him during get-togethers in the evenings. Conversation with the English cricketers was restricted to the Baigs, the Pataudis, the Bedis ... the Oxbridge brigade, the princes and the exceptionally confident. Today most of the sides interact without stumbling on a baggage of the past that predates their births. New financial muscle allows Indian cricketers to shed the £3-a-day yoke of 1971 that put them on the back foot even before John Snow ran in.

Today Virat Kohli can be as fluently eloquent in his speech and sledges as he is with his cover drives. Today Ravi Ashwin can directly ask why the English definition of a good wicket is sacrosanct.

Having grown up in an India with an open-economy, satellite television and Sachin Tendulkar, they are neither reticent nor submissive.

The Indian team had won just 16 Tests in the 39 years before the 1971 series kicked off, while losing 49. From 2015 until the time of writing (2022), after stepping into the Kohli-era, they have won 44 and lost just 17. A victory was rare in those days, a cause of celebration. Today it is expected.

There is no question that it is a far greater team today than it had been in those days. However, I doubt that their deeds will ever be touched with such magical-mythical retelling as we have seen in the case of the 1971 pioneers.

Part of it definitely has to do with the sketchy extrapolation of the Test matches from static-filled airwaves and grainy newspaper pictures, which brought home the great tidings without throwing light on the chinks and weaknesses. Much of the perceived invulnerability of past cricketers can be explained in this way; the heroes of the older days never had the nervous swishes outside the off stump and long hops on the leg stump beamed to every home from every corner of the world. All followers of the game saw were giant headlines when they succeeded.

But much of it has to do with the unexpectedness of the event, the huge and historical backdrop of despair, the deep-rooted prevailing perceptions about the Indians and their cricket, the colonial past and the illusion of superiority on the other side of the world.

It was not just about 1971. It has never been just about 1971. History, be it cultural or cricketing, is never just about one event.

In a completely different context, singer, bassist and songwriter Lemmy Kilmister reflected, 'That was a great time, the summer of '71. I can't remember it, but I'll never forget it.'

The same is true for legions of Indian cricket fans.

APPENDICES

Appendix A

Tour Averages – India in England, 1971
India in Tests – Batting and Fielding

	T	R	HS	Ave	100	50	Ct/St
S Abid Ali	3	50	26	12.50	0	0	2
BS Bedi	3	12	8	4.00	0	0	0
BS Chandrasekhar	3	4	4*	–	0	0	3
FM Engineer	3	172	59	43.00	0	1	8/1
SM Gavaskar	3	144	57	24.00	0	2	5
AV Mankad	3	42	11	7.00	0	0	2
DN Sardesai	3	147	54	29.40	0	1	0
ED Solkar	3	168	67	42.00	0	2	5
S Venkataraghavan	3	62	24	15.50	0	0	3
GR Viswanath	3	128	68	25.60	0	1	1
AL Wadekar	3	204	85	34.00	0	1	5

India in Tests – Bowling

	Wkts	BB	Ave	5wI	10wM
S Abid Ali	5	4/64	53.80	0	0
BS Bedi	11	4/70	29.54	0	0
BS Chandrasekhar	13	6/38	29.15	1	0
SM Gavaskar	0	–	–	0	0
ED Solkar	6	3/28	22.83	0	0
S Venkataraghavan	13	4/52	26.92	0	0

England in Tests – Batting and Fielding

	T	R	HS	Ave	100	50	Ct/St
DL Amiss	1	9	9	4.50	0	0	2
G Boycott	1	36	33	18.00	0	0	1
BL D'Oliveira	3	88	30	17.60	0	0	1
JH Edrich	3	180	62	30.00	0	2	2
KWR Fletcher	2	30	28*	10.00	0	0	1
N Gifford	2	32	17	16.00	0	0	1
RA Hutton	3	129	81	32.25	0	1	5
R Illingworth	3	175	107	35.00	1	0	4
JA Jameson	2	141	82	35.25	0	1	0
APE Knott	3	223	90	44.60	0	2	10/1
P Lever	1	88	88*		0	1	0
BW Luckhurst	3	244	101	40.66	1	1	1
JSE Price	3	9	5*	3.00	0	0	1
JA Snow	2	85	73	21.25	0	1	1
DL Underwood	1	33	22	16.50	0	0	1

England in Tests – Bowling

	Wkts	BB	Ave	5wI	10wM
BL D'Oliveira	3	2-40	27.67	0	0
N Gifford	8	4-43	15.87	0	0
RA Hutton	4	2-38	32.75	0	0
R Illingworth	7	5-70	28.85	1	0
P Lever	5	5-70	16.80	1	0
BW Luckhurst	1	1-9	9.00	0	0
JSE Price	8	2-30	25.87	0	0
JA Snow	6	2-64	28.16	0	0
DL Underwood	4	3-72	30.25	0	0

Indians in Tour Matches – Batting and Fielding

	M	R	HS	Ave	100	50	Ct/St
S Abid Ali	14	552	102*	32.47	1	2	11
AA Baig	13	526	64	25.04	0	2	6
BS Bedi	13	50	8	6.25	0	0	5
BS Chandrasekhar	13	16	6	2.66	0	0	9
FM Engineer	4	262	62*	52.40	0	2	8/1
SM Gavaskar	15	1141	194	43.88	3	6	15
DD Govindraj	12	172	40*	19.11	0	0	5
HK Jayantilal	10	237	84	16.92	0	2	7
SMH Kirmani	7	118	37*	23.6	0	0	7
P Krishnamurthy	9	56	32	8.00	0	0	16/8
AV Mankad	13	795	154*	41.84	2	4	8
EAS Prasanna	9	33	10*	8.25	0	0	1
DN Sardesai	15	495	120	23.57	1	3	5
ED Solkar	16	802	113	44.55	1	6	14
S Venkataraghavan	14	303	57	15.15	0	1	12
GR Viswanath	16	946	122	41.13	3	5	4
AL Wadekar	16	1057	150	40.65	2	6	23

Indians in Tour Matches – Bowling

	Wkts	BB	Ave	5wI	10wM
S Abid Ali	16	4-64	57.87	0	0
AA Baig	0	-	-	-	-
BS Bedi	58	7-111	25.63	4	0
BS Chandrasekhar	50	6-34	24.86	5	1
SM Gavaskar	4	2-8	47.50	0	0
DD Govindraj	11	2-37	61.27	0	0
HK Jayantilal	0	-	-	-	-
SMH Kirmani	0	-	-	-	-

AV Mankad	2	1-8	61.00	0	0
EAS Prasanna	26	5-137	33.80	1	0
DN Sardesai	0	-	-	-	-
ED Solkar	14	3-28	49.42	0	0
S Venkataraghavan	63	9-93	24.90	2	1
AL Wadekar	0	-	-	-	-

Appendix B
Full Scorecard of the deciding Test

Third Test, The Oval – 19, 20, 21, 23, 24 August, 1971
Balls per over   6
England won the toss and decided to bat
India won by 4 wickets
Umpires   CS Elliott, AEG Rhodes

Close of play day 1   England (1) 355 all out
Close of play day 2   No play
Close of play day 3   India (1) 234/7 (Abid Ali 2*,
                       Venkataraghavan 3*)
Close of play day 4   India (2) 76/2 (Wadekar 45*, Sardesai 13*)

England First Innings		Runs	Balls	Mins	4s	6s
BW Luckhurst	c Gavaskar b Solkar	1	6	6	-	-
JA Jameson	run out	82	152	162	10	2
JH Edrich	c Engineer b Bedi	41	118	124	4	-
KWR Fletcher	c Gavaskar b Bedi	1	15	21	-	-
BL D'Oliveira	c Mankad b Chandra	2	19	16	-	-
+APE Knott	c and b Solkar	90	116	117	11	1
*R Illingworth	b Chandra	11	35	39	1	-
RA Hutton	b Venkataraghavan	81	125	132	13	-
JA Snow	c Engineer b Solkar	3	16	15	-	
DL Underwood	c Wadekar b Venkat	22	47	54	2	
JSE Price	not out	1	3	4	-	-

Extras (4 b, 15 lb, 1 w) 20
Total (all out, 108.4 overs) 355
Fall of wickets:
1-5 (Luckhurst), 2-111 (Edrich), 3-135 (Fletcher), 4-139 (Jameson),
5-143 (D'Oliveira), 6-175 (Illingworth), 7-278 (Knott), 8-284 (Snow),
9-352 (Underwood), 10-355 (Hutton, 108.4 ov)

India Bowling	Overs	Mdns	Runs	Wkts
Abid Ali	12	2	47	0
Solkar	15	4	28	3
Gavaskar	1	0	1	0
Bedi	36	5	120	2
Chandra	24	6	76	2
Venkata	20.4	3	63	2

India First Innings		Runs	Balls	Mins	4s	6s
SM Gavaskar	b Snow	6	35	49	1	-
AV Mankad	b Price	10	28	38	1	-
*AL Wadekar	c Hutton b Illingworth	48	133	171	2	-
DN Sardesai	b Illingworth	54	139	135	7	-
GR Viswanath	b Illingworth	0	8	6	-	-
ED Solkar	c Fletcher b D'Oliveira	44	125	129	3	-
+FM Engineer	c Illingworth b Snow	59	111	124	-	-
S Abid Ali	b Illingworth	26	40	60	3	-
S Venkat	lbw b Underwood	24	66	62	4	-
BS Bedi	c D'Oliveira b Illingworth	2	18	17	-	-
BS Chandrasekhar	not out	0	4	3	-	-
Extras	(6 b, 4 lb, 1 nb)	11				
Total	**(all out, 117.3 overs)**	**284**				

Fall of wickets:
1-17 (Mankad), 2-21 (Gavaskar), 3-114 (Sardesai), 4-118 (Viswanath), 5-125 (Wadekar), 6-222 (Solkar), 7-230 (Engineer), 8-278 (Abid Ali), 9-284 (Venkataraghavan), 10-284 (Bedi, 117.3 ov)

England bowling	Overs	Mdns	Runs	Wkts
Snow	24	5	68	2
Price	15	2	51	1
Hutton	12	2	30	0
D'Oliveira	7	5	5	1
Illingworth	34.3	12	70	5
Underwood	25	6	49	1

England Second Innings

		Runs	Balls	Mins	4s	6s
BW Luckhurst	c Venkat b Chandra	33	111	110	3	-
JA Jameson	run out	16	25	35	2	-
JH Edrich	b Chandra	0	5	5	-	
KWR Fletcher	c Solkar b Chandra	0	1	1	-	-
BL D'Oliveira	c sub (Jayantilal) b Venkat	17	28	26	2	-
+APE Knott	c Solkar b Venkat	1	4	9	-	=
*R Illingworth	c and b Chandra	4	17	15	-	-
RA Hutton	not out	13	44	49	1	-
JA Snow	c and b Chandras	0	4	1	-	-
DL Underwood	c Mankad b Bedi	11	27	28	2	-
JSE Price	lbw b Chandra	3	5	5	-	-
Extras	(3 lb)	3				
Total	**(all out, 45.1 overs)**	**101**				

Fall of wickets:

1-23 (Jameson), 2-24 (Edrich), 3-24 (Fletcher), 4-49 (D'Oliveira),
5-54 (Knott), 6-65 (Illingworth), 7-72 (Luckhurst), 8-72 (Snow),
9-96 (Underwood), 10-101 (Price, 45.1 ov)

India Bowling	Overs	Mdns	Runs	Wkts
Abid	3	1	5	0
Solkar	3	1	10	0
Bedi	1	0	1	1
Chandra	18.1	3	38	6
Venkat	20	4	44	2

India second innings		Runs	Balls	Mins	4s	6s
SM Gavaskar	lbw b Snow	0	9	10	-	-
AV Mankad	c Hutton b Underwood	11	74	78	-	-
*AL Wadekar	run out	45	118	125	4	-
DN Sardesai	c Knott b Underwood	40	156	159	4	-
GR Viswanath	c Knott b Luckhurst	33	171	175	-	-
ED Solkar	c and b Underwood	1	16	22	-	-
+FM Engineer	not out	28	59	50	3	-
S Abid Ali	not out	4	4	1	1	-
Extras	(6 b, 5 lb, 1 nb)	12				
Total	**(6 wickets, 101 overs)**	**174**				

Fall of wickets:

1-2 (Gavaskar), 2-37 (Mankad), 3-76 (Wadekar), 4-124 (Sardesai), 5-134 (Solkar), 6-170 (Viswanath)

England Bowling	Overs	Mdns	Runs	Wkts
Snow	11	7	14	1
Price	5	0	10	0
D'Oliveira	9	3	17	0
Illingworth	36	15	40	0
Underwood	38	14	72	3
Luckhurst	2	0	9	1

Appendix C
Demystifying the Ranji Teams
(compiled by Abhishek Mukherjee)

Team	Original Name	Also played as	First appearance	Last appearance
Andhra			1953/54	
Arunachal Pradesh			2018/19	
Assam (Part of Bengal till 1937/38)			1948/49	
Baroda			1937/38	
Bengal			1935/36	
Bihar Played as Jharkhand from 2004/05, separately from 2018/19		Jharkhand	1936/37 2004/05	
Delhi			1934/35	
Goa			1985-86	
Gujarat			1934-35	
Haryana (originally Part of Southern Punjab)			1970-71	
Himachal Pradesh			1985-86	
Hyderabad			1934-35	
Jammu and Kashmir			1959-60	
Karnataka		Mysore	1934-35	
Kerala		Travancore-Cochin	1951-52	
Madhya Pradesh		Holkar	1941-42	1954-55
		Central India	1934-35	1940-41
		Central Provinces & Berar	1934-35	1949-50
		Chhattisgarh	2016-17	
		Gwalior	1943-44	1943-44
		Madhya Bharat	1955-56	1955-56
Maharashtra			1934-35	
Manipur			2018-19	
Meghalaya			2018-19	
Mizoram			2018-19	
Mumbai		Bombay	1934-35	
Nagaland			2018-19	

Northern India (now in Pak)		1934-35	1947-48
NWFP (now in Pak)		1937-38	1947-48
Odisha (Part of Bihar till 1948/49)	Orissa	1949-50	
Punjab		1968-69	
Lost East Punjab in 1947-48	PEPSU	1956-57	1956-57
PEPSU Patiala and Eastern Punjab States Union		1948-49	1958-59
Northern Punjab and Southern Punjab split into Punjab and Haryana	Northern Punjab	1950-51	1959-60
		1960-61	1967-68
	Southern Punjab	1934-35	1967-68
Puducherry		2018-19	
Railways		1958-59	
Rajasthan	Rajputana	1935-36	
Saurashtra	Nawanagar	1936-37	
	Western India	1934-35	1946-47
	Kathiawar	1946-47	1949-50
Services	Army	1934-35	
Sikkim		2018-19	
Sind (Now in Pak)		1934-35	
Tamil Nadu	Madras	1934-35	
Tripura		1985-86	
Uttar Pradesh	United Provinces	1934-35	
	Uttarakhand	2018-19	
Vidarbha		1957-58	

BIBLIOGRAPHY

Addison, Paul, *Now that the War is Over* (London: Faber & Faber, 2012)

Ali, Mushtaq, *Cricket Delightful* (New Delhi: Rupa, 1967)

Allen, David-Rayvern, *Arlott: The Authorised Biography* (London: Harper Collins, 1996)

Amiss, Dennis, *In Search of Runs* (Newton Abbot: Readers Union, 1977)

Arlott, John, *Indian Summer* (London: Longmans, 1947)

Arlott, John, *Basingstoke Boy* (London: Harper Collins, 1992)

Arlott, Timothy, *John Arlott, a Memoir* (London: André Deutsch, 1994)

Baden-Powell, Robert, *Scouting for Boys* (London: Horace Cox, 1908)

Barkwai, Tarak, *Soldiers of Empire* (Cambridge: Cambridge University Press, 2017)

Barnes, Sidney, *Eye on The Ashes* (London: Kimber, 1953)

Basu, Sankari Prasad, *Not Out* (Calcutta: Ananda Publishers, 1965)

Berry, Scyld, *Crciketwallah* (London: Hodder & Stoughton, 1982)

Bharatan, Raju, *Indian Cricket: The Vital Phase* (New Delhi: Vikas, 1977)

Birley, Derek, *A Social History of English Cricket* (London: Aurum Press, 1999)

Blofeld, Henry, *A Thirst for Life* (London: Hodder & Stoughton, 2001)

Bose, Mihir, *A History of Indian Cricket* (London: André Deutsch, 2002)

Bose, Mihir, *The Maidan View: Magic of Indian Cricket* (London: George Allen and Unwin, 1986)

Bose, Mihir, *From Midnight to Glorious Morning* (London: Haus Publishing, 2018)

Bowen, Rowland, *Cricket: A History of its Growth and Development Throughout the World* (London: Eyre and Spottiswoode, 1970)

Bradman, Don, *Farewell to Cricket* (London: Hodder & Stoughton, 1950)

Brantlinger, Patrick, *Rule of Darkness* (Ithaca: Cornell University Press, 1990)

Buruma, Ian, *Playing the Game* (New York: Farrar Straus and Giroux, 1991)

Cannadine, David, *Class in Britain* (New Haven: Yale University Press, 1998)

Cannadine, David, *Ornamentalism: How the British Saw their Empire* (Oxford: Oxford University Press, 2002)

Cannadine David, *The Decline and Fall of the British Aristocracy* (London: Vintage, 1999)

Cardus, Neville, *Cardus in the Covers* (London: Souvenir, 2013)

Chalke, Stephen, *At the Heart of English Cricket: The Life and Memories of Geoffrey Howard* (Bath: Fairfield Books, 2001)

Chamberlain, Muriel, *Britain and India: The Interaction of Two Peoples* (London: David & Charles, 1974)

Chamberlain, Paul Thomas, *The Cold War's Killing Fields: Rethinking the Long Peace* (New York: Harper, 2018)

Coldham, James D, *Lord Harris* (London: Allen and Unwin, 1983)

Cowdrey, Colin, *MCC* (London: Coronet Books, 1977)

Crocker, Walter, *Nehru: A Contemporary's Estimate* (London: Allen and Unwin, 1966)

Darwin, John, *The Empire Project: The Rise and Fall of the British World-System, 1830–1970* (Cambridge: Cambridge University Press, 2011)

Davis, Mike, *Late Victorian Holocausts: El Niño Famines and the Making of the Third World* (London: Verso, 2017)

DeGroot, Gerard J, *The Sixties Unplugged: A Kaleidoscopic History of a Disorderly Decade* (Boston: Harvard University Press, 2010)

DeGroot, Gerard J, *The Seventies Unplugged: A Kaleidoscopic Look at a Violent Decade* (New York: Picador, 2011)

Denman, Roy, *Missed Chances: Britain and Europe in the Twentieth Century* (London: Cassell Illustrated, 1995)

Dexter, Ted, *85 Not Out* (Stroud: Quiller, 2020)

Dorling, Donny and Tomlinson, Sally *Rule Britannia: Brexit and the End of Empire* (London: Biteback Publishing, 2019)

Frith, David, *Paddington Boy* (Amstelveen: CricketMASH, 2021)

Frith, David, *Bodyline Autopsy* (London: Aurum Press, 2003)

Gandhi, Indira, *India and Bangladesh: Selected Speeches and Statements* (Calcutta: Orient Longman, 1972)

Gandhi, M.K., *Hind Swaraj* (Natal: The International Printing Press, Phoenix, 1910)

Gavaskar, Sunil, *Sunny Days* (New Delhi: Rupa, 1976)

Gavaskar, Sunil, *Run 'n Ruins* (New Delhi: Rupa, 1984)

Ghosh, Mayukh, *In a League of their Own* (Amstelveen: CricketMASH, 2019)

Gibson, Anthony, *Of Didcot and the Demon: The Cricketing Life and Times of Alan Gibson* (Bath: Fairfield Books, 2009)

Giliomee, Hermann, *The Last Afrikaner Leaders: A Supreme Test of Power* (Charlottesville: University of Virginia Press, 2013)

Gilmour, David, *The Ruling Caste: Imperial Lives in the Victorian Raj* (New York: Farrar, Straus and Giroux, 2007)

Gilmour, David, *The Long Recessional: The Imperial Life of Rudyard Kipling* (New York: Farrar, Straus and Giroux, 2002)

Gordon, Paul, *Different Worlds: Racism and Discrimination in Britain* (London: Runnymede Trust, 1986)

Grob-Fitzgibbon, Benjamin, *Imperial Endgame: Britain's Dirty Wars and the End of Empire* (London: Palgrave Macmillan, 2016)

Guha, Ramchandra, *A Corner of a Foreign Field* (Gurgaon: Penguin Random House, 2004)

Haigh, Gideon, *The Summer Game: Australia in Test Cricket 1949-71* (Sydney: ABC Books, 2006)

Hain, Peter and Odendaal, Andre *Pitch Battles* (London: Rowman and Littlefield Publishers, 2021)

Hain, Peter, *Don't Play with Apartheid* (London: Allen and Unwin, 1971)

Halsey, A.H. *Change in British Society* (Oxford: Oxford University Press, 1978)

Harris, Lord, *A Few Short Runs* (London: John Murray, 1921)

Hawke, Lord, *Recollections and Reminiscences* (London: William and Norgate, 1924)

Headlam, Cecil, *Ten thousand miles through India & Burma* (London: J.M. Dent, 1903)

Heald, Tim, *Jardine's Last Tour* (London: Methuen, 2011)

Hennessy, Peter, *Having it So Good: Britain in the Fifties* (London: Penguin, 2007)

Hennessy, Peter, *Winds of Change: Britain in the Early Sixties* (London: Penguin, 2020)

Hennessy, Peter, *Never Again: Britain, 1945-1951* (London: Pantheon, 1994)

Heyhoe Flint, Rachael and Rheinberg, Netta, *Fair Play* (London: Angus and Robertson, 1976)

Hill, Alan, *Jim Laker: A Biography* (London: André Deutsch, 2002)

Hobbs, Jack, *Test Match Surprise* (London: Readers Library, 1913)

Holmes, Colin, *John Bull's Island: Immigration and British Society, 1871-1971* (London: Routledge, 2015)

Howatt, Gerald, *Len Hutton* (London: Methuen, 1988)

Hughes, Simon, *A lot of Hard Yakka* (Eastbourne: Gardners Books, 1998)

Hyam, Ronald, *Britain's Imperial Century* (London: B.T. Batsford, 1976)

Hyam, Ronald, *Britain's Declining Empire: The Road to Decolonisation* (Cambridge: Cambridge University Press, 2007)

Illingworth, Ray, *Yorkshire and Back* (London: Queen Anne Press, 1980)

Imran Khan, *All Round View* (London: Chatto and Windus, 1988)

Inden, Ronald B., *Imagining India* (Bloomington: Indiana University Press, 2001)

James, C.L.R., *Beyond a Boundary* (London: Hutchinson, 1963)

Johnson, Paul, *Twentieth-Century Britain: Economic, Social and Cultural Change* (Boston: Addison-Wesley Longman Ltd, 1994)

Keay, John, *India: A History* (New York: Atlantic Monthly, 2000)

Keay, John, *Midnight's Descendants: South Asia from Partition to the Present Day* (London: HarperCollins, 2014)

Kidambi, Prasahant, *Cricket Country: An Indian Odyssey in the Age of Empire* (Oxford: Oxford University Press, 2019)

Kipling, Rudyard, *Kim* (London: Everyman New Edition, 1995)

Kipling, Rudyard and Fletcher, C.R.L., *A History of England* (London: Clarendon Press, 1911)

Kynaston, David, *Austerity Britain 1945-51* (London: Walker Books, 2008)

Kynaston, David, *Family Britain 1951-57* (London: Walker Books, 2010)

Kynaston, David, *Modernity Britain 1957-62* (London: Walker Books, 2014)

Laker, Jim, *Over to Me* (London: Frederick Muller, 1960)

Laker, Jim, *Spinning Round the World* (London: Frederick Muller, 1957)

Lang, John, *Wanderings in India and Other Sketches of Life in Hindostan* (New Delhi: Rupa, 2015)

Layton-Henry, Zygmunt, *The Politics of Race in Britain* (London: Allen and Unwin, 1984)

Layton-Henry, Zygmunt, *The Politics of Immigration: Race and Race Relations in Postwar Britain* (New York: Wiley-Blackwell, 1992)

Levin, Bernard, *The Pendulum Years* (London: Hodder & Stoughton, 1989)

Litchfield, Eric, *Cricket Grand-Slam* (Auckland: Howard Timmins, 1970)

Luckhurst, Brian, *Boot boy to President* (Chartham: KOS Media, 2004)

Lumby, E.W.R., *The Transfer of Power in India* (London: George Allen and Unwin, 1954)

Macaulay, Thomas Babington, *Sketches of some distinguished Anglo-Indians: (second series) including Lord Macaulay's great minute on education in India; with Anglo-Indian anecdotes and incidents.* (London: W.H. Allen and Co, 1888)

Mackenzie, John, *Propaganda and Empire: The Manipulation of British Public Opinion, 1880-1960* (Manchester: Manchester University Press, 1988)

Magee, Bryan, *Clouds of Glory: A Hoxton Childhood* (London: Penguin Random House, 2004)

Majeed, Javed, *Ungoverned Imaginings. James Mill's The History of British India and Orientalism* (Oxford: Oxford University Press, 1982)

Malhotra, Inder, *Indira Gandhi: A Personal and Political Biography* (New Delhi: Hay House, 2014)

Malik, Yogendra K., *India: The Years of Indira Gandhi* (Leiden: E.J. Brill, 1988)

Manley, Michael, *A History of West Indies Cricket* (London: André Deutsch, 2002)

Marwick, Arthur, *British Society Since 1945* (London: Penguin, 1990)

McKinstry, Leo, *Geoff Boycott: A Cricketing Hero* (London: Harper non-fiction, 2005)

Metcalf, Barbara D. and Metcalf, Thomas R., *A Concise History of Modern India* (Cambridge: Cambridge University Press, 2006)

Modi, Rusi, *Cricket Forever* (Bombay: self-published, 1964)

Morris, Jan, *Heaven's Command: An Imperial Progress* (Boston: Houghton Miffin Hartcourt, 1980)

Morris, Jan, *Pax Brittania: Climax of an Empire* (Boston: Houghton Miffin Hartcourt, 1989)

Morris, Jan, *Farewell the Trumpets: An Imperial Retreat* (Eastbourne: Gardners Books, 2003)

Mukherjee, Abhishek and Sengupta, Arunabha, *Sachin and Azhar at Cape Town: Indian and South African Cricket Through the Prism of a Partnership* (Worthing: Pitch Publishing, 2021)

Mukherjee, Madhusree, *Churchill's Secret War* (New York: Basic Books, 2011)

Mukherjee, Sujit, *The Romance of Indian Cricket* (New Delhi: Hind Pocket Books, 1968)

Mulholland, Marc, *The Longest War: Northern Ireland's Troubled History* (Oxford: Oxford University Press, 2002)

Neal, Steve, *Over and Out: Albert Trott: The Man Who Cleared the Lord's Pavilion* (Worthing: Pitch Publishing, 2017)

Oborne, Peter, *Basil D'Oliveira: Cricket and Conspiracy: The Untold Story* (London: Little, Brown, 2004)

Oborne, Peter, *Wounded Tiger* (London: Simon & Schuster, 2015)

Oborne, Peter and Heller, Richard, *White on Green: Celebrating the Drama of Pakistan Cricket* (London: Simon & Schuster, 2016)

Odendaal, André; Reddy, Krish and Merrett, Christopher, *Divided Country: The History of South African Cricket Retold 1914–1950s* (Cape Town: BestRed, 2018)

Odendaal, André; Reddy Krish; Merrett, Christopher and Winch, Jonty, *Cricket and Conquest: The History of South African Cricket Retold 1795–1914* (Cape Town: BestRed, 2016)

Osborne, John, *The Entertainer* (London: Faber & Faber, 1974)

Pandey, Gyanendra, *Remembering Partition: Violence, Nationalism and History in India* (Cambridge: Cambridge University Press, 2008)

Pataudi, M.A.K., *Tiger's Tale* (London: Stanley Paul, 1969)

Patel, J.M. Framjee, *Stray Thoughts on Indian Cricket* (Bombay: Times Press, 1905)

Pavri, M.E., *Parsi Cricket* (Mumbai: K.R. Cama Oriental Institute, 2006)

Pearson, Harry, *Connie: The Marvellous Life of Learie Constantine* (London: Abacus, 2018)

Peel, Mark, *England Expects* (London: Kingswood, 1992)

Peel, Mark, *The Last Roman* (London: André Deutsch, 1999)

Peel, Mark, *Ambassadors of Goodwill: MCC tours 1946/47-1970/71* (Worthing: Pitch Publishing, 2018)

Pugh, Martin, *We Danced All Night: A Social History of Britain Between the Wars* (London: Vintage, 2009)

Pugh, Martin, *State and Society: A Social and Political History of Britain Since 1870* (London: Bloomsbury, 2017)

Raghavan, Srinath, *1971 A Global History of the Creation of Bangladesh* (Boston: Harvard University Press, 2013)

Rajan, Sundar, *India vs England 1971* (Bombay: Jaico Books, 1972)

Raskin, Jonah, *The Mythology of Imperialism* (New York: Random House, 1971)

Read, Donald, *Edwardian England* (London: The Historical Association, 1972)

Reeve, Dermot, *Dermot Reeve's Winning Ways* (Basingstoke: Boxtree, 1996)

Rickson, Barry, *Duleepsinhji: A Prince of Cricketers* (Eastbourne: Gardners Books, 2005)

Roberts, Robert, *The Classic Slum: Salford Life in the First Quarter of the Century* (Harmondsworth: Penguin, 1973)

Robinson, Ray, *The Wildest Tests*, (London: Pelham, 1972)

Ross, Alan, *West Indies at Lord's* (London: Constable, 1986)

Ross, Alan, *Ranji* (London: Collins, 1983)

Said, Edward W, *Orientalism* (New York: Pantheon Books, 1978)

Sandbrook, Dominic *Never Had It So Good: A History of Britain from Suez to the Beatles* (London: Little, Brown, 2006)

Sandbrook, Dominic, *White Heat 1964-1970* (London: Abacus, 2007)

Sandbrook, Dominic, *State of Emergency: The Way We Were* (London: Penguin, 2011)

Sarkar, Sumit, *Modern India 1885-1947* (Madras: MacMillan India, 1984)

Savage, Mike, *Identities and Social Change in Britain since 1940: The Politics of Method* (Oxford: Oxford University Press, 2010)

Segal, Ronald, *The Anguish of India* (New York: Stein & Day, 1965)

Sengupta, Arunabha, *Apartheid: A Point to Cover* (Amstelveen: CricketMASH, 2020)

Sivanandan, A, *A Different Hunger: Writings on Black Resistance* (London: Pluto Press, 1991)

Snow, John, *Cricket Rebel* (London: Hamlyn, 1976)

Stevenson, John, *British Society 1914-1945* (London: Penguin, 1984)

Stollmeyer, Jeff, *Everything Under the Sun: My Life in West Indies Cricket* (London: Stanley Paul, 1983)

Swanton, Jim, *Gubby Allen: Man of Cricket* (London: Arrow, 1985)

Tennyson, Lionel, *From Verse to Worse* (London: Cassell, 1933)

Tennyson, Lionel, *Sticky Wickets* (Christopher Johnson, 1950)

Titmus, Fred, *My Life in Cricket* (London: Blake, 2005)

Wadekar, Ajit as told to K.N. Prabhu, *My Cricketing Years* (New Delhi: Vikas, 1973)

West, Peter, *The Fight for The Ashes 1953* (London: George G. Harrap, 1953)

Williams, Jack, *Cricket and Race* (Oxford: Berg Publishers, 2001)

Wilson, Harold, *A Personal Record: The Labour Government, 1964-1970* (London: Little, Brown, 1971)

Other sources

Bhala B, Bhala A & Bhala N, *A Historical look at Indian healthcare professionals in the NHS* 2019 (Nov) 19-21 (https://www.sushruta.net/november-2019)

Davis, Charles, *Z-score's Cricket Stats Blog,* (http://www.sportstats.com.au/)

Mettyear, James, *The Joy of '71, (https://www.thecricketmonthly.com/story/1103284/the-joy-of--71)*

Mukherjee, Abhishek, *Mansur Ali Khan 'Tiger' Pataudi,* (https://www.cricketcountry.com/articles/mansur-ali-khan-tiger-pataudi-the-enigmatic-nawab-233137)

Sengupta, Arunabha, *Bhagwat Chandrasekhar: Diasbility became dangerous weapon, (http://cricmash.com/biographies/bhagwat-chandrasekhar-diasbility-became-dangerous-weapon)*

Williamson, Martin, *The Denness Affair,* (https://www.espncricinfo.com/magazine/content/story/496743.html)

Wisden Almanacks

Wikipedia

Association of Cricket Statisticians and Historians

The Cricket Statistician

The Cricketer

ESPNCricinfo

The Cricket Monthly

Cricketarchive

CricketCountry

CricMASH

YouTube

The Guardian Archives

The Times Archives

British Newspaper Archives

MCC Library

Trent Bridge Library

Sussex CCC Museum

INDEX

ABOUT THE AUTHOR

Arunabha Sengupta is a cricket historian, analyst and writer for numerous cricket publications. He is the author of *Apartheid: A Point to Cover – South African cricket 1948–1970 and the Stop The Seventy Tour* and the co-author (with Abhishek Mukherjee) of *Sachin and Azhar at Cape Town – Indian and South African Cricket Through the Prism of a Partnership.*

He has also written a cricket-based Sherlock Holmes pastiche *Sherlock Holmes and the Birth of The Ashes.*